TERRY & JOYCE LOSONSKY

McDonald's®

HAPPY MEAL® TOYS
AROUND THE WORLD

McWORLD

SEE THE WORLD
with Ronald McDonald

1982 RONALD McDONALD STICKER FUN
Coloring Calendar

Schiffer Publishing Ltd

77 Lower Valley Road, Atglen, PA 19310

Printed in Hong Kong

ISBN: 0-88740-835-4

Published by Schiffer Publishing, Ltd.
77 Lower Valley Road
Atglen, PA 19310
Please write for a free catalog.
This book may be purchased from the publisher.
Please include $2.95 postage.
Try your bookstore first.

We are interested in hearing from authors
with book ideas on related subjects.

Library of Congress Cataloging-in-Publication Data

Losonsky, Terry.
    McDonald's Happy Meal toys around the world / Terry & Joyce Losonsky.
        p.   cm.
    Includes index.
    ISBN 0-88740-835-4 (paper)
    1. McDonald's Corporation--Collectibles--Catalogs.
2. Lunchboxes--Collectors and collecting--Catalogs. 3.
Premiums (Retail trade)--Collectors and collecting--
Catalogs.   I. Losonsky, Joyce.
II. Title
NK6213.L679   1995
688.7'2'075--dc20   95-37442
                                                    CIP

Acknowledgments and Thanks

We would like to express our sincere appreciation to our family and friends for their endearing support. We especially would like to thank our four children who are the Best kids a Mom and Dad could ask for. This book and our other McDonald's books are written especially for them to attempt to make sense out of our collection. It is our small legacy to our children in the hope they will have as much fun in their lives as we have had in ours. We sincerely apologize for any names and familiar faces left off our list.

BEST KIDS
Andrea Losonsky
Natasha Losonsky
Nicole Losonsky
Ryan Losonsky

ADVISORY BOARD
Ron & Eileen Corbett
John & Eleanor Larsen
Rich & Laurel Seidelman
Jimmy & Pat Futch
Bill & Pat Poe
David Tuttle
E. J. Ritter
Pat Sentell
Ken Clee

THANK YOU!
McDonald's Corporation
Helen Farrell - USA McDonald's Archives
Lois Doughtery - USA McDonald's Archives
Kees & Conny Versteeg - Holland
Daphne Veerendad - Holland
Robin Murray - New Zealand
Ryoji Okamoto - Japan
Takao Ezawa - Japan
Nigel Thomas - England
David Beaumont - England
Brian Gildea - England
Gordon & Kath Fairgrieve - UK
Taylor & Cindy Wagon - Hawaii
Frank Duessel - Germany
Jurgen Seifried - Germany
Frank Schneidewind - Germany
Peter Peterson - Austria
Tracy Cavanach - Australia
Lexie Keady - Ireland
Irv & Robin Kirstein - Canada
Joyce Klassen - Canada
Don Wilson - Canada
Dave Archer - Canada
Gerry Acaster - Canada
Claire Savoy - Canada
Larry & Manuella Poli - France
Rene & Anne Marie Naim - France
David & Patrine Tang - Singapore

Bonnie Garnett - Australia
Stephen & Ann Zurko
Steve & Linda Zurko
Max Zurko
Chad Zurko
Nancy & Peter Schiffer
Frank & Nancy Losonsky
Phil & Alana Losonsky
Chris & Toni Losonsky
Leslie Bockol
Doug Congdon-Martin
Dawn Stoltzfus
Charles & Julia Fritz
John & Olga Harcarik
Mildred Cunane Smith
Julia Fritz
John Z Schurko
Nicholas Schurko
Ursula Shows
Jonathan Miller
Charles DuBal
Meredith Williams
Gary & Shirley Henriques

Thank you one and all.
Have fun!

- Joyce & Terry Losonsky

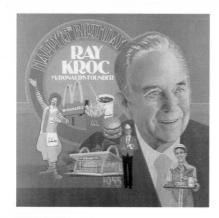

McDONALD'S AT 40, STILL GREEN AND GROWING
(1955-1995)

Welcome to the world of McDonald's Happy Meal Toys Around the World. From humble beginnings, on April 15, 1955, the late Ray Kroc opened his first McDonald's Drive-thru Restaurant in Des Plaines, Illinois (USA). That day, rain and all, launched the sites and sounds of a chain of restaurants heard around the world. From downtown Tokyo, to London, to the Bavarian Alps in Germany, McDonald's restaurants around the world strive to offer the same quality food, quick service, clean surroundings as well as value that customers have enjoyed for the last 40 years (1955 - 1995).

The late Mr. Ray Kroc, the founder of McDonald's Restaurants, had a saying: "When you're green, you're growing..." As the world's leading fast food restaurant organization marked its 40th birthday, April 15, 1995, it couldn't be greener. The McDonald's Restaurant story is not that simple; it is one with many innovative twists and much marketing genius. It is the spirit and the people, employees and customers as well as the newest customers, the collectors who enhance the operation. McDonald's story is the story of people helping people. It is the story of how the world's biggest small business grew...

1948 - Dick and Mac McDonald, known as the McDonald brothers, opened their first limited menu, self-service McDonald's drive-in restaurant in San Bernardino, California (USA). Ray Kroc, a salesman for milk-shake machines strikes an agreement with the McDonald brothers to franchise the concept of the restaurant. The menu: 15 cent hamburgers, 10 cent french fries and 20 cent shakes. The restaurant is called "McDonald's" and the global chapter on the History of Fast Food Restaurants is beginning to unfold.

1952 - Dick and Mac McDonald officially franchise their McDonald's Speedee Service System. The initial building design was red and white tile with yellow neon arches going through the roof. The Golden Arches were born. The first eight McDonald's restaurants were in southern California with Speedee as their mascot.

PRESS ON

NOTHING IN THE WORLD CAN TAKE THE PLACE OF PERSISTENCE. TALENT WILL NOT: NOTHING IS MORE COMMON THAN UNSUCCESSFUL MEN WITH TALENT. GENIUS WILL NOT: UNREWARDED GENIUS IS ALMOST A PROVERB'S. EDUCATION ALONE WILL NOT: THE WORLD IS FULL OF EDUCATED DERELICTS. PERSISTENCE AND DETERMINATION ALONE ARE OMNIPOTENT.

HONORARY PALLBEARERS: "ALL OF US HE TOUCHED."

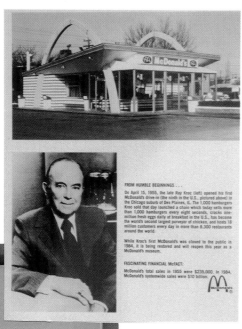

FROM HUMBLE BEGINNINGS...

On April 15, 1955, the late Ray Kroc (left) opened his first McDonald's drive-in (the ninth in the U.S., pictured above) in the Chicago suburb of Des Plaines, IL. The 1,000 hamburgers Kroc sold that day launched a chain which today sells more than 1,000 hamburgers every eight seconds, cracks one-million fresh eggs daily at breakfast in the U.S., has become the world's second largest purveyor of chicken, and hosts 18 million customers every day in more than 8,300 restaurants around the world.

While Kroc's first McDonald's was closed to the public in 1984, it is being restored and will reopen this year as a McDonald's museum.

FASCINATING FINANCIAL McFACT:

McDonald's total sales in 1955 were $235,000. In 1984, McDonald's systemwide sales were $10 billion.

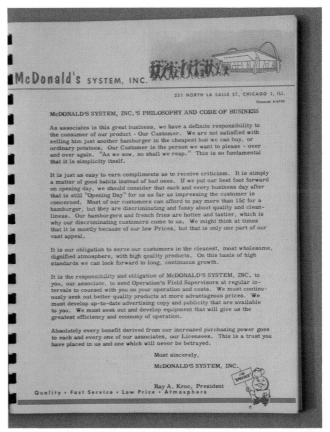

McDonald's SYSTEM, INC.

221 NORTH LA SALLE ST., CHICAGO 1, ILL.
Financial 6-6750

McDONALD'S SYSTEM, INC.'S PHILOSOPHY AND CODE OF BUSINESS

As associates in this great business, we have a definite responsibility to the consumer of our product - Our Customer. We are not satisfied with selling him just another hamburger in the cheapest bun we can buy, or ordinary potatoes. Our Customer is the person we want to please - over and over again. "As we sow, so shall we reap." This is so fundamental that it is simplicity itself.

It is just as easy to earn compliments as to receive criticism. It is simply a matter of good habits instead of bad ones. If we put our best foot forward on opening day, we should consider that each and every business day after that is still "Opening Day" for us as far as impressing the customer is concerned. Most of our customers can afford to pay more than 15¢ for a hamburger, but they are discriminating and fussy about quality and cleanliness. Our hamburgers and french fries are hotter and tastier, which is why our discriminating customers come to us. We might think at times that it is mostly because of our low Prices, but that is only one part of our vast appeal.

It is our obligation to serve our customers in the cleanest, most wholesome, dignified atmosphere, with high quality products. On this basis of high standards we can look forward to long, continuous growth.

It is the responsibility and obligation of McDONALD'S SYSTEM, INC, to you, our associate, to send Operation's Field Supervisors at regular intervals to counsel with you on your operation and costs. We must continuously seek out better quality products at more advantageous prices. We must develop up-to-date advertising copy and publicity that are available to you. We must seek out and develop equipment that will give us the greatest efficiency and economy of operation.

Absolutely every benefit derived from our increased purchasing power goes to each and every one of our associates, our Licensees. This is a trust you have placed in us and one which will never be betrayed.

Most sincerely,

McDONALD'S SYSTEM, INC.

Ray A. Kroc, President

Quality · Fast Service · Low Price · Atmosphere

nothing succeeds like success

McDonald's

Manual

No. 0001

1955 - Ray Kroc opens his first restaurant in Des Plaines, Illinois (USA) on April 15, 1955. It is the ninth McDonald's to open in the USA, the other eight being in the southern California area. April 15th each year is officially known as Founder's Day. A little hamburger man called "Speedee" was the company symbol. By the end of the year, Ray Kroc had opened a second McDonald's in Fresno, California (USA).

1956 - A dozen more McDonald's restaurants are added in Chicago, Illinois and California (USA). Fred Turner, a very essential person, is hired to be the one man Operations Department. Mr. Turner initially worked as a grillman in the Des Plaines store.

1957 - Q.S.C. concept is instituted: Quality, Service and Cleanliness.

1959 - The 100th McDonald's restaurant is opened near Chicago's Midway Airport (USA).

1960-The 200th McDonald's restaurant is opened and "Look for the Golden Arches" jingle is played on radio. The first company owned and operated restaurant is opened in Columbus, Ohio (USA).

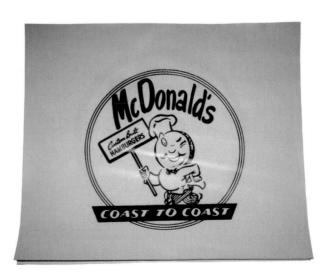

1961 - The All American Meal is launched for 45 cents and Ray Kroc buys out the McDonald brothers for $2.7 million. Hamburger University is opened in Elk Grove Village, Illinois. The first graduating class received degrees in "Bachelor Hamburgerology." The management training center strived to standardize the product, place, price and promotions along with the most important element, the selling agents, the employees. The All American Menu featured hamburgers, fries and shakes. The bisected arches are introduced, "M" slashed with a line symbolizes the Golden Arches and restaurant roof design. BOG - Be Our Guest cards are introduced. Economist and marketing experts in attempting to explain the secret of McDonald's early success agree that it was simply the controlled, meticulous way in which it was operated which led to the success.

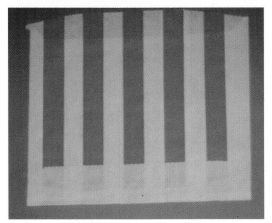

1962 - The Golden Arches replaced Speedee as the McDonald's company's symbol on packaging in January. "Go For Goodness at McDonald's" advertising slogan appeared as McDonald's advertised nationally in LIFE magazine (USA).

1963 - Willard Scott appears as the first local Ronald McDonald, making his debut in Washington, D.C. at the Cherry Blossom Parade. Filet-O-Fish sandwich is added to the menu at 24 cents. National advertisement appears in Reader's Digest magazine. The advertising blitz begins. Double hamburger and double cheeseburger introduced. Ronald's Flying Hamburger is tested in Rockville, Maryland restaurant.

1964 - Archy McDonald logo is used on a limited number of premiums and bags. Arch Madden of DesMoines, Illinois turned the one day receipts of his six stores over to the Children's Zoo.

1965 - 10th Anniversary of McDonald's restaurants in the USA. McDonald's was on its way to becoming a "way of life." The building blocks for the coming years—training, research, advertising—were being anchored firmly into place.

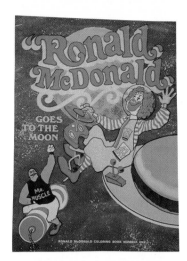

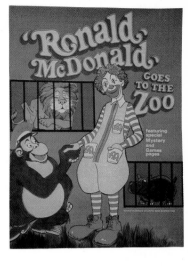

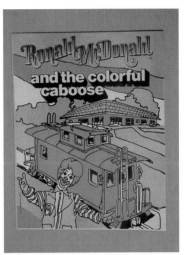

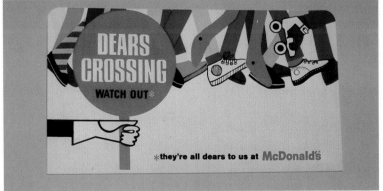

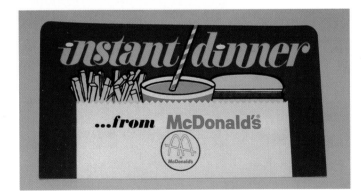

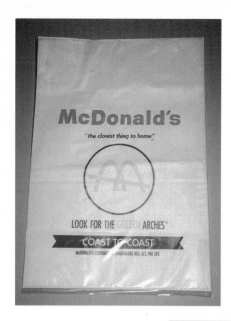

1966 - Ronald McDonald makes his first national television appearance as the spokesman for McDonald's. McDonald's Corporation is listed on the New York Stock Exchange. In September of 1966, Ronald McDonald and his Flying Hamburger were introduced nationally as the new spokesman for McDonald's. Advertising jingle: "McDonald's—Where Quality Starts Fresh Everyday. Look for the Golden Arches." McDonald's was entrenched as a national name. Rather than concentrating on individual menu items, the advertising focused on creating a total quality image.

1967 - Canada (June 1) and Puerto Rico (November 10) open their first McDonald's restaurants. British Columbia (Canada) was the first international restaurant for McDonald's outside the USA. OPNAD (The Operators' National Advertising Fund) was formed; it was the voluntary cooperative of McDonald's restaurants that purchased national advertising. Cooperative purchasing of products was instituted; Cooperative warehousing developed among the stores in order to solve the storage problems created by the increasing volume. McDonald's All-American High School band debuts in the Macy's Thanksgiving Day Parade in New York City. Ad theme: "McDonald's is Your Kind of Place" was introduced. Price of hamburgers increased from 15 cents to 18 cents on January 1, 1967. The roast beef sandwich was in test. Visitors to the Toronto Zoo in Canada enjoy McDonald's food in snack bars designed in natural wood to blend in with the environment. In 1993, McDonald's of Canada supported the NHL/Upper Deck trading card promotion which involved picturing the first female goalie ever to play NHL Pre-season hockey, Manon Rheaume.

1968 - Hawaii opens its first McDonald's. The Big Mac sandwich and Hot Apple Pie are introduced. "Give up a pack for a Big Mac" theme slowly began to take hold in the USA.

1969 - Red and white tile design is replaced with a "New Modern Design-The Mansard Roof". Changing designs with the times became a McDonald's standard practice. "QSC" is joined with "V" for value. Ronald McDonald received a new costume design.

1970 - Virgin Islands (September 4) and Costa Rica (December 2) opens their first McDonald's restaurants. "You Deserve A Break Today" advertising slogan is born along with McDonaldland. Christmas gift certificates were introduced. Price of a hamburger in the USA increased from 18 cents to 20 cents. With the opening of a McDonald's in Anchorage, Alaska, McDonald's was in all 50 states in the USA.

1971 - Guam (June 10), Japan (July 20), Holland (August 21), Panama (September 1), Germany (November 22), and Australia (December 20) open their first McDonald's. Ronald McDonald's cast of characters begins to grow—Hamburglar, Grimace, Mayor McCheese, Captain Crook and The Professor join Ronald McDonald in McDonaldland. McDonaldland is the imaginary place where the characters live and play, their playland. First McDonald's Playland opens in Chula Vista, California (USA). Playlands play an important role in restaurants globally. "You Deserve A Break Today —So Get Up and Get Away to McDonald's" is the advertising theme. Cherry and Shamrock shakes introduced. Quarter Pounder, Egg McMuffin, Tripple Ripple Ice cream, Fish 'n Chips, Cookies, Onion Rings and Fried Chicken in test sites in USA. Some of the world's most beautiful McDonald's restaurants are located in international markets. The "Oldest" McDonald's was located in Freiburg, West Germany, in a building which dates back to 1250 A.D.

HOLLAND

1972 - France (June 30) and El Salvador (July 20) open restaurants. 145 restaurants were operating outside the USA with Canada having 96 restaurants operating in 1972. Ray Kroc received Horatio Alger Award and celebrated his 75th birthday. Large Fries were introduced. McDonald's participated in the Jerry Lewis Muscular Dystrophy Telethon for the first time. Danish were being tested as a breakfast item. In the USA, McDonald's restaurants are operated either by independent business people or by the company. Expansion outside the USA is accomplished through the development of restaurants operated by: (1) the company through subsidiaries; (2) franchisees - individuals granted franchises by the company, a subsidiary or an affiliate; and (3) affiliates - companies where McDonald's equity is 50 percent or less and the remaining equity is generally owned by a resident national.

CANADA

CANADA

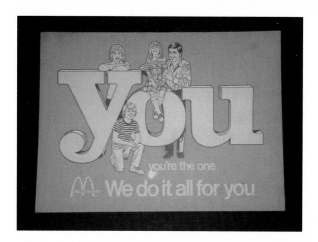

1973 - Sweden (November 5) opens first restaurant. McDonald's makes the cover of TIME magazine and Canada's store #100 opens in St. John, New Brunswick. Hot Cakes, Sausage and Soft Serve Cones were in test. Egg McMuffin is added to the menu.

1974 - Guatemala (June 19), Netherlands Antilles (August 16), England (October 1) and St. Thomas, VI (November 25) open restaurants. England adds the 3000th store in Woolwich, England. The first Ronald McDonald House is opened in Philadelphia, Pennsylvania (USA). McDonaldland Cookies become a menu item. QLT/HLT, Iced Tea, Sundaes and Diet Drinks in test stage. International McDonald's strives to strengthen local economies by supporting local charitable, civic, educational and community service programs. This approach is in keeping with Ray Kroc's original philosophy of "putting something back into the communities where McDonald's does business."

1975 - McDonald's Systems of Europe, Inc., based in Frankfort, Germany was formed. Stockholm, Sweden restaurant first to reach $2 million in annual sales. The Drive-thru concept is opened in Sierra Vista, AZ and Oklahoma City, Oklahoma (USA). The Honorary Meal of McDonaldland is introduced in the USA and Canada. "Twoallbeefpattiesspecialsaucelettuce cheesespicklesonionsonasesameseedbun" promotional jingle catches the imagination of the country. The direct relationship between advertising and sales is rooted. McDonald's celebrates 20th Anniversary. Ad campaign, "We Do It All For You" introduced. New polystyrene packaging begins. McFeast, Salad Bar, Scrambled Eggs, McChicken Sandwich, Chili in testing stage.

1976 - New Zealand (June 7) and Switzerland (October 20) open first restaurants. Montreal, Canada opens McDonald's 4000th restaurant (4000 Ste-Catherin Quest, Montreal, QUE on July 13, 1976). Kisarazu, Japan opens Japan's 100th restaurant. "You, You're The One" advertising campaign focuses on individual attention to detail, the customer. The breakfast menu was instituted. McDonald's becomes the official sponsor of Olympic Games in Montreal, Canada. New Zealand does not specifically distribute a Happy Meal premium for children under the age of 3 (USA) or the age of 5, like in Germany. In the 1990s in New Zealand, about 8-10 different Happy Meal boxes tended to appear and disappear with various promotions. These same box designs just kept rotating around in the different cities, not in any specific distribution cycle. New Zealand provides "Lobby Toys" which compensates for the lack of U-3 toys.

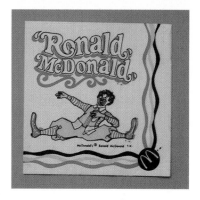

The Club That Treats Kids Extra Special!

Ronald McDonald fun club

FOR KIDS UNDER 10 YEARS OLD

Ask for details at the counter.

1976 Ronald McDonald McFavorite Clown Coloring Calendar

YOU CAN BE A REAL MAGICIAN WITH FREE McDONALDLAND Magic Tricks

COLLECT ALL FOUR
A DIFFERENT ONE EVERY WEEK AT THE COUNTER

Ronald McDonald Happy Hat

Ronald McDonald HAPPY HAT

Ronald McDonald HAPPY HAT

GRIMACE™

HAMBURGLAR™

1977 - Ireland (May 9) and Austria (July 21) open restaurants. The Happy Meal concept is test marketed in the USA. From the Happy Plate, Happy Cup, and Happy Hat, the overall Happy Meal concept evolved. The initial boxes were designed like round top metal lunch boxes. McDonald's owns over half of all of its real estate sites by the end of the year; a key marketing decision for future success. Chocolaty Chip Cookies, Chopped Beef Sandwich, Sausage McMuffin, Chicken Pot Pie, Onion Nuggets in test stage.

1978 - Belgium (March 21) opens first restaurant. Osaka, Japan was the first to reach $3 million in sales. Kanagawa, Japan (Fujisawa City) opens store #5000 on October 17, 1978.

1979 - Brazil (February 13) and Singapore (October 20) open restaurants. The 100th McDonald's in Australia, featuring a Drive-thru opens in Sunnybank. The 100th German McDonald's opened in Hamburg. New advertising theme, "Nobody Can Do It Like McDonald's Can" hits the airwaves. Chicken McNuggets, Ham Biscuits, McCola, McPizza and Cinnamon Streusel in testing stages. Happy Meal Tests were conducted in the USA while the advertising slogans focused on children and the "Collect all..." theme.

1980 - 25th Anniversary (Silver) celebrated. Birdie the Early Bird joins McDonaldland and Ronald's Cast of Characters. Ronald McDonald Houses are providing shelter for 33,000 families in the USA, Canada and Australia. The 1000th International McDonald's opened in Hong Kong. Store #6000 opened on June 23, 1980 in Munich, Germany. In 1994, McDonald's of Germany held the first ever world press conference in Munich, Germany to announce outstanding financial results from the 500 restaurants in Germany. Newest advertising slogan: "You Deserve a Break Today, and Nobody Makes Your Day Like McDonald's Can" appear on mass media.

BRAZIL

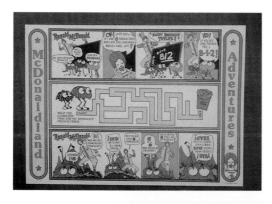

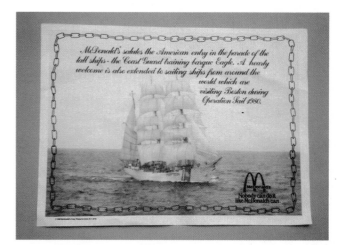

CANADA

15

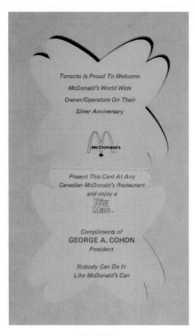

CANADA

CANADA

CANADA

1981 - Spain (March 10), Denmark (April 15) and Philippines (September 27) open restaurants. McDonald's becomes the largest food service organization in Canada. The first Ronald McDonald House opens in Toronto, Canada. Australia, Germany, Guam, Holland, Japan and Panama celebrated their 10th Anniversary. Japan is involved in an extensive test market program for the Happy Meal/promotions and Kid's give-away premiums. The items are tested and then run about 9 months to a year later if they are successful in drawing an interest and increasing sales.

1982 - Malaysia (April 29) opens a McDonald's. Soft serve cones were added to the menu.

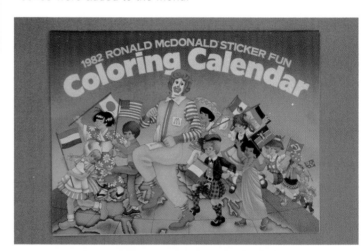

CANADA

CANADA

1983 - Norway (November 18) opens its first McDonald's. Yugoslavia signs joint venture to open a McDonald's restaurant. The 100th McDonald's in England opens in Manchester. McNugget Mania promotes Chicken McNuggets addition to the menu. "McDonald's and You" advertising campaign introduced. Diet Coke added to menu; while McDLT in testing stage. Ronald McDonald learned Italian and communicates in at least 18 languages. England typically distributed 4 different Happy Meal boxes with the Kid's Meal. These are designed to serve as a themed backdrop with punchout pieces to enhance the 3-D effect of the packaging.

1984 - Taiwan (January 28), Andorra (June 29), Finland (December 14) and Wales (December 3) add their first restaurants. Ray Kroc dies at the age of 81. His vision lives on. Newest ad campaign "It's Good Time For the Great Taste of McDonald's" refreshes the global thirst for McDonald's. At year's end there were 73 Ronald McDonald Houses operating in USA, Canada and Australia. McDonald's and its franchisees provide money to build the Olympic Swim Stadium in Los Angeles. RMCC - Ronald McDonald Children's Charities founded in memory of Ray Kroc. "When the US Wins, You Win" promotion in conjunction with the Summer Olympics wins customers. Pecan roll and Bacon/Egg/Cheese Biscuit in testing stage. There are 1,709 restaurants in 34 countries and territories outside the USA in 1984. Five previously opened international markets—Japan, Hong Kong, Sweden, Taiwan and Switzerland in 1984 represented 20 percent of McDonald's systemwide sales. RMCC: Ronald McDonald Children's Charities (RMCC) was founded in 1984 upon Mr. Kroc's death. The cornerstone of RMCC is the Ronald McDonald House program. A Ronald McDonald House is a "home away from home" for out of town families of children receiving hospital treatment for life threatening illnesses such as cancer. The houses provide a supportive environment for parents and siblings of sick children. Introduced in Philadelphia, Pennsylvania (USA) in 1974, by 1984 there are more than 150 Ronald McDonald Houses around the world and many more under development. The New Zealand Ronald McDonald House became McDonald's 151st house; located beside the Wellington Hospital. The first Ronald McDonald House opened in the former communist East Bloc in 1993. McDonald's of Finland (in conjunction with the Finnish Ministry for Internal Affairs, The Ministry of Transportation and Finland's First Alert Company "Torres") developed a program to inform residents of the new "112" emergency number, which functions like the "911" number in the USA.

1985 - Thailand (February 23), Luxembourg (July 17), Bermuda (July 24), Venezuela (August 31), Italy (October 15), Mexico (October 29), Aruba (April 4) open stores and help McDonald's celebrate their 30th Anniversary. The Ronald McDonald House program offers a "home away from home" for families of children being treated for serious illnesses. The first European Ronald McDonald House opened in March 1985 in Amsterdam. New braille menu assisted visually impaired. Customers sing, "The Hot Stays Hot and the Cool Stays Cool" as McDonald's introduced the McDLT sandwich. Ad theme, "Good Time for Great Taste" encourages customers to visit their local McDonald's. Sausage McMuffin added to menu. The 1984 famous picture of the Buddhist priest eating french fries on the steps of an ancient Japanese temple (1985 McDonald's Calendar) amply illustrates the worldwide appeal of McDonald's French Fries. Mexico calls their Happy Meal, "La Cajita Feliz."

CANADA

CANADA

17

HOLLAND

GERMANY

FRANCE

1986 - Cuba (Navy Base-April 24), Turkey (October 24) and Argentina (November 24) open McDonald's. Store #9000 opens in Sydney, Australia. Three varieties of biscuit sandwiches and Sausage McMuffin with Egg introduced. Special McNuggets Shanghai promotion featured chopsticks and McFortune cookies. Germany began to call their children's menu Kindermenu in 1986 with their Ship Shape promotion.

1987 - Macau (April 11), Scotland (November 23) open first McDonald's. Salads become the newest menu item. Monopoly game was the most successful national promotion and Muppet Babies was the most successful Happy Meal to date. Rome, Italy restaurant reaches $5 million in sales. Rock 'n Roll McDonald's in Chicago, Illinois (USA) became 1st USA store to reach $5 million in sales. Mac tonight debuts in promotional literature and ad campaign. McDonald's of Canada celebrated 20th Anniversary. Canada's boxes and bags for the "Joyuex Festin" Happy Meal are the same as the USA except are printed in English and French.

AUSTRALIA

CANADA

18

1988 - Yugoslavia (March 22), Korea (March 29) and Hungary (April 30) open restaurants. At year's end there are 118 Ronald McDonald Houses worldwide. Newest ad theme premieres: "Good Time, Great Taste, That's Why This is My Place" appears in commercials. CosMc, the little space alien joined McDonaldland. New breakfast theme, "America's Morning Place" encourages breakfast market. Cheddar Melt added to menu. McMasters program to recruit older workers is introduced. Bonus size fries and super size soft drinks are standard menu items in the USA. German archives indicate January-April 1988 in Augsburg, Germany is where the Junior-Tute (Happy Meal) officially was test marketed.

1989 - Barbados (August 24) opens with fanfare. McChicken sandwich is introduced nationally in the USA after 10 years of testing. McDonald's sold 35 million plush Muppet Baby Dolls to raise nearly $9 million for RMCC and Ronald Houses. 126 Ronald Houses open in USA, Canada, Australia, Austria, Germany and the Netherlands; while serving over 1 million families members per year. Store #11,000 opened on October 20th in Hong Kong.

GERMANY

JAPAN

CANADA

19

THE GOLDEN ARCHES OF MOSCOW

15 MONTHS AFTER ITS GRAND OPENING, McDONALD'S FAST FOOD FANTASIA IS STILL WOWING IVAN

1990 - Russia (January 31), China-Shenzhen (October 8) and Chile (November 19) open restaurants to long lines of customers. Environmental concerns reflect movement to recycled paper products. 35th Anniversary is celebrated. McDonald's food is being served in two restaurant cars on the Swiss Federal RR Basel-Geneva run. Newest ad campaign: "Food, Folks and Fun" introduced. McDonald's opened in Shenzhen, a special economic zone of People's Republic of China just across the border from Hong Kong.

CHINA

UK

RUSSIA

RUSSIA

RUSSIA

RUSSIA

HOLLAND

JAPAN

1991 - 427 international restaurants added. Germany was issuing Junior-Tute (Happy Meal) in a brown bag with comics on the back. McDonald's international goal is to make the Golden Arches the customer's first choice around the globe.

1992 - Poland (June 17) opened, making it the 62nd country in which McDonald's does business. 25th Anniversary of McDonald's International. McDonald's of Sweden developed educational maps/trayliner to illustrate the changes which occurred in Europe, including a picture of the thirteen "New Countries" which were created. The New Europe Map was distributed as a trayliner in September 1992. Food, Folks and Fun along with a geography lesson were the offerings.

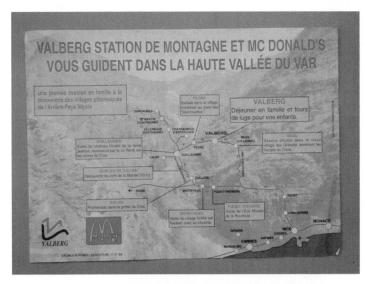

FRANCE

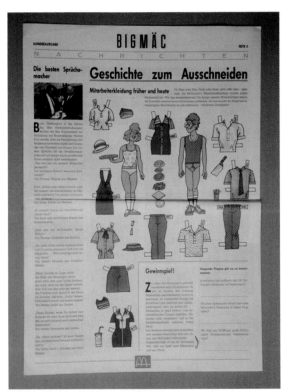

GERMANY

GERMANY

CANADA

GERMANY

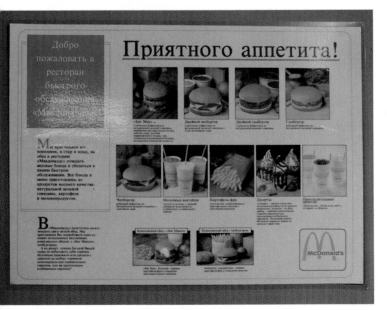

LATVIA

GERMANY

CANADA

JAPAN

HONG KONG   UK

1993 - Iceland, Israel, Saipan, Slovenia and Saudi Arabia are added to the roster of new restaurants. McDonald's participates in the exhibition, "DESIGN, MIRROR OF THE CENTURY" at the Grand Palais in Paris, France. They construct an exact replica of the old red and white restaurant in Des Plaines, Illinois to serve as a fully operational restaurant at the Grand Palais. A special trayliner was issued which depicted the outstanding success of the operation. The Minister of Culture, Mr. Jacques Toubon declared the exhibit, "C'EST MAGNIFIQUE!" McDonald's provided something more than food, they consistently provided a quality approach, 38 years later. German Junior-Tute Happy Meal changed to white numbered bags with comics on the back. McWorld advertising emphasized the global relationship between McDonald's and the Earth.

MONACO

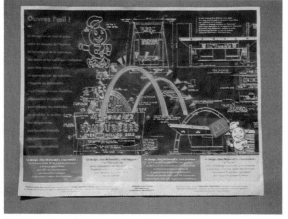

FRANCE

FRANCE

JAPAN

CANADA

CANADA

CANADA

FRANCE

1994 - Egypt and New Caledonia plus Kuwait, Bahrain, the United Arab Emirates, Oman are the newest places McDonald's calls home. The 500th McDonald's in Germany opened and the new McDonald's in Budapest becomes the 22nd in the capital of Hungary. It is the 100th restaurant in Central Europe. McDonald's announces planned operation of restaurants in the 1996 Olympic Village in Atlanta, Georgia (USA). McWorld Environmental Stamp Design Contest drew over 150,000 entries from the USA children; produced a series of four USA 32 cent stamps in 1995. The Kids Care stamps

AUSTRALIA

KOREA

JAPAN

GERMANY

UK

JAPAN

about the environment depicted ways to preserve, protect or restore the environment. 10th Anniversary of Ronald McDonald Children's Charities (RMCC) and the 20th anniversary of the first Ronald McDonald House is celebrated. There are over 162 Ronald McDonald houses worldwide with houses in Rio de Janeiro, Brazil and Auckland, New Zealand. Satellite restaurants in Wal Mart and limited space locations continues to grow in number. There are over 100 satellite locations in Canada, 10 in Mexico and 2 in Puerto Rico. These low-cost units serve a simplified menu. By year's end, China had over 30 restaurants and was growing rapidly to meet the population demands of 30 million people. In the Asia/Pacific region, McDonald's has only one restaurant for every 900,000 people, compared to one for every 25,000 people in the USA. Japan had opened its 1,000th restaurant in 1994 and the United Kingdom and Germany are already 500 restaurants and growing. They employ more then 650,000 people around the world. Ronald McDonald speaks well over 26 languages. Menu selections vary slightly in adapting traditional McDonald's offerings to local tastes—special chicken dishes in Japan, veggie burgers in the Netherlands or Kahuna burgers in Australia. Germany distributed: Batman, The Animated Series Happy Meal, 1994 in a Happy Meal Box (4 different boxes). This was the only Happy Meal in Germany distributed in a box due to ecological concerns. Boxes and toys are made in Germany and distributed in other European countries.

1995 - Beijing, Buenos Aires, Lisbon, Budapest combine to make the total 80 international countries and still growing! The aim is over 100 countries by the year 2000. McDonald's has just begun to communicate the McDonald's way in the USA; as well as communicate the process on an international scale. By 1995, over half of McDonald's income stream came from outside the USA. In the USA and in the international markets McDonald's is expanding into smaller sales units with McStop and McSnack operations in retail stores and limited space locations. McDonald's restaurants span the globe and are located on all continents except Antarctica. McDonald's believes that preserving and enhancing the integrity of one's environment benefits everyone. As Ray Kroc had stated, "None of us is as good as all of us." Ray Kroc reflected in 1965, "...I like to try to dream of what this Company of ours will be like on its 50th anniversary—the golden anniversary of the Golden Arches. I try to imagine but I admit I cannot. After all, who ten years ago could have predicted we would be where we are today..." Looking back over the last 40 years Ray Kroc would be justifiably proud of the amazing record of growth and success. McDonald's is an institution, a way of life and is world class. McDonald's is a global beacon, a global lighthouse!

There is no single coordinated program for distribution of Happy Meal toys globally. Each country is different with various countries joining together at times. Each Pacific Rim country is independent as are Central and South America. Eastern Europe, with the exception of Hungary and the Middle East, is not specifically involved in a coordinated program. The UK (United Kingdom) coordinates programs for England, Scotland, Wales, Ireland, and Iceland. Germany, France, Spain, Portugal, Italy and Andorra are independent. Scandanavia, Switzerland, Belgium and Holland are coordinated by the London based McDonald's Development Corporation. In essence, all Europe may run the same program, like the World Cup Promotion, but have different premiums with different packaging. The packaging tends to be multilingual with multilingual graphics and/or totally different for each country. Europe and Japan tend to run National and Test Programs and rerun Happy Meal promotions from the USA, which were run 2-3 years prior and reduce the number of toys from 8 to 4. The USA tends to distribute 8 premiums on an average each month, with the exception being Barbie/Hot Wheels which have 8 of each.

There is a kind of cross-pollination with customers, collectors and restaurants all over the world exchanging their specialties with each other—like the Australian meat pie being sold in England. The same thing is happening with collectors all over the world, exchanging their Happy Meal toys and promotional items with each other—like the New Zealand Big Buddies being traded for a set of USA Moveables. McDonald's success story is one of recognition and respect for multicultural differences. It is more than the story of business, it has been the story of people helping people. Collectors from every corner of the globe have joined together in a dedicated and common purpose: to have McFun exchanging Happy Meal toys, promotional items, buttons, pins, anything with the McDonald's logo on it. Why? For the McFun of it! Spanning the globe, McDonald's collecting is World Class McFun!

JAPAN

In response to the often asked question, "What is the earliest International Happy Meal?" A Happy Meal is a hamburger or cheeseburger, fries, and a drink with a toy within a designated carton or bag; the answer is difficult because of cultural difference between countries. Some countries, like Canada, did not include the toy in the Happy Meal price. It was sold separately. Notice the prices on the Canadian translites. In the USA the toy is included with the price of the Happy Meal. At differing times, the toys may be included and/or sold separately; for example, in the USA during June 1995, Power Ranger figures will be sold along with the Power Ranger Happy Meal. So, the answer is not straightforward but cloudy. The earliest called "International Happy Meal" the USA McDonald's Archives can validate is "Ronald McDonald Children's Meal" from Australia, the Caribbean, Hong Kong, Latin America and New Zealand in 1980. This meal offered a hamburger or cheeseburger, fries, soft drink and possibly a toy or premium in a "Happy Meal" style box. There were seven Happy Meal boxes with possible assorted generic premiums. In 1980, the focus was on collecting the box as the premium/toy and not collecting an individual toy within the box. The next recorded "Happy Meal" promotion was the "Airplane" meal which ran in 1982. This promotion consisted of boxes with punch out wings to form airplanes from the boxes, the toy being the box after it is perforated and put together. Many countries have given premiums not specifically associated with the words "Happy Meal." Some of these promotion are called self-liquidators which are tied to offers to purchase a particular product with the purchase of a food item or Value Meal. Prior to 1995, there was no coordinated program for International Happy Meal offerings globally. It looks like McDonald's is moving in the direction of coordinating large segments of the global population. In late 1995, Canada, USA and Mexico will be a coordinated promotion with the premiums being multiligual packaged. For reasons of continuity between our USA and International books, we have chosen to start our International Happy Meal listing with the 1975 Honorary Meal of McDonaldland— when **Ronald McDonald Proclaims everyone "AN HONORARY CITIZEN OF McDONALDLAND, AND IS ENTITLED TO FUN AND HAPPINESS FOREVER, SIGNED AND WITNESSED THIS DAY BY RONALD McDONALD."** It is our feeling that McDonaldland is where the fun should begin!

USA

Kids really care about the environment! These four stamp designs — chosen from some 150,000 entries in a 1994 national design contest among kids age 8 to 13 — depict ways to preserve, protect or restore our environment.

USA

JAPAN

HELPFUL INFORMATION FOR USING THIS BOOK

Realizing that McDonald's is the largest and best-known global foodservice retailer, with more than 15,000 locations in 80 countries, the process of organizing the collectible items is global and geometric. The following codes were used to identify the systemwide restaurants:

COUNTRY	ALPHABETIC ABBREVIATION	NUMBER OF RESTAURANTS IN 1994
EUROPE/AFRICA/MIDDLE EAST		**2,197**
Andorra	AND	1
Austria	ATA	56
Bahrain	BAH	1
Belgium	BEL	32
Czech Republic	CZE	15
Denmark	DEN	39
Egypt	EGY	4
England	UK	526
Finland	FIN	31
France	FRA	350
Germany	GER	570
Greece	GRE	7
Hungary	HUN	27
Iceland	ICE	1
Ireland	IRE	21
Isreal	ISR	7
Italy	ITA	23
Kuwait	KUW	1
Latvia	LAT	1
Luxembourg	LUX	3
Monaco	MON	1
Morocco	MOR	2
Netherlands	NET	110
Northern Ireland	NIR	7
Norway	NOR	20
Oman	OMA	1
Poland	POL	23
Portugal	POR	11
Russia	RUS	3
Saudi Arabia	SAU	10
Scotland	SCO	29
Slovenia	SLO	3
Spain	SPA	80
Sweden	SWE	79
Switzerland	SWI	49
Turkey	TUR	29
United Arab Emirates	UAE	1
Wales	WAL	16
Yugoslavia	YUG	6
ASIA/PACIFIC		**2,111**
Australia	AUS	454
Brunei	BRU	1
China	CHN	27
Guam	GUA	5
Hong Kong	HON	82
Indonesia	IND	23
Japan	JPN	1,133
Macau	MAC	4
Malaysia	MAL	46
New Caldonia	CAL	1
New Zealand	ZEA	80
Phillipines	PHI	55
Saipan	SAI	1
Singapore	SIN	59
South Korea	KOR	31
Taiwan	TAI	81
Thailand	THA	28
NORTH AMERICA		**10,461**
Canada	CAN	717
United States	USA	9,744
LATIN AMERICA		**436**
Antilles	ANT	3
Argentina	ARG	44
Aruba	ARU	1
Bahamas	BAH	4
Barbados	BAR	1
Bermuda/Navy Base	BER	1
Brazil	BRA	149
Chile	CHI	11
Costa Rico	COS	10
Cuba/Navy Base	CUB	1
El Salvador	SAL	4
Guadeloupe	GUD	1
Guatemala	GUA	9
Martinique	MAR	1
Mexico	MEX	102
Nicaragua	NIC	1
Panama	PAN	12
Puerto Rico	PUE	59
Trinidad	TRI	2
Uruguay	URU	6
Venezuela	VEN	12
Virgin Islands	VIR	4

PRICING - The price range listed is for MINT IN THE PACKAGE AND/OR MINT ON THE TREE. Loose toys are generally 50% less than mint in the package. Damaged, chipped or broken toys tend to have little value with a collector. The real value of any collectible is what a buyer is willing to pay for a particular item at a particular time. This value may exceed the stated mint in the package (MIP) or mint on tree (MIT) range. Likewise, since McDonald's makes millions of toys, value may be over inflated based on regional or global markets. Price ranges vary by geographical regions, continents and availability. The price range listed can be used as a relative guide to draw relative comparisons between items.

Premium Names - The toys are listed by the names on the packaging whenever possible.

Check-Off Blocks - The check-off blocks are provided for record keeping; mark one block for mint in package; one block for loose.

Box Names - The boxes were named by the authors with the accompanying identifying numbering system. Whenever possible, the names were taken from the front panel of the Happy Meal box, where the words, "Happy Meal" are displayed.

Numbering System - The numbering system reflects:
   Country of Origin/Country whose name is marked on the item. In some cases, the country of distribution is the country of origin; in most cases the country of origin is not the country of distribution. Many European Happy Meal premiums and Happy Meal boxes and bags are made in Germany and not specifically distributed in Germany and/or other parts of Europe. If the box, toy or item is marked, "Made in Germany" it is listed as: GER for Germany with the accompanying date.

Happy Meal Alphabetic code; two letters. In most cases, this code is made up of the first two letters of the Happy Meal name.

Year of distribution is the first year item was distributed; dates vary among the countries listed.

Numerical listing of item; each general item is assigned a numerical number;

Example: CAN HO7501 = CANADA, HONORARY MEAL OF MCDONALDLAND PROMOTION, 1975, ITEM #01

CAN HO7501

CAN = CANADA - COUNTRY OF ORIGIN
HO = HONORARY MEAL OF MCDONALDLAND PROMOTION
75 = 1975 - YEAR OF DISTRIBUTION
01 = NUMERICAL LISTING OF ITEM -i.e. first item given out

Numerical designator - Last two numbers of identification code; whenever possible the following last two numbers have been used:

TOYS/PREMIUMS	1-9
HM BOXES	10-13
DISPLAY	26
HM BAG	30
CEILING DANGLER	41
COUNTER CARD	42
CREW CARD	43
CREW POSTER	44
REGISTER TOPPER	45
BUTTON	50
TRAYLINER	55
TABLE TENT	56
COUNTER MAT	60
MESSAGE CENTER INSERT	61
HEADER CARD	62
LUG-ON	63
TRANSLITE/SMALL	64
TRANSLITE/LARGE	65
PIN	95

Whenever conflict in selecting the alphabetical/numerical designator arose, the first letter of the first two names of the Happy Meal was used and/or the generic alphabetic representation/combination of letter representing the item was used. For example, Batman, The Animated Series became: BT. Likewise, some Happy Meal Promotions seem to be repeated over the years. These are consistently assigned alphabetic listings, Attack Pack = AP; Barbie = BA; Cabbage Patch = CP; Funny Fry Friends = FF; Halloween = HA; Hot Wheels = HW and Tonka = TK. As time progresses, it is hoped these alphabetic/numeric listings will become standard. The authors apologize for all past inconsistencies in developing a system which identifies each and every item from each and every country with an individual alpha/numeric label.

McDonald's Collecting Language
HM = Happy Meal
MIP = Mint in Package
MIT = Mint on Tree/mint on plastic holder
MOC = Mint on card
ND = No date listed on item
NP = Not packaged/given out in loose form
JT = Junior Tute/Happy Meal/German

Clean-up Week - open time period following a Happy Meal when no specific designated toy is distributed. The stock room backlog is given out in no particular order.

Counter Card - advertising or customer information card or board which sits on the counter.

Display - advertising medium which holds/displays the toys being promoted and distributed during specific time frame. These range from older bubble type displays to 1990s cardboard fold-up type. These are displayed in stand-up Ronald McDonald's cases and/or in the lobby display holder.

Generic - item such as a box or a toy not specifically associated with a specific theme Happy Meal or promotion. The item(s) may be used in several different promtions over a period of time; it may appear and reappear.

Header card - used in older Happy Meal promotions as advertising on top of the permanent display or ceiling dangler to display Happy Meal boxes or toys.

Insert card - advertising card within/along with the premium packaging.

Lug-on - sign added to the menu board.

McDonaldland - imaginary place where all Ronald McDonald's cast of characters live and play; a playland area.

National - all stores in the geographical area distribute the same Happy Meal at the same time; supported with national advertising.

Register Topper - advertising item placed on the top of the register; cardboard advertising sign.

Regional - geographical distribution limited to specific cities, states or stores; restricted distribution area.

Self-liquidator - item intended to be sold over the counter which may or may not be included in the Happy Meal promotion.

Table tent - rectangle shaped advertising sign placed on the tables and counters in the lobby.

Translite - advertising transparent sign used on overhead or drive-thru menu boards to illustrate the current promotion.

U-3 or U-5 - toys or premiums specifically designed for children under the age of 3 or 5; packaging is typically in zebra stripes around the outside of the package; the colors of the zebra stripes vary; typically a soft rubber toy.

USA

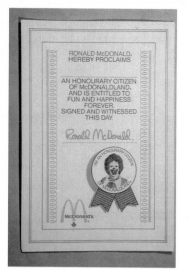

1975

HONORARY MEAL OF McDONALDLAND PROMOTION, 1975
❑ ❑ CAN HO7501 **CITIZENSHIP CERTIFICATE/ENGLISH -**
RONALD PROCLAIMS "HONORARY CITIZEN/MCDLAND",
1975 $15-20
❑ ❑ CAN HO7502 **CITIZENSHIP CERTIFICATE/FRENCH -**
RONALD PROCLAIMS "HONORARY CITIZEN/MCDLAND",
1975 $15-20

COMMENTS: REGIONAL DISTRIBUTION: QUEBEC, CANADA AND
LIMITED AREAS OF CANADA - 1975. NOTE; IN USA, MAYOR
MCCHEESE PROCLAIMS "CUSTOMER AS HONORARY
CITIZEN OF McDONALDLAND". FOCUS WAS CHANGED
FROM MAYOR MCCHEESE TO RONALD McDONALD. See
USA - HONORARY MEAL OF McDONALDLAND, 1975.
CANADA OPENED IT'S FIRST McDONALD'S RESTAURANT
IN 1967.

KLEIDERBUGEL/CLOTHES HANGERS PROMOTION, 1975
❑ ❑ GER KL7501 **CLOTHES HANGER - RONALD,** ND, SMILING/
FULL FACE/HEAVY PAPER/SET OF 3 $25-40

COMMENTS: REGIONAL DISTRIBUTION: GERMANY - 1975 AS
SELF LIQUIDATOR. ADVERTISING ENCOURAGED ONE TO
"LUSTIGE RONALD McDONALD'S/KLEIDERBUGEL. 3 STUCK
NUR DM 2.45."

CAN HO7501   CAN HO7502

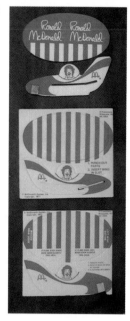

1977

GERMANY/UK GENERIC PROMOTION, 1977
❑ ❑ UK GE7721 **GLIDER - RONALD,** ND, STYRO/PUNCH-OUT/
RED/YEL 4 3/8" W METAL WT $8-10
❑ ❑ GER GE7701 **PLANT ID - HAMB,** 1977, WHT/PAPER $20-25

COMMENTS: REGIONAL DISTRIBUTION: EUROPE/UK -1977.
GLIDER AIRPLANE WAS FREE WITH ANY PURCHASE. UK
GE7721 IS THE SAME AS USA GE7921, HAPPY MEAL TEST -
PART IV - GENERIC HAPPY MEAL, 1979. GER GE7701 CAME
IN DIFFERENT CHARACTER VERSIONS, DATED 1977;
MADE BY SIMON MARKETING, GERMANY.

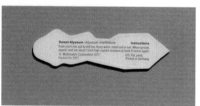

GER GE7701   USA GE7921

1978

RONALD/FULL FIGURE DOLL PROMOTION, 1978
❑ ❑ GER RO7801 **RONALD STUFFED DOLL,** ND, CLOTH/3 RED
STRIPES ON LEG/OUTLINED IN BLK/4" $8-12

COMMENTS: REGIONAL DISTRIBUTION: GERMANY - 1978 AS
SELF LIQUIDATOR. STUFFED RONALD DOLL IS NOT
DATED; "RONALD McDONALD" PRINTED IN RED ON THE
BACK.

RING/BEAD TOSS TREAT-OF-THE WEEK PROMOTION, 1981/1978
❑ ❑ CAN RI7801 **CAPTAIN,** 1978, TRIPPLE BALL TOSS/YEL BASE
$7-10
❑ ❑ CAN RI7802 **RONALD,** 1978, DOUBLE RING TOSS/YEL BASE
$7-10
❑ ❑ CAN RI8101 **CAPTAIN,** 1981, TRIPPLE BALL TOSS $6-8
❑ ❑ CAN RI8102 **RONALD,** 1981, DOUBLE RING TOSS $6-8
❑ ❑ CAN RI8103 **BIG MAC,** 1981, DOUBLE RING TOSS/2 BALLS
$6-8
❑ ❑ CAN RI8104 **MAYOR,** 1981, SINGLE RING TOSS/2 BALLS $6-8
❑ ❑ CAN RI8105 **HAMBURGLAR,** 1981, DOUBLE RING TOSS
$6-8

CAN RI7802   CAN RI7801

CAN RI8103   CAN RI8104   CAN RI8105

COMMENTS: REGIONAL DISTRIBUTION: CANADA - 1978 AND AGAIN IN 1981 AS TREAT-OF-THE WEEK PROMOTION. THESE PREMIUMS CAME WITH A YELLOW BASE. EACH SET IS DATED. CAN RI7801/02 IS SIMILAR TO USA SA8027 AND USA SA8030. EACH IS MARKED DIFFERENTLY WITH COUNTRY AND DATE. See USA SAFARI HAPPY MEAL, 1980.

CAN FT7903

1979

CANADA/GENERIC PROMOTION, 1979

☐ ☐ CAN FT7901 **FUN TIMES - VOLUME 1,** 1979, SPRING/ MAGAZINE/PAPER $20-25
☐ ☐ CAN FT7902 **FUN TIMES - VOL 1 NO 2,** 1979, FALL/MAGA- ZINE/PAPER $20-25
☐ ☐ CAN FT7903 **FUN TIMES - VOL 1 NO 3,** 1979, WINTER/ MAGAZINE/PAPER $20-25
☐ ☐ CAN FT7904 **FUN TIMES - VOL 1 NO 4,** 1980, SPRING/ MAGAZINE/PAPER $20-25
☐ ☐ CAN GE7905 **COMIC - PICNIC PANIC,** 1979, PAPER $10-15

COMMENTS: REGIONAL DISTRIBUTION: CANADA - 1979. CAN FT7901-04 ARE THE FIRST SET OF FUN TIMES MAGAZINES ISSUED IN CANADA. STARTING WITH VOLUME 1 NO 4, FUN TIMES COULD HAVE BEEN ISSUED IN THE USA AND CANADA. EACH FUN TIMES MAGAZINE IS MARKED ON THE BACK COVER WITH THE COUNTRY OF ORIGIN/DISTRIBU- TION. CAN GE7905 IS SIMILAR TO USA RO7940/41/42. (See USA ROUND TOP TEST III HAPPY MEAL, 1978/1978).

CAN FT7904

CAN FT7901

CAN FT7902

CAN GE7905

USA

1980

BISCUITS/McDONALDLAND COOKIES CARD PROMOTION, 1980

❏ ❏ CAN BI8001 **CARD-BIG MAC/L'OFFICIER BIG MAC,** 1980
$3-4

❏ ❏ CAN BI8002 **CARD-CAPTAIN CROOK/CAPTAINE CROCHU,** 1980 $3-4

❏ ❏ CAN BI8003 **CARD-GOBBLINS/LES GLOUTONS,** 1980 $3-4

❏ ❏ CAN BI8004 **CARD-GRIMACE/ROSSE DOUCEUR,** 1980, ON TRAIN $3-4

❏ ❏ CAN BI8005 **CARD-GRIMACE/GROSSE DOUCEUR,** 1980, IN ROW BOAT $3-4

❏ ❏ CAN BI8006 **CARD-HAMBURGLAR/PIQUE-BURGER,** 1980 $3-4

❏ ❏ CAN BI8007 **CARD-MAYOR MCCHESE/MAIRE RU FROMAGE,** 1980 $3-4

❏ ❏ CAN BI8008 **CARD-PROFESSOR/LE PROFESSEUR,** 1980 $3-4

❏ ❏ CAN BI8009 **CARD-RONALD McDONALD,** 1980, W HAND CART $3-4

❏ ❏ CAN BI8010 **CARD-RONALD McDONALD,** 1980, ON BICYCLE $3-4

COMMENTS: NATIONAL DISTRIBUTION: CANADA - 1980. CANADA'S BISCUITS/COOKIES ARE SIMILAR TO USA McDONALDLAND COOKIES.

CAN BI8001   CAN BI8002   CAN BI8003   CAN BI8004

CAN BI8005   CAN BI8006

USA

CAN BI8007   CAN BI8008   CAN BI8009   CAN BI8010

USA

CANADA/GENERIC PROMOTION, 1980
❏ ❏ CAN GE8001 **COLORING BOOK,** 1980, COLOURING BOOK
$15-25

COMMENTS: REGIONAL DISTRIBUTION: CANADA - 1980.

GERMANY/GENERIC PROMOTION, 1980
❏ ❏ GER GE8001 **COMIC BOOK,** 1980, RONALD MCD SUPER COMICS $15-25
❏ ❏ GER GE8016 **PEN - RONALD**, 1980, YEL/RED/WHT W RED CORD $6-8

COMMENTS: REGIONAL DISTRIBUTION: AUGSBURG, GERMANY - AUGUST 1980. GER GE8016 IS CALLED PEN TOPPER/ TOLLER SCHREIBER. IT WAS GIVEN/SOLD AS A SELF LIQUIDATOR IN GERMANY. GER GE8016 = USA GE8016 = UK PE8316 (See USA/GENERIC PROMOTION, 1980 AND UK PENFRIENDS PROMOTION 1989/1983).

PENCIL HOLDERS PROMOTION, 1986/1980
❏ ❏ CAN PE8001 **BIG MAC/L'OFFICER,** 1980, ORG or RED or GRN or YEL HOLDING LF HAND PENCIL $2-3
❏ ❏ CAN PE8002 **CAPITAINE CROCHU,** 1980, ORG or RED or GRN or YEL HOLDING RT HAND PENCIL $2-3
❏ ❏ CAN PE8003 **PIQUE-BURGER,** 1980, ORG or RED or GRN or YEL HOLDING RT HAND PENCIL $2-3
❏ ❏ CAN PE8004 **RONALD McDONALD,** 1980, ORG or RED or GRN or YEL HOLDING LF HAND PENCIL $2-3

COMMENTS: REGIONAL DISTRIBUTION: CANADA - 1980 AND AGAIN IN 1986 AS TREAT-OF-THE-WEEK. EACH SET IS DATED.

USA

USA

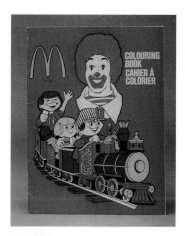

CAN GE8001

CAN PE8001   CAN PE8002   CAN PE8003   CAN PE8004

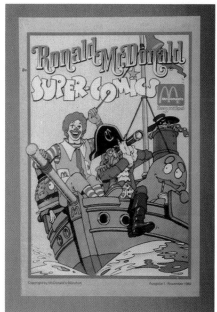

GER GE8001

GER GE8016

CAN PE8601   CAN PE8602   CAN PE8603   CAN PE8604

*** DI8001   *** DI8002   *** DI8003

*** DI8016

RONALD McDONALD FLYER/FRISBEE/DISC PROMOTION, 1992/1980

*** IDENTICAL FLYERS: AUS/UK DI8001/02/03/16

❑ ❑ *** DI8001 **FRISBEE - GRIMACE,** 1980, RED or YEL or BLU
$2-3

❑ ❑ *** DI8002 **FRISBEE - HAMBURGLAR,** 1980, RED or YEL or BLU
$2-3

❑ ❑ *** DI8003 **FRISBEE - BIG MAC,** 1980, RED or YEL or BLU
$2-3

❑ ❑ *** DI8016 **FRISBEE - RONALD,** 1980, R M FLYER/THIN RON/ARMS OUTSTRETCHED/RED or YEL or BLU $2-3

❑ ❑ AUS DI9204 **FRISBEE - BIRDIE,** 1992, YEL $1.50-2.50

COMMENTS: REGIONAL DISTRIBUTION: UK - AUGUST 16-SEPTEMBER 1980. FLYER WAS FREE WITH ANY PURCHASE TO ANYONE 12 OR UNDER. UK DI8016 IS VERY SIMILAR TO USA DI8216 (See USA DINOSAUR DAYS HAPPY MEAL, 1982). UK FLYERS ARE MARKED, "MADE IN UK 1980." AUSTRALIA FLYERS DO NOT HAVE MARKINGS ON BACK.

1981

MINI-CINEMA PROMOTION, 1981

❑ ❑ CAN CI8101 **HAMBURGLAR,** 1981, ON SLED $2-3
❑ ❑ CAN CI8102 **MAYOR,** 1981, ON SKIS $2-3
❑ ❑ CAN CI8103 **RONALD,** 1981, ON SKATES $2-3

COMMENTS: REGIONAL DISTRIBUTION: CANADA - 1981 AS TREAT-OF-THE-WEEK.

RONALD McDONALD CHILDREN'S MEAL HAPPY MEAL, 1981

❑ ❑ AUS CI8110 **HM BOX,** 1979, **AT THE BEACH** $20-25
❑ ❑ AUS CI8111 **HM BOX,** 1979, **AT A PICNIC** $20-25
❑ ❑ AUS CI8112 **HM BOX,** 1979, **AT THE ZOO** $20-25
❑ ❑ AUS CI8113 **HM BOX,** 1979, **AMUSEMENT PARK**

$20-25
❑ ❑ AUS CI8114 **HM BOX,** 1979, **COLLECTING LITTER** $20-25
❑ ❑ AUS CI8115 **HM BOX,** 1979, **SPACE** $20-25
❑ ❑ AUS CI8116 **HM BOX,** 1979, $20-25

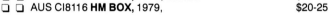

AUS DI9204

CAN CI8101   CAN CI8102   CAN CI8103

USA

32

COMMENTS: LIMITED REGIONAL DISTRIBUTION: AUSTRALIA, NEW ZEALAND, LATIN AMERICA AND HONG KONG - 1981. THE SEVEN BOX GRAPHICS DIFFERED SOMEWHAT/ LANGUAGE FROM USA CIRCUS WAGON HAPPY MEAL, 1979. LIKE USA CIRCUS WAGON HM, 1979 THIS HAPPY MEAL IS CONSIDERED TO BE THE "FIRST INTERNATIONAL HAPPY MEAL PROMOTION" BY McDONALD'S ARCHIVES.

USA

USA

USA

AUSTRALIA

1982

AIRPLANE PROMOTION, 1982

❏ ❏ *** AI8210 **HM BOX,** 1982, **BIG MAC/PUNCH-OUT PLANE**
$20-25
❏ ❏ *** AI8211 **HM BOX,** 1982, **GRIMACE/PUNCH-OUT PLANE**
$20-25
❏ ❏ *** AI8212 **HM BOX,** 1982, **HAMBURGLAR/PUNCH-OUT PLANE**
$20-25
❏ ❏ *** AI8213 **HM BOX,** 1982, **MAYOR/PUNCH-OUT PLANE**
$20-25
❏ ❏ *** AI8214 **HM BOX,** 1982, **RONALD/PUNCH-OUT PLANE**
$25-25
❏ ❏ *** AI8215 **HM BOX,** 1982, **R/HM/M/PUNCH-OUT PLANE**
$20-25
❏ ❏ *** AI8265 TRANSLITE/LG, 1982
$45-60

COMMENTS: LIMITED REGIONAL DISTRIBUTION: AUSTRALIA/ HONG KONG/NEW ZEALAND/SWEDEN/SOUTH AMERICA - 1982. PAPER WINGS FIT THROUGH THE BOX FORMING AN AIRPLANE. MARKINGS ON THE BOXES ARE UNKNOWN. REGIONAL DISTRIBUTION COULD HAVE OCCURED IN THE USA.

AUSTRALIA

AUSTRALIA

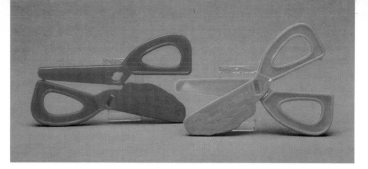

CAN GE8201

USA

CANADA/GENERIC PROMOTION, 1982

❏ ❏ CAN GE8201 **SCISSOR-RON,** 1982, ORG or RED $3-4
❏ ❏ CAN GE8202 **MCDLAND HOCKEY-FRY GUY,** 1982, RED or ORG or TURQ or YEL $3-5
❏ ❏ CAN GE8203 **HARDWORKING BURGER BULLDOZER,** 1982, LT GRN or YEL $4-6
❏ ❏ CAN GE8204 **HARDWORKING BURGER DUMP TRUCK,** 1982, LT GRN or YEL $4-6
❏ ❏ CAN GE8205 **BIKE BUDDY RING - GRIMACE,** 1982, YEL or ORG $4-5

COMMENTS: REGIONAL DISTRIBUTION: CANADA - 1982 AS TREAT-OF-THE-WEEK. CAN GE8205 IS SAME AS USA BIKE BUDDY RING, EXCEPT COLORS VARY. CAN GE8203/04 = USA GE8213/14, EXCEPT COLORS. THE USA VERSIONS CAME IN DARK GREEN AND ORANGE; CANADA IN LIGHT GREEN AND YELLOW. See USA/GENERIC PROMOTIONS, 1982.

MASKEN I/FACE MASKS JUNIOR TUTE, 1982

❏ ❏ GER MA8201 **MASK - GRIMACE,** 1982, PAPER/SHAKY $7-10
❏ ❏ GER MA8202 **MASK - BIG MAC,** 1982, PAPER $7-10
❏ ❏ GER MA8203 **MASK - HAMBURGLAR,** 1982, PAPER/ HAMBURGERKLAU $7-10
❏ ❏ GER MA8204 **MASK - FRY GUY,** 1982, PAPER/ POMMMESFRITZCHEN $12-15
❏ ❏ GER MA8205 **MASK - RONALD,** 1982, PAPER $7-10

COMMENTS: LIMITED REGIONAL DISTRIBUTION: GERMANY - FEBRUARY 1-26, 1982. FIRST JUNIOR TUTE/HAPPY MEAL TEST DISTRIBUTED IN GERMANY, ALTHOUGH GERMAN ARCHIVES INDICATE JANUARY-APRIL 1988 IN WURZBURG, GERMANY IS WHERE THE JUNIOR TUTE/HAPPY MEAL WAS OFFICIALLY TESTED. CALLED "MASKIERT EUCH!/ GESICHTSMASKEN" ON ADVERTISING WITH 5 MASKS PICTURED. THESE HALLOWEEN STYLE MASKS WERE RUN AGAIN IN JANUARY 15-FEBRUARY 15, 1983, WITHOUT GER MA8204 - FRY GUY MASK.

TRUCK/BIG MAC JUNIOR TUTE, 1982

❏ ❏ GER TR8201 **TRUCK - BIG MAC,** 1982, **PAPER**/PUNCH OUT/ BASTELBOGEN $25-40

COMMENTS: LIMITED REGIONAL DISTRIBUTION: GERMANY - SEPTEMBER 1982. DISTRIBUTED AS A JUNIOR TUTE/ HAPPY MEAL WITH PREMIUM AND FOOD ASSOCIATED TOGETHER.

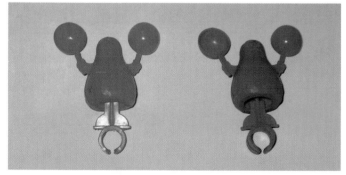

CAN GE8205   USA

USA

USA

CANADA

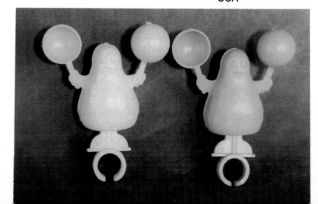

34

1983

MASKEN II/FACE MASKS JUNIOR TUTE/HAPPY MEAL, 1983

- ❑ ❑ GER MA8301 **MASK - GRIMACE,** 1982, PAPER/**SHAKY**/WHT BACKGROUND $7-10
- ❑ ❑ GER MA8302 **MASK - BIG MAC,** 1982, PAPER/WHT BACK-GROUND $7-10
- ❑ ❑ GER MA8303 **MASK - HAMBURG,** 1982, PAPER/ HAMBURGERKLAU/WHT BACKGROUND $7-10
- ❑ ❑ GER MA8305 **MASK - RONALD,** 1982, PAPER/WHT BACK-GROUND $7-10

COMMENTS: LIMITED REGIONAL DISTRIBUTION: GERMANY - JANUARY-FEBRUARY 1983. PAPER FACE MASKS JUNIOR TUTE/HAPPY MEAL WAS REPEATED IN GERMANY IN 1983 WITH ONLY 4 FACE MASKS THIS SECOND TIME, EX- CLUDED FRY GUY FACE MASK (See MASKEN/FACE MASKS, 1982). LOOSE/PUNCHED OUT, GER MA8301/02/03/ 05 = GER MA8201/02/03/05. GRIMACE IS CALLED SHAKY IN GERMANY.

McDONALDLAND EXPRESS/McDONALD'S EXPRESS HAPPY MEAL, 1988/1983

*** IDENTICAL CARS: CAN/NET EX8200/01/02/03
- ❑ ❑ *** EX8200 **ENGINE,** 1982, VACUFORMED/RED or BLU $15-20
- ❑ ❑ *** EX8201 **COACH,** 1982, VACUFORMED/BLU or ORG $15-20
- ❑ ❑ *** EX8202 **FREIGHT CAR,** 1982, VACUFORMED/GRN or ORG $15-20
- ❑ ❑ *** EX8203 **CABOOSE,** 1982, VACUFORMED/RED or GRN $15-20
- ❑ ❑ NET EX8806 **STICKER SHEET-ENGINE,** 1982 $6-10
- ❑ ❑ NET EX8807 **STICKER SHEET-COACH,** 1982 $6-10
- ❑ ❑ NET EX8808 **STICKER SHEET-FREIGHT,** 1982 $6-10
- ❑ ❑ NET EX8809 **STICKER SHEET-CABOOSE,** 1982 $6-10

COMMENTS: REGIONAL DISTRIBUTION: CANADA: 1983; NETH- ERLANDS: JANUARY 1988. VACUFORM TRAIN CARS SERVED AS THE FOOD CONTAINER AND PREMIUM. NETHERLANDS NET EX8800-03 = USA EX8200-03. NOTICE McDONALDLAND EXPRESS CARS ON THE OVERHEAD MENU BOARD PICTURE FROM EDMONTON, CANADA. See USA McDONALDLAND EXPRESS HAPPY MEAL, 1982.

USA EX8809 USA EX8808 USA EX8807 USA EX8806
USA EX8203 USA EX8202 USA EX8201 USA EX8200

USA EX8226

Edmonton, Canada 1983

Edmonton, Canada 1983

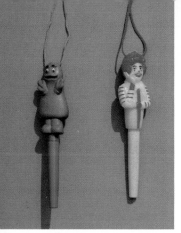
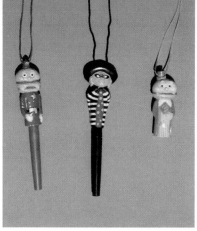

*** PE8318   *** PE8316   *** PE8314   *** PE8315   UK PE8317

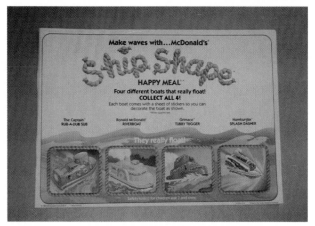

USA

USA SH8303   USA SH8304   USA SH8302
                  USA SH8301

USA SH8505

PENFRIENDS/FILZSTIFTE/UMHANGESTIFTE JUNIOR TUTE, 1989/1983

*** IDENTICAL PENS: GER/UK PE8314/15/16/18

❑ ❑ *** PE8314 **PEN - BIG MAC,** 1983, BLU PEN/BLU CORD $6-8
❑ ❑ *** PE8315 **PEN - HAMBURGLAR,** 1983, BLK PEN/BLK or WHT CORD $6-8
❑ ❑ *** PE8316 **PEN - RONALD,** 1983, YEL PEN/RED CORD $6-8
❑ ❑ *** PE8318 **PEN - GRIM/SHAKY,** 1983, PURP PEN/PURP CORD $6-8
❑ ❑ UK PE8317 **PEN - MAYOR,** 1983, PNK PEN/PNK CORD $6-8

COMMENTS: REGIONAL DISTRIBUTION: GERMANY - NOVEMBER-DECEMBER 1983; UK 1983/1989. UK - 4 PEN FRIENDS IN 1983 - PE8314/15/16/17 COST 27p EACH WITH ANY PURCHASE IN 1983. UK PE8314/15/16/17 = USA GE8014/15/16 AND USA GE8216. USA GE8013 = GER PE8318 = UK PE8918. THE SAME PENS WERE DISTRIBUTED IN THE USA IN 1980/1982; IN GERMANY IN 1983 AND UK IN 1983/1989. THIS PROMOTION WAS REPEATED IN THE UK IN 1989 WITH THE ADDITION OF GRIMACE UK PE8918. THE UK - 5 PENFRIENDS IN 1989 COST 44p EACH. IT IS POSSIBLE THAT THE COLORS OF THE ATTACHED CORDS VARIED, THE PENS REMAINED THE SAME IN THE VARIOUS COUNTRIES.

SAMMELBECHER/PLASTIC CUP JUNIOR TUTE, 1983

❑ ❑ GER SA8301 **PLASTIC CUP - RONALD,** 1983, FLYING A KITE/WHT $3-5
❑ ❑ GER SA8302 **PLASTIC CUP - HAMBURGLAR,** 1983, HIGH JUMPING/WHT $3-5
❑ ❑ GER SA8303 **PLASTIC CUP - SHAKY,** 1983, SPINNING/WHT $3-5
❑ ❑ GER SA8304 **PLASTIC CUP - BIG MAC,** 1983, PLAYING BAND INSTRUMENTS/WHT $3-5

COMMENTS: REGIONAL DISTRIBUTION: GERMANY - APRIL 1983.

SHIP SHAPE I JUNIOR TUTE, 1986/1983

❑ ❑ GER SH8301 **HAMBURGLAR SPLASH DASHER,** 1983, WHT TOP/YEL BOTTOM $10-15
❑ ❑ GER SH8302 **GRIMACE TUBBY TUGGER,** 1983, BLU TOP/BLU BOTTOM $10-15
❑ ❑ GER SH8303 **CAPT RUB-A-DUB SUB,** 1983, RED TOP/BLU BOTTOM $10-15
❑ ❑ GER SH8304 **RONALD RIVER BOAT,** 1983, YEL TOP/BLU BOTTOM $10-15
❑ ❑ GER SH8505 **STICKER SHEET - SPLASH DASHER,** 1985 $4-6
❑ ❑ GER SH8506 **STICKER SHEET - TUBBY TUGGER,** 1985 $4-6
❑ ❑ GER SH8507 **STICKER SHEET - RUB-A-DUB-SUB,** 1985 $4-6
❑ ❑ GER SH8508 **STICKER SHEET - RIVER BOAT,** 1985 $4-6

COMMENTS: NATIONAL DISTRIBUTION: GUATEMALA: JUNE 6-JULY 18, 1983; GERMANY: JUNE/JULY 1986. THE VACUUM FORM CONTAINERS ARE THE SAME AS USA SH8301/02/03/04 - USA SHIP SHAPE HM, 1983/1985 CONTAINERS. NOTE: GERMAN COLORS ARE DIFFERENT FROM USA COLORS.

1984

CANADA/GENERIC PROMOTION, 1984

❑ ❑ CAN GE8401 **FREEZE POP MOLD,** 1984, RON/GRN or BLU TOP/CLEAR BASE $4-5
❑ ❑ CAN GE8402 **COIN PURSE,** 1984, RON FACE/BLU or GRN or ORG $1-1.50
❑ ❑ CAN GE8450 BUTTON/ENGLISH, 1984, HA! HA! $7-10
❑ ❑ CAN GE8451 BUTTON/FRENCH, 1984, OFFREZ-VOUS UN JOYEUX $7-10

COMMENTS: REGIONAL DISTRIBUTION: CANADA - 1984 AS TREAT-OF-THE-WEEK. CAN GE8450-51 DEPICTS USA CIRCUS WAGON HM BOX FROM 1979. See USA CIRCUS WAGON HAPPY MEAL, 1979.

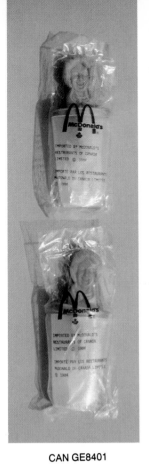

CAN GE8402

CAN GE8401

CAN GE8450   CAN GE8451

FAST MAC/SPEEDIES/MCMINI BUGGIES/BURGER BUGGY HAPPY MEAL, 1992/1987/1986/1985/1984

CANADA

*** **IDENTICAL TOYS: CAN/GUA/UK FA8505/06/07**
- ❏ ❏ *** FA8505 **CAR - BIG MAC,** 1985, IN WHT SQUAD/POLICE CAR $4-6
- ❏ ❏ *** FA8506 **CAR - BIRDIE,** 1985, IN PNK SUN CRUISER/PNK ARCHES WINDSHIELD $4-6
- ❏ ❏ *** FA8507 **CAR - HAMB,** 1985, IN RED SPORTS CAR $4-6

*** **IDENTICAL TOY: CAN/GUA FA8508**
- ❏ ❏ *** FA8508 **CAR - RONALD,** 1985, **IN YEL JEEP/NO WINDSHIELD** $4-6

- ❏ ❏ UK FA8409 **CAR - RONALD,** 1984, IN YEL JEEP W **WHT RECTANGLE WINDSHIELD** $15-20

*** **IDENTICAL TOYS: AUS/FRA/GER/JPN FA8710/11/12/13**
- ❏ ❏ *** FA8710 **CAR - BIG MAC,** 1985, IN **WHT/GRN SQUAD/ POLICE CAR**/GRY BUMPER $4-6
- ❏ ❏ *** FA8711 **CAR - HAMB,** 1985, IN RED SPORTS CAR W RED FINS/GRY BUMPER $4-6
- ❏ ❏ *** FA8712 **CAR - RONALD,** 1985, IN YEL JEEP W GRY BUMPER $4-6
- ❏ ❏ *** FA8713 **CAR - SHAKY/GRIM,** 1985, IN PNK CRUISER/GRY BUMPER $4-6

- ❏ ❏ AUS FA9243 COUNTER CARD, 1992 $4-6
- ❏ ❏ CAN FA8550 BUTTON, 1985, FAST MAC! $4-7
- ❏ ❏ CAN FA8565 TRANSLITE/LG, 1985 $15-20

CAN FA8505   CAN FA8506   CAN FA8508   CAN FA8507

UK FA8710   UK FA8713

UK FA8711   UK FA8712

37

AUS

COMMENTS: LIMITED REGIONAL DISTRIBUTION: UK: 1984. NATIONAL DISTRIBUTION: CANADA/UK - 1985; GERMANY - TEST MARKED IN NOVEMBER 1-23,1986; AGAIN IN OCTOBER 30-NOVEMBER 29, 1987; BELGIUM, DENMARK, FINLAND, FRANCE, ITALY, HOLLAND, SPAIN, SWEDEN, SWITZERLAND: 1987; GUATEMALA: 1985/1986; JAPAN: 1988; AUSTRALIA - 1992. CALLED "MCMINI BUGGIES PROMOTION" IN SOUTH AMERICA; CALLED "SPEEDIES" IN GERMANY, SELF LIQUIDATING PROMOTION. CALLED "BURGER BUGGIES" IN AUSTRALIA IN 1992. IN ENGLAND/ UK THIS WAS THE FIRST HM TEST PROMOTION WHERE TOYS WERE SOLD/GIVEN WITH A FOOD PURCHASE. CANADA'S FAST MACS CARS WERE SOLD FOR 69 CENTS. CAN FA8505-7 = UK FA8505-7. AUSTRALIA/GERMANY GER FA8710/11/12/13 ARE DIFFERENT FROM USA AND UK VERSION. BLISTER PACK CARDS/CARS CARRY 1984 DATE. CARS WERE SOLD ON A BLISTER PACK. UK FA8507 = USA FA8402, USA FAST MACS I PROMOTION, 1984. UK FA8506 AND UK FA8409 WERE REDESIGNED FOR NATIONAL DISTRIBUTION IN USA IN 1985.

AUS FA9243

CAN FA8565

FRA FA8713   FRA FA8710   FRA FA8712   FRA FA8711

CAN FA8550

AUS FA9412   AUS FA9413   AUS FA9410   AUS FA9411

FUN PAILS HAPPY MEAL, 1984

❑ ❑ CAN PA8401 **PAIL - RON,** 1983, BEIGE/RON JOGGING/RED SHOVEL $5-7
❑ ❑ CAN PA8402 **PAIL - RON,** 1983, YEL RON BIKING/YEL SHOVEL $5-7
❑ ❑ CAN PA8403 **PAIL - RON,** 1983, WHT/RON W BEACH BALL/ GRN SHOVEL $5-7
❑ ❑ CAN PA8404 **PAIL - RON,** 1983, BLU/RON IN SAIL BOAT/BLU SHOVEL $5-7
❑ ❑ CAN PA8450 BUTTON/ENGLISH, 1983, COLLECT McDONALD'S FUN PAILS $4-7
❑ ❑ CAN PA8451 BUTTON/FRENCH, 1983, COLLECTIONNEZ LES PETITES CHAUDIERES $4-7

COMMENTS: REGIONAL DISTRIBUTION: CANADA - 1984.

GERMANY/GENERIC PROMOTION, 1984

❑ ❑ GER GE8401 **STUFFED DOLL - RONALD,** 1981, CLOTH/2 STRIPES ON LEG/4 1/2"/BLK CORD $8-12
❑ ❑ GER GE8402 **STENCIL/ZAUBERSCHREIBER,** 1984, SQ W CIRCLE CUTOUT/YEL DISC/2P $3-5
❑ ❑ GER GE8403 **NOSE CARD/NASENSPIEL,** 1984, RON W STRING NOSE/PAPER $5-7
❑ ❑ GER GE8404 **SLATE BOARD/ZAUBERTAFEL,** 1984, DRAW RONALD $3-5
❑ ❑ GER GE8405 **AIRPLANE/STYROPORFLUGZEUG,** 1984, YEL GLIDER/RED-YEL WINGS/RED PLASTIC WT $7-10
❑ ❑ GER GE8406 **PATCH/SEW,** 1984, I LIKE McDONALD'S/RECT/ RED/YEL $5-7
❑ ❑ GER GE8407 **STICKER/SAFETY/SICHERHEITSAUFKLEBER,** 1984, ROUND/RON W LG YEL GLOVE/HAND $5-7
❑ ❑ GER GE8408 **COIN PURSE/KINDERBORSE,** 1984, RONALD'S FACE/RED $1-1.50
❑ ❑ GER GE8409 **ADVENT CALENDAR/ADVENTSKALENDER,** 1984, RON ON SLEIGH $12-15

COMMENTS: REGIONAL DISTRIBUTION: GERMANY - 1984. STUFFED RONALD DOLL (DISTRIBUTED IN FEBRUARY 1984) IS DATED 1981 WITH McDONALD'S LOGO ON THE BACK. GENERIC ITEMS WERE REGIONALLY DISTRIBUTED IN GERMANY DURING 1984. GER GE8408 RONALD'S SMILE IS DIFFERENT FROM CANADA'S AND USA'S VERSIONS.

CAN PA8403   CAN PA8401   CAN PA8404

CAN PA8450   CAN PA8451

Laudsburt, Germany

Wiesbaden, Germany

Lünenburg, Germany

39

GER GE8408

GLOW'N DARK PUZZLE TREAT-OF-THE WEEK, 1984

❏ ❏ CAN GL8401 **PUZZLE - HAMB/MAYOR,** 1984, PLAYING
BASEBALL/9P $5-7
❏ ❏ CAN GL8402 **PUZZLE - RON/HAMB,** 1984, IN SPEED BOAT/
9P $5-7
❏ ❏ CAN GL8403 **PUZZLE - RON/BIRDIE,** 1984, IN AIRPLANE/
HOT AIR BALLOON $5-7

COMMENTS: REGIONAL DISTRIBUTION: CANADA - 1984.

LEGO BUILDING SET HAPPY MEAL, 1984

❏ ❏ CAN LE8410 HM BOX, 1984, AT THE DOCK/THE GARAGE
$4-5
❏ ❏ CAN LE8401 **SET 1 RACE CAR,** 1984, RED PACKAGED 16P
$5-8
❏ ❏ CAN LE8402 **SET 2 TANKER,** 1984, BLUE PACKAGED 27P
$5-8
❏ ❏ CAN LE8403 **SET 3 HELICOPTER,** 1984, YELLOW PACK-
AGED 19P $5- 8
❏ ❏ CAN LE8404 **SET 4 AIRPLANE,** 1984, GREEN PACKAGED
18P $5-8

COMMENTS: REGIONAL DISTRIBUTION: CANADA - 1984. HM
BOX, SETS 1/2/3/4 RAN AGAIN IN 1986 AS LEGO BUILDING
SET HAPPY MEAL, 1986 WITH BUTTONS. PACKAGING IS
DATED AND MARKED WITH CANADIAN MCD LOGO.
CANADA LEGO 1984 IS VERY SIMILAR TO USA LEGO
BUILDING SETS, 1984, NUMBER OF PIECES VARY AND SET
1 USA IS A TRUCK; WHEREAS SET 1 CANADA IS A RACE
CAR (See USA LEGO BUILDING SETS HM, 1984).

CAN

CAN GL8401

CAN GL8402

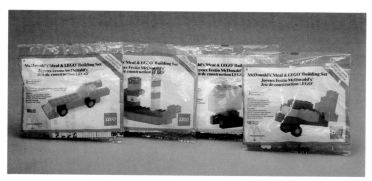

CAN LE8401   CAN LE8402   CAN LE8403   CAN LE8404

CAN GL8403

Front, CAN GE8403

USA LE8426

40

USA LE8465

CAN LE8410

USA WI8304   USA WI8305

USA WI8301   USA WI8302   USA WI8303

RONALD & FRIENDS HAPPY MEAL, 1984

- ☐ ☐ GUA WI8401 **ORNAMENT-BIRDIE,** 1983, YEL/PNK VINYL 4" W LOOPED CORD $3-5
- ☐ ☐ GUA WI8402 **ORNAMENT-GRIMACE,** 1983, PUR VINYL 4" W LOOPED CORD $3-5
- ☐ ☐ GUA WI8403 **ORNAMENT-HAMBURGLAR,** 1983, BLK W WHT STRIPES/VINYL 4" W LOOPED CORD $3-5
- ☐ ☐ GUA WI8404 **ORNAMENT-MAYOR,** 1983, YEL/PNK/PUR VINYL 4" W LOOPED CORD $3-5
- ☐ ☐ GUA WI8405 **ORNAMENT-RONALD,** 1983, RED/YEL VINYL 4" W LOOPED CORD $3-5

COMMENTS: REGIONAL DISTRIBUTION: GUATEMALA - 1984. GUA WI8401-05 = USA WI8301-05 (See USA WINTER WORLDS HAPPY MEAL, 1983).

SPACESHIP (HAVE LANDED HERE) / FLIEGENDE UNTERTASSEN/MCSPACESHIP I/UFO HAPPY MEAL/ JUNIOR TUTE, 1990/1989/1988/1986/1985/1984

*** IDENTICAL SPACESHIPS: CAN/GER/FRA/MAL/NET/UK SP8230/31/32/33

- ☐ ☐ *** SP8230 **SPACESHIP #1 - STARLIGHT - 8 WINDOWS,** 1981, BLU or GRN or RED or YEL W DECALS $15-20
- ☐ ☐ *** SP8231 **SPACESHIP #2 - GALAXIS - REAR ENGINE,** 1981, BLU or GRN or RED or YEL W DECALS $15-20
- ☐ ☐ *** SP8232 **SPACESHIP #3 - HYPERSPLASH - POINTED FRONT,** 1981, BLU or GRN or RED or YEL W DECALS $15-20
- ☐ ☐ *** SP8233 **SPACESHIP #4 - FLASHPOINT - 4 KNOBS,** 1981, BLU or GRN or RED or YEL W DECALS $15-20

- ☐ ☐ GER SP8504 SPACESHIP STICKER SHEET #1, 1984, #1 BLAU $4-5
- ☐ ☐ GER SP8505 SPACESHIP STICKER SHEET #2, 1984, #2 ROT $4-5
- ☐ ☐ GER SP8506 SPACESHIP STICKER SHEET #3, 1984, #3 GRUN $4-5
- ☐ ☐ GER SP8507 SPACESHIP STICKER SHEET #4, 1984, #4 GELB $4-5

- ☐ ☐ UK SP8404 SPACESHIP STICKER SHEET #1, 1984, 8 WINDOWS/UK FLAG $4-5
- ☐ ☐ UK SP8405 SPACESHIP STICKER SHEET #2, 1984, REAR ENGINE/UK FLAG $4-5
- ☐ ☐ UK SP8406 SPACESHIP STICKER SHEET #3, 1984, POINTED FRONT/UK FLAG $4-5
- ☐ ☐ UK SP8407 SPACESHIP STICKER SHEET #4, 1984, FOUR KNOBS/UK FLAG $4-5

USA

USA   *** SP8230

USA   *** SP8231

USA SP8233

USA SP8232

FRA SP8465

CAN SP8450   CAN SP8451

USA

☐	☐	UK SP8441 CEILING DANGLER, 1984	$20-25
☐	☐	UK SP8444 CREW/COMPETITION POSTER, 1984	$3-5
☐	☐	UK SP8445 REGISTER TOPPER, 1984	$6-8
☐	☐	CAN SP8450 BUTTON/ENGLISH, 1984, HAVE YOUR NEXT MEAL IN A SPACESHIP	$15-20
☐	☐	CAN SP8451 BUTTON/FRENCH, 1984, OFFREZ-YOUS UN FESTIN McDONALD'S...	$15-20
☐	☐	FRA SP8465 TRANSLITE/POSTER/UN HAPPY MEAL, 1984, SPACESHIPS	$75-100
☐	☐	UK SP8465 TRANSLITE/LG, 1984	$45-60
☐	☐	FRA SP8466 WALL SIGN, 1984	$45-60

COMMENTS: REGIONAL DISTRIBUTION: CANADA/FRANCE/ UNITED KINGDOM - 1984; TEST MARKETED IN BREMEN, GERMANY - FEBRUARY 1984 AND REGIONALLY IN GERMANY - MAY-JULY 1985; NETHERLAND - 1986; AUSTRALIA - 1988; MALAYSIA - 1988-1990. CALLED "MCSPACESHIP" IN MALAYSIA. THE FIRST HAPPY MEAL IN THE NETHERLANDS WAS THE UFO HAPPY MEAL, 1986. NETHERLANDS ADVERTISED, "MET EEN HAMBURGER, FRANSE FRIETJES EN EEN DRINK IN EEN ECHT RUIMTESCHIP; EEN UFO." SPACESHIP HM WAS THE "FIRST REGIONAL HAPPY MEAL PROMOTION" IN THE UK AND HOLLAND WHERE A SPECIFIC PREMIUM WAS IDENTIFIED WITH NAME AND FOOD ITEMS AND CALLED A HAPPY MEAL. IN UK DURING 1984, FAST MACS PROMOTION I (NOT SPECIFICALLY CALLED A HAPPY MEAL) ALSO ASSOCIATED A PREMIUM WITH FOOD ITEMS. CAN/FRA/UK SPACESHIPS ***SP8230/31/32/33 ARE THE SAME AS USA SP8230/31/32/33 (See USA SPACESHIP HAPPY MEAL, 1982). IT IS LIKELY THAT ALL COLORS OF ALL SPACESHIPS WERE DISTRIBUTED INTERNATIONALLY, BASED ON AVAILABILITY IN THE WAREHOUSES; TOTAL OF 16 SPACESHIPS (4 DIFFERENT SPACESHIPS/ 4 COLORS). STICKER SHEETS WERE MARKED WITH THE COUNTRY OF DISTRIBUTION. IT IS CONCEIVABLE THAT IN MALAYSIA, THE COLOR PURPLE WAS SUBSTITUTED FOR THE GREEN SPACESHIPS. COLOR SHADES VARY WITHIN THE COUNTRIES OF DISTRIBUTION, FROM LIGHT TO DARK AND NEON TO DULL. THE SPECIFIC DIFFERENT SPACESHIPS ARE THE GLO-TRON SPACESHIPS WITH METALLIC FLAKE COLORS AND GLOW IN THE DARK STICKERS.

1985

CANADA/GENERIC PROMOTION, 1985

❏ ❏ CAN GE8501 **POP CAR/AUTO - BIRDIE,** 1985, RED or GRN
AUTO/6P $5-7
❏ ❏ CAN GE8502 **POP CAR/AUTO - RONALD,** 1985, RED or GRN
AUTO/6P $5-7
❏ ❏ CAN GE8503 **STENCIL - RONALD,** 1985, W AUTO/CANOE/
BALLOON/AIRPLANE $3-4

COMMENTS: REGIONAL DISTRIBUTION: CANADA = 1985 AS
TREAT-OF-THE-WEEK.

CRAYOLA CRAYONS & MARKERS PROMOTION, 1985

❏ ❏ CAN CR8510 HM BOX, 1985, CRAYOLA/BIRD W MCD
CANADA LOGO $10-15

❏ ❏ CAN CR8501 **SET 1 CRAYONS/BOX/3 REGULAR,** 1985,
ORG/YEL/GRN CRAYONS/BINNEY SMITH BOX $4-6
❏ ❏ CAN CR8526 **SET 2 THICK GREEN OR BLUE MARKER,**
1985, **NUMBERED** THICK MARKERS/#2 ON COLOR BAND
                                                                $4-5
❏ ❏ CAN CR8527 **SET 3 CRAYONS/BOX/6 REGULAR,** 1985,
WHT/GRN/BLU/PURP/VIO/ORG "COLOURS"/BOX $4-6
❏ ❏ CAN CR8528 **SET 4 THIN BLU OR RED MAGIC MARKER,**
1985 $2-5

❏ ❏ CAN CR8550 BUTTON, 1985, COLLECT CRAYOLA/RECT-
ANGLE $4-6
❏ ❏ CAN CR8555 TRAYLINER, 1985, COLLECT CRAYOLA
CRAYONS & MARKERS/29 CENTS $4-6

COMMENTS: REGIONAL DISTRIBUTION: CANADA: 1985. NOTE:
CAN CR8510 SHOWS RED CRAYOLA MARKER; CAN
CR8555 SHOWS THICK GREEN CRAYOLA MARKER WITH
THE #2 ON ITS SIDE; CRAYOLA CRAYON BOXES HAVE
WORDS, "BRILLANT COLOURS" ON FRONT OF EACH.
THESE THICK MARKERS, CRAYON BOXES AND HAPPY
MEAL BOX ARE NOT EXACTLY THE SAME AS USA CRAY-
OLA II HAPPY MEAL, 1987, THOUGH VERY SIMILAR.

USA

CAN CR8527

CAN CR8855

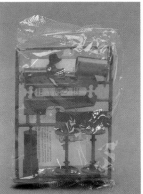

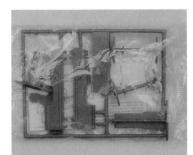

CAN GE8501

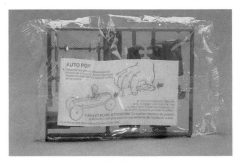

CAN GE8502

CAN CR8850

USA

43

Erlangen, Germany

GER GE8501

USA

GER GE8502

GER GE8503

GER GE8504

GERMANY/GENERIC PROMOTION, 1985

❏ ❏ GER GE8501 **PUZZLE - RONALD,** 1985, YEL/WHT W SLIDING SQUARES/15P $3-5

❏ ❏ GER GE8502 **STRAW - RONALD,** 1985, W BUBBLE CHARACTER HEAD $5-7

❏ ❏ GER GE8503 **BEAD GAME - RONALD,** 1985, RON JUGGLING/HEELS $5-7

❏ ❏ GER GE8504 **BEAD GAME - RONALD,** 1985, RON JUGGLING/FLAT SHOES/PINBALL $5-7

❏ ❏ GER GE8505 **MEASURING TAPE,** 1985, PAPER/RON CLIMBING LADDER $2-3

❏ ❏ GER GE8506 **FRISBEE,** 1985, FULL FIG RONALD/THIN RON/ NEON COLORS $1-2

❏ ❏ GER GE8507 **PLANT MARKER,** 1985, RONALD/PLASTIC $2-3

❏ ❏ GER GE8508 **AIRPLANE,** 1985, RON FLYING/STRYO/2P W 2P CLEAR WTS $8-12

❏ ❏ GER GE8509 **NOSE - RONALD,** 1985, RED W ELASTIC $5-7

❏ ❏ GER GE8510 **PAINT CARD,** 1985, FLOWERS W PAINT STRIP $2-3

❏ ❏ GER GE8511 **STICKER - PUFFY RONALD,** 1985, WHT W RONALD FACE $2-3

❏ ❏ GER GE8512 **WINDOW/WUNDERBILD,** 1985, DISAPPEARING RON $3-4

❏ ❏ GER GE8513 **STAMP PAD,** 1985, RONALD/RECTANGLE $3-4

❏ ❏ GER GE8514 **COOKIE CUTTER,** 1985, ORG/RONALD McDONALD $2-3

❏ ❏ GER GE8515 **ADVENT CALENDAR,** 1985, RON W CHRISTMAS TREE $5-8

COMMENTS: REGIONAL DISTRIBUTION: GERMANY: 1985. TOYS ARE MARKED SIMON MARKETING OR MADE IN GERMANY. PAPER INSERTS IN MINT PACKAGING IS WRITTEN IN GERMAN. GER GE8502 IS SIMILAR TO USA BUBBLE CHARACTER STRAWS; NOTING EXCEPTION, BOTTOM OF USA STRAW IS STRAIGHT AND NOT CURLED.

GLO-TRON SPACESHIPS HAPPY MEAL, 1985

❏ ❏ ATA SP8601 **SPACESHIP 8 WINDOWS,** 1985, METALLIC YEL/ GREY W GLOW STICKERS $35-50

❏ ❏ ATA SP8602 **SPACESHP W REAR ENGINE,** 1985, METALLIC BLUE W GLOW STICKERS $35-50

❏ ❏ ATA SP8603 **SPACESHIP W POINTED NOSE,** 1985, METALLIC GREEN W GLOW STICKERS $35-50

❏ ❏ ATA SP8604 **SPACESHIP 4 HUMPS,** 1985, METALLIC RED W GLOW STICKERS $35-50

❏ ❏ ATA SP8607 **STICKER SHEET/EACH,** 1985 $20-25

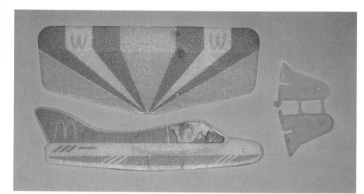
GER GE8508

GER GE8514

USA SP8607

Salzburg, Austria

COMMENTS: REGIONAL DISTRIBUTION: AUSTRIA (ATA): APRIL-MAY 1985. THE SPACESHIPS HAVE A SHINY METALLIC FLAKE FINISH. THE SPACESHIPS WERE THE VACUFORM HAPPY MEAL CONTAINERS AND THE PREMIUM. THE STICKERS ARE GLOW-IN-DARK, NOT SPACESHIPS THEMSELVES. See USA GLO-TRON SPACESHIP TEST MARKET HAPPY MEAL, 1986.

LUGGAGE TAGS PROMOTION, 1985
❑ ❑ FRA LU8501 **TAG - BIRDIE,** 1985, WHT W RED STRAP $2-3
❑ ❑ FRA LU8502 **TAG - GRIMACE,** 1985, WHT W RED STRAP $2-3
❑ ❑ FRA LU8503 **TAG - HAMBURG,** 1985, WHT W RED STRAP
$2-3
❑ ❑ FRA LU8504 **TAG - RONALD,** 1985, WHT W RED STRAP $2-3

COMMENTS: REGIONAL DISTRIBUTION: FRANCE/EUROPE - 1985.

McDONALDLAND FIGURINES PROMOTION, 1985
❑ ❑ CAN FI8501 **GRIMACE,** 1985, PURP/STANDING $4-5
❑ ❑ CAN FI8502 **HAMBURGLAR,** 1985, BLK/WHT W OPEN CAPE
$4-5
❑ ❑ CAN FI8503 **BIG MAC,** 1985, BLU/BEIGE STANDING W ARMS BEHIND BACK $4-5
❑ ❑ CAN FI8504 **RONALD,** 1985, RED/YEL/WHT STANDING/ WAVING $5-7
❑ ❑ CAN FI8550 BUTTON/ENGLISH, 1985, GRI/HAMB/MAYOR/ RON $12-15
❑ ❑ CAN FI8551 BUTTON/FRENCH, 1985, GRI/HAMB/MAYOR/ RON $12-15
❑ ❑ CAN FI8565 TRANSLITE/LG, 1985 $15-20

COMMENTS: REGIONAL DISTRIBUTION: CANADA 1985. FIGURINES CAN FI8501-04 WERE SOLD FOR 39/45 CENTS WITH A FOOD PURCHASE. FIGURINES WERE SOLD ON TWO DIFFERENT DATES. MILK IS NOW AVAILABLE IN THE HAPPY MEAL.

Frieburg, Germany

CAN FI8565

FRA LU8504

CAN FI8501   CAN FI8502   CAN FI8503   CAN FI8504

CAN FI8551   USA

CAN PL8550

CAN PL8552

PLAYMOBIL HAPPY MEAL, 1985

❑ ❑ CAN PL8550 **SET 1 SHERIFF**/"**PLAYMO SPACE**" **IN YEL,**
1982 W CHAIR/RIFLE/BLK HAT/CAPE $7-10
❑ ❑ CAN PL8551 **SET 2 INDIAN**/"PLAYMO SPACE" IN YEL, 1982,
W SHIELD/GUN/SPEAR/PEACE PIPE/HEADDRESS $7-10
❑ ❑ CAN PL8552 **SET 3 HORSE**/"PLAYMO SPACE" IN YEL, 1982,
BRN/ATTACHED SADDLE/OVAL TROUGH $12-15
❑ ❑ CAN PL8553 **SET 4 UMBRELLA GIRL**/"PLAYMO SPACE" IN
YEL, 1982, W UMBRELLA/SUITCASE/HAT $12-15
❑ ❑ CAN PL8554 **SET 5 FARMER**/"PLAYMO SPACE" IN YEL, 1982,
W HOE OR PICK/RAKE/YEL HAT/BRN DOG $12-15

❑ ❑ CAN PL8555 **SET 1 SHERIFF**/"**PLAYMO SPACE**" **IN WHT,**
1982 W CHAIR/RIFLE/BLK HAT/CAPE $7-10
❑ ❑ CAN PL8556 **SET 2 INDIAN**/"PLAYMO SPACE" IN WHT, 1982,
W SHIELD/2 SPEARS/PEACE PIPE $7-10
❑ ❑ CAN PL8557 **SET 3 HORSE**/"PLAYMO SPACE" IN WHT, 1982,
BRN/ATTACHED SADDLE/OVAL TROUGH $12-15
❑ ❑ CAN PL8558 **SET 4 UMBRELLA GIRL**/"PLAYMO SPACE" IN
WHT, 1982, W UMBRELLA/SUITCASE/HAT $12-15
❑ ❑ CAN PL8559 **SET 5 FARMER**/"PLAYMO SPACE" IN WHT,
1982, W HOE OR PICK/RAKE/YEL HAT/BRN DOG $12-15

❑ ❑ CAN PL8572 BUTTON, 1982, STAR W PLAYMOBIL MEAL
DEAL $10-15
❑ ❑ CAN PL8573 ACCESSORY SET, 1985, 18P VILLAGE $35-50

COMMENTS: REGIONAL DISTRIBUTION: CANADA - FALL 1985.
CAN PL8550-54 IS FRENCH CANADIAN SET WITH "PLAYMO
SPACE" IN YELLOW WRITING ON THE PACKAGE. CAN
PL8555-59 IS THE CANADIAN/ENGLISH SET WITH "PLAYMO
SPACE" IN WHITE WRITING ON THE PACKAGE. NOTE,
PLAYMOBIL COUPON VALID UNTIL DECEMBER 31, 1985. A
$1.98 ACCESSORY SET (18 PIECES) WAS OFFERED BY
COUPON WITHIN THE PACKAGES. THIS ACCESSORY SET
WAS AN INDIAN VILLAGE. SEE USA PLAYMOBILE HAPPY
MEAL, 1981 (TEST) AND 1982. CAN PL8572 = USA PL8272,
DISTRIBUTED REGIONALLY IN BOTH USA AND CANADA.

USA

USA

USA

USA

USA

CAN PL8557

CAN PL8572

USA

RONALD McDONALD & HAMBURGLAR TOOTHBRUSHES PROMOTION, 1985

❏ ❏ UK FE8501 **TOOTHBRUSH - RONALD BUST,** 1985, WHT-RED/POLYBAGGED $4-5

❏ ❏ UK FE8502 **TOOTHBRUSH - HAMB BUST,** 1985, WHT-BLK/POLYBAGGED $4-5

COMMENTS: REGIONAL DISTRIBUTION: UK - 1985. TOOTH-BRUSHES COST 23p EACH WITH ANY PURCHASE. UK FE8501/02 = USA FE8501/02 (See USA FEELING GOOD HAPPY MEAL, 1985).

USA

USA FE8501

USA

GUA SC8504

GER SC8607   GER SC8608   GER SC8610   GER SC8611

GER SM8501   GER SM8503

GER SM8502

GER SM8504   GER SM8506

GER SM8505

GER SM8507   GER SM8509   GER SM8510

GER SM8513   GER SM8508

GER SM8511

GER SM8512

SANTA CLAUS THE MOVIE/HAPPY HOLIDAYS MEAL , 1985

❑ ❑ *** SA8510 HM BOX, 1985, SANTA'S COTTAGE $5-8
❑ ❑ *** SA8511 HM BOX, 1985, WORKSHOP $5-8
❑ ❑ *** SA8504 CARD/COLOR, 1985, W CRAYONS/5 TYPES $2-3

COMMENTS: NATIONAL DISTRIBUTION: HONG KONG - NOVEMBER 15-24, 1985. IT IS CONCEIVABLE THAT USA HM BOXES WERE USED. See USA SANTA CLAUS THE MOVIE HAPPY MEAL, 1985. COLOR CARDS ARE OF UNDETERMINED ORIGIN.

SCHOOL KIT/SCHOOL DAYS/SCHULERSET PROMOTION, 1991/1990/1989/1988/1987/1986/1985

*** IDENTICAL TOYS: GER/UK SC8604/07
❑ ❑ *** SC8604 ERASER - RONALD, 1984, ONE ARM TO FACE
$3-4
❑ ❑ *** SC8607 PENCIL/2 - RONALD, ND, W YEL RON MCD LOGO $2-3

*** IDENTICAL TOYS: GER/GUA/UK SC8608/10/11
❑ ❑ *** SC8608 PENCIL CASE - RON AT BLACKBOARD, 1984, THIN CLEAR VINYL
$2-4
❑ ❑ *** SC8610 PENCIL SHARPENER - RONALD BUST, 1984
$3-5
❑ ❑ *** SC8611 RULER/METRIC, 1984, WHT W CUTOUTS
$3-4
❑ ❑ GUA SC8504 ERASER - RONALD, 1984, W HISTORY BOOK
$3-4
❑ ❑ GUA SC8507 PENCIL/2 - RONALD, ND, 2 SCRIP WHT/RED LOGO $2-3
❑ ❑ GUA SC8512 TABLET, 1984, WHT/PAPER W RONALD PICTURE $3-4

COMMENTS: REGIONAL DISTRIBUTION: TEST MARKETED IN GERMANY - JUNE 6-JULY 20, 1986; REGIONAL DISTRIBUTION: GERMANY - APRIL 24-MAY 24, 1987; GERMANY AND UK SETS WERE THE SAME. DISTRIBUTED IN GUATEMALA - 1985-1989, REGIONALLY; COSTA RICA: FEBRUARY 1991; CHILE: MARCH 1993. CALLED "SCHULERSET" HAPPY MEAL IN GERMANY. GERMANY AND UK DISTRIBUTED THE SAME BASIC SET OF SCHOOL PREMIUMS. COST 33p EACH WITH A FOOD PURCHASE IN THE UK. SOLD ONLY AS A SET IN GERMANY. TOYS ARE SIMILAR TO USA SCHOOL DAYS HAPPY MEAL, 1985. USA RULER DID NOT HAVE METRIC.

SMURF/SCHLUMPFE PROMOTION, 1985

❑ ❑ GER SM8501 CAPTAIN - KAPITANSCHLUMPF, 1985, W GOLD EYEGLASS $4-5
❑ ❑ GER SM8502 GIFT - GESCHENKSCHLUMPF, 1985, W WHT/RED GIFT $4-5
❑ ❑ GER SM8503 ICE CREAM - EISSCHENLUMPF, 1985, HOLDING RED/WHT POPSIC $4-5
❑ ❑ GER SM8504 LYRE/HARP - LEIERSCHLUMPF, 1985, W YEL INSTRUMENT $4-5
❑ ❑ GER SM8505 HAMBURGER - HAMBURGERSCHLUMP, 1985, W HAMBURGER $4-5
❑ ❑ GER SM8506 BASEBALL - BASEBALLSCHLUMPF, 1985, ON GRN BASE W BASEBALL/MIT/CATCHER $4-5
❑ ❑ GER SM8507 CONDUCTOR - DIRIGENTENSCHLUM, 1985, W YEL BATON $4-5
❑ ❑ GER SM8508 CRAFTSMAN - HANDWERKERSCHLUM, 1985, W GRY/BLK HAMMER BRN/WHT TOOL BOX $4-5
❑ ❑ GER SM8509 BRUSHING TEETH - ZAHNPUTZSCH, 1985, W YEL BRUSH/RED PASTE $4-5
❑ ❑ GER SM8510 FLOWERS/GIFT - GESCHENK/BL, 1985, W YEL GIFT/YEL/RED FLOWERS $4-5
❑ ❑ GER SM8511 MIRROR - SPIEFELSCHLUMPF, 1985, W RED/WHT MIRROR $4-5
❑ ❑ GER SM8512 SOCCER - FUSSBALLSCHLUMPF, 1985, W WHT SOCCER BALL $4-5
❑ ❑ GER SM8513 SLEEPWALKER - SCHLAFWANDEL, 1985, W WHT BED CAP/EYES CLOSED $4-5
❑ ❑ GER SM8544 POSTER W 9 SMURFS PICTURED, 1985, W MCD LOGO $35-50

COMMENTS: REGIONAL DISTRIBUTION: GERMANY: NOVEMBER-DECEMBER 1985 AS A SELF-LIQUIDATOR. SMURFS WERE DISTRIBUTED IN GERMANY—i.e. GERMAN SMURFS. GER SM8501-13 ARE NOT THE SAME AS USA AS8571-83 ASTROSNIKS. GERMAN ADVERTISING MCD POSTER DOES NOT SHOW GER SM8502/03/04/06/13. SMURFS WERE MANUFACTURED/MARKED BY PEYO/BULLY WITHOUT McDONALD'S LOGO. FIGURINES ARE MARKED PEYO, BULLY. COLOR VARIATIONS AND MARKINGS DIFFER BETWEEN COUNTRIES: HONG KONG, PORTUGAL, GERMANY.

CAN ST8501   CAN ST8502   CAN ST8503   CAN ST8504

STENCIL PROMOTION, 1985

❏ ❏ CAN ST8501 **STENCIL - GRIMACE,** 1985, GRN/CIRCLE/COMPASS $2-3
❏ ❏ CAN ST8502 **STENCIL - HAMBURGLAR,** 1985, GRN/CIRCLE/COMPASS $2-3
❏ ❏ CAN ST8503 **STENCIL - MAYOR,** 1985, GRN/CIRCLE/COMPASS $2-3
❏ ❏ CAN ST8504 **STENCIL - RONALD,** 1985, GRN/CIRCLE/COMPASS $2-3

COMMENTS: REGIONAL DISTRIBUTION: CANADA - 1985 AS TREAT-OF-THE-WEEK.

USA AI8651   USA AI8652   USA AI8653   USA AI8654

AIRPORT HAPPY MEAL, 1986

*** IDENTICAL TOYS: BEL/DEN/FIN/FRA/NOR/SPA/SWE/SWI AI8651/52/53/54
❏ ❏ *** AI8651 **BIG MAC HELICOPTER,** 1982, 3P GRN HELICOPTER $4-6
❏ ❏ *** AI8652 **FRY GUY FLYER,** 1986, 3P BLU AIRPLANE $4-6
❏ ❏ *** AI8653 **RONALD SEAPLANE,** 1986, 4P RED PLANE $4-6
❏ ❏ *** AI8654 **GRIMACE ACE,** 1986, 3P PUR BIPLANE $4-6

❏ ❏ CAN AI8651 **BIG MAC HELICOPTER,** 1982, RED BIG MAC HELICOPTER $4-6
❏ ❏ CAN AI8652 **FRY GUY FLYER,** 1986, 3P DARK GRN AIRPLANE $4-6
❏ ❏ CAN AI8654 **GRIMACE ACE,** 1986, 3P DARK PURPLE BIPLANE $4-6
❏ ❏ CAN AI8655 **BIRDIE BENT W BRAZER,** 1986, 5P YEL BIRDIE BENT WING BLAZER $4-6

COMMENTS: REGIONAL DISTRIBUTION: CANADA - 1986; REGIONAL DISTRIBUTION: BELGIUM, DENMARK, FINLAND, FRANCE, NORMAY, SPAIN, SWEDEN, SWITZERLAND - APRIL-MAY 1987. THE PLANES ARE SIMILAR TO USA AI8651-52-53-54-55 EXCEPT THE COLORS ARE DIFFERENT IN CANADA. See USA AIRPORT HAPPY MEAL, 1986.

CAN AI8651   CAN AI8652   CAN AI8654   CAN AI8655

USA AI8965

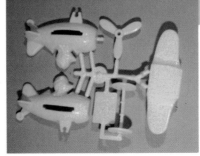

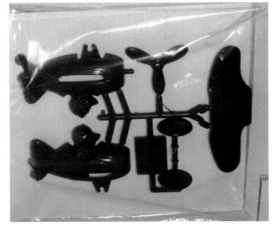

USA PROTOTYPE

USA PROTOTYPE

PROTOTYPE

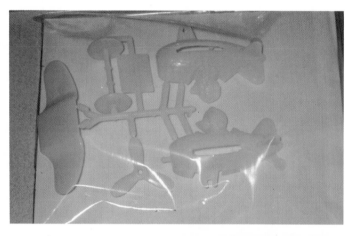

USA

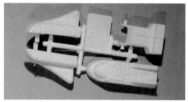

CANADA/GENERIC PROMOTION, 1986
❑ ❑ CAN GE8601 **MIGHTY MAC,** 1986, YEL/ROBOT SHUTTLE
$3-4
❑ ❑ CAN GE8602 **MIGHTY MAC,** 1986, LT BLU/ROBOT SHUTTLE
$3-4
❑ ❑ CAN GE8603 **HELL0! COPTER,** 1986, BLU/HELICOPTER $3-4
❑ ❑ CAN GE8604 **MIX & MATCH BOOK,** 1986, LIVRET A RABATS
$1-2
❑ ❑ CAN GE8605 **CIRQUE SCENES,** 1986, 20 DIFFERENT
SCENES $1-1.25

COMMENTS: LIMITED REGIONAL DISTRIBUTION: CANADA - 1986.
GIVEN AS TREAT-OF-THE-WEEK WITH GENERIC BAG;
USED DURING CLEAN-UP WEEKS.

CHRISTMAS BEARS PROMOTION, 1986
❑ ❑ CAN BE8601 **BROTHER BEAR,** 1986, BLU JUMPER/RED
CHRISTMAS BOOK $4-6
❑ ❑ CAN BE8602 **SISTER BEAR,** 1986, PNK DRESS $4-6
❑ ❑ CAN BE8603 **FATHER BEAR,** 1986, GRN SHORTS $4-6
❑ ❑ CAN BE8604 **MOTHER BEAR,** 1986, RED APRON $4-6
❑ ❑ CAN BE8650 BUTTON/ENGLISH, 1986, MCD CHRISTMAS
BEARS $3-5

CAN GE8604

CAN GE8602   CAN GE8601

CAN

CAN GE8603

CAN GE8605

□ □ CAN BE8651 BUTTON/FRENCH, 1986, OURSONS DE NOEL
DE MCD $3-5
□ □ CAN BE8655 TRAYLINER, 1986, 99 CENTS/MCD CHRISTMAS
BEARS $3-4
□ □ CAN BE8665 TRANSLITE/LG, 1986 $8-12

COMMENTS: REGIONAL DISTRIBUTION: CANADA - 1986. BEARS
WERE SOLD FOR 99 CENTS WITH A FOOD PURCHASE.
THE USA ARCHIVES REPORTS THAT IN 1992, SINGAPORE
DISTRIBUTED FOUR BEARS WITH MOVING ARMS, CALLED
"TIP TOE TEDDY" PROMOTION. THESE WERE NOT THE
SAME BEARS.

COMMANDRONS HAPPY MEAL, 1986
□ □ CAN CO8600 **COMMANDER/COMMANDANT MAGNA,** 1985,
RED/WHT/BLU PLANE/DK BLU BOX $8-12
□ □ CAN CO8601 **MOTRON/MOTRON,** 1985, RED/WHT/BLU CAR
W DARK BLU BOX $8-12
□ □ CAN CO8602 **SOLARDYN/SOLARIUS,** 1985, RED/WHT/BLU
SPACESHIP W DARK BLU BOX $8-12
□ □ CAN CO8603 **VELOCITOR/VELOSTELLA,** 1985, RED/WHT/
BLU ROCKETSHIP W DARK BLU BOX $8-12
□ □ CAN CO8650 BUTTON/ENGLISH, 1986, COMMANDRONS
                                                          $3-5
□ □ CAN CO8651 BUTTON/FRENCH, 1986, LES COMMANDRONS
                                                          $3-5
□ □ CAN CO8652 BUTTON/X-0-GRAPHIC, 1986,
COMMANDRONS $10-15
□ □ CAN CO8655 TRAYLINER, 1986, 99 CENTS/COMMANDRONS
                                                          $3-4
□ □ CAN CO8656 TRAYLINER, 1986, SOLARDYN $2-3
□ □ CAN CO8665 TRANSLITE/LG, 1986 $25-40

COMMENTS: REGIONAL DISTRIBUTION: CANADA - MAY 9, 1986

CAN BE8665

CAN BE8655

CAN BE8601   CAN BE8602   CAN BE8603   CAN BE8604

CAN CO8600   CAN CO8601   CAN CO8602   CAN CO8603

CAN BE8650   CAN BE8651

CAN CO8650   CAN CO8651

CAN CO8652

CAN CO8648

CAN CO8649

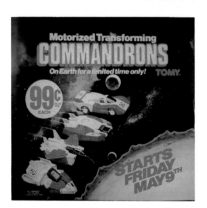

CAN CO8665

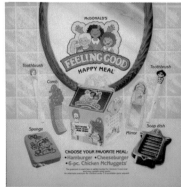

USA FE8565

FEELING GOOD HAPPY MEAL, 1986

❑ ❑ *** FE8515 HM BOX, 1985, CHILD IN MIRROR/GUESS WHO
$5-7

❑ ❑ *** FE8516 HM BOX, 1985, HIDDEN TOOTHBRUSHES/FIND THE PAIRS $5-7

❑ ❑ *** FE8517 HM BOX, 1985, CHAR WARM UP EXERCISES/ SNOOZE BLUES $5-7

❑ ❑ *** FE8518 HM BOX, 1985, REVERSE MESSAGE/THE BIRDIE PATH $5-7

*** **IDENTICAL TOYS: FRA/HOL/ITA/NOR/SWI FE8501/02**

❑ ❑ *** FE8501 **TOOTHBRUSH - RONALD BUST,** 1985, WHT-RED/ POLYBAGGED $4-5

❑ ❑ *** FE8502 **TOOTHBRUSH - HAMB BUST,** 1985, WHT-BLK/ POLYBAGGED $4-5

❑ ❑ *** FE8503 **SOAP DISH,** 1985, GRIMACE W SPREAD ARMS/ PUR $4-5

❑ ❑ *** FE8504 **SPONGE - FRY KID,** 1985, TURQ $2-3

❑ ❑ *** FE8505 **MIRROR - BIRDIE,** 1985, YEL RECTANGLE MIRROR/POLYBAGGED $3-5

❑ ❑ *** FE8506 **COMB,** 1985, RONALD or GRIMACE $1-2

COMMENTS: REGIONAL DISTRIBUTION: FRANCE, HOLLAND, ITALY, NORWAY, SWITZERLAND - 1986. OTHER CHARAC-TER COMBS COULD HAVE BEEN DISTRIBUTED WITH THIS HM. See USA FEELING GOOD HAPPY MEAL, 1985.

GERMANY/GENERIC PROMOTION, 1986

❑ ❑ GER GE8601 **BIKE REFLECTOR,** 1986, YEL STRAP/ORG REFLECTOR $5-7

❑ ❑ GER GE8602 **POPCYCLE MOLD - RONALD,** 1986, RED or YEL RON W CLEAR BOTTOM/2P $3-4

❑ ❑ GER GE8603 **BOX - CHANGE HOLDER,** 1986, RED TOP/YEL BOTTOM/RECTANGLE W RED CORD $3-4

❑ ❑ GER GE8604 **TAG - IDENTIFIER,** 1986, RED W RON PIC $3-4

❑ ❑ GER GE8605 **CLICK-KLACK,** 1986, 2 SWING BALLS W YEL PRESS $4-5

❑ ❑ GER GE8606 **STENCIL - RONALD,** 1986, RON FACE/RED DISC $2-3

❑ ❑ GER GE8607 **BOOK MARK,** 1986, PAPER/RON W RED CORD $2-3

❑ ❑ GER GE8608 **GAME - TIDDLY WINKS,** 1986, PAPER BOARD W RED/YEL DISC $3-4

❑ ❑ GER GE8609 **BEAD GAME,** 1986, RON JUMPING W 2 BEADS/YEL DISC $3-4

❑ ❑ GER GE8610 **ADVENT CALENDAR,** 1986, SNOWMAN $7-10

*** FE8503   *** FE8504   *** FE8505   *** FE8506

COMMENTS: REGIONAL DISTRIBUTION: GERMANY/EUROPE - 1986 DURING CLEAN-UP WEEKS. TOYS ARE MARKED SIMON MARKETING AND/OR MADE IN GERMANY. GER GE8602 IS THE SAME AS USA AND CANADA VERSIONS, MINT IN PACKAGING DESIGNATES THE COUNTRY OF ORIGIN. DISTRIBUTION IS WORLDWIDE ON A FEW OF THESE ITEMS.

LEGO BUILDING SET HAPPY MEAL, 1991/1990/1987/1986

❏ ❏ CAN LE8410 HM BOX, 1984, AT THE DOCK/THE GARAGE $4-5

❏ ❏ MEX LE9110 HM BOX, 1991, VEHICULOS LEGO $4-5

❏ ❏ ZEA LE9004 **U-3 BIRD W EYE,** 1986, DUPLO/RED PACKAGED 5P AGES 1 1/2-4 $5-8
❏ ❏ ZEA LE9005 **U-3 BOAT W SAILOR,** 1986, DUPLO/BLU PACKAGED 5P AGES 1 1/2-4 $5-8

    *** **IDENTICAL TOYS: CAN/MEX/ZEA LE8601/02/03/04**
❏ ❏ *** **LE8601 SET 1 RACE CAR,** 1986, RED PACKAGED 16P $5-8
❏ ❏ *** **LE8602 SET 2 TANKER,** 1986, BLUE PACKAGED 27P $5-8
❏ ❏ *** **LE8603 SET 3 HELICOPTER,** 1986, YELLOW PACKAGED 19P $5- 8
❏ ❏ *** **LE8604 SET 4 AIRPLANE,** 1986, LEGO/GREEN PACKAGED 18P $5-8

❏ ❏ *** **LE8605 TRUCK,** 1986, PICTURED ON BUTTON $10-15

❏ ❏ CAN LE8648 BUTTON/ENGLISH, 1986, CAR/BOAT/59 CENTS $3-5
❏ ❏ CAN LE8649 BUTTON/FRENCH, 1986, CAR/BOAT/59 CENTS $3-5
❏ ❏ CAN LE8650 BUTTON/ENGLISH, 1986, COLLECT LEGO BLDG SETS $3-5
❏ ❏ CAN LE8651 BUTTON/FRENCH, 1986, JEUX LEGO CONSTRUCTION COLLEDCTIONNEZ-LES $3-5
❏ ❏ CAN LE8652 BUTTON/ENGLISH, 1986, HELICOPTER/ AIRPLANE $3-5
❏ ❏ CAN LE8653 BUTTON/FRENCH, 1986, HELICOPTER/ AIRPLANE $3-5
❏ ❏ CAN LE8655 TRAYLINER, 1986, 59 CENTS/LEGO BUILDING SETS W RACE CAR PIC $3-4
❏ ❏ CAN LE8665 TRANSLITE/LG, 1986 $25-40

COMMENTS: REGIONAL DISTRIBUTION: CANADA: 1986: NEW ZEALAND: 1990; MEXICO: SEPTEMBER 1991; COSTA RICA: DECEMBER 1991; VENEZUELA: OCTOBER 1991; MALAYSIA OCTOBER 1987. CANADA SETS 1/2/3/4 ARE DATED 1986. CAN LE8410 HM BOX AND CAN LEGO SETS 1/2/3/4 WERE REPEATED FROM 1984 LEGO BUILDING SET TEST (MIP PACKAGED WITH 1986 DATE). CAN LE8410 HM BOX WITH PLAYMOBIL CHARACTERS COULD HAVE BEEN DESIGNED FOR PLAYMOBILE HM/CANADA AND THEN DISTRIBUTION CANCELLED DUE TO RECALL OF USA PLAYMOBIL HAPPY MEAL, 1982. NEW ZEALAND'S MINT IN THE PACKAGE SET DATES VARY-1984 AND 1986. IT APPEARS USA LEGO BUILDING SETS WERE USED WITH MEX LE9110 HM BOX (SEE USA LEGO BUILDING SETS HAPPY MEAL, 1986). IT IS CONCEIVABLE THAT THE RACE CAR AND THE TRUCK WERE GIVEN OUT IN CANADA OVER A PERIOD OF TIME. THE 1986 DATED TRANSLITE AND TRAYLINER SHOW THE RACE CAR, THE BLUE BUTTON ILLUSTRATES THE TRUCK. IN 1984 IN CANADA, THE RACE CAR WAS GIVEN OUT, WITH 1984 DATE.

GER GE8601

GER GE8608

MEX LE9110

*** LE8604   *** LE8605

CAN LE8650   CAN LE8651

CAN LE8652   CAN LE8653

CAN LE8555

CAN LE8665

Back, CAN MU8600-MU8604

MUPPET BABIES HAPPY MEAL (CANADA I / NEW ZEALAND I), 1989/1986

    *** IDENTICAL TOYS: CAN/ZEA MU8600/01/02/03/04

❑ ❑ ***** MU8600 GONZO,** 1986, **W/O SHOES** ON GRN BIG WHEELS/"MCD" ON BOTTOM TRIKE/2P $6-8

❑ ❑ ***** MU8601 FOSSIE,** 1986, ON YEL ROCKING HORSE/2P $2.50-4

❑ ❑ ***** MU8602 MISS PIGGY,** 1986, **W/O BOW ON BACK DRESS/** IN PINK CAR/2P $6-8

❑ ❑ ***** MU8603 KERMIT,** 1986, GRN FROG ON RED SKATE BOARD/2P $2.50-4

❑ ❑ ***** MU8604 ANIMAL,** 1986, **PNK FACED BABY MUPPET IN RED WAGON/**2P $4-6

COMMENTS: REGIONAL DISTRIBUTION: CANADA: EARLY 1986; NEW ZEALAND: 1989. CAN MU8600/01/02/03 = USA MU8600/ 01/02/03, LOOSE OUT OF PACKAGE. USA MUPPET BABIES I TEST MARKETED SET CAME OUT IN AUGUST/SEPTEMBER 1986 WITHOUT ANIMAL.

*** MU8600   *** MU8601   *** MU8602   *** MU8603   *** MU8604

CAN MU8603   CAN MU8601   CAN MU8602   CAN MU8600

CAN MU8600   CAN MU8602   CAN MU8604

CAN MU8602

PENCIL HOLDERS PROMOTION, 1986

☐ ☐ CAN PE8601 **BIG MAC/L'OFFICER,** 1986, ORG or RED or GRN or YEL HOLDING LEFT HAND FOR PENCIL $2-3

☐ ☐ CAN PE8602 **CAPITAINE CROCHU,** 1986, ORG or RED or GRN or YEL CAPTAIN CROOK HOLDING RIGHT HAND PENCIL $2-3

☐ ☐ CAN PE8603 **PIQUE-BURGER,** 1986, ORG or RED or GRN or YEL HAMBURGLAR HOLDING RIGHT HAND PENCIL $2-3

☐ ☐ CAN PE8604 **RONALD McDONALD,** 1986, ORG or RED or GRN or YEL HOLDING LEFT HAND FOR PENCIL $2-3

COMMENTS: REGIONAL DISTRIBUTION: CANADA - 1986 AS TREAT-OF-THE-WEEK. ORIGINALLY PROMOTED IN 1980. EACH SET IS DATED.

CAN PE8601   CAN PE8602   CAN PE8603   CAN PE8604

STICKER CLUB HAPPY MEAL, 1987/1986

*** **IDENTICAL PREMIUMS: BEL/FIN/FRA/HOL/NOR/SPA/ SWI ST8501/02/03/04/05**

☐ ☐ *** ST8501 **STICKER - PAPER,** 1985, 5 STICKERS/RON/ HAMB/BIG MAC/MAYOR/FRY GUYS $4-6

☐ ☐ *** ST8502 **STICKER - SCENTED/SCRATCH & SNIFF,** 1985, 5 STICKERS/HAMBURGLAR/BIRDIE/RONALD/FRY GUY/ GRIMACE $4-6

☐ ☐ *** ST8504 **STICKER - SHINY/PRISMATIC,** 1985, 4 STICK-ERS/RONALD/GRIMACE/ARCHES/LG RED FRIES BOX $4-6

☐ ☐ *** ST8505 **STICKER - PUFFY,** 1985, 4 STICKERS/RONALD/ GRIMACE/HAMBURGLAR/MAYOR $4-6

COMMENTS: REGIONAL DISTRIBUTION: BELGIUM, FINLAND, FRANCE, HOLLAND, NORWAY, SPAIN, SWITZERLAND: 1986-1987. SIMILAR TO/NOT THE SAME AS: USA STICKER CLUB HAPPY MEAL, 1985. LANGUAGE ON STICKERS VARIED WITH THE COUNTRY OF DISTRIBUTION.

USA ST8501

USA ST8504

TOOTH CARE HAPPY MEAL, 1986

☐ ☐ CAN TO8601 **TOOTH CARE KIT,** 1986 $7-12

☐ ☐ GUA TO8601 **TOOTHBRUSH,** 1986, RONALD $4-5

☐ ☐ GUA TO8602 **DRINKING CUP,** 1986, PLASTIC $4-5

☐ ☐ *** TO8603 **TOOTHBRUSH HOLDER,** 1986, RONALD/WHT PLASTIC $4-5

☐ ☐ GUA TO8604 **TOOTHPASTE,** 1986, COLGATE $4-5

COMMENTS: REGIONAL DISTRIBUTION: CANADA/GUATEMALA - 1986. *** TO8603 WAS GIVEN OUT IN MEXICO, GUATEMALA AND AUSTRALIA. A SPANISH VERSION COULD HAVE BEEN GIVEN OUT TOO.

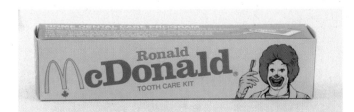

CAN TO8601

USA ST8502

USA ST8505

FRANCE

GUA TO8603

USA ST8565

MCWATCH PROMOTION, 1986

❑ ❑ UK WA8601 **RONALD McDONALD WATCH,** 1986, DARK BLU/
LCD $4-6
❑ ❑ UK WA8602 **RONALD McDONALD WATCH,** 1986, RED/LCD
$4-6

COMMENTS: REGIONAL DISTRIBUTION: UK - 1986. EACH WATCH
HAS FOUR FUNCTIONS: TIME, DATE, SECONDS AND
RAISING £1.00 FOR THE RONALD McDONALD HOUSE AT
GUY'S HOSPITAL. WATCHES COST £2.40 EACH.

1987

BUCKETS OF FUN/HAPPY PAIL III HAPPY MEAL, 1987

❑ ❑ UK HP8790 **PAIL - BEACH,** 1986, BLU HANDLE/TOP/YEL
SHOVEL $5-7
❑ ❑ UK HP8792 **PAIL - PICNIC,** 1986, YEL HANDLE/TOP/RED
RAKE $5-7
❑ ❑ UK HP8795 **PAIL - FUN FAIR,** 1986, RED HANDLE/TOP/YEL
SHOVEL $5-7
❑ ❑ UK HP8796 **PAIL - GARDEN,** 1986, GRN HANDLE/TOP/RED
RAKE $5-7

  *** **IDENTICAL PAILS: BEL/DEN/FIN/FRA/HOL/NOR/SPA/
SWE/SWI/IRE/AND/PAN HP8692/94/97**
❑ ❑ *** HP8692 **PICNIC,** 1986, YEL HANDLE/TOP/RED RAKE $5-7
❑ ❑ *** HP8694 **VACATION,** 1986, GRN HANDLE/TOP/RED RAKE
$5-7
❑ ❑ *** HP8697 **MOUNTAINS,** 1986 $5-7

COMMENTS: REGIONAL DISTRIBUTION: UK - MAY 1987; EU-
ROPE: JULY 1987; BELGIUM, DENMARK, FINLAND,
FRANCE, HOLLAND, NORWAY, SPAIN, SWEDEN, SWITZER-
LAND, IRELAND, ANDORRA, AND PANAMA: JULY 1987. ***
HP8692/94 ARE THE SAME PAILS GIVEN OUT IN USA
HAPPY PAILS III HAPPY MEAL, 1986. PAILS COST 49p AND
CAME WITH EITHER A BRIGHT YELLOW SHOVEL OR RED
RAKE. UK HP8790/92 = USA HP8690/92 See USA HAPPY
PAIL III HAPPY MEAL, 1986.

USA

USA

Collect All Five!

USA HP8626

USA HP8690

USA HP8692

USA HP8694

USA HP8665

CANADA/GENERIC PROMOTION, 1987

❑ ❑ CAN GE8701 **VALVE STEM,** 1987, RON/YEL 1P $4-5
❑ ❑ CAN GE8702 **COIN/WALLET,** 1987, RON/YEL $1-1.25
❑ ❑ CAN GE8703 **PHOTO STICKER,** 1987, HAMBURGLAR or
RONALD $2-3

COMMENTS: REGIONAL DISTRIBUTION: CANADA- 1987 AS
TREAT-OF-THE WEEK.

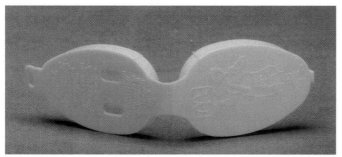

CAN GE8701   CAN GE8702

GERMANY/GENERIC PROMOTION, 1987

❑ ❑ GER GE8701 **PAGE W CRAYONS/12/MALSET,** 1987, PAPER/
BOX 12 CRAYONS/COLOR PAGE $3-4

❑ ❑ GER GE8702 **PENNANT - BIKE FLAG/WIMPEL,** 1987, RON
RESTING/PENNANT/WHT $3-4

❑ ❑ GER GE8703 **CATAMARAN,** 1987, YEL/PLASTIC W RUBBER
BAND/5P $7-10

❑ ❑ GER GE8704 **DICTIONARY/HOLIDAY,** 1987, CHILDREN'S
HOLIDAY WORDS/PAPER $3-4

❑ ❑ GER GE8705 **CARD GAME - CHARS,** 1987, PAPER CARDS/
32P $5-7

❑ ❑ GER GE8706 **YO YO,** 1987, WHT W RON W ARMS OPEN $3-4

❑ ❑ GER GE8707 **DICE,** 1987, PLASTIC W CHARACTERS ON
CUBES/3P $3-4

❑ ❑ GER GE8708 **ADVENT CALENDAR,** 1987, CLOUDS/STARS
$7-10

❑ ❑ GER GE8709 **DOOR HANGER/SIGN,** 1987, RON W TIE/
PAPER $3-4

❑ ❑ GER GE8710 **DISC,** 1987, YEL/4P $3-4

COMMENTS: REGIONAL DISTRIBUTION: GERMANY - 1987
DURING CLEAN-UP WEEKS AND/OR FOR CHILDREN
UNDER THE AGE OF 5. TOYS MUST BE SAFETY TESTED/
APPROVED FOR DISTRIBUTION TO CHILDREN UNDER THE
AGE OF 5 IN GERMANY.

GER GE8706

CAN GE8703

GER GE8703

GER GE8710

GER GE8707

MAGIC HAPPY MEAL, 1987

❏ ❏ *** MA8710 HM BOX, 1987 $4-5
❏ ❏ *** MA8711 HM BOX, 1987 $4-5
❏ ❏ *** MA8712 HM BOX, 1987 $4-5
❏ ❏ *** MA8713 HM BOX, 1987 $4-5

    *** IDENTICAL TOYS: BEL/DEN/FIN/FRA/HOL/NOR/SWE/
SWI *** MA8701/02/03/04
❏ ❏ *** MA8701 **MAGIC ROPE**, 1987, RONALD $4-5
❏ ❏ *** MA8702 **DISAPPEARING BALL**, 1987 $4-5
❏ ❏ *** MA8703 **CHANGING CARD**, 1987 $4-5
❏ ❏ *** MA8704 **FANTASTIC CUBE,** 1987 $4-5

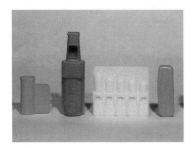

USA MA8500

USA MA8565

COMMENTS: REGIONAL DISTRIBUTION: BELGIUM, DENMARK, FINLAND, FRANCE, HOLLAND, NORWAY, SWEDEN, SWITZERLAND: 1987. McDONALD'S ARCHIVES INDICATES 4 BOXES WERE GIVEN WITH THIS PROMOTION. NOTE: 4 BOXES WERE GIVEN WITH USA MAGIC SHOW HAPPY MEAL, 1985; IT IS LIKELY THE SAME FOUR BOXES WERE USED IN THIS PROMOTION.

McDONALDLAND BAND HAPPY MEAL, 1987

❏ ❏ USA MC8702 **SIREN**, 1986, HAMB/ORG $1-1.50
❏ ❏ USA MC8703 **TRAIN ENGINE WHISTLE**, 1986, RONALD/
PURP $1-1.50
❏ ❏ USA MC8704 **PAN PIPES**, 1986, RONALD/YEL $1.50-2
❏ ❏ USA MC8705 **HARMONICA**, 1986, RONALD/RED $2.50-4

USA

COMMENTS: REGIONAL DISTRIBUTION: BELGIUM, DENMARK, FINLAND, FRANCE, HOLLAND, NORWAY, SPAIN, SWEDEN, SWITZERLAND: FEBRUARY-APRIL 1987. NONE WERE POLYBAGGED. IN THE USA DURING THE 1990s THE PREMIUMS WERE SOLD IN RETAIL STORES ON BLISTER PACKS AND SOLD IN HALLOWEEN TREAT BAGS BY RETAIL STORES. See USA McDONALDLAND BAND HAPPY MEAL, 1987 FOR 4 ADDITIONAL PREMIUMS GIVEN WITH THIS HM.

MUPPET BABIES HAPPY MEAL (CANADA II), 1987

❏ ❏ CAN MU8701 **SET 1 GONZO,** 1986, ON GRN BIG WHLS **W SHOES** $4-6
❏ ❏ CAN MU8702 **SET 2 FOZZIE,** 1986, ON YEL HORSE $4-6
❏ ❏ CAN MU8703 **SET 3 MISS PIGGY,** 1986, W PNK CAR/PNK BOW ON BACK OF DRESS $4-6
❏ ❏ CAN MU8704 **SET 4 KERMIT,** 1986, ON RED SKATEBOARD $4-6
❏ ❏ CAN MU8705 **SET 5 ANIMAL,** 1986, ON RED WAGON/2P $5-8
❏ ❏ CAN MU8752 BUTTON/ENGLISH, 1986, MUPPET BABIES/ THEY'RE BACK/49 CENTS $4-6
❏ ❏ CAN MU8753 BUTTON/FRENCH, 1986, BEBES MUPPET/ILS SONT DE RETOUR! $4-6
❏ ❏ CAN MU8765 TRANSLITE/LG, 1986 $20-25

COMMENTS: REGIONAL DISTRIBUTION: CANADA - LATE 1986/ EARLY 1987 - COLLECT ALL 5. REDESIGNED GONZO WITH SHOES AND MISS PIGGY WITH PNK RIBBON IN HAIR AND DRESS BOW ON BACK OF DRESS. NOTICE BUTTON POINTS OUT - THEY'RE BACK / 49 CENTS. THEY WERE REDESIGNED AND REINTRODUCED IN SOME REGIONAL AREAS. CAN MU8701-04 = USA MU8701-04. See USA MUPPET BABIES II HAPPY MEAL, 1987.

USA

USA

CAN MU8752   CAN MU8753

USA

USA

USA

PLACEMATS HAPPY MEAL, 1987
- ❏ ❏ UK PL8701 **PART 1 - A TOUGH ACT TO FOLLOW,** 1987, START/HOW TO PLAY $4-6
- ❏ ❏ UK PL8702 **PART 2 - A CUT ABOVE THE REST,** 1987, RONALD'S SECRET STAIRCASE $4-6
- ❏ ❏ UK PL8703 **PART 3 - A FLYING VISIT,** 1987, RONALD CATAPULTS YOU $4-6
- ❏ ❏ UK PL8704 **PART 4 - NO BUSIN/SNOW BUSIN,** 1987, YOU'VE FALLEN FOR HAMB TRAP $4-6

COMMENTS: REGIONAL DISTRIBUTION: UK - 1987. SET OF FOUR WIPEABLE PLACEMATS COST 46p EACH. THEY ARE LAMINATED AND FORM THE RONALD McDONALD ADVENTURES - GAME FOR A McDONALD'S.

RONALD McDONALD HAPPY MEAL, 1987
- ❏ ❏ *** RO8710 HM BOX, 1987, PICNIC $4-5
- ❏ ❏ *** RO8711 HM BOX, 1987, MYSTERY $4-5
- ❏ ❏ *** RO8712 HM BOX, 1987, SCHOOL $4-5

*** IDENTICAL TOYS: BEL/DEN/FIN/FRA/GER/ITA/HOL/NOR/ SPA/SWE/SWI RO8701/02/03/04
- ❏ ❏ *** GE8501 **PUZZLE - RONALD,** 1985, YEL/WHT W SLIDING SQUARES/15P $3-5
- ❏ ❏ *** GE8502 **STRAW - RONALD,** 1985, W BUBBLE CHARACTER HEAD $5-7

CAN MU8765

UK PL8704

UK PL8703

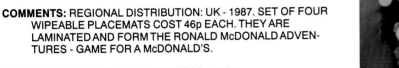

UK PL8701

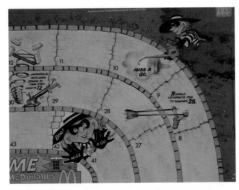

UK PL8701

UK PL8702

❑ ❑ *** GE8503 **BEAD GAME - RONALD,** 1985, RON JUGGLING/
HEELS $5-7
❑ ❑ *** GE8504 **BEAD GAME - RONALD,** 1985, RON JUGGLING/
FLAT SHOES/PINBALL $5-7
❑ ❑ *** GE8506 **FRISBEE,** 1985, FULL FIG RONALD/THIN RON/
NEON COLORS $1-2

COMMENTS: REGIONAL DISTRIBUTION: BELGIUM, DENMARK,
FINLAND, FRANCE, GERMANY, ITALY, HOLLAND, NORWAY,
SPAIN, SWEDEN, SWITZERLAND - 1987. THESE PREMIUMS
WERE PREVIOUSLY GIVEN OUT IN GERMANY IN 1985-87
TIME PERIOD WITHOUT A BAG. See GERMANY/GENERIC,
1987 FOR PICTURES. ORIGIN OF THE HAPPY MEAL BOXES
IS UNDETERMINED. IT IS CONCEIVABLE THAT THE BOXES
USED WERE: USA STORYBOOK MUPPET BABIES, 1988
BOXES.

*** GE8802   *** GE8803

1988

BEARS PROMOTION, 1988
❑ ❑ JPN BE8801 **SET 1 SISTER,** 1987 $5-7
❑ ❑ JPN BE8802 **SET 2 PAPA,** 1987 $5-7
❑ ❑ JPN BE8803 **SET 3 BROTHER,** 1987 $5-7
❑ ❑ JPN BE8804 **SET 4 MAMA,** 1987 $5-7
❑ ❑ JPN BE8805 **SET 5 BABY,** 1987 $5-7

COMMENTS: REGIONAL DISTRIBUTION: JAPAN - FEBRUARY
1988. FROM LIMITED INFORMATION, IT APPEARS BEARS
ARE SIMILIAR TO CANADA'S CHRISTMAS BEARS WITH AN
ADDITIONAL ONE ADDED, BABY BEAR. See CAN CHRIST-
MAS BEARS PROMOTION, 1986.

BOATS 'N FLOATS HAPPY MEAL, 1988

*** **IDENTICAL CONTAINERS: AND/ATA/BEL/DEN/GER/FIN/
FRA/HOL/IRE/LUX/NOR/SPA/SWE/SWI**
❑ ❑ *** BO8700 **HM CONTAINER - GRIMACE SKI BOAT,** 1986,
PUR $6-8
❑ ❑ *** BO8701 **HM CONTAINER - FRY KIDS ON RAFT,** 1986,
GRN $6-8
❑ ❑ *** BO8702 **HM CONTAINER - MCNUGGET BUDDIES LIFE
BOAT,** 1986, ORG $6-8
❑ ❑ *** BO8703 **HM CONTAINER - BIRDIE ON RAFT,** 1986, YEL
$6-8
❑ ❑ *** BO8704 STICKER SHEET - SKI BOAT, 1986 $3-5
❑ ❑ *** BO8705 STICKER SHEET - FRY KIDS ON RAFT, 1986
$3-5
❑ ❑ *** BO8706 STICKER SHEET - LIFE BOAT, 1986 $3-5
❑ ❑ *** BO8707 STICKER SHEET - BIRDIE ON RAFT, 1986 $3-5

COMMENTS: REGIONAL DISTRIBUTION: ANDORRA, AUSTRIA,
BELGIUM, DENMARK, GERMANY, FINLAND, FRANCE,
HOLLAND, IRELAND, LUXEMBOURG, NORWAY, SPAIN,
SWEDEN, SWITZERLAND - MAY 1988. VACUFORM BOATS
SERVED AS THE FOOD CONTAINER AND PREMIUM.

BOOK MARKER JUNIOR TUTE, 1988
❑ ❑ GER BO8801 **BIRDIE,** 1988, YEL PLASTIC MARKER/BIRDIE
STICKER $4-6
❑ ❑ GER BO8802 **FRY GIRL,** 1988, YEL PLASTIC MARKER/FRY
GIRL STICKER $4-6
❑ ❑ GER BO8803 **GRIMACE/SHAKY,** 1988, YEL PLASTIC
MARKER/SHAKY STICKER $4-6
❑ ❑ GER BO8804 **HAMBURGLAR,** 1988, YEL PLASTIC MARKER/
HAMB STICKER $4-6
❑ ❑ GER BO8805 **RONALD,** 1988, YEL PLASTIC MARKER/RON
STICKER $4-6

COMMENTS: REGIONAL DISTRIBUTION: GERMANY - 1988.
YELLOW PLASTIC BOOK MARKERS CAME WITH WHITE
DECALS.

*** GE8804   *** GE8805

CANADA/GENERIC PROMOTION, 1988
❑ ❑ CAN GE8801 **HAT/MONOPOLY,** 1988, PAPER $2.50-4
❑ ❑ *** GE8802 **WINDOW DECAL,** 1988, BIG MAC $3-4
❑ ❑ *** GE8803 **WINDOW DECAL,** 1988, CAPTAIN $3-4
❑ ❑ *** GE8804 **WINDOW DECAL,** 1988, HAMBURGLAR $3-4
❑ ❑ *** GE8805 **WINDOW DECAL,** 1988, RONALD $3-4

COMMENTS: REGIONAL DISTRIBUTION: CANADA - 1988.

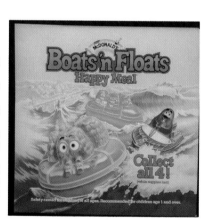

USA BO8765

CAN GE8801

GER BO8801 GER BO8802 GER BO8803 GER BO8804 GER BO8805

CASTLEMAKERS/SAND CASTLE PROMOTION, 1988

❏ ❏ JPN CA8700 **SAND MOLD - CYLINDRICAL,** 1987, YEL/8"
$20-30
❏ ❏ JPN CA8701 **SAND MOLD - DOMED,** 1987, BLU/8" $20-30
❏ ❏ JPN CA8702 **SAND MOLD - RECTANGLE,** 1987, RED/9"
$20-30
❏ ❏ JPN CA8703 **SAND MOLD - SQUARE,** 1987, DK BLU/5 1/2"
$20-30

COMMENTS: REGIONAL DISTRIBUTION: JAPAN - 1988. MCD LOGO "M" WAS MOLDED INTO EACH TOP SECTION.

COLORING FUN HAPPY MEAL, 1988

❏ ❏ *** CO8810 **HM BOX,** 1988, COLOR YOUR OWN $4-5
❏ ❏ *** CO8811 **HM BOX,** 1988, COLOR YOUR OWN $4-5
❏ ❏ *** CO8812 **HM BOX,** 1988, COLOR YOUR OWN $4-5

*** **IDENTICAL CRAYON BOXES: BEL/FIN/FRA/ITA/HOL/ NOR/SPA/SWE/SWI CO8801/02/03**
❏ ❏ *** CO8801 **CRAYONS/6 PK,** 1988, GRN/BLK/YEL/RED/BLU/ BLK $2-3
❏ ❏ *** CO8802 **CRAYONS/FLOURESCENT,** 1988, ULTRA YEL/ CHARTREUSE/ULTRA PNK/ULTRA GRN $2-3
❏ ❏ *** CO8803 **CRAYONS/METALLIC,** 1988, COPPER/SILVER/ GOLD/METALLIC GOLD $2-3

COMMENTS: REGIONAL DISTRIBUTION: BELGIUM, FINLAND, FRANCE, ITALY, HOLLAND, NORWAY, SPAIN, SWEDEN, SWITZERLAND - SEPTEMBER 1988.

DUCK TALES I HAPPY MEAL, 1989/1988

❏ ❏ GER DT8901 **MAGNIFYING GLASS,** 1987, RED W DECAL/ RON FACE $3-4
❏ ❏ GER DT8902 **MAGNIFYING GLASS,** 1987, RED W DECAL/ RON W MAGNIFYING GLASS $3-4
❏ ❏ DEN DT8802 **MAGNIFYING GLASS,** 1987, RED W DUCK TALES DECAL $3-4
❏ ❏ JPN DT8802 **MAGNIFYING GLASS,** 1987, GRN W GRIMACE DECAL/INSECT IDENTIFIER CARD $3-4
❏ ❏ *** DT8802 **MAGNIFYING GLASS,** 1987, BLU W DUCK TALES DECAL $3-4
❏ ❏ JPN DT8803 **SPY GLASS,** 1987, YEL/RED W HAMBURGLAR DECAL/VERTICAL $2-3

COMMENTS: REGIONAL DISTRIBUTION: DENMARK/GERMANY/ JAPAN AS CLEAN-UP WEEK PROMOTIONS. DEN/GER/JPN DT8802/03 = USA DT8802/03 (See USA DUCK TALES I HAPPY MEAL, 1988), EXCEPT FOR DECALS AND COLORS.

USA CA8700   USA CA8703   USA CA8701   USA CA8702

JPN DT8802   GER DT8802

DEN DT8802

JPN GE8802   GER GE8801

*** DT8802

JPN DT8802   GER DT8802   DEN DT8802

AUS DU8831   DU8833   DU8830   DU8832

USA DU8831   USA DU8833   USA DU8832   USA DU8830   USA DU8834

AUS DU8834

HOL DU9044

GER DU9065

DUCK TALES II HAPPY MEAL, 1992/1991/1990/1988

❑ ❑ AUS DU8834 **U-3 HUEY ON SKATES**, 1988, **W SILVER ON SKATES**/YEL-ORG-GRN $15-25

   *** IDENTICAL TOYS: AUS/ZEA DU8830/31/32/33

❑ ❑ *** DU8830 **SCROOGE**, 1988, W BLK TOP HAT IN RED CAR/2P $4-6

❑ ❑ *** DU8831 **LAUNCHPAD**, 1988, ORG AIRPLANE(1/4" SMALLER THAN USA VERSION) W DUCK PILOT $4-6

❑ ❑ *** DU8832 **WEBBY**, 1988, W PINK BOW IN BLU TRICYCLE W PINK WHEELS/2P $4-6

❑ ❑ *** DU8833 **NEPHEWS,** 1988, 3 NEPHEWS ON YEL/GRN SKI BOAT/1P $4-6

   *** IDENTICAL TOYS: GER/HOL DU9030/31/32/33

❑ ❑ *** DU9030 **SET 1 UNCLE SCROOGE**, 1988, IN RED CAR/2P $4-6

❑ ❑ *** DU9031 **SET 2 WEBBY**, 1988, ON TRICYCLE/BLU-PNK-WHT/2P $4-6

❑ ❑ *** DU9032 **SET 3 LAUNCHPAD**, 1988, IN ORG PLANE(SM)/ORG-BRN-BLU/1P $4-6

❑ ❑ *** DU9033 **SET 4 HUEY DUEY LOUIE**, 1988, ON SKI BOAT W WHEELS/YEL-GRN/1P $4-6

❑ ❑ HOL DU9044 POSTER/SM, 1990 $5-8
❑ ❑ GER DU9065 TRANSLITE/LG, 1990 $25-40

COMMENTS: REGIONAL DISTRIBUTION: AUSTRALIA - 1988; GERMANY - MARCH 16-APRIL 16, 1990; NEW ZEALAND - MAY 1991; HOLLAND - SEPTEMBER 24-NOVEMBER 25, 1990. BELGIUM, DENMARK, FINLAND, FRANCE, ITALY, NORWAY, SWEDEN, SWITZERLAND: AUGUST-OCTOBER 1990. AUS/ZEA FIGURINES ARE NOT THE SAME SIZE AS USA DU8830-34 (See USA DUCK TALES II HAPPY MEAL, 1988). ZEA DU91131 AND EUROPE'S LAUNCHPAD ORANGE AIRPLANE IS 1/4" SMALLER PLANE THAN USA VERSION. AUS/NEW ZEALAND DUCK TALES TOYS HAVE REMOVABLE FIGURINE CHARACTERS; AUS DU8834 (U-3) HAS SILVER PAINT ON SKATES, USA VERSION DOES NOT.

FLIEG & SPAR/FRISBEE PROMOTION, 1988

❑ ❑ GER FL8830 HM BAG, 1988, NUMBERED/WHT #1-20
❑ ❑ GER FL8801 **FRISBEE**, 1988, GREEN $3-4
❑ ❑ GER FL8802 **FRISBEE**, 1988, RED $3-4
❑ ❑ GER FL8803 **FRISBEE**, 1988, YELLOW $3-4

COMMENTS: REGIONAL DISTRIBUTION: GERMANY - APRIL 10-MAY 30, 1988.

USA

USA

FRAGGLE ROCK HAPPY MEAL, 1988

❏ ❏ CAN FR8820 **GOBO**, 1988, GOBO IN ORG CARROT $3-5
❏ ❏ CAN FR8821 **RED**, 1988, RED FRAGGLE IN RED RADISH $3-5
❏ ❏ CAN FR8822 **MOKEY**, 1988, TURQ/GRN FRAGGLE IN PURP EGG PLANT $3-5
❏ ❏ CAN FR8823 **BOOBER**, 1988, GRN CUCUMBER W BOOBER ET WEMBLEY $3-5
❏ ❏ CAN FR8850 BUTTON/ENGLISH, 1988, 4 CHAR VEHICLES $4-6
❏ ❏ CAN FR8851 BUTTON/FRENCH, 1988, 4 CHAR VEHICLES/CHACUNE $4-6
❏ ❏ CAN FR8855 TRAYLINER, 1988, 49 CENTS/JIM HENSON'S FRAGGLE ROCK $3-4
❏ ❏ CAN FR8865 TRANSLITE/LG, 1 $25-40
❏ ❏ CAN FR8896 COFFEE MUG, 1988 $5-7

COMMENTS: REGIONAL DISTRIBUTION: CANADA - 1988. CAN FR8820-23 = USA FR8820-23 (See USA FRAGGLE ROCK HM, 1988).

GERMANY/GENERIC PROMOTION, 1988

❏ ❏ GER GE8830 HM BAG, 1988, RON W RAINBOW $3-4
❏ ❏ GER GE8801 **PEN**, 1986, WHT PEN/SNAKE SHAPED $4-6
❏ ❏ GER GE8802 **PEN**, 1986, BLU PEN/SNAKE SHAPED $4-6
❏ ❏ GER GE8803 **ZIPPER PULL**, 1987, RON or BIRDIE or GRIM or HAMB or BIG MAC W METAL CLASP $2-3
❏ ❏ GER GE8807 **MONEY BAG - RONALD**, 1988, PURSE/PLASTIC/RON SITTING $3-4
❏ ❏ GER GE8808 **CARD GAME - MEMORY**, 1988, 30 CARDS/CHARS/PLACES $5-7
❏ ❏ GER GE8809 **CRAYONS/4**, 1988, 4 RECTANGLE/RED/YEL/GRN/BLU W FF BOX $3-4
❏ ❏ GER GE8810 **MAGNET - FRENCH FRIES**, 1988, PLASTIC/FRIES $2-3
❏ ❏ GER GE8811 **MAGNET - BIG MAC**, 1988, PLASTIC/BIG MAC $2-3
❏ ❏ GER GE8812 **SOAP BUBBLE BLOWER**, 1988, CONTAINER W RED BUBBLE BLOWER $5-7
❏ ❏ GER GE8813 **PENCIL SHARPENER**, 1984, RONALD BUST $5-8

CAN FR8850   CAN FR8851

CAN FR8865   CAN FR8896

CAN FR8855

CAN

USA FR8821 USA FR8820   USA FR8823 USA FR8822

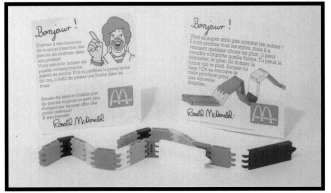

GER GE8801   GER GE8802

GER GE8813

GER GE8803

GER GE8807

CAN HW8850   CAN HW8851

COMMENTS: REGIONAL DISTRIBUTION: GERMANY - 1988 DURING CLEAN-UP WEEKS. GER GE8812 = USA SC8410 (See USA SCHOOL DAYS HAPPY MEAL, 1984). THE WHITE GERMAN HAPPY MEAL BAG WAS DISTRIBUTED: JANUARY 1 - APRIL 30, 1988.

HOT WHEELS PROMOTION, 1988

❑ ❑	CAN HW8330	**CORVETTE STINGRAY** NO.9241		$8-10
❑ ❑	CAN HW8331	**JEEP CJ-7** NO.3259		$8-10
❑ ❑	CAN HW8332	**3-WINDOW '34** NO 1132		$8-10
❑ ❑	CAN HW8333	**56 HI-TAIL HAULER** NO.9647		$8-10
❑ ❑	CAN HW8334	**57 T-BIRD** NO.2013		$8-10
❑ ❑	CAN HW8335	**BAJA BREAKER** NO.2022		$8-10
❑ ❑	CAN HW8336	**CADILLAC SEVILLE** NO.1698		$8-10
❑ ❑	CAN HW8337	**CHEVY CITATION "X-11"** NO.3362		$8-10
❑ ❑	CAN HW8338	**DATSUN 200 SX** NO.3255		$8-10
❑ ❑	CAN HW8339	**DIXIE CHALLENGER** NO.3364		$8-10
❑ ❑	CAN HW8340	**FIREBIRD FUNNY CAR** NO.3250		$8-10
❑ ❑	CAN HW8341	**FRONT RUNNING FAIRMONT** NO.3257		$8-10
❑ ❑	CAN HW8342	**LAND LORD** NO.3260		$8-10
❑ ❑	CAN HW8343	**MALIBU GRAND PRIX "GOODYEAR 9999"** NO.9037+		$8-10
❑ ❑	CAN HW8344	**MERCEDES 380/SILVER SEL** NO.3261+		$8-10
❑ ❑	CAN HW8345	**MINITREK "GOOD TIME CAMPER"/WHITE** NO.1697+		$8-10
❑ ❑	CAN HW8346	**PORSCHE 928** NO.5180+		$8-10
❑ ❑	CAN HW8347	**RACE BAIT 308** NO.2021		$8-10
❑ ❑	CAN HW8348	**SHERIFF PATROL/BLK/WHT** NO.2019		$8-10
❑ ❑	CAN HW8349	**SPLIT WINDOW '63** NO.1136+		$8-10
❑ ❑	CAN HW8350	**TRICAR X8** NO.1130		$8-10
❑ ❑	CAN HW8351	**TURISMO "10"** NO.1694+		$8-10
❑ ❑	CAN HW8352	**STUTZ BLACKHAWK** NO.1126		$8-10
❑ ❑	CAN HW8800	**57 T-BIRD - TURQ**, 1988		$8-10
❑ ❑	CAN HW8801	**57 T-BIRD - WHT**, 1988		$8-10
❑ ❑	CAN HW8802	**80'S FIREBIRD - BLU**, 1988		$8-10
❑ ❑	CAN HW8803	**80'S FIREBIRD - BLK/NO.3972**, 1988		$8-10
❑ ❑	CAN HW8804	**FIRE CHIEF - RED**, 1988		$8-10
❑ ❑	CAN HW8805	**P-911 TURBO - BLACK/NO.3968**, 1988		$8-10
❑ ❑	CAN HW8806	**P-911 TURBO - WHT**, 1988		$8-10
❑ ❑	CAN HW8807	**SHERIFF PATROL - BLK**, 1988		$8-10

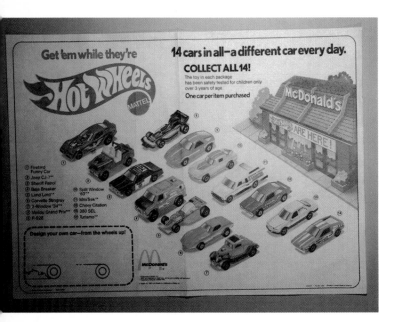

USA HW8355

USA HW8326

		CAN HW8808 **SPLIT WINDOW '63 - BLACK,** 1988	$8-10
		CAN HW8809 **SPLIT WINDOW '63 - SILVER,** 1988	$8-10
		CAN HW8810 **STREET BEAST - RED,** 1988	$8-10
		CAN HW8811 **STREET BEAST - SILVER,** 1988	$8-10
		CAN HW8812 **CJ7 JEEP - WHT/ORG/NO.3953,** 1988	$8-10
		CAN HW8813 **CJ7 JEEP - YEL/ORG/NO.3954,** 1988	$8-10
		CAN HW8814 **CORVETTE STINGRAY - WHT/RED STRIPE/ NO.3973*,** 1988	$8-10
		CAN HW8815 **CORVETTE STINGRAY - YEL/ORG STRIPE/ NO.3974*,** 1988	$8-10
		CAN HW8816 **THUNDER STREEK - BURGAN/PURP/ NO.3998*,** 1988	$8-10
		CAN HW8817 **THUNDER STREEK - BLU/YEL/NO.3999*,** 1988	$8-10
		CAN HW8818 **FIRE EATER - RED TRUCK/BLU/NO.4000*,** 1988	$8-10
		CAN HW8819 **FIRE EATER - YEL TRUCK/BLU/NO.4001*,** 1988	$8-10
		CAN HW8850 BUTTON/ENGLISH, 1988	$7-10
		CAN HW8851 BUTTON/FRENCH, 1988	$7-10

USA HW8826

COMMENTS: REGIONAL OPTIONAL DISTRIBUTION: CANADA - 1988. HOT WHEELS WERE USED AS A SELF-LIQUIDATING PROMOTION. DIFFERENT CARS (MARKED BY + COULD HAVE BEEN GIVEN OUT AND/OR SOLD IN DIFFERENT REGIONS. CARS COULD BE PURCHASED FOR $.69. "COLLECT ALL 14. A DIFFERENT CAR EVERY DAY". NO UNDER 3 (U-3) PREMIUMS WERE FURNISHED. THIS WAS A REGIONAL OPTION. DATES STAMPED ON CARS DO NOT ALWAYS MATCH THE MIP PACKAGE DATE. CAN GO8330-31 CARRY 1981 DATES/MADE IN USA, ALL OTHERS CARRY 1982 DATES. CAN GO8352 STUTZ BLACK HAWK NO. 1126 COULD HAVE BEEN SUBSTITUTED FOR CAN GO8333 HIGH TAIL HAULER NO. 9647 AND/OR CAN GO8345 MINITREK GOOD TIME CAMPER NO. 1697. THIS PROMOTION WAS RUN REGIONALLY AS A SELF-LIQUIDATOR IN 1983 AND AGAIN IN 1988 REGIONALLY IN THE USA AND CANADA. SOME/ALL OR NONE OF THE ABOVE CARS COULD HAVE BEEN DISTRIBUTED SINCE THE CARS WERE RANDOMLY SELECTED. THE LIST INCLUDES THE ENTIRE USA 1983 AND 1988 PROMOTIONS.

JUNGLE FACE/ZOO FACES/TIERNASIN JUNIOR TUTE/ HAPPY MEAL, 1992/1991/1989/1988

| | | AUS ZO9210 HM BAG, 1992, RON W SAFARI HAT/IN JUNGLE | $2-3 |
| | | GER ZO9110 HM BAG, 1991, AFRICAN ANIMAL GRAPHICS | $3-4 |

GER ZO9202

AUS ZO9202

*** IDENTICAL FACE: AUS/GER/ZEA ZO8802/03
| | | *** ZO8802 **SET 2 APE/MONKEY,** 1988, PNK/BRN W PAAS MAKE-UP KIT | $5-7 |
| | | *** ZO8803 **SET 3 TIGER,** 1988, ORG/PNK W PAAS MAKE-UP KIT | $5-7 |

*** IDENTICAL FACES: AUS/ZEA ZO8801/04
| | | *** ZO8801 **SET 1 TOUCAN,** 1988, RED/YEL W PAAS MAKE-UP KIT | $5-7 |
| | | *** ZO8804 **SET 4 ALLIGATOR,** 1988, GRN/PNK W PAAS MAKE-UP KIT | $5-7 |

USA ZO8803   USA ZO8801

| | | GER ZO9115 **SET 1 DINOSAUR,** 1990, GRN/BLK W PAAS MAKE-UP KIT | $5-7 |
| | | GER ZO9118 **SET 4 DUCK,** 1990, YEL/ORG W PAAS MAKE-UP KIT | $5-7 |

| | | AUS ZO9245 REGISTER TOPPER/COUNTER CARD, 1992 | $7-10 |
| | | GER ZO9165 TRANSLITE/LG, 1991 | $25-40 |

AUSTRALIA

COMMENTS: REGIONAL DISTRIBUTION: NEW ZEALAND - 1988; AUSTRALIA - 1989 W/O HM BAG AND AGAIN IN 1991 WITH HM BAG; GERMANY: JANUARY 12-FEBRUARY 7, 1989 WITH HM BAG; BELGIUM, DENMARK, ITALY, SPAIN, SWEDEN, SWITZERLAND - JANUARY 1990 WITH USA PREMIUMS. PREMIUMS ARE THE SAME AS USA ZO8801-04. CALLED "TIERNASEN JUNIOR TUTE/HAPPY MEAL" IN GERMANY; GERMANY RAN TIERNASEN II HM AGAIN - JANUARY 17- FEBRUARY 12, 1991 W 3 NEW MASKS.

GER ZO9118

AUS ZO9245

GER ZO9165

USA LI8701

USA LI8702   USA LI8703   USA LI8704

USA LI8765

USA NU8800
USA NU8812
USA NU8811
USA NU8801
USA NU8802
USA NU8803
USA NU8805
USA NU8804
USA NU8806
USA NU8807
USA NU8808
USA NU8809

USA

66

KID'S WEEK PROMOTION, 1988
- ❑ ❑ SIN KI8810 HM BOX, 1988, KID'S PROMO $4-5
- ❑ ❑ SIN KI8801 **IDENTIFICATION/NAME TAG,** 1988, RONALD $2.50-3

COMMENTS: REGIONAL DISTRIBUTION: SINGAPORE - 1988.

LITTLE ENGINEER HAPPY MEAL, 1988
- ❑ ❑ *** LI8710 HM BOX, 1986, ROUND HOUSE TRAIN GARAGE/ REPAIR PAIRS $4-5
- ❑ ❑ *** LI8711 HM BOX, 1986, STATION/WAITING ROOM $4-5
- ❑ ❑ *** LI8712 HM BOX, 1986, TRESTLE/A PLACE FOR EVERY-THING $4-5
- ❑ ❑ *** LI8713 HM BOX, 1986, TUNNEL/TUNNEL PROJECT $4-5

*** IDENTICAL TRAIN CAR: EUROPE LI8701/02/03/04
- ❑ ❑ *** LI8701 **FRY GIRL EXPRESS,** 1986, TRAIN ENGINE/BLU 3P W STICKERS $5-7
- ❑ ❑ *** LI8702 **FRY GUY FLYER,** 1986, TRAIN ENGINE/DAY GLO ORG 3P W STICKER $5-7
- ❑ ❑ *** LI8703 **GRIMACE PURPLE STREAK,** 1986, TRAIN ENGINE/PUR 3P W STICKERS $5-7
- ❑ ❑ *** LI8704 **RONALD'S RAILWAY,** 1986, TRAIN ENGINE/RED 3P W STICKERS $5-7

COMMENTS: REGIONAL DISTRIBUTION: EUROPE - 1988. IT IS NOT DOCUMENTED YET WHICH COUNTRY PRODUCED THE 4 BOXES. IN THE USA, 4 BOXES WERE USED ALONG WITH THE 4 PREMIUMS LISTED: *** LI8701/02/03/04. See USA LITTLE ENGINEER HAPPY MEAL, 1987 FOR A FIFTH PREMIUM WHICH WAS ONLY USED IN THE USA.

MCNUGGET BUDDIES HAPPY MEAL, 1989/1988
- ❑ ❑ ZEA MC8811 **U-3 SLUGGER,** 1988, BRN W BASEBALL GLOVE/2P $4-5
- ❑ ❑ ZEA MC8812 **U-3 DAISY,** 1988, BRN/BEAR W DAISEY FLOWER ON HAT/2P $4-5
- ❑ ❑ HON NU8803 **DRUMMER MCNUGGET,** 1988, 3P DRUM MAJOR HAT W DRUM BELT $3-4

*** IDENTICAL MCNUGGET: HONG KONG/SIN MC8804
- ❑ ❑ *** NU8804 **CORNY MCNUGGET,** 1988, 3P STRAW HAT W RED POPCORN BELT $3-4

- ❑ ❑ ZEA MC8806 **SPARKY MCNUGGET,** 1988, FIRE HAT W HATCHET/EXTINGUISH BELT/3P $3-4

*** IDENTICAL MCNUGGET: SIN/ZEA NU8807
- ❑ ❑ *** NU8807 **BOOMERANG MCNUGGET,** 1988, 3P AUSIE HAT W BOOMERANG $3-4

*** IDENTICAL MCNUGGET: HONG KONG/SIN/ZEA MC8809
- ❑ ❑ *** NU8809 **SNORKEL MCNUGGET,** 1988, 3P MASK W KNIFE/LITE BELT $3-4

*** IDENTICAL MCNUGGET HONG KONG/SIN MC8810

❏ ❏ ***** NU8810 ROCKER MCNUGGET,** 1988, 3P ORG W HAIR & GUITAR BELT $3-4

❏ ❏ **ZEA MC8808 VOLLEY MCNUGGET,** 1988, HEAD BAND E TENNIS BELT/3P $3-4

COMMENTS: NATIONAL DISTRIBUTION: NEW ZEALAND - 1988; HONG KONG MARCH-APRIL 1989; SINGAPORE JULY-AUGUST 1989. THE FIRST NEW ZEALAND McDONALD'S OPENED IN PORIRVA, NEW ZEALAND IN 1976. MCNUGGET BUDDIES HM, 1988 WAS THE FIRST NATIONAL HAPPY MEAL IN NEW ZEALAND.

MCROULI MCROULLY TREAT-OF-THE-WEEK, 1988

❏ ❏ CAN RO8801 **GRIMACE BEAD GAME,** 1988, ROUND/PNK $2-3

❏ ❏ CAN RO8802 **FRY KID BEAD GAME,** 1988, ROUND/GRN $2-3

❏ ❏ CAN RO8803 **HAMB BEAD GAME,** 1988, ROUND/BLU $2-3
❏ ❏ CAN RO8804 **RONALD BEAD GAME,** 1988, ROUND/YEL $2-3

COMMENTS: REGIONAL DISTRIBUTION: CANADA - 1988

MUPPET BABIES (CANADA III) HAPPY MEAL, 1988

❏ ❏ CAN MU8600 **GONZO,** 1986, ON GRN BIG WHLS/**NO SHOES**/ 2P $15-20
❏ ❏ CAN MU8601 **FOSSIE,** 1986, ON YEL HORSE/2P $2-3
❏ ❏ CAN MU8602 **MISS PIGGY,** 1986, IN PNK CAR W SEAT RIBS/ **NO BOW AT WAIST**/2P $15-20
❏ ❏ CAN MU8603 **KERMIT,** 1986, ON RED SKATEBOARD/2P $2-3
❏ ❏ CAN MU8850 BUTTON/ENGLISH, 1987, MUPPET BABIES/49 CENTS $4-5
❏ ❏ CAN MU8851 BUTTON/FRENCH, 1987, BEBES MUPPET/49 CENTS $4-5
❏ ❏ CAN MU8855 TRAYLINER, 1987, MUPPET BABIES/COLLECT ALL FOUR $3-4
❏ ❏ CAN MU8865 TRANSLITE/LG, 1986 $25-40

COMMENTS: REGIONAL DISTRIBUTION: CANADA: 1988. CAN MU8601 AND CAN MU8603 = USA MU8601 AND USA MU8603. CAN MU8602 PINK CAR IS SLIGHTLY DIFFERENT RIBS/CROSS BARS UNDER SEAT THAN USA TEST SET - USA MU8602.

CANADA

CAN MU8600   CAN MU8601   CAN MU8602   CAN MU8603

CAN MU8850   CAN MU8851

CAN RO8801   CAN RO8802   CAN RO8803

CAN MU8855

CAN RO8804

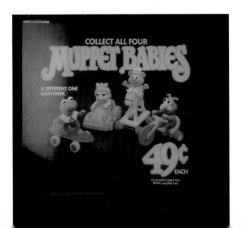

CAN MU8865

67

USA MU8701   USA MU8702   USA MU8703   USA MU8704

GER MU8865

CAN MU8955

CAN MU8950   CAN MU8951

USA MU8803   USA MU8801   USA MU8802

68

MUPPET BABIES (GERMANY I/II) JUNIOR TUTE/HAPPY MEAL, 1988

   *** **IDENTICAL TOYS: AUSTRIA/FIN/FRA/GER/ITA/HOL/NOR/ SPA/SWE/SWI/JPN MU8701/02/03/04**

❑ ❑ *** MU8701 **SET 1 GONZO,** 1987, ON GRN BIG WHLS/W
    SHOES/2P $3-5
❑ ❑ *** MU8702 **SET 2 FOZZIE,** 1987, ON YEL HORSE/2P $3-5
❑ ❑ *** MU8703 **SET 3 MS PIGGY,** 1987, IN PNK CAR/PNK
    RIBBON/2P $3-5
❑ ❑ *** MU8704 **SET 4 KERMIT,** 1987, ON RED SKATEBOARD/2P
                                     $3-5

❑ ❑ GER MU8865 TRANSLITE/LG, 1987 $25-40

COMMENTS: REGIONAL DISTRIBUTION: GERMANY: MARCH 25-
APRIL 17, 1988 AND NOVEMBER 25-DECEMBER 13, 1988;
AUSTRIA - APRIL-MAY 1988; BELGIUM, FINLAND, FRANCE,
ITALY, HOLLAND, NORWAY, SPAIN, SWEDEN, SWITZER-
LAND - 1988. HONG KONG SOLD MUPPET BABIES AS A
SELF LIQUIDATOR IN 1988; GUATEMALA - 1987 AND 1988.
GER MU8701-04 = USA MU8701-04, LOOSE OUT OF
PACKAGE. See USA MUPPET BABIES II HAPPY MEAL, 1987.

MUPPET BABIES HOLIDAY/PLUSH DOLLS PROMOTION, 1994/1989/1988

   *** **IDENTICAL DOLLS: CAN/GER MU8801/02**

❑ ❑ *** MU8801 **FOSSIE,** 1987, BRN/GOLD STUFFED DOLL/RED
    HAT/HOLLY LEAVES $2-2.50
❑ ❑ *** MU8802 **KERMIT,** 1987, GRN/WHT/RED STUFFED DOLL
                                   $2-2.50

❑ ❑ GER MU8803 **MISS PIGGY,** 1987, RED/WHT/PNK STUFFED
    DOLL/**WITH HAIR** $2-2.50
❑ ❑ CAN MU8804 **MISS PIGGY,** 1987, RED/WHT/PNK STUFFED
    DOLL/**WITHOUT HAIR** $2.50-3

❑ ❑ CAN MU8950 BUTTON/ENGLISH, 1987 $3-5
❑ ❑ CAN MU8951 BUTTON/FRENCH, 1987 $3-5
❑ ❑ CAN MU8955 TRAYLINER, 1987, BE A SOFTIE, ADOPT JH'S
    MB/MISS P-NO HAIR $1-1.25

COMMENTS: REGIONAL DISTRIBUTION: CANADA: 1989. TEST
DISTRIBUTION: GERMANY NOVEMBER 1988 AND MARCH
1989; NATIONAL DISTRIBUTION: GERMANY: JANUARY 1-
APRIL 30, 1988; REGIONAL DISTRIBUTION: GERMANY -
JULY-AUGUST 1989; CANADA: 1989; EUROPE - JANUARY-
FEBRUARY 1990. MEXICO, COSTA RICA, GUATEMALA,
VENEZUELA, ARGENTINA: DECEMBER 1994. GER MU8801/
02/03 = USA MU8801/02/03 (See USA MUPPET BABIES
HOLIDAY PROMOTION, 1988). DOLLS WERE SOLD FOR
$2.69 DURING HOLIDAY PROMOTION IN CANADA. FOSSIE
AND KERMIT ARE SAME AS USA VERSION. MISS PIGGY
DID NOT HAVE HAIR UNDER RED CHRISTMAS CAP IN
CANADA; i.e. CAN MU8804 DOES NOT HAVE HAIR LIKE IN
USA AND GERMAN/EUROPEAN SETS.

USA MU8864

ON THE GO II / LUNCH BOX / McLUNCH HAPPY MEAL, 1988

*** IDENTICAL LUNCH BOXES: FRA/JP/MAL/SIN ***
ON8801/03
- ❏ ❏ *** ON8801 **RED LUNCH BOX,** 1988, GRIM/RM RAISED SCENE W BULLETIN BOARD $3-5
- ❏ ❏ *** ON8803 **GRN LUNCH BOX,** 1988, GRIM/RM RAISED SCENE W BULLETIN BOARD $3-5

*** ON8801   *** ON8803

COMMENTS: REGIONAL DISTRIBUTION: FRANCE: OCTOBER 1988; JAPAN: 1990; MALAYSIA: FEBRUARY 1992; SINGAPORE: AUGUST 1989. THIS HAPPY MEAL WAS CALLED, "McLUNCH BOX" IN MALAYSIA AND "LUNCH BOX" IN SINGAPORE. IN THE USA, 2 VELCRO CLOSURE BAGS WERE ALSO USED. See USA ON THE GO II LUNCH BOX/ BAGS HAPPY MEAL, 1988.

PLAY-DOH HAPPY MEAL, 1988
- ❏ ❏ UK PL8676 **BLUE PLAY-DOH,** 1988, YEL CONT/BLU LID/ 2 OZ $4-5
- ❏ ❏ UK PL8678 **RED PLAY-DOH,** 1988, YEL CONT/RED LID/ 2 OZ $4-5
- ❏ ❏ UK PL8680 **YELLOW PLAY-DOH,** 1988, YEL CONT/YEL LID/ 2 OZ $4-5
- ❏ ❏ UK PL8682 **WHITE PLAY-DOH,** 1988, YEL CONT/YEL LID/ 2 OZ $4-5
- ❏ ❏ UK PL8865 TRANSLITE/LG, 1988 $15-20
- ❏ ❏ UK PL8806 CEILING DANGLER, 1988 $15-20
- ❏ ❏ UK PL8807 REGISTER TOPPER, 1988 $6-8

USA PL8676

USA PL8678

USA PL8682

USA PL8680

COMMENTS: REGIONAL DISTRIBUTION: UK - 1988. THE 2 OUNCE PLAY-DOH CONTAINERS DO NOT HAVE RONALD/CHARAC-TER MARKINGS. THE BOXES USED WERE IDENTICAL TO THE USA PL8690-93 AND THE PLAY-DOH CONTAINERS: USA PL8676/78/80/82. See USA PLAY-DOH HAPPY MEAL, 1986.

POCKET VIEWERS/DISNEY PROMOTION, 1993/1989/ 1988
- ❏ ❏ JPN VI8801 **VIEWER - PINOCCHIO,** ND, RED $5-7
- ❏ ❏ JPN VI8802 **VIEWER - SLEEPING BEAUTY,** ND, PNK $5-7
- ❏ ❏ JPN VI8803 **VIEWER - WINNIE THE POOH,** ND, YEL W HONEY POT $5-7
- ❏ ❏ JPN VI8804 **VIEWER - MICKEY MOUSE,** ND, RED $5-7
- ❏ ❏ JPN VI8805 **VIEWER - DONALD DUCK,** ND, BLU $5-7
- ❏ ❏ JPN VI8806 **VIEWER - WINNIE THE POOH,** ND, YEL WAVING $5-7
- ❏ ❏ JPN VI8807 **VIEWER - MICKEY MOUSE,** ND, BLU $5-7
- ❏ ❏ JPN VI8808 **VIEWER - GOOFY,** ND, BLU $5-7

USA PL8665

JPN VI8805   JPN VI8806

JPN VI8801   JPN VI8802

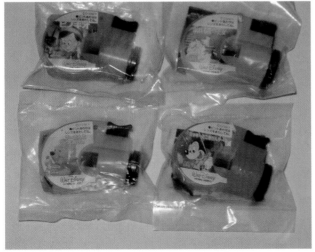

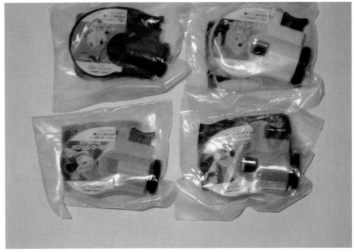

JPN VI8807   JPN VI8808

JPN VI8803   JPN VI8804

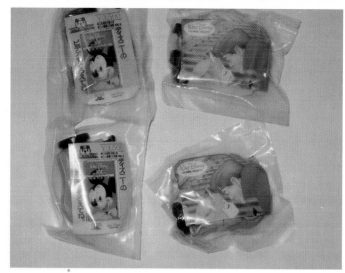

JAPAN

JPN VI8808

CAN RF8801

GER RF9202   GER RF9301

COMMENTS: REGIONAL DISTRIBUTION: JAPAN - DECEMBER 1988, DECEMBER 1989 AND AGAIN IN 1993; MEXICO: JUNE 1993. COLORS LISTED ARE FOR ILLUSTRATION, PICTURE. EACH VIEWER CAME IN COMBINATION OF COLORS: RED, YEL, LIGHT BLUE AND DARK BLUE AND PNK.

REFLECTOR PROMOTION, 1993/1992/1991/1990/1989/1988

❑ ❑ CAN RF8801 **CAPTAIN CROOK,** 1988, BLU/BIKE REFLECTOR $3-4
❑ ❑ GER RF9202 **RONALD,** 1992, RED/BIKE REFLECTOR $3-4
❑ ❑ GER RF9203 **RONALD,** 1992, YEL/BIKE REFLECTOR $3-4
❑ ❑ GER RF9301 **CAPTAIN CROOK,** 1993, YEL/BIKE REFLECTOR $2-3

COMMENTS: REGIONAL DISTRIBUTION: CANADA - 1988/1989/1990/1991 AS TREAT-OF-THE-WEEK; GERMANY - 1992 FOR UNDER THE AGE OF 5 PREMIUM (U-5).

RONALD McDONALD MUG & BOWL/DISHES PROMOTION, 1988

❑ ❑ UK DI8801 **MUG,** 1988, CERAMIC W RONALD SITTING W LEGS CROSSED $4-6
❑ ❑ UK DI8802 **BOWL,** 1988, CERAMIC W RONALD SITTING W LEGS CROSSED $4-6

COMMENTS: REGIONAL DISTRIBUTION: UK - 1988. MUG AND BOWL SOLD FOR 63p EACH WITH A PURCHASE. ADVERTISING REQUESTED ONE TO SIT DOWN TO BREAKFAST WTIH RONALD McDONALD.

SAILORS HAPPY MEAL, 1988

❑ ❑ SIN SA8810 HM BOX, 1987, FRY GUY AFLOAT $4-5
❑ ❑ SIN SA8811 HM BOX, 1987, WHICH HOUSEBOAT IS WHOSE/OUR LINES ARE CROSSED $4-5
❑ ❑ SIN SA8812 HM BOX, 1987, ISLAND EYES $4-5
❑ ❑ SIN SA8813 HM BOX, 1987, RONALD FISHING/CROSSWORD $4-5

*** IDENTICAL TOYS: BEL/CAN/FIN/FRA/HOL/MEX/NOR/SPA/SWE/SWI SA8800/01/02/03

USA SA8810

USA SA8811

USA SA8812   USA SA8813   CAN SA8802   CAN SA8801   *** SA8803   *** SA8800

□ □ *** SA8800 **GRIMACE SUBMARINE,** 1987, PUR TOP/
   BOTTOM/PROP/3P $3-5
□ □ *** SA8803 **RONALD MCD AIRBOAT,** 1987, RED BOTTON/
   RONALD/PROP/3P $3-5

   ***IDENTICAL TOYS: BEL/FIN/FRA/HOL/MEX/NOR/SPA/
   SWE/SWI SA8801/02**
□ □ *** SA8801 **FRY KIDS FERRY,** 1987, GRN TOP/BOTTON/
   FERRY CAR/3P $4-5
□ □ *** SA8802 **HAMBURGLAR PIRATE SHIP,** 1987, BLU TOP/
   BOTTON/SAIL/3P $3-5

□ □ CAN SA8801 **FRY KIDS FERRY,** 1987, **ORG TOP/BOTTOM/**
   FERRY CAR/3P $5-8
□ □ CAN SA8802 **HAMB PIRATE SHIP,** 1987, **YEL TOP/BOTTOM/**
   SAIL/3P $5-8

USA   CAN SA8801

COMMENTS: REGIONAL DISTRIBUTION: CANADA/SINGAPORE -
1988; BELGIUM, FINLAND, FRANCE, HOLLAND, NORWAY,
SPAIN, SWEDEN, SWITZERLAND - JANUARY 1989; MEXICO
- JUNE 1989. IN MEXICO, SAILORS HAPPY MEAL WAS THE
FIRST NATIONAL HAPPY MEAL PROMOTION (JUNE 1989).
CAN SA8800/03 = USA SA8800/03. CAN SA8801 IS ORANGE
WHEREAS USA SA8801 IS GREEN; CAN SA8802 IS YELLOW
WHEREAS USA SA8802 IS BLUE (See USA SAILORS HAPPY
MEAL, 1988).

SKIMMERS/FRISBEE DISC PROMOTION, 1988
□ □ UK SK8801 **SKIMMER - RED,** 1988, 8" DISC FRISBEE W LG
   ARCHES $3-4
□ □ UK SK8802 **SKIMMER - YEL,** 1988, 8" DISC FRISBEE W LG
   ARCHES $3-4

COMMENTS: REGIONAL DISTRIBUTION: UK - 1988. COST 22p
WITH ANY FOOD PURCHASE.

USA   CAN SA8802

SUPER SUMMER/SUMMER TOYS/SUMMER FUN HAPPY MEAL, 1988
□ □ CAN SU8825 **PAIL/SAND,** 1987, WHT SAND PAIL/RED LID W
   YEL RAKE or RED SHOVEL $2.50-4

   ***IDENTICAL SUMMER TOYS: BEL/CAN/DEN/FIN/FRA/ITA/
   HOL/NOR/SPA/SWE/SWI *** SU8826/27 AND *** BT8973**
□ □ *** SU8826 **BEACH BALL,** 1987, WHT/FRY KIDS $2.50-3
□ □ *** SU8827 **BOAT/SAIL,** 1988, INFLATABLE SAIL BOAT/
   GRIMACE $.50-1
□ □ *** BT8973 **SET 3 FRISBEE/RONALD FUN FLYER,** 1987, RON
   ON GRN/ORG FRISBEE FLYER/INFLA $1-1.50
□ □ *** SU8932 **SUN VISOR,** 1988, FOAM $1-1.50
□ □ JPN SU8826 **BEACH BALL,** 1987, BIG SUMMER/WHT/RON
   ON SURF BOARD $4-6

JPN SU8826

CAN SU8865

USA TU9065

USA TU9000   USA TU9001   USA TU9002   USA TU9003

CAN TU8802   CAN TU8803   CAN TU8805   CAN TU8801

UK

❑ ❑ CAN SU8865 TRANSLITE/LG, 1987 $15-25

COMMENTS: REGIONAL DISTRIBUTION: CANADA - 1988;
BELGIUM, DENMARK, FINLAND, FRANCE, ITALY, HOLLAND,
NORWAY, SPAIN, SWEDEN, SWITZERLAND - 1988. IT IS
CONCEIVABLE THAT *** SU8826/27 AND ***BT8973 ARE THE
SAME PREMIUMS USED IN 1989 IN THE USA IN BEACH TOY
"COLLECT ALL 4" TEST MARKET HAPPY MEAL, 1989 OR
USA SUPER SUMMER HM, 1988. See USA BEACH TOY
"COLLECT ALL 4"/TEST MARKET HAPPY MEAL, 1989;
SUPER SUMMER HM, 1988. CANADIAN SUMMER TOYS
SOLD FOR 69 CENTS EACH. See USA SUPER SUMMER II
HAPPY MEAL, 1988.

TURBO MACS JUNIOR TUTE/HAPPY MEAL, 1993/1990/ 1989/1988

❑ ❑ GER TU9030 HM BAG, 1990, WHT/AUTO GRAPHICS $1-1.50

*** IDENTICAL CARS: CAN/UK TU8801/02/03/04
❑ ❑ *** TU8801 **GRIMACE,** 1988, IN WHITE CAR W LG RED
ARCHES $4-7
❑ ❑ *** TU8802 **HAMBURG,** 1988, IN YEL CAR W LG RED
ARCHES $4-7
❑ ❑ *** TU8803 **RONALD,** 1988, IN RED CAR W LG YEL ARCHES/
NO TEAR DROP $4-7
❑ ❑ *** TU8805 **BIG MAC,** 1988, IN **BLU SPORTS CAR** W LG
YELLOW ARCHES $4-7

*** IDENTICAL CARS: GER/NET TU9000/01/02/03
❑ ❑ *** TU9000 **BIRDIE,** 1988, IN PINK RACER W LG YEL
ARCHES $4-7
❑ ❑ *** TU9001 **GRIMACE,** 1988, IN WHITE CAR W LG RED
ARCHES $4-7
❑ ❑ *** TU9002 **HAMBURG,** 1988, IN YEL SPORTS CAR W LG
RED ARCHES $4-7
❑ ❑ *** TU9003 **RONALD,** 1988, IN RED RACER W LG RED
ARCHES/NO TEAR DROP $4-7

❑ ❑ CAN TU8850 BUTTON/ENGLISH, 1988, TURBOMACS
RACING TEAM $3-4
❑ ❑ CAN TU8851 BUTTON/FRENCH, 1988, TURBOMACS/
L'EQUIPE $3-4
❑ ❑ CAN TU8852 REGISTER TOPPER, 1988, TURBOMACS $4-7
❑ ❑ CAN TU8855 TRAYLINER, 1988, TURBOMACS $3-4

COMMENTS: REGIONAL DISTRIBUTION: CANADA - 1988 AS A
KID'S PROMOTION; UK - AUGUST-SEPTEMBER 1989;
GERMANY - AUGUST 24-SEPTEMBER 16 1990; GUATE-
MALA: 1990; HOLLAND (NETHERLANDS) - FEBRUARY 4-
MARCH 17, 1993. BELGIUM, DENMARK, FINLAND, FRANCE,
ITALY, HOLLAND, NORWAY, SPAIN , SWEDEN, SWITZER-
LAND: MARCH 1989. COST 38p WITH ANY FOOD PUR-
CHASE IN THE UK. CANADA'S SET OF BIG MAC HAVE THE
MAPLE LEAF LOGO AND SOLD FOR 59 CENTS IN 1988.
GERMANY'S SET OF TURBO MACS DO NOT HAVE GER-
MAN LOGO ON THE CARS, ONLY ON THE PAPER INSERT.
GER TU9000-03 = USA TU9000-03. See USA TURBO MAC I
HAPPY MEAL, 1988 FOR RONALD WITH TEARDROP; AND
USA TURBO MAC II HAPPY MEAL, 1990.

CAN TU8850   CAN TU8851

CAN TU8855

CANADA

1989

ADVENT CALENDAR/CHRISTMAS BALLS PROMOTION, 1989

- ❏ ❏ UK AD8901 HM BOX, 1989, ADVENT CALENDAR/1990 CALENDAR $5-7
- ❏ ❏ UK AD8902 **RONALD/ORNAMENT,** 1989, 1P PAPER/ "JUMPING" RONALD McDONALD $8-10
- ❏ ❏ UK AD8903 **GRIM/RON/ORNAMENT,** 1989, 1P PAPER/ RONALD/GRI ON SLEIGH $8-10
- ❏ ❏ UK AD8904 **GRIMACE BALL,** 1989, GLASS/PURPLE CHRIST- MAS BALL $6-8
- ❏ ❏ UK AD8905 **HAMBURGLAR BALL,** 1989, GLASS/SILVER CHRISTMAS BALL $6-8
- ❏ ❏ UK AD8906 **RONALD BALL,** 1989, GLASS/RED CHRISTMAS BALL $6-8

   *** IDENTICAL CHRISTMAS BALLS: GER/FRA/NET/SPA AD8904/06

- ❏ ❏ *** AD8904 **GRIMACE BALL,** 1989, PLASTIC/WHT CHRIST- MAS BALL/GRI PICT $6-8
- ❏ ❏ *** AD8906 **RONALD BALL,** 1989, PLASTIC/WHT CHRIST- MAS BALL/RON PICT $6-8

- ❏ ❏ UK AD8964 TRANSLITE/SM, 1989 $8-10
- ❏ ❏ UK AD8965 TRANSLITE/LG, 1989 $15-20
- ❏ ❏ UK AD8909 CEILING DANGLER, 1989 $12-15
- ❏ ❏ UK AD8910 REGISTER TOPPER, 1989 $5-8

COMMENTS: NATIONAL DISTRIBUTION: UK - DECEMBER 1989. THIS WAS THE VERY "FIRST NATIONAL HAPPY MEAL IN THE UK". GER/UK/SCOTLAND/WALES NATIONAL DISTRIBU- TION: DECEMBER 1989. GERMANY'S CHRISTMAS BALL WAS WHITE PLASTIC. NETHERLANDS NL AD8904/06 WAS DISTRIBUTED IN SPAIN. INSERT CARDS ARE MARKED IN LOWER RIGHT HAND CORNER WITH COUNTRY OF DISTRIBUTION.

USA

UK AD8902

UK AD8906

UK AD8903

1st UK Promo

73

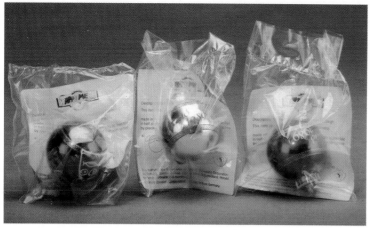

UK AD8904   UK AD8905   *** AD8906

NET AD8904   NET AD8906

GER AD8906   GER AD8904

SPA AD8904

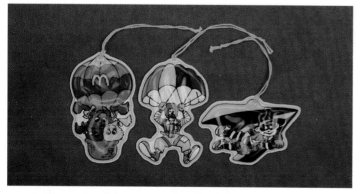

CAN RA8901   CAN GE8901

BEAU TEMPS/MAUVAIS TEMPS/RAIN OR SHINE HAPPY MEAL, 1989

❑ ❑ CAN RA8901 HM BOX, 1989, BULLES/BUBBLES/RON ET ZOISO $3-4

COMMENTS: REGIONAL DISTRIBUTION: CANADA: 1989 DURING CLEAN-UP WEEKS. See USA RAIN OR SHINE HAPPY MEAL, 1989.

CANADA/GENERIC PROMOTION, 1989

❑ ❑ CAN GE8901 **COMB-VROOMER GROOMER,** 1989, RON IN GRN CAR $1-1.25

COMMENTS: REGIONAL DISTRIBUTION: CANADA: 1989 AS TREAT OF THE WEEK.

CRAZY CLINGERS/WALL CRAWLERS PROMOTION, 1989

❑ ❑ GER CR8901 **BIRDIE,** 1989, W BUNCH BALLOONS $4-5
❑ ❑ GER CR8902 **F KIDS,** 1989, W HOT AIR BALLOON $4-5
❑ ❑ GER CR8903 **GRIMACE,** 1989, W ORG/YEL HOT AIR BALLOON $4-5
❑ ❑ GER CR8904 **HAMBURG,** 1989, ON HANG GLIDER $4-5
❑ ❑ GER CR8905 **RONALD,** 1989, W PARACHUTE $5-7

❑ ❑ JPN CR8901 **BIRDIE,** 1989 $5-7
❑ ❑ JPN CR8902 **GRIMACE,** 1989, W GRN/ORG HOT AIR BALLOON/SET 2 $5-7
❑ ❑ JPN CR8903 **HAMBURG,** 1989, W BLU HANG GLIDER/SET 4 $5-7
❑ ❑ JPN CR8904 **RONALD,** 1989 $5-7

COMMENTS: REGIONAL DISTRIBUTION: FRANCE, JAPAN: 1989. COULD HAVE BEEN DISTRIBUTED IN LIMITED REGIONAL AREAS IN USA IN 1989, UNCONFIRMED. PROMOTION WAS A SELF LIQUIDATING PROMOTION IN EUROPE WITH GERMAN MARKINGS; DISTRIBUTED IN VARIOUS EUROPEAN COUNTRIES.

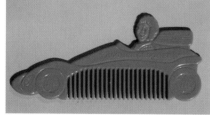

GER CR8902   GER CR8905   GER CR8904

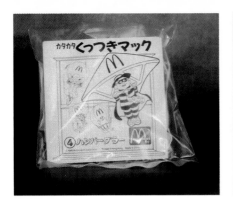

JPN CR8903   JPN CR8902

FIESTA MEXICANA JUNIOR TUTE, 1989
❏ ❏ GER FI8930 HM BAG, 1989, RON IN SOMBRERO/CACTUS
    GRAPHICS $1-2
❏ ❏ GER FI8901 **FRIENDSHIP BRACELET,** 1989, THREADS
    WOVEN/WRIST BRACELET $2-3
❏ ❏ GER FI8902 **PLASTIC CUP,** 1989, FIESTA MEXICANA $2-3
❏ ❏ GER FI8965 TRANSLITE/LG, 1989, RON W SOMBRERO
                                 $10-15

COMMENTS: NATIONAL DISTRIBUTION: GERMANY - NOVEMBER
1989.

FUN WITH FOOD HAPPY MEAL, 1989
❏ ❏ CAN FU8900 **SET 1 HAMBURGER GUY,** 1988, 3P ORG BUNS
    W BRN HAMB W STICKER $4-6
❏ ❏ CAN FU8901 **SET 2 FRENCH FRY GUY,** 1988, 3P FF/1P WHT
    HOLDER W 2P FF W STICKER $4-6
❏ ❏ CAN FU8902 **SET 3 SOFT DRINK CUP,** 1988, 2P/WHITE CUP
    W LID W STICKER $4-6
❏ ❏ CAN FU8903 **SET 4 CHICKEN MCNUGGETS,** 1988, 2P BRN
    YEL BOX/STICKER/3 MCCROQUETTES $4-6
❏ ❏ CAN FU8950 BUTTON/ENGLISH, 1989, FUN WITH FOOD HM
    ARE HERE $5-7
❏ ❏ CAN FU8951 BUTTON/FRENCH, 1989, PETITS GOURMETS
                                   $5-7

COMMENTS: REGIONAL DISTRIBUTION: CANADA - 1989. CAN
FU8900-03 SAME AS USA FU8900-03 (See USA FUN WITH
FOOD HAPPY MEAL, 1989).

USA

MEXICO

CAN FU8900   CAN FU8901   CAN FU8902   CAN FU8903

CAN FU8950

MEXICO

CANADA

CAN FU8951

CAN FU8951

GER FF9102   GER FF9101

FRA FF9411

FUNNY FRY FRIENDS/GLOUTONS RIGOLOS/POMMES FRITZCHEN/FRANSJES & DE FRIETJES JUNIOR TUTE/ HAPPY MEAL, 1993/1992/1991/1990/1989

❏ ❏ FRA FF9411 HM BOX, 1994, TOO TALL $2-3
❏ ❏ FRA FF9412 HM BOX, 1994, GADZOOKS $2-3

*** IDENTICAL BOXES: CAN/GER/UK GL8915/18
❏ ❏ *** FF8915 HM BOX, 1989, COOL DAY AT SCHOOL/UNE CHOUETTE ECOLE $2-3
❏ ❏ *** FF8918 HM BOX, 1989, SNOW DAY PLAY/DES FLOCONS PLEIN LA TETE $2-3

❏ ❏ UK FF9117 HM BOX, 1991, SKI HOLIDAY $2-3
❏ ❏ UK FF9116 HM BOX, 1991, CITY SIGHTS $2-3

❏ ❏ AUS FF9009 **U-3 HOP-A-LONG/LITTLE DARLING**, 1989, YEL KID COW GIRL $3-5
❏ ❏ AUS FF9010 **U-3 LIL' CHIEF**, 1989, ORG KID INDIAN CHIEF $3-5

*** IDENTICAL TOYS: CAN/GER/HOL/UK/ZEA FF9001
❏ ❏ *** FF9001 **HOOPS**, 1989, PURPLE KID W SWEAT B W BASKETBALL $2-3
*** IDENTICAL TOY: AUS/CAN/GER/GUA/HOL/UK/ZEA FF9002
❏ ❏ *** FF9002 **ROCKIN' ROCKER**, 1989, YEL GIRL W HEAD PHONES W SKATES $2-3

*** IDENTICAL TOYS: CAN/GER/GUA/HOL/ZEA FF9003
❏ ❏ *** FF9003 **MATEY**, 1989, RED KID W PIRATE HAT $2-3

*** IDENTICAL TOYS: CAN/GER/HOL/ZEA FF9004
❏ ❏ *** FF9004 **GADZOOKS**, 1989, BLU KID W EYEGLASSES $2-3

*** IDENTICAL TOYS: AUS/CAN/GER/GUA/HOL/ZEA FF9005
❏ ❏ *** FF9005 **TRACKER**, 1989, BLU KID W SAFARI HAT W SNAKE $2-3

*** IDENTICAL TOY: AUS/CAN/GER/GUA FF9006
❏ ❏ *** FF9006 **ZZZ'S**, 1989, TURQ KID W SLEEPING CAP W BEAR $2-3

*** IDENTICAL TOYS: AUS/CAN/GER/HOL/UK FF9007
❏ ❏ *** FF9007 **TOO TALL**, 1989, GRN KID W CLOWN HAT $2-3

*** IDENTICAL TOYS: CAN/GER/HOL/UK FF9008
❏ ❏ *** FF9008 **SWEET CUDDLES**, 1989, PNK KID W BABY BONNET W BOTTLE $2-3

FRA FF9412

USA FF9015   USA FF9016

USA FF9002

USA FF9017   USA FF9018

*** FF9009   *** FF9004   *** FF9005   *** FF9008

Take one of us   Take one of us
home today!   home today!

USA   USA

*** FF9002   *** FF9006
*** FF9010   *** FF9003   *** FF9007

Nu bij je Happy Meal:
de Fransjes & de Frietjes!

VAN 15 JULI T/M 25 AUGUSTUS.

HOLLAND

AUS FF9009

AUS FF9005   AUS FF9002   AUS FF9007   AUS FF9006

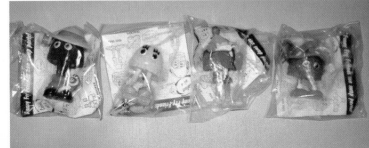

GER FF9165

❏	❏	GER FF9165 TRANSLITE/LG, 1991, 4 FFF		$25-40
❏	❏	UK FF9141 CEILING DANGLER, 1991		$15-20
❏	❏	HOL FF9144 POSTER/SM, 1991		$5-8
❏	❏	UK FF9145 REGISTER TOPPER, 1991		$5-8
❏	❏	UK FF9146 SHEET 4 WINDOW STICKERS, 1991		$8-10
❏	❏	UK FF9164 TRANSLITE/SM, 1991		$5-8
❏	❏	UK FF9165 TRANSLITE/LG, 1991		$8-12

COMMENTS: REGIONAL DISTRIBUTION: QUEBEC, CANADA - 1989. CANADA'S PREMIUMS WERE THE SAME AS: USA FF9001-08, FUNNY FRY FRIENDS II (COLLECT ALL 8) HAPPY MEAL, 1990. CANADA'S PACKAGING WAS NOT IN FRENCH, ONLY IN ENGLISH EXACTLY LIKE THE USA VERSIONS. NATIONAL DISTRIBUTION: UK - FEBRUARY 15-MARCH 4, 1991; GERMANY/HOLLAND: JULY 15-AUGUST 25, 1991 AND JANUARY 2-24, 1993; GUATEMALA: 1990; HONG KONG: JANUARY 1990 AS SELF LIQUIDATOR; NEW ZEALAND, MALAYSIA, MEXICO: JANUARY-FEBRUARY 1990. IN NEW ZEALAND, GADZOOKS WAS GIVEN AS A BIRTHDAY PARTY GIFT. GERMANY REPEATED DISTRIBUTION OF FFF HM AGAIN IN 1993 W 4 ADDITIONAL PREMIUMS. PREMIUMS SAME AS USA FF901-08, USA FUNNY FRY FRIENDS HM, 1990. GERMAN/HOLLAND PREMIUMS = USA PREMIUMS, LOOSE OUT OF PACKAGE.

GARFIELD HAPPY MEAL, 1991/1990/1989

		*** IDENTICAL TOYS: CAN/GER/ZEA GA9101/02/03	
❏	❏	*** GA9101 **GAR/PUSH SCOOTER,** 1989, ON YEL/PUR WHEELS SCOOTER/2P	$6-8
❏	❏	*** GA9102 **GAR/CAR,** 1989, IN BLU CAR/2P	$6-8
❏	❏	*** GA9103 **GAR/SKATEBOARD,** 1989, ON PNK/YEL SKATEBOARD 2P	$6-8
		*** IDENTICAL TOY: CAN/ZEA GA8904	
❏	❏	*** GA8904 **GAR/MOTOR SCOOTER,** 1989, ON RED MOTOR BIKE W ODIE/2P	$6-8
❏	❏	CAN GA9105 **GAR/BIG WHEELS,** 1989, ON GRN/PURP BIG WHEELS/2P	$6-8
❏	❏	GER GA9006 **GAR/MOTOR SCOOTER,** 1989, ON BLU MOTORSCOOTER/2P	$6-8
❏	❏	CAN GA9145 REGISTER TOP, 1989, GARFIELD/2 FOR 99 CENTS	$2-4
❏	❏	CAN GA8950 BUTTON/ENGLISH, 1989, GARFIELD COLLECTIBLES	$3-5
❏	❏	CAN GA8951 BUTTON/FRENCH, 1989, GARFIELD ROULEZ AVEC	$3-5
❏	❏	CAN GA8955 TRAYLINER, 1989, GARFIELD/59 CENTS	$3-4
❏	❏	CAN GA9165 TRANSLITE/LG, 1989	$25-40

GER FF9008   GER FF9001

GER FF9004   GER FF9002   GER FF9007   GER FF9006

UK FF9001   UK FF9008   UK FF9002   UK FF9007

GER GA9101

CAN. GA9101   CAN. GA9102

GER GA9006

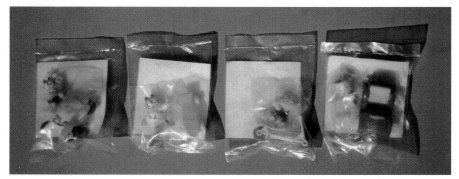

CAN GA8904   CAN GA8903   CAN GA8901   CAN GA8902

USA

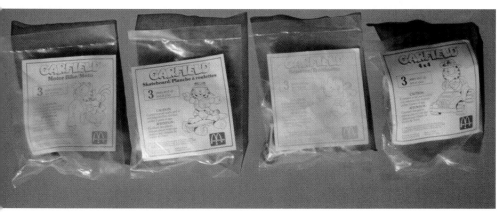

CAN GA8904   CAN GA8903   CAN GA8901   CAN GA8902

USA

CAN GA8901   CAN GA8902   CAN GA8903   CAN GA8904

CAN GA8950   CAN GA8951

USA

CAN GA8955

USA

USA

MEXICO

GER GE8901

COMMENTS: REGIONAL DISTRIBUTION: CANADA/NEW ZEALAND - 1989. NATIONAL DISTRIBUTION: CANADA - 1989 AND AGAIN IN 1991 WITH CAN GAA9105 REPLACING CAN GA8904; GERMANY - NOVEMBER 16-DECEMBER 6, 1990.

GERMANY/GENERIC PROMOTION, 1989

❏ ❏ GER GE8901 **CRAYON MARKER,** 1989, RECT/CRAYON MIXTURE/MCD LOGO $3-4

*** IDENTICAL STUFFED ORNAMENTS: GER/MEX GE8902/ 03

❏ ❏ *** GE8902 **ORNAMENT - OLIVER,** 1989, CLOTH CAT/ MUSICAL W BOX $3-4

❏ ❏ *** GE8903 **ORNAMENT - DODGER,** 1989, CLOTH DOG/ MUSICAL W BOX $3-4

❏ ❏ GER GE8904 **YO YO,** 1989, YEL/RED W MCD LOGO $2-3
❏ ❏ GER GE8905 **YO YO,** 1989, YEL/YEL W MCD LOGO $2-3
❏ ❏ GER GE8906 **YO YO,** 1989, YEL/RED W "ESSEN MIT SPAB" $2-3
❏ ❏ GER GE8907 **BIRDIE/SHAKY WALKER,** 1989, YEL M/ STRING/PURP WABBEL WALKER $5-7
❏ ❏ GER GE8908 **CLICK-CLACKER,** 1989, RONALD FACE/ PRESS CLACKER ON BACK $2-3
❏ ❏ GER GE8909 **SOFT SOFTBALL,** 1989, RED or YEL SOFT SOFTBALL W MCD LOGO $1-2
❏ ❏ GER GE8910 **GRIM ROLLING WHEEL,** 1989, PURP GRI/2 YEL WHEELS/SKAKY AUF RADERN/3P $3-5
❏ ❏ GER GE8911 **TRACING ALPHA/NUM,** 1989, RED RECT W ALPHABET/NUMBERS $1-2
❏ ❏ GER GE8912 **FRISBEE/WURFSCHEIBE,** 1989, NEON COLORS FRISBEES $1-1.25
❏ ❏ GER GE8913 **SUNGLASSES/ARCHES,** 1989, LG PAPER LOGO $2-3
❏ ❏ GER GE8914 **DRINK HOLDER,** 1989, WHT DRINK HOLDER FOR AUTO DOOR $1-1.25
❏ ❏ GER GE8915 **PUZZLE,** 1989, RON ON TRAIN/32P $2-4
❏ ❏ GER GE8916 **LOLLIPOP,** 1989, W WHT RON STICKER/ FRUCHTLUTSCHER $1-1.25
❏ ❏ GER GE8917 **RULER,** 1989, CENTIMETERS/XO GRAPHIC $3-5

USA

GER GE8903   GER GE8902

GER GE8905   GER GE8904

GERMANY

GERMANY

GERMANY

GER GE8907

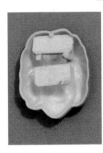

GER GE8908

GER GE8910

GER GE8913

COMMENTS: REGIONAL DISTRIBUTION: GERMANY/MEXICO -
1989 AS SELF LIQUIDATOR AND GIVE-AWAYS. TOYS ARE
NOT ASSOCIATED WITH A SPECIFIC JUNIOR TUTE/HAPPY
MEAL. GER GE8902/03 GIVEN OUT DURING NOVEMBER/
DECEMBER 1989 WERE CLOTH DOLLS WITH MUSICAL
ORNAMENTS; CAME PACKAGED IN A BLUE CARDBOARD
BOX. GER GE8902/03 = USA MUSICAL ORNAMENTS GIVEN
FREE WITH A PURCHASE OF A $5.00 GIFT CERTIFICATE
BOOK, 1989.

HAPPY HATS HAPPY MEAL, 1994/1989

*** **IDENTICAL HATS:** BEL/DEN/FIN/FRA/ITA/NOR/SPA/SWE/
SWI HT8900/01/02/03

☐ ☐	*** HT8900	**BIG MAC-CONSTABLE**, 1989, BLUE	$12-15
☐ ☐	*** HT8901	**GRIM-SHOW BIZ**, 1989, PURP	$12-15
☐ ☐	*** HT8902	**F KID-CONSTRUCTION HAT**, 1989, YEL	$12-15
☐ ☐	*** HT8903	**RONALD-FIREMAN HAT**, 1989, RED	$12-15

AUS HT9442

USA HT9003   USA HT9002   USA HT9001   USA HT9000

USA HT9065

☐	☐	AUS HT9401 **FIREMAN HAT,** 1994, RED/PLASTIC	$7-10
☐	☐	AUS HT9402 **SCOUT/GUIDES HAT,** 1994, YEL/PLASTIC	$7-10
☐	☐	AUS HT9403 **SAFARI HAT,** 1994, WHT/PLASTIC	$7-10
☐	☐	AUS HT9404 **DERBY,** 1994, BLK/PLASTIC	$7-10
☐	☐	AUS HT9442 COUNTER CARD, 1994	$5-7

COMMENTS: REGIONAL DISTRIBUTION: BELGIUM, DENMARK, FINLAND, FRANCE, ITALY, NORWAY, SPAIN, SWEDEN, SWITZERLAND: SEPTEMBER 1989. REGIONAL DISTRIBUTION: AUSTRALIA: 1994. AUS HT9401-04 ARE SIMILAR TO USA HT9000-03 IN CONCEPT. USA HATS HAPPY MEAL (SEE HATS HAPPY MEAL, 1990) PREMIUMS CAME WITH A PLASTIC INSERT/2P.

KARNEVALSMADKEN/FACE MASK JUNIOR TUTE, 1989

☐ ☐ GER KA8901 **FACE MASK - HAMBURGLAR,** 1989, PLASTIC
$10-12
☐ ☐ GER KA8902 **FACE MASK - RONALD,** 1989, PLASTIC $10-12
☐ ☐ GER KA8903 **FACE MASK - SHAKY/GRIM,** 1989, PLASTIC
$10-12
☐ ☐ GER KA8904 **FACE MASK - BIG MAC,** 1989, PLASTIC $10-12
☐ ☐ GER KA8965 TRANSLITE/LG, 1989, FACE MASK/JT $25-40

COMMENTS: NATIONAL DISTRIBUTION: GERMANY - FEBRUARY 1-27, 1990. THESE ARE SIMILIAR TO/NOT THE SAME AS AUSTRALIAN FACE MASKS, 1995.

CAN LO8901   CAN LO8902   CAN LO8903   CAN LO8904

LOONEY TUNES HAPPY MEAL, 1989

☐ ☐ CAN LO8901 **BUGS BUNNY,** 1989, GREY STANDING ON GRN/RED SCOOTER/2P $3-5
☐ ☐ CAN LO8902 **COYOTE/ROAD RUNNER,** 1989, BRN STANDING ROAD RUNNER ON RED RR HAND CART/2P $3-5
☐ ☐ CAN LO8903 **DAFFY DUCK,** 1989, BLK DUCK SITTING IN YEL CAR/2P $3-5
☐ ☐ CAN LO8904 **SYLVESTER/TWEETY,** 1989, BLK CAT SITTING W TWEETY IN BLU AIRPLANE/2P $3-5

☐ ☐ CAN LO8945 REGISTER TOPPER, 1989, "WHAT'S UP DOC?"/ 59 CENTS $2-4
☐ ☐ CAN LO8950 BUTTON/ENGLISH, 1989, LOONEY TUNES COLLECTIBLES $3-5
☐ ☐ CAN LO8951 BUTTON/FRENCH, 1989, LOONEY TUNES/ FIGURINES A COLLECTIONNER $3-5
☐ ☐ CAN LO8955 TRAYLINER, 1989, "WHAT'S UP DOC?"/59 CENTS $1-1.50
☐ ☐ CAN LO8965 TRANSLITE/LG, 1989 $25-40

COMMENTS: REGIONAL DISTRIBUTION: CANADA - 1989. COST 59 CENTS EACH IN CANADA.

CAN LO8965

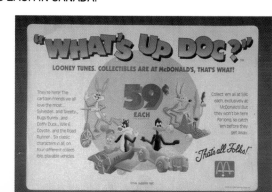

CAN LO8955

CAN LO8950   CAN LO8951

82

LUNAR NEW YEAR/RONALD McDONALD FIGURINES PROMOTION, 1989

❑ ❑ SIN RO8901 **RONALD HOLDING SCROLL/BANNER,** ND, RED BANNER $15-20

❑ ❑ SIN RO8902 **RONALD HOLDING HONG BAO,** ND, RED BANNER $15-20

❑ ❑ SIN RO8903 **RONALD W GONG,** ND, GOLD BELL $15-20

❑ ❑ SIN RO8904 **RONALD W ACCORDIAN/FIRE CRACKER,** ND, RED ACCORDIAN $15-20

COMMENTS: REGIONAL DISTRIBUTION: SINGAPORE - JANUARY 19-FEBRUARY 15, 1989. FIGURINES ARE NOT DATED.

MAC TONIGHT TREAT-OF-THE WEEK, 1989

❑ ❑ CAN MA8901 **BEAD GAME - MAC IS BACK,** 1989, RECT/BLK/ MAC W PIANO $2-3

❑ ❑ CAN MA8902 **BEAD GAME - MAKE IT MAC TONIGHT,** 1989, RECT/YEL/MAC W SKYLINE $2-3

❑ ❑ CAN MA8903 **BEAD GAME - MAC TONIGHT,** 1989, CIRCLE/ BLU/MAC AS MOON $2-3

❑ ❑ CAN MA8904 **BEAD GAME - MAKE IT MAC TONIGHT,** 1989, CIRCLE/ORG/MAC AT PIANO $2-3

❑ ❑ CAN MA8805 **MAC TONIGHT DECAL,** 1988, LIGHT SWITCH DECAL $3-4

COMMENTS: REGIONAL DISTRIBUTION: CANADA - 1989.

USA

CAN MA8901   CAN MA8902   CAN MA8903   CAN MA8904

SIN RO8901

SIN RO8902

CAN MA8805

USA

SIN RO8904

SIN RO8903

USA

USA

83

MICKEY'S BIRTHDAYLAND/DISNEY RACERS HAPPY MEAL, 1990/1989

USA MB8900   USA MB8901   USA MB8902   USA MB8903   USA MB8904

USA MB8926   USA MB8965

COMMENTS: REGIONAL DISTRIBUTION: JAPAN - MAY 1989; TAIWAN - JULY 1990. PREMIUMS CALLED, "DISNEY RACERS" IN JAPAN IN 1989. See USA MICKEY'S BIRTHDAYLAND HAPPY MEAL, 1989 FOR ADDITIONAL U-3 PREMIUMS. IT IS CONCEIVABLE THAT THE VARIOUS COLORS OF THE USA U-3 MICKEY'S BIRTHDAYLAND PREMIUMS ORIGINATED IN JAPAN. THE VARIOUS PASTEL COLORS OF THE U-3 CARS COULD HAVE BEEN MADE FOR THE INTERNATIONAL MARKET, NOT THE USA MARKET WHICH ONLY HAD OFFICIALLY, 6 U-3 CARS.

Mickey's Birthdayland U-3   USA

NEW FOOD CHANGEABLES/CHANGEABLES HAPPY MEAL, 1994/1992/1990/1989

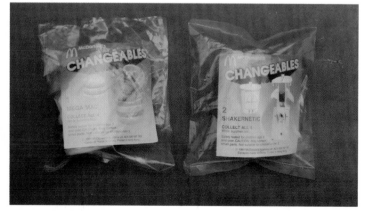

JAPAN NE8904   JAPAN CH8706

COMMENTS: REGIONAL DISTRIBUTION: JAPAN - MARCH-APRIL 1988 AND 1989 (SET OF 6) AND AGAIN IN 1994; AUSTRALIA - MARCH 1991; CHINA 1994. IT IS BELIEVED THAT ALL CHANGEABLES AND NEW FOOD CHANGEABLES. (See USA CHANGEABLES HM, 1987 AND See USA NEW FOOD CHANGEABLES HAPPY MEAL, 1989) WERE GIVEN OUT, BASED ON AVAILABILITY IN WAREHOUSES; MARKETING OF FOOD ITEMS. PRICE/MIP VARIANCE IS DUE TO DISTRIBUTION WORLDWIDE. SET NUMBERS VARY ACCORDING TO COUNTRY DISTRIBUTED. JAPAN'S SET SAYS, "COLLECT ALL 4." AND SECOND SET ILLUSTRATED SAYS, "#5/#6". See NEW FOOD CHANGEABLES/MCROBOTS, 1990.

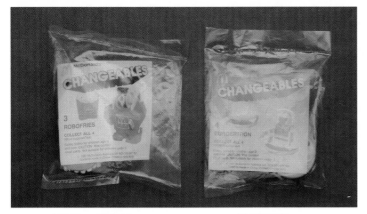

JAPAN   NE8906   *** NE8902

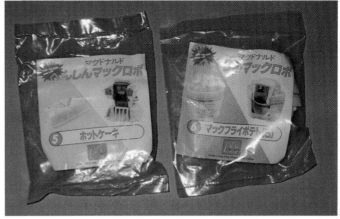

JAPAN   NE8900   *** NE8907

CH8701   *** CH8702   *** CH8703   *** CH8704   *** CH8705   USA CH8706

USA NE8900   USA NE8901   USA NE8902   USA NE8903

USA NE8904   USA NE8905   USA NE8906   USA NE8907

OLIVER & COMPANY HAPPY MEAL, 1989

❏ ❏	*** OC8810 HM BOX, 1988, FUNNY BONES	$4-5
❏ ❏	*** OC8811 HM BOX, 1988, NOISY NEIGHBORHOOD	$4-5
❏ ❏	*** OC8812 HM BOX, 1988, SHADOW SCRAMBLE	$4-5
❏ ❏	*** OC8813 HM BOX, 1988, TRICKY TRIKE	$4-5

    *** IDENTICAL FINGER PUPPETS: BEL/FIN/FRA/ITA/HOL/
NOR/SPA/SWE/SWI *** OC8801/02/03/04

❏ ❏ *** OC8800 **SET 1 OLIVER**, 1988, KITTEN/FINGER PUPPET

                                                     $2-3

❏ ❏ *** OC8801 **SET 2 FRANCIS**, 1988, BULLDOG/FINGER
PUPPET $2-3

❏ ❏ *** OC8802 **SET 3 GEORGETTE**, 1988, FRENCH POODLE/
FINGER PUPPET $2-3

❏ ❏ *** OC8803 **SET 4 DODGER**, 1988, DOG W GOGGLES/
FINGER PUPPET $2-3

❏ ❏ *** OC8895 PIN, 1988, OLIVER & COMPANY/ROUND $3-4

USA OC8800   USA OC8801   USA OC8802   USA OC8803

USA   OC8895

USA

MEX PE9210

PEANUTS/POPMOBILES/SNOOPY & FRIENDS HAPPY MEAL, 1993/1991/1989

❏	❏	MEX PE9210 HM BOX, 1992, RN W BLACKBOARD	$3-4
❏	❏	MEX PE9211 HM BOX, 1992, RN W JUNGLE	$3-4
		*** IDENTICAL TOYS: CAN/GER/JP/MEX PE8901/02/03/04	
❏	❏	*** PE8901 **CHARLIE BROWN,** 1989, IN BLU/YEL TRAIN ENGINE	$5-8
❏	❏	*** PE8902 **LUCY,** 1989, IN GREEN FIRE TRUCK	$5-8
❏	❏	*** PE8903 **SNOOPY,** 1989, IN RED/YEL DOG HOUSE/AIRPLANE	$5-8
❏	❏	*** PE8904 **WOODSTOCK,** 1989, IN PURP/GRN CAR	$5-8
❏	❏	CAN PE8945 REGISTER TOPPER, 1989, POPMOBILES/69 CENTS	$2-4
❏	❏	CAN PE8950 BUTTON/ENGLISH, 1989, PEANUTS POPMOBILES	$3-5
❏	❏	CAN PE8951 BUTTON/FRENCH, 1989, POPMOBILES PEANUTS/CHACUNE	$3-5
❏	❏	CAN PE8955 TRAYLINER, 1989, POPMOBILES/69 CENTS	$3-4
❏	❏	CAN PE8965 TRANSLITE/LG, 1989	$25-40
❏	❏	GER PE9165 TRANSLITE/LG, 1991	$25-40

CAN PE8901   CAN PE8902   CAN PE8903   CAN PE8904

GER PE9165

CAN PE8955

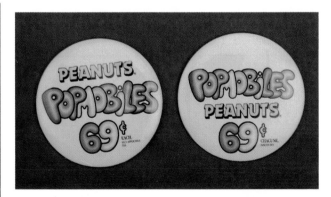

CAN PE8950   CAN PE8951

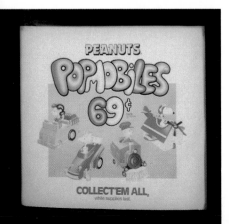

CAN PE8965

JPN PE9401   JPN PE9402   JPN PE9403

SAFARIBECHER/SAFARI PLASTIC CUP JUNIOR TUTE, 1989

❑ ❑ GER SA8905 HM BAG, 1989, SAFARIBECHER/AFRICAN
ANIMALS $2-3
❑ ❑ GER SA8901 **PLASTIC CUP - GIRAFFE,** 1989, W ANIMAL
GRAPHICS $3-5
❑ ❑ GER SA8902 **PLASTIC CUP - ALLIGATOR,** 1989, W ANIMAL
GRAPHICS $3-5
❑ ❑ GER SA8903 **PLASTIC CUP - TIGER,** 1989, W ANIMAL
GRAPHICS $3-5
❑ ❑ GER SA8904 **PLASTIC CUP - FLAMINGO,** 1989, W ANIMAL
GRAPHICS $3-5

COMMENTS: NATIONAL DISTRIBUTION: GERMANY: JUNE 2-JULY
2, 1989.

1990

AIRPORT/FLUGZEUG PROMOTION, 1990

❑ ❑ GER AI9056 **BIPLANE - DOPPELDECKER,** 1986, 6P RED/YEL
BIPLANE/YEL WINGS/RED BODY $4-6
❑ ❑ GER AI9057 **BIPLANE - DOPPELDECKER,** 1986, 6P RED/YEL
BIPLANE/RED WINGS/YEL BODY $4-6
❑ ❑ GER AI9058 **STEERMAN - FLUGZEUG,** 1986, 5P RED/YEL
STEERMAN/YEL BODY/RED WING $4-6
❑ ❑ GER AI9059 **STEERMAN - FLUGZEUG,** 1986, 5P RED/YEL
STEERMAN/RED BODY/YEL WING $4-6

COMMENTS: REGIONAL DISTRIBUTION: GERMANY: 1990.
AIRPLANES CAME WITH STICKER SHEET AND ARE DATED
1986.

BEACH BALL HAPPY MEAL, 1990

❑ ❑ *** BE8607 HM BOX, 1986, HAVING A WONDERFUL TIME/BY
THE SEA $4-5
❑ ❑ UK BE8601 **BEACH BALL - BIRDIE,** 1986, BLU/ON BEACH W
SAND CASTLE/SAILBOAT $7-10
❑ ❑ UK BE8602 **BEACH BALL - GRIMACE,** 1986, YEL/W BEACH
UMBRELLA W BIRD/FISH/SAILBOAT $7-10
❑ ❑ UK BE8603 **BEACH BALL - RONALD,** 1986, RED/WAVING
ON BEACH W PELICAN/SEAHORSE/SUN $7-10

COMMENTS: REGIONAL DISTRIBUTION: UK: JULY 1990. MIP
PACKAGE CAME POLYBAGGED WITH SCOTCH TAPE
ENCLOSURE. BEACH BALLS UK BE8601/02/03 = USA
BE8601/02/03. See USA BEACH BALL HAPPY MEAL, 1986.
USA BE8607 HAPPY MEAL BOX COULD HAVE BEEN
DISTRIBUTED IN THE UK WITH THIS PROMOTION, ON A
REGIONAL BASIS.

BEACH TIME/AUFBLASBARES SCHIFF/VAKANTIE HAPPY MEAL/JUNIOR TUTE, 1991/1990

❑ ❑ FRA BT9030 HM BAG, 1990, RON W SNORKEL $2-3
❑ ❑ GER BT9030 HM BAG, 1990, RON IN SAIL BOAT/BLU/WHT
$2-3
❑ ❑ UK BT9130 HM BAG, 1991, BEACH TIME/PLASTIC $3-5

*** IDENTICAL TOYS: GER/HOL/UK BE9070/71/72/73
❑ ❑ *** BT9072 **SET 1 BEACH BALL/GRIMACE BOUNCIN,** 1988,
YEL/INFLATABLE $1-2
❑ ❑ *** BT9071 **SET 2 CATAMARAN/FRY KID SUPER SAILER,**
1991, F KIDS ON RED/PURP CATAMARAN BOAT/INFLA $1-2
❑ ❑ *** BT9073 **SET 4 FRISBEE/RONALD FUN FLYER,** 1991, RON
ON GRN/ORG FRISBEE FLYER/INFLA $1-1.50
❑ ❑ *** BT9070 **SET 5 SUBMARINE/BIRDIE SEASIDE SUB,** 1988,
SUBMARINE/PINK/INFLA $1-2

❑ ❑ HOL BT9074 **SET 3 COIN CONTAINER,** 1991, RED/WHT
CONTAINER W NECK STRING/2P $3-5
❑ ❑ GER BT9075 **SET 3 SAILBOAT - RONALD,** 1990, YEL/RED
SAILBOAT W RON ON WHT SAIL $2-3

MEXICO

GER AI9056   GER AI9057   GER AI9058   GER AI9059

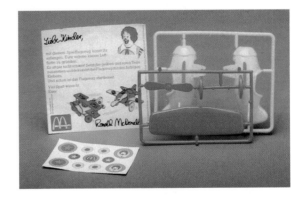

GER AI9056

USA BT8665

COMMENTS: NATIONAL DISTRIBUTION - GERMANY: JULY 6-29, 1990; UK: AUGUST 2, 1991; HOLLAND: JUNE 25-AUGUST 19, 1990. GER BT9075 IS SIMILAR TO USA SU8827, EXCEPT GERMANY HAS RONALD ON THE SAIL; USA HAS GRIMACE ON THE WHITE SAIL (See USA SUPER SUMMER HAPPY MEAL, 1988; USA BEACH TOY I HM, 1989; USA BEACH TOY II HM, 1990). UK BT9170-73 AND HOL BT9070-73 = USA BT9070-73, LOOSE OUT OF PACKAGE. FRA BT9030 HM BAG WAS USED IN SEVERAL COUNTRIES, IN SEVERAL DIFFERENT HM PROMOTIONS. CALLED "SCHIFF AHOI HM" IN GERMANY; "VAKANTIE HM" IN HOLLAND; "BEACH TIME" IN UK. GERMANY GAVE 5 PREMIUMS, HOLLAND GAVE 5 WITH #3 CHANGED TO A COIN HOLDER AND UK GAVE 4 PREMIUMS, LEAVING OUT #3 ALTOGETHER. JAPAN TESTED IN JULY 1990 AND RAN AGAIN IN JULY 1991, AS WELL AS AN EARLIER VERSION IN 1988. BELGIUM, DENMARK, FINLAND, FRANCE, ITALY, HOLLAND, NORWAY, SPAIN, SWEDEN, SWITZERLAND: JUNE-AUGUST 1990. CALLED, "BEACHTIME" IN SCANDINAVIAN COUNTRIES WITH 5 GENERIC TYPE HM BOXES USED. See GENERIC/COUNTRY PROMOTIONS.

FRA BT9030

HOLLAND

HOL BT9072

HOL BT9071

HOL BT9078

HOL BT9073

HOL BT9070

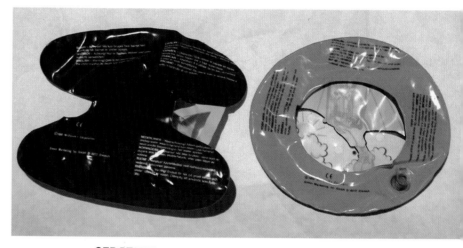

GER BT9071

GER BT9073

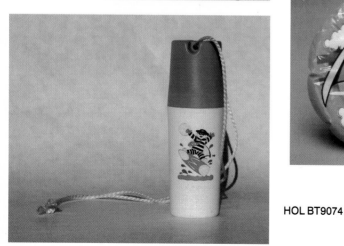

HOL BT9074

UK BT9073

GER BT9065

Schiff ahoi!
Junior-Tüte jetzt mit einem lustigen Segelschiff
nur DM 6,10

88

CANADA POST CORPORATION / MCD'S LEGENDARY CREATURES, 1992/1990

❑ ❑ CAN PO9001 **LEGENDARY CREATURES**, 1990, BLU BOOKLET/OGOPOGO $7-10
❑ ❑ CAN PO9002 **LEGENDARY CREATURES**, 1990, GRN BOOKLET/LOUP-GAROU $7-10
❑ ❑ CAN PO9201 **STAMPS-DINOSAURES**, 1992 $4-7

COMMENTS: REGIONAL DISTRIBUTIOIN: CANADA: OCTOBER 1990 AND AGAIN IN 1992 IN CONJUNCTION WITH THE CANADIAN POST OFFICE.

CAMP McDONALDLAND/BUSH CAMP KIT HAPPY MEAL, 1991/1990

❑ ❑ AUS CM9030 HM BAG, 1990, GENERIC $1-1.25

     *** IDENTICAL PREMIUM: HONG KONG/TAI/JP/AUS CM9000/01/02/03
❑ ❑ USA CM9000 **SET 1 GRIMACE CANTEEN**, 1989, 2P BLU W YEL TOP $1-1.50
❑ ❑ USA CM9001 **SET 2 BIRDIE CAMPER/MESS KIT**, 1989, 3P GRN W ORG HANDLE $1-1.50
❑ ❑ USA CM9002 **SET 3 FRY KID UTENSILS**, 1989, 3P TURQ FK/ YEL SP/PURP KN W OR W/O 5 BANDAIDS $1-1.50
❑ ❑ USA CM9003 **SET 4 COLLAPSIBLE CUP/RONALD**, 1989, 2P RED CUP W LID $1-1.50
❑ ❑ USA CM9050 BUTTON, 1990, CAMP MCDLAND HM $3-5

COMMENTS: REGIONAL DISTRIBUTION: HONG KONG, TAIWAN: SEPTEMBER 1990; SINGAPORE: OCTOBER 1990; JAPAN TESTED IN MAY 1990 AND RAN A YEAR LATER IN MAY 1991; AUSTRALIA RAN AS "BUSH CAMP KIT" IN SEPTEMBER-OCTOBER 1991 WITH A SPECIAL BAG. See USA CAMP McDONALDLAND HAPPY MEAL, 1990 FOR ADDITIONAL PREMIUMS GIVEN WITH THIS HM.

HOL BT9044

CAN PO9001   CAN PO9002

CAN PO9201

CANADA

USA

USA CM9050

89

USA

CANADA/GENERIC PROMOTION, 1990

❑ ❑ CAN GE9001 **PUZZLE - RON ON SWING**, 1990, GLOW IN DARK $2-3

COMMENTS: REGIONAL DISTRIBUTION: CANADA: 1990.

DESIGN-O-SAURS/DESIGN-O-SAURUS/DINOSAURUS/ LAND OF THE DINOSAURS HAPPY MEAL, 1991/1990

*** **IDENTICAL TOYS: CAN/HOL DE8710/11/12/13**

❑ ❑ *** DE8710 **SET 1 RONALD**, 1987, **ON tyRONALDsaurus rex TYRANNOSAURUS**/5P RED W STICKERS $5-8

❑ ❑ *** DE8711 **SET 2 GRIMACE**, 1987, **ON GRIMACEsaur PTERODACTYL**/5P PURP W STICKERS $5-8

❑ ❑ *** DE8712 **SET 3 FRY GUY**, 1987, **ON brontoFRY GUY BRONTOSAURUS**/5P GRN W STICKERS $5-8

❑ ❑ *** DE8713 **SET 4 HAMBURG**, 1987, **ON triceraHAMBURGLAR TRICERATOPS**/5P YEL W STICKERS $5-8

❑ ❑ HOL DE9144 POSTER, 1990 $5-8

COMMENTS: REGIONAL DISTRIBUTION: CANADA: 1990. CANADA DE8710-13 = USA DE8710-13 EXCEPT USA VERSION HAD NO STICKERS. HOLLAND - JANUARY 29-MARCH 25, 1990; BELGIUM, DENMARK, FRANCE, HOLLAND, NORWAY, SPAIN, SWEDEN, SWITZERLAND: JANUARY 29-APRIL 1, 1990. USA PROTO-TYPES/PRE-PRODUCTION MODELS EXIST OF THESE PREMIUMS.

CAN DE8710   CAN DE8711   CAN DE8712   CAN DE8713

CAN GE9001

USA PROTOTYPE-Designosaurus

HOL DE9144

GERMANY/EUROPE/JPN GENERIC HAPPY MEAL, 1990

- ☐ ☐ GER GE9001 **COIN HOLDER/RON,** 1990, RED/RONALD'S FACE/PLASTIC $1-2
- ☐ ☐ GER GE9002 **ICE CUBE/RONALD,** 1990, YEL MOLD/RONALD ICE CUBE/EISFIGUR $3-4
- ☐ ☐ GER GE9003 **FRISBEE/RONALD,** 1990, WHT W RON WAVING/4 1/2" $3-4
- ☐ ☐ GER GE9004 **KINDER-PFLASTER,** 1990, BANDAGE $1-2
- ☐ ☐ GER GE9005 **ACROBAT-RON,** 1990, YEL RON/CROSS BAR/ STICKERS/6P $8-12
- ☐ ☐ GER GE9006 **PAINT SET,** 1990, WATERCOLORS W BRUSH/ PAPER/WASSERFARBENSET/2P $3-4
- ☐ ☐ GER GE9007 **JUMPING RON,** 1990, YEL RON W PULL HANDLE/6P $7-10
- ☐ ☐ GER GE9008 **TELESCOPE,** 1990, RED/YEL or BLU/YEL W RON PIC $2-3
- ☐ ☐ GER GE9009 **JACK/SPACE,** 1990, NEON COLORS SPIN- NING JACK/OUTER SPACE TOP $2-3
- ☐ ☐ GER GE9010 **SPINNING TOP,** 1990, ASSORTED COLORS DISC W STRING $2-3
- ☐ ☐ GER GE9011 **KALEIDOSCOPE,** 1990, RED or GRN SCOPE W ARCHES ON LENSE $3-4
- ☐ ☐ DEN GE9005 **ACROBAT/RON,** 1990, YEL/4P $3-4
- ☐ ☐ JPN GE9001 **MAC TONIGHT,** 1990, IRON-ON DECAL $7-10
- ☐ ☐ JPN GE9002 **PLATE,** 1990, WHT/CHARS $3-4
- ☐ ☐ *** GE9001 **DOLL-RONALD,** 1990, ORIGIN UNKNOWN $——

COMMENTS: REGIONAL DISTRIBUTION: GERMANY/EUROPE - 1990 DURING CLEAN-UP WEEKS AND/OR AS U-5 PREMI- UMS. DEN GE9005 = USA CI8305 (See USA CIRCUS HAPPY MEAL, 1983). THE DATES ON THE ACROBAT PREMIUMS DIFFER. CANADA ALSO DISTRIBUTED THE ACROBAT PREMIUMS, DATES VARY. ITEM PRODUCED WHICH ARE NOT UP TO McDONALD'S HIGH STANDARDS ARE CONSID- ERED, "KNOCK-OFF" ITEMS. KNOCK-OFF ITEMS ARE ITEMS MADE WITHOUT McDONALD'S PERMISSION. SOME COLLEC- TORS SHUN THESE ITEMS, OTHERS ENJOY THEM. McDON- ALD'S WILL SUE ANYONE WHO PRODUCES A KNOCK-OFF ITEM. THE RONALD DOLL MAY BE A KNOCK-OFF ITEM

USA PROTOTYPES

GER GE9001

GER GE9002

GERMANY

GER GE9004

GER GE9003

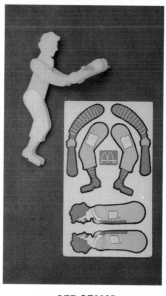

GER GE9005

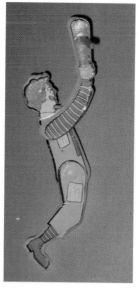

USA

GER GE9010

GER GE9011

GERMANY

DEN GE9005

JPN GE9001

JPN GE9002

*** GE 9001

SEE THE WORLD
with Ronald McDonald

**LITTLE MERMAID/ARIELLE/KLEINE ZEEMEERMIN
JUNIOR TUTE/HAPPY MEAL, 1991/1990**

❑ ❑ GER LI9010 HM BOX, 1990, SEA GARDEN/ARIEL W FLOUN-
     DER AND SEBASTIAN $4-5
❑ ❑ GER LI9011 HM BOX, 1990, URSULA'S DOMAIN/ARIEL W
     URSULA $4-5
❑ ❑ GER LI9012 HM BOX, 1990, VILLAGE LAGOON/ARIEL AND
     PRINCE ERIC IN BOAT $4-5
❑ ❑ GER LI9013 HM BOX, 1990, ARIEL'S GROTTO $4-5

*** IDENTICAL TOYS: GER/HOL/UK LI9000/02/03

❏ ❏ *** LI9000 **FLOUNDER,** 1990, YEL SOFT RUBBER SQUIRT
TOY FISH $3-5
❏ ❏ *** LI9002 **ERIC,** 1990, ERIC(PRINCE) W CRAB(SEBASTIAN)
IN YEL BOAT/2P $3-5
❏ ❏ *** LI9003 **ARIEL,** 1990, ARIEL THE LITTLE MERMAID $3-5

*** IDENTICAL TOY: HOL/UK LI9001

❏ ❏ *** LI9001 **URSULA,** 1990, SEA WITCH OCTOPUS W
SUCTION CUP $3-5

❏ ❏ UK LI9041 CEILING DANGLER, 1990 $15-20
❏ ❏ HOL LI9044 POSTER/SM, 1990 $5-8
❏ ❏ UK LI9045 REGISTER TOPPER, 1990 $5-8
❏ ❏ UK LI9063 LUG-ON/BOARD, 1990 $6-8
❏ ❏ UK LI9064 TRANSLITE/SM, 1990 $8-12
❏ ❏ UK LI9065 TRANSLITE/LG, 1990 $15-20

COMMENTS: NATIONAL DISTRIBUTION: UK: NOVEMBER 1990;
GERMANY: DECEMBER 4-24, 1990; GUATEMALA: 1989;
BELGIUM, DENMARK, FINLAND, FRANCE, ITALY, HOLLAND,
NORWAY, SPAIN, SWEDEN, SWITZERLAND: NOVEMBER 26-
JANUARY 20, 1991. UK/GER/HOL LI9000-03 = USA LI8900-03
(See USA LITTLE MERMAID HAPPY MEAL, 1989), LOOSE
OUT OF PACKAGE. TOYS GIVEN IN UK/GERMANY/HOL-
LAND WERE IDENTICAL TO USA TOYS EXCEPT FOR
PACKAGING DATED 1990; USA PACKAGING DATED 1989.
UK DISTRIBUTED BOXES MARKED, "MADE IN GERMANY".

MAC TONIGHT HAPPY MEAL, 1993/1990

❏ ❏ AUS MA9310 HM BOX, 1993, SKYLINE/MACTONIGHT $4-6

❏ ❏ AUS MA9301 **CUP/PLASTIC,** 1993, MAC TONIGHT $2-3
❏ ❏ AUS MA9302 **PENCIL,** 1993, W MAC TONIGHT HEAD $4-6
❏ ❏ AUS MA9303 **MASK/PAPER,** 1993, PAPER MASK/17 CM $4-6
❏ ❏ AUS MA9304 **PHOTO FRAME,** 1993, PHOTO FRAME/11 CM
$5-7

❏ ❏ ZEA MA8800 **SET 1 JEEP/OFF ROADER,** 1988, 4 WHEELER
W MAC GRN $4-6
❏ ❏ ZEA MA8801 **SET 2 SPORTS CAR,** 1988, PORCHE W MAC
RED $4-6
❏ ❏ ZEA MA8803 **SET 3 SURF SKI,** 1988, SKIBOAT W MAC W YEL
WHEELS (1990) $7-10
❏ ❏ ZEA MA8804 **SET 4 SCOOTER,** 1988, SCOOTER W MAC BLK
$4-6
❏ ❏ ZEA MA8805 **SET 5 MOTORCYCLE,** 1988, RED W MAC
TONIGHT $4-6
❏ ❏ ZEA MA8807 **SET 6 AIRPLANE,** 1988, GRN PLANE W MAC/
BLK SUNGLASSES $4-6

COMMENTS: REGIONAL DISTRIBUTION: NEW ZEALAND:
OCTOBER 1990; VENEZUELA: JUNE 1991; AUSTRALIA:
1993. NEW ZEALAND/S ZEA MA8800-05/07 = USA MA8800-
05/07. See USA MAC TONIGHT TRAVEL TOYS HAPPY MEAL,
1988. USA VERSION HAD AN ADDITIONAL TOY, MAC
TONIGHT ON THE AIRPLANE WITH BLUE SUNGLASSES;
PLUS USA U-3, MAC TONIGHT ON A SKATEBOARD.

GER LI9010   GER LI9011   GER LI9012

UK LI9001   UK LI9003   UK LI9002   UK LI9000

GERMANY

AUS MA9301   HOL LI9044

93

AUS MA9304

USA MA8800 USA MA8801 USA MA8803 USA MA8804

USA MA8867

USA MA8866

USA MA8805 USA MA8807 USA MA8806 USA

GER MA9003

CAN FI9005   CAN FI9007   CAN FI9006   CAN FI9008

MASKEN III JUNIOR TUTE, 1990
- ❏ ❏ GER MA9001 **MASK - GRIMACE,** 1990, PAPER/**SHAKY**/WHT BACKGROUND $3-4
- ❏ ❏ GER MA9002 **MASK - BIG MAC,** 1990, PAPER/WHT BACKGROUND $3-4
- ❏ ❏ GER MA9003 **MASK - HAMBURGLAR,** 1990, PAPER/HAMBURGERKLAU/WHT BACKGROUND $3-4
- ❏ ❏ GER MA9005 **MASK - RONALD,** 1990, PAPER/WHT BACKGROUND $3-4

COMMENTS: LIMITED REGIONAL DISTRIBUTION: GERMANY - FEBRUARY 1-27, 1990. PAPER FACE MASKS JUNIOR TUTE/ HAPPY MEAL WAS REPEATED IN 1982 AND 1983, EACH WITH DIFFERING GRAPHICS ON THE PAPER MASKS.

McDONALDLAND FIGURINES PROMOTION, 1990
- ❏ ❏ CAN FI9005 **BIRDIE,** 1990, YEL W MAPLE LEAF UNDER ARCHES $4-5
- ❏ ❏ CAN FI9006 **HAMBURGLAR,** 1990, WHT W ARMS DOWN TO SIDE $4-5
- ❏ ❏ CAN FI9007 **GRIMACE,** 1990, PURP/STANDING W BASEBALL CAP TURNED TO SIDE $4-5
- ❏ ❏ CAN FI9008 **RONALD,** 1990, RED/STANDING W ARMS OUTSTRETCHED $5-7

COMMENTS: REGIONAL DISTRIBUTION: CANADA - 1990.

McDONALDLAND FLYER PROMOTION, 1990
- ❏ ❏ UK FL9001 **FLYER - BIG MAC,** 1990, YEL CUTOUT FRISBEE W ARMS UP FIG $3-4
- ❏ ❏ UK FL9002 **FLYER - GRIMACE,** 1990, PURP CUTOUT FRISBEE W FULL FIGURE GRIMACE $3-4

❏ ❏ UK FL9003 **FLYER - HAMBURGLAR,** 1990, ORG CUTOUT
FRISBEE W HAMB W ARMS UP FIG $3-4
❏ ❏ UK FL9004 **FLYER - RONALD,** 1990, RED CUTOUT FRISBEE
W FULL FIGURE RONALD $3-4

COMMENTS: REGIONAL DISTRIBUTION: UK - 1990. FRISBEES
WERE FREE WITH ANY PURCHASE.

MCSPACESHIP II/HYPER UFO HAPPY MEAL, 1992/1990
❏ ❏ FRA VA9001 **BIG MAC,** 1990, VACUUM FORM W STICKERS
$50-65
❏ ❏ FRA VA9002 **BIRDIE,** 1990, VACUUM FORM W STICKERS
$50-65
❏ ❏ FRA VA9003 **GRIMACE,** 1990, VACUUM FORM W STICKERS
$50-65
❏ ❏ FRA VA9004 **HAMBURGLAR,** 1990, VACUUM FORM W
STICKERS $50-65
❏ ❏ FRA VA9005 **RONALD,** 1990, VACUUM FORM W STICKERS
$50-65
❏ ❏ FRA VA9006 STICKER SHEET, 1990 $10-12

COMMENTS: VERY LIMITED REGIONAL DISTRIBUTION: BEL-
GIUM, DENMARK, FINLAND, FRANCE, NORWAY, SPAIN,
SWEDEN, SWITZERLAND: OCTOBER-NOVEMBER 1990 AND
AGAIN IN PARIS WITH VERY LIMITED REGIONAL DISTRIBU-
TION: PARIS, FRANCE - DECEMBER-JANUARY 1992.
VACUUM FORM CONTAINERS SERVED AS THE FOOD
CONTAINER AND PREMIUM. EACH CAME WITH A STICKER
SHEET. CALLED, "HYPER UFO'S" IN FRANCE. HONG KONG
MIGHT HAVE DISTRIBUTED THESE VACU-FORM CHARAC-
TERS IN APRIL 1990 WITH CHINESE WRITING ON THE
STICKER SHEETS.

FRA VA9002

FRA VA9001

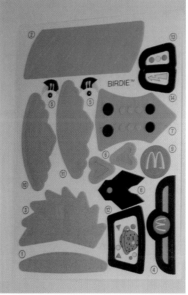

FRA-Birdie Sticker Sheet

FRA-Birdie Vacuum Form

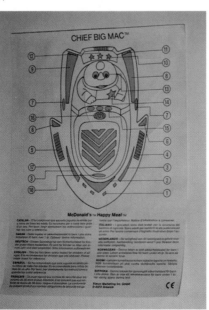

FRA VA9006

FRA VA9005

95

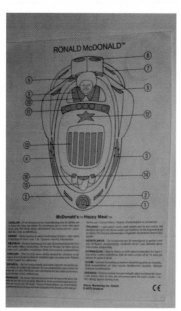

FRA-Ronald Sticker Sheet

FRA-Ronald Vacuum Form

MCSURPRISE HAPPY MEAL, 1990

- ❏ ❏ USA BB8721 **SET 2 PAPA,** 1987, W BRN WHEELBARROW/ FLOCKED $3-4
- ❏ ❏ USA BB8723 **SET 4 MAMA,** 1987, W DRESS W YEL SHOP CART/FLOCKED $3-4
- ❏ ❏ USA LE8900 **SET 1A GYRO BIRD HELICOPTER,** 1989, LEGO/PACKAGED 19P $3-4
- ❏ ❏ USA LE8903 **SET 2B LIG STRIKER AIRPLANE,** 1989, LEGO/ PACKAGED 14P $3-4
- ❏ ❏ USA CH8950 **SET 1 CHIP'S ROTO-CUPTER,** 1989, 3P/RED PROP/BLU-RED-ORG/YEL RULER FOR BLADES $2-3
- ❏ ❏ USA CH8951 **SET 2 DALE'S ROTO ROADSTER,** 1989, 4P/ ORG PROP/GRN PIPE/PURP BRUSH PROP/YEL COPT $2-3
- ❏ ❏ USA NU8811 **U-3 SLUGGER,** 1988, 2P BRN W BASEBALL GLOVE $5-7
- ❏ ❏ USA NU8812 **U-3 DAISY,** 1988, 2P BRN/BEAR W DAISEY FLOWER ON HAT $6-10
- ❏ ❏ USA NU8804 **CORNY MCNUGGET,** 1988, 3P STRAW HAT W RED POPCORN BELT $3-4
- ❏ ❏ USA NU8809 **SNORKEL MCNUGGET,** 1988, 3P MASK W KNIFE/LITE BELT $3-4

COMMENTS: REGIONAL DISTRIBUTION: MALAYASIA 1990. PREMIUMS WERE USA PREVIOUSLY ISSUED HM TOYS FROM DIFFERENT HAPPY MEALS. SURPRISE PREMIUM COULD HAVE BEEN WHATEVER WAS AVAILABLE IN THE WAREHOUSES. See USA, *HAPPY MEAL TOYS IN THE USA* FOR FULL LISTING.

USA BB8723

USA BB8721

USA LE8900

USA LE8901

USA LE8902

USA LE8903

USA CH8965

USA NU8865

MEGA BLOCKS HAPPY MEAL, 1990

❏ ❏ CAN ME9001 **BIRDIE,** 1990, 9 BLOCKS W/STICKERS (2 SM PNK 2 LG;4 SM YEL 1 LG) $7-10
❏ ❏ CAN ME9002 **GRIMACE,** 1990, 9 BLOCKS W/STICKERS (5 SM PURP 3 LG;1 SM YEL) $7-10
❏ ❏ CAN ME9003 **HAMBUR,** 1990, 9 BLOCKS W/STICKERS (3 SM RED 1 LG;3 SM WHT 1 LG;1 SM BLK 1 LG) $7-10
❏ ❏ CAN ME9004 **RONALD,** 1990, 9 BLOCKS W/STICKERS (3 SM RED 2 LG;2 SM YEL 1 LG;1 SM WHT $7-10

COMMENTS: REGIONAL DISTRIBUTION: CANADA - 1990.

MIX'EM UP MONSTERS/MONSTERTJES/EINEM LUSTIGEN MONSTER JUNIOR TUTE/HAPPY MEAL, 1992/1991/1990

❏ ❏ GER MI9011 HM BAG, 1990, RON W BALLOONS/GENERIC BAG $2-3
❏ ❏ UK MI9110 HM BOX, 1990, BIBBLE/GRN $3-4
❏ ❏ UK MI9111 HM BOX, 1990, CORKLE/BLU $3-4
❏ ❏ UK MI9112 HM BOX, 1990, THUGGER/PURP $3-4

　　*** **IDENTICAL BOX: GER/UK MI9113**
❏ ❏ *** MI9113 HM BOX, 1990, GROPPLE/YEL $3-4

　　*** **IDENTICAL TOYS: GER/HOL/UK/USA MI9200/01/02/03**
❏ ❏ *** MI8900 **BLIBBLE,** 1986, GREEN/EXTENDED EYES/3P $4-6
❏ ❏ *** MI8901 **CORKLE,** 1986, BLUE/FOLDED ARMS/3P $4-6
❏ ❏ *** MI8902 **GROPPLE,** 1986, YEL/2 HEADS/3P $4-6
❏ ❏ *** MI8903 **THUGGER,** 1986, PUR/LARGE TUSKS/3P $4-6

❏ ❏ UK MI9141 CEILING DANGLER, 1991 $15-20
❏ ❏ HOL MI9144 POSTER/SM, 1991 $5-8
❏ ❏ UK MI9145 REGISTER TOPPER, 1991 $5-8
❏ ❏ UK MI9164 TRANSLITE/SM, 1991 $8-12
❏ ❏ UK MI9165 TRANSLITE/LG, 1991 $5-8
❏ ❏ GER MI9065 TRANSLITE/LG, 1988 $25-40

COMMENTS: NATIONAL DISTRIBUTION: GERMANY: MAY 10-JUNE 3, 1990; UK: MAY 1991; BELGIUM, DENMARK, FINLAND, FRANCE, GREECE, ITALY, HOLLAND, NORWAY, PORTUGAL, SPAIN, SWEDEN, SWITZERLAND: FEBRUARY 20-APRIL 1, 1992; AUSTRIA: TESTED MARCH 1989. 4 PREMIUMS ARE IDENTICAL TO USA MI8900-03 (See USA MIX'EM UP MONSTERS HAPPY MEAL, 1989). CALLED "LUSTIGE MONSTER" IN GERMANY. UK PACKAGING IS MARKED 1991.

CAN ME9001　　CAN ME9002　　CAN ME9003　　CAN ME9004

HOL MI9144

GER MI9113　　　　　HOLLAND

Junior-Tüte

GER MI9065

THANK YOU FOR COMING TO McDONALD'S.

UK MI9112　　UK MI9110　　UK MI9113

UK MI8903   UK MI8901   UK MI8900   UK MI8902

AUSTRIA

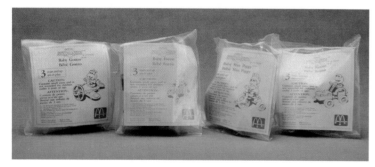

CAN MU9000   CAN MU9001   CAN MU9002   CAN MU9003

CANADA

MUPPET BABIES CONNECTIBLES (CANADA IV) HAPPY MEAL, 1990

- ❑ ❑ CAN MU9000 **GONZO/BEBE GONZO,** 1986, W SHOES IN GRN AIRPLANE $3-4
- ❑ ❑ CAN MU9001 **FOSSIE/BEBE FOZZIE,** 1986, IN RED/ORG/YEL HANDLE WAGON $3-4
- ❑ ❑ CAN MU9002 **MISS PIGGY/BEBE MISS PIGGY,** 1986, ON BLU/PNK/YEL TRICYCLE $3-4
- ❑ ❑ CAN MU9003 **KERMIT,** 1986, ON YEL/RED/BLU SOAP BOX CAR $3-4
- ❑ ❑ CAN MU9045 REGISTER TOPPER, 1990, MB CONNECTIBLES/59 CENTS $2-4
- ❑ ❑ CAN MU9055 TRAYLINER, 1990, MB CONNECTIBLES/59 CENTS $1.50-3

COMMENTS: REGIONAL DISTRIBUTION: CANADA - 1990; MEXICO: JULY 1991; GUATEMALA: SEPTEMBER 1991. CAN MU9000-03 VEHICLES/ONLY (NOT CHARACTERS) ARE THE SAME AS USA CONNECTIBLES/LINKABLES HAPPY MEAL VEHICLES. CAN MU9000-03 = USA MU9100-03 LOOSE OUT OF PACKAGE, USA MUPPET BABIES III HAPPY MEAL, 1991.

NEW FOOD CHANGEABLES/MCROBOTS/ROBOMAC/ MCTRANSFORMERS JUNIOR TUTE/HAPPY MEAL, 1992/ 1991/1990

- ❑ ❑ CAN NE9010 HM BOX, 1990, PERDUS DANS LESPACE/ OMBRES SPATIALES $2-3
- ❑ ❑ CAN NE9011 HM BOX, 1990, OUVRONS LOEIL!/BIZARD GROTTE $2-3
- ❑ ❑ DEN RO9010 HM BOX, 1990, MCNUGGETS $2-3
- ❑ ❑ DEN RO9011 HM BOX, 1990, SHAKE $2-3
- ❑ ❑ UK RO9010 HM BOX, 1990, BIG MAC $2-3
- ❑ ❑ UK RO9011 HM BOX, 1990, LARGE RIES $2-3
- ❑ ❑ UK RO9012 HM BOX, 1990, QUARTER POUNDER W CHEESE $2-3
- ❑ ❑ UK RO9013 HM BOX, 1990, SOFT DRINK $2-3

- ❑ ❑ CAN RO8900 **HOTCAKES,** 1988, ROBOCAKES/HOTCAKES/ SAUSAGE
- ❑ ❑ UK RO8901 **QUARTER POUNDER,** 1988, GALLACTA BURGER $2-3

USA MU9100   USA MU9101   USA MU9102   USA MU9103

CANADA

CAN MU9055

CAN NE9011   CAN NE9010

*** IDENTICAL TOYS: CAN/GER/SIN/UK/ZEA RO8902/04
- ☐ ☐ *** RO8904 **BIG MAC,** 1987, MACRO MAC/SUPER MAC W PAINTED HANDS $2-3
- ☐ ☐ *** RO8902 **LG/MED FRIES,** 1987, FRY FORCE $2-3

*** IDENTICAL TOYS: CAN/GER/SIN/UK RO8903
- ☐ ☐ *** RO8903 **SHAKE/SOFT DRINK,** 1988, KRYPTO CUP/OPENS FROM SIDE $2-3

- ☐ ☐ GER RO8905 **TURBO CONE,** 1988, ICE CREAM CONE $2-3

*** IDENTICAL TOY: CAN/GER/ZEA RO8906
- ☐ ☐ *** RO8906 **C2-CHEESBURGER,** 1988, BURGERTRON/CHEESEBURGER $2-3

*** IDENTICAL TOY: CAN/SIN RO8907
- ☐ ☐ *** RO8907 **SMALL FRIES,** 1988, FRY-BOT $2-3

*** IDENTICAL TOY: SIN/ZEA RO8908
- ☐ ☐ *** RO8908 **MCNUGGETS,** 1988, CHICKEN MCNUGGETS $2-3

- ☐ ☐ HON RO8909 **BIG BREAKFAST,** 1991, MAC CHARGER $2-3
- ☐ ☐ UK RO9041 CEILING DANGLER, 1990 $15-20
- ☐ ☐ UK RO9045 REGISTER TOPPER, 1990 $4-7
- ☐ ☐ UK RO9063 LUG-ON/MENU BOAR, 1990 $5-8
- ☐ ☐ UK RO9064 TRANSLITE/SM, 1990 $5-8
- ☐ ☐ UK RO9065 TRANSLITE/LG, 1990 $10-15
- ☐ ☐ GER RO9065 TANSLITE/LG, 1990 $25-40

DEN RO9010

DEN RO9011

COMMENTS: NATIONAL DISTRIBUTION: CANADA: QUEBEC/UK-DECEMBER 1990; REGIONAL DISTRIBUTION: GERMANY: MAY-JUNE 1990 AND FEBRUARY 21-MARCH 17, 1991; IRELAND - APRIL 6-MAY 6, 1990; TAIWAN: JANUARY 1990; AUSTRALIA: 1991; GUATEMALA - 1990; NEW ZEALAND - 1992; JAPAN JULY 1989; HONG KONG: MARCH 1990/1991; SINGAPORE: APRIL 1989 AND JULY 1990 AS A SELF LIQUIDATOR; UK: APRIL-MAY 1990 AND AGIN IN 1994 DURING CLEAN-UP PERIODS. BELGIUM, DENMARK, FINLAND, FRANCE, HOLLAND, ITALY, NORWAY, SPAIN, SWEDEN, SWITZERLAND: NOVEMBER 1989; PORTUGAL: OCTOBER-NOVEMBER 1989. THE PREMIMUMS ARE ALMOST IDENTICAL TO USA NEW FOOD CHANGEABLES HM, 1989 - USA NE8900-07; EXCLUDING VARIATIONS IN COLORS OF ARCHES, SIZES OF ARCHES. IT APPEARS THAT DIFFERENT COUNTRIES GAVE OUT AN ASSORT-MENT OF THE 8 BASIC PREMIUMS, BASED ON AVAILABIL-ITY IN LOCAL WAREHOUSES. ROBOCAKES IS MISSING FROM THE EUROPE BECAUSE EUROPEAN COUNTRIES IN 1990 WERE JUST INTRODUCING THIS MENU ITEM. IT IS CONCEIVABLE THAT ALL 8 NEW FOOD CHANGEABLES TOYS WERE GIVEN OUT WORLDWIDE, BASED ON AVAILABILITY IN WAREHOUSES DURING CLEAN-UP WEEKS.

GER RO9005   GER RO9006   GER RO9011

GER RO9065

USA NE8964

USA NE8926

CAN NE8904

USA

USA

PLAY-DOH JUNIOR TUTE, 1990
❑ ❑ GER PL9030 HM BAG, 1990, WHITE/#21-30
❑ ❑ GER PL9001 **BLUE PLAY-DOH,** 1988, YEL CONT/BLU LID/ 2 OZ $4-5
❑ ❑ GER PL9002 **RED PLAY-DOH,** 1988, YEL CONT/RED LID/ 2 OZ $4-5
❑ ❑ GER PL9003 **YELLOW PLAY-DOH,** 1988, YEL CONT/YEL LID/ 2 OZ $4-5
❑ ❑ GER PL9004 **GREEN PLAY-DOH,** 1988, YEL CONT/GRN LID/ 2 OZ $4-5

COMMENTS: NATIONAL DISTRIBUTION: GERMANY: OCTOBER 12-NOVEMBER 4, 1990. VERY SIMILAR TO UK PLAY-DOH, 1988, EXCEPT GREEN SUBSTITUTED FOR WHITE. CANS ARE MARKED (CE) GERMANY W PAPER LEAFLET ON TOP OF CAN.

RALLYE HAPPY MEAL, 1990
❑ ❑ GER RA9010 HM BOX, 1990, RONALD ON CAR $3-4
❑ ❑ FRA RA9010 HM BOX, 1990, GRIMACE ON SKATEBOARD $3-4

    *** IDENTICAL TOYS: FRA/HOL/JPN RA9001/02.03/04
❑ ❑ *** RA9001 **GRIMACE,** 1988, ON GRN/BLU SCOOTER/#1 STICKER $10-12
❑ ❑ *** RA9002 **BIRDIE,** 1988, ON BLUE SCOOTER/#2 STICKERS $10-12
❑ ❑ *** RA9003 **HAMBUR,** 1988, ON YEL/RED SCOOTER/#3 STICKERS $10-12
❑ ❑ *** RA9004 **RONALD,** 1988, ON RED/YEL CAR/#4 STICKERS $10-12
❑ ❑ HOL RA9044 POSTER/SM, 1990 $5-8

COMMENTS: NATIONAL DISTRIBUTION: BELGIUM, DENMARK, FINLAND, FRANCE, ITALY, HOLLAND, NORWAY, SPAIN, SWEDEN, SWITZERLAND: APRIL 2-MAY 13, 1990.

FRA RA9010

HOL RA9002   HOL RA9003   HOL RA9004

SCHOOL KIT II/BACK TO SCHOOL PROMOTION, 1991/1990

- ❑ ❑ UK SC9001 **CASE,** ND, RED/YEL/WHT W DIAGONAL STRIPES/2 POCKET　　　　　　　$2-3
- ❑ ❑ UK SC9002 **ERASER,** ND, YEL W LG RED M LOGO　$1-1.50
- ❑ ❑ UK SC9003 **INFO CARD,** 1990, TIMETABLE/TAKING CARE OF THE EARTH　　　　　　　$1-1.25
- ❑ ❑ UK SC9004 **NOTE PAD,** ND, RED/YEL/WHT W DIAGONAL STRIPES/YEL M LOGO　　　　　$1.50-2
- ❑ ❑ UK SC9005 **PENCIL,** ND, McDONALD'S MAKES YOUR DAY!　　　　　　　　　　　　$1-1.50
- ❑ ❑ UK SC9006 **P SHARPENER,** ND, RED W #3 INSIDE/MOR GERMANY　　　　　　　　　　$1-1.50
- ❑ ❑ UK SC9007 **RULER,** ND, RED/6" W INCHES/METRIC　$1-1.50

- ❑ ❑ HON SC9101 **TIME TABLE,** 1991, RONALD McDONALD　$3-4
- ❑ ❑ HON SC9102 **SET SQUARE,** 1991, HAMBURGLAR　$3-4
- ❑ ❑ HON SC9103 **RULER,** 1991, GRIMACE　　　　　$2-3
- ❑ ❑ HON SC9104 **PENCIL CLIPPER,** 1991, FRY GUY　$2-3
- ❑ ❑ HON SC9105 **STENCIL,** 1991, BIRDIE　　　　　$3-4

COMMENTS: REGIONAL DISTRIBUTION: UK: AUGUST 1990; HONG KONG: 1991. COST 65p WITH A FOOD PURCHASE IN THE UK.

SUMMER TOYS/BEACH TOY HAPPY MEAL, 1991/1990

- ❑ ❑ CAN BE9071 **SET 1 FRY KID SUPER SAILOR,** 1989, RED-PUR CATAMARAN/YEL SAIL　　　　　$1-1.50
- ❑ ❑ CAN BE9076 **SET 2 FRY KIDS SAND PAIL,** 1989, WHT/RED LID/BEACH TOY HM　　　　　　　$3-5
- ❑ ❑ CAN BE9072 **SET 3 GRI BOUNCIN BEA BALL,** 1989, YEL-BLU-GRN　　　　　　　　　　　　$1-2
- ❑ ❑ CAN BE9075 **SET 4 SAND PROPELLOR,** 1989, RED W YEL/SAND PROPELLER/2P　　　　　　$1-2
- ❑ ❑ CAN BE9073 **SET 5 RONALD FUN FLYER,** 1989, INFLATABLE TUR-ORG RING　　　　　　$1-1.50
- ❑ ❑ CAN BE9065 TRANSLITE/LG, 1989　　　　$15-20

COMMENTS: REGIONAL DISTRIBUTION: CANADA - 1990. JAPAN DISTRIBUTED: *** BE9071 FRY KID SUPER SAILOR CATAMARAN BOAT IN 1991. CAN BE9071/72/73/75/76 = USA BE9071/72/73/75/76, USA BEACH TOY II HM, 1990 (COLLECT ALL 8).

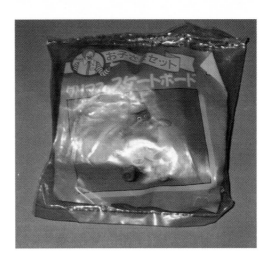

JPN RA9001

HOL RA9044

JAPAN

USA

UK

USA

CAN BE9065

USA BE9072   USA BE9075

USA BE9073   USA BE9076

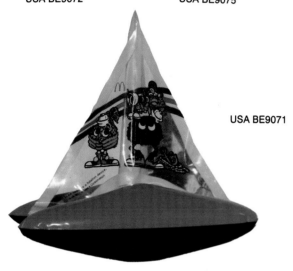

USA BE9071

TRAVEL BUG/JUNIOR DRIVERS HAPPY MEAL, 1994/1993/1990

❏ ❏ AUS TR9001 **JEEP/4 WHEEL DRIVE,** 1990, VACU-FORM/BLU LID/BLUE BASE $10-15
❏ ❏ AUS TR9002 **SPEEDBOAT,** 1990, VACU-FORM/YEL LID/RED BASE $10-15
❏ ❏ AUS TR9003 **TRAIN,** 1990, VACU-FORM/GRN LID/GRN BASE $10-15
❏ ❏ AUS TR9004 **AIRPLANE,** 1990, VACU-FORM/WHT LID/ORG BASE $10-15

❏ ❏ AUS TR9301 **AIRPLANE-HAMBURGLAR,** 1993, VACUFORM 3" YEL AIRPLANE W STICKERS $4-6
❏ ❏ AUS TR9302 **CAR-RONALD,** 1993, VACUFORM 3" RED AUTO W STICKERS $4-6
❏ ❏ AUS TR9303 **TRAIN -BIRDIE,** 1994, VACUFORM/3" GRN TRAIN W STICKERS $4-6
❏ ❏ AUS TR9304 **BOAT-GRIMACE,** 1994, VACUFORM/3" PURP BOAT W STICKERS $4-6

COMMENTS: REGIONAL PROMOTIONAL: AUSTRALIA - 1990: AGAIN IN MARCH-APRIL 1993 AND 1994/1995 DURING CLEAN-UP WEEKS AND TO CHILDREN UNDER THE AGE OF 5 (U-5). DIFFERENT PREMIUMS WERE GIVEN OUT IN DIFFERING YEARS.

TUINPRET/BRITAIN IN BLOOM/LITTLE GARDENER HAPPY MEAL, 1992/1991/1990

❏ ❏ UK LG9110 HM BOX, 1990, BIRDIE W TROWEL $3-4
❏ ❏ UK LG9111 HM BOX, 1990, FRY GIRL/GRIMACE W FLOWER POT $3-4
❏ ❏ UK LG9112 HM BOX, 1990, RONALD W WATERING CAN $3-4
❏ ❏ UK LG9113 HM BOX, 1990, GRIMACE W RAKE $3-4

*** **IDENTICAL TOYS: BEL/DEN/FIN/FRA/ITA/HOL/NOR/SPA/SWE/SWI/UK LG9075/76/77/78**
❏ ❏ *** LG8975 **BIRDIE'S TROWEL,** 1988, ORG SHOVEL W MARIGOLD SEEDS $2-4
❏ ❏ *** LG8976 **FRY KIDS PLANTER,** 1988, TURQ FLOWER POT W PURP LID/HANDLE W NASTURTIUM SEEDS $2-4
❏ ❏ *** LG8977 **GRIMACE/RAKE,** 1990, GRN RAKE W SWEET PEA SEEDS $2-4
❏ ❏ *** LG8978 **RON WATERING CAN,** 1988, RED WATERING CAN/YEL HANDLE W FORGET-ME-NOT SEEDS $2-4
❏ ❏ UK LG8985 **CALENDAR/1991,** 1990, BRITAIN IN BLOOM $7-10

❏ ❏ HOL LG9044 POSTER/SM, 1990 $5-8

AUS TR9301   AUS TR9302

AUS TR9303

HOLLAND

COMMENTS: NATIONAL DISTRIBUTION: BELGIUM, DENMARK, FINLAND, FRANCE, ITALY, HOLLAND, NORWAY, SPAIN, SWEDEN, SWITZERLAND: MAY 14-JUNE 24, 1990; TAIWAN: APRIL 1990; UK: MARCH 15-APRIL 11, 1991 AND MAY 1992. MIP PREMIUMS MARKED "MADE IN ITALY". HOL/UK LG8975-78 = USA LG8975-78 (See USA LITTLE GARDENER HAPPY MEAL, 1989). CALENDARS WERE GIVEN OUT AND/OR SOLD SEPARATELY.

ZAUBERSCHREIBER/STENCIL PROMOTION, 1990
- ❏ ❏ GER ZA9001 **STENCIL**, 1990, NEON YEL/6 AREAS/ ZAUBERSCHREIBER $3-5
- ❏ ❏ GER ZA9002 **STENCIL**, 1990, NEON PNK/6 AREAS/ ZAUBERSCHREIBER $3-5
- ❏ ❏ GER ZA9003 **STENCIL**, 1990, NEON RED/6 AREAS/ ZAUBERSCHREIBER $3-5

COMMENTS: REGIONAL DISTRIBUTION: GERMANY - 1990.

GER ZA9001

HOL LG9044

GER ZA9002   GER ZA9003

1991

UK LG8985

USA AL9105

ALVIN AND THE CHIPMUNKS HAPPY MEAL, 1992/1991
- ❏ ❏ MEX AL9110 HM BOX, 1990, ALVIN/SPANISH GRAPHICS $3-4

IDENTICAL TOYS: MEX/SIN/PUE AL9101/02/03/04
- ❏ ❏ *** AL9101 **ALVIN**, 1990, 2P/RED ALVIN W BLU GUITAR $8-10
- ❏ ❏ *** AL9102 **BRITTNEY**, 1990, 2P/PNK BRIT W GRN JUKEBOX $8-10
- ❏ ❏ *** AL9103 **SIMON**, 1990, 2P/YEL SIMON W PNK MOVIE CAMERA $8-10
- ❏ ❏ *** AL9104 **THEODORE**, 1990, 2P/TURQ/YEL THEO W RAP MACHINE $8-10

COMMENTS: REGIONAL DISTRIBUTION: MEXICO: MAY 1991; SINGAPORE: MARCH 1992; PUERTO RICO: MAY 1991. PREMIUM MARKINGS "KH CHINA 1990 M-B SALES" OR "1990 BAGDASARIAN PROD CHINA" OR "DY CHINA." See USA ALVIN AND THE CHIPMUNKS HAPPY MEAL, 1991.

USA AL9101   USA AL9102   USA AL9103   USA AL9104

USA BE8901   USA BE8902   USA BE8903   USA BE8904

USA BE8965

GERMANY

BEDTIME HAPPY MEAL, 1990/1989

   *** **IDENTICAL PREMIUMS: HON/MAL/SIN/ZEA BE9101/02/03/04**

❑ ❑ *** **BE9101 SET 1 TOOTHBRUSH,** 1988, YEL/RON W .85 OZ. CREST SPARKLE PASTE $6-8

❑ ❑ *** **BE9102 SET 2 DRINKING CUP,** 1988, RONALD W FRIENDS/1P/12OZ $3-5

❑ ❑ *** **BE9103 SET 3 FOAM WASH MIT,** 1988, RONALD SCRUBBING/1P/12OZ $3-5

❑ ❑ *** **BE9104 SET 4 NITE STAND RN,** 1988, GLOW IN THE DARK STAR/1P $3-5

COMMENTS: NATIONAL DISTRIBUTION: HONG KONG/MALAYSIA - OCTOBER 1989; SINGAPORE - FEBRUARY 1990; NEW ZEALAND - NOVEMBER 1991. See USA BEDTIME HAPPY MEAL, 1991.

BERNARD & BIANCA/RESCUERS DOWN UNDER/DE REDDERTJES IN KANGOEROELAND HAPPY MEAL, 1992/1991

❑ ❑ GER RE9110 HM BOX, 1991, EAGLE/BERNARD/MISS BIANCA $3-4

❑ ❑ GER RE9111 HM BOX, 1991, FIREFLIES/TO LIGHT THE NIGHT $3-4

❑ ❑ GER RE9112 HM BOX, 1991, LIZARD/FRANK THE FRILL-NECKED $3-4

❑ ❑ GER RE9113 HM BOX, 1991, ROPE/MCLEACH THE VILLAIN/TOP SECRET $3-4

❑ ❑ FRA RE9110 HM BOX, 1991, MCLEACH/JOANNA $3-4

   *** **IDENTICAL TOYS: GER/HOL/UK RE9101/02/03/04**

❑ ❑ *** **RE9101 BERNARD,** 1991, RED SHIRT/GRY CAP MOUSE $4-7

❑ ❑ *** **RE9102 BIANCA,** 1991, PURP CAP/SCARF MOUSE $4-7

❑ ❑ *** **RE9103 FRANK,** 1991, GRN LIZARD $4-7

❑ ❑ *** **RE9104 WILBUR,** 1991, BLK CAP/SCARF DUCK $4-7

❑ ❑ HOL RE9144 POSTER/SM, 1991 $5-8

FRA RE9110

GER   RE9103   *** RE9104   *** RE9102

GER RE9112

*** RE9101

UK RE9101   UK RE9103   UK RE9102   UK RE9104

COMMENTS: REGIONAL DISTRIBUTION: GERMANY/UK: DECEMBER 1991; BELGIUM, DENMARK, FINLAND, FRANCE, GREECE, ITALY, HOLLAND, NORWAY, PORTUGAL, SPAIN, SWEDEN, SWITZERLAND: NOVEMBER 28-JANUARY 8, 1992; NETHERLANDS - DECEMBER 2-JANUARY 12, 1993. THIS IS A SET OF HARD FIGURINES; SOMETIMES CALLED, "RESCUERS BENDABLES" TO DIFFERENCIATE THEM FROM ANOTHER SET OF CLOTH DOLLS CALLED BERNHARD & BICANCA IM KANGRUHLAND, 1991.

BERNARD & BIANCA IM KANGURUHLAND PROMOTION, 1991

❏ ❏ GER RE9105 **BERNARD,** 1991, CLOTH/RED SHIRT/GRY CAP
MOUSE $4-7
❏ ❏ GER RE9106 **BIANCA,** 1991, CLOTH/PURP CAP/PURP
SCARF MOUSE $4-7
❏ ❏ GER RE9107 **JAKE,** 1991, CLOTH/SAFARI STYLE HAT W BLK
BELT $4-7
❏ ❏ GER RE9108 **WILBUR,** 1991, CLOTH/BLK CAP/BLU SCARF/
DUCK $4-7
❏ ❏ GER RE9165 TRANSLITE/BERNARD & BIANCA/LG, 1991
                                                        $20-30

COMMENTS: NATIONAL DISTRIBUTION: GERMANY - DECEMBER 1991 AS A SELF LIQUIDATOR. CLOTH DOLLS WERE ADVERTISED IN CONJUNCTION WITH THE MOVIE "RESCUERS DOWN UNDER".

HOL RE9144

1991

GERMANY

GER RE9165

GERMANY

GER RE9101

GER RE9106   GER RE9105

GER RE9108   GER RE9107

105

UK BI9301

ZEA BI9103

*** BI9105

BIG MAC & COMPANY/FUN AT SCHOOL/SCHOOL KIT HAPPY MEAL, 1994/1992/1991

☐ ☐ UK BI9301 **MCFUN BOX**, 1993, $10-15
☐ ☐ JPN BI9101 **SCHOOL KIT/BOX**, ND, METAL W SUPPLIES
                                                                        $7-10
☐ ☐ ZEA BI9101 **BIG MAC SANDWICH NOTEPAD**, 1991, PAPER
                                                                        $5-8
☐ ☐ ZEA BI9102 **ICE CREAM SUNDAE ERASER**, 1991, STRAW-
         BERRY SUNDAE/2P $7-10
☐ ☐ ZEA BI9103 **FF BOX/PAPER CLIP FRIES**, 1991, IN RED
         CONTAINER $7-10
☐ ☐ ZEA BI9104 **PICTURE FRAME**, 1991, RED $5-8
☐ ☐ *** BI9105 **MAGNET**, ND, BIG MAC & CO. $1-1.50

COMMENTS: REGIONAL DISTRIBUTION: UK: 1993/1994; NEW
     ZEALAND: JULY 1991 AND AGAIN IN JULY 1992; URUGUAY:
     1994. CALLED "BIG MAC & COMPANY HM" IN NEW
     ZEALAND; "FUN AT SCHOOL HM" IN URUGUAY. JAPAN
     TESTED SCHOOL SUPPLIES GIVE-AWAYS IN AUGUST 1991;
     SINGAPORE TESTED SCHOOL SUPPLIES IN JANUARY
     1992. JAPAN GAVE OUT THE JPN BI9102 ERASER AS A
     GENERIC PREMIUM IN 1993.

CANADA/MEXICO GENERIC PROMOTION, 1991

☐ ☐ CAN GE9130 **HM BAG**, 1991, FUN BAG/BRN W RED/YEL/
         PUR/KIDS COMBO MEAL $1-1.25
☐ ☐ MEX GE9110 **HM BOX**, 1991, RONALD McSHOW $3-4

COMMENTS: REGIONAL DISTRIBUTION: CANADA/MEXICO - 1991/
     1992 DURING CLEAN-UP WEEKS.

CARNIVAL/McCARNIVAL HAPPY MEAL, 1991

   *** **IDENTICAL TOYS:** JPN/ZEA CA9100/01/02/03
☐ ☐ *** CA9000 **BIRDIE**, 1990, ON SWING/ORG SWING/5P $4-6
☐ ☐ *** CA9001 **GRIMACE**, 1990, IN TURN-AROUND/BLU/GRN/5P
                                                                        $4-6
☐ ☐ *** CA9002 **HAMBURGLAR**, 1990, ON FERRIS WHEEL/PURP
         ARCH/5P $4-6
☐ ☐ *** CA9003 **RONALD**, 1990, ON CAROUSEL/GRN TEETER
         TOTTER/4P $4-6

☐ ☐ JPN CA9120 **COUNTER CARD**, 1990 $15-20

CAN GE9130

MEX GE9110

JPN CA9120

USA CA9000   USA CA9001   USA CA9002   USA CA9003

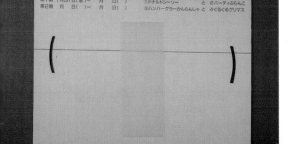

USA CA9065

COMMENTS: REGIONAL TEST DISTRIBUTION: JAPAN: TESTED IN MARCH 1991 AND RAN IN JANUARY 1992; NATIONAL DISTRIBUTION: MEXICO: FEBRUARY 1992; COSTA RICA APRIL 1991; PANAMA MARCH 1991; NEW ZEALAND - SEPTEMBER 1991. CALLED, "McCARNIVAL" IN MALAYSIA. PREMIUMS ARE THE SAME AS USA CA9000-03. USA GAVE OUT AN U-3 TOY, USA CA9004 (See USA McDONALDLAND CARNIVAL HAPPY MEAL, 1990/1991).

CIRCUS PARADE HAPPY MEAL, 1991
- ❑ ❑ UK CI9111 HM BOX, 1991, BIRDIE $3-4
- ❑ ❑ UK CI9112 HM BOX, 1991, FRY GUY IN ANIMAL CAGE $3-4
- ❑ ❑ UK CI9113 HM BOX, 1991, HAMBURGLAR ON HORSEBACK $3-4
- ❑ ❑ UK CI9114 HM BOX, 1991, RINGMASTER $3-4

    *** IDENTICAL TOYS: HOL/FRA/UK/USA CI9101/02/03/04
- ❑ ❑ *** CI9101 **RONALD RINGMASTER,** 1989, IN BLU CAR $2-3
- ❑ ❑ *** CI9102 **BIRDIE BAREBACK,** 1989, BAREBACK RIDER $2-3
- ❑ ❑ *** CI9103 **FRY GUY TRAINER,** 1989, ELEPHANT TRAINER $2-3
- ❑ ❑ *** CI9104 **GRIMACE DANCING,** 1989, W CALLIOPE $2-3

- ❑ ❑ HOL CI9144, POSTER, 1991 $5-8
- ❑ ❑ UK CI9164 TRANSLITE/SM, 1989 $4-7
- ❑ ❑ UK CI9165 TRANSLITE/LG, 1989 $8-12
- ❑ ❑ UK CI9166 EXTENSION PACK, 1989 $4-7

COMMENTS: NATIONAL DISTRIBUTION: UK: DECEMBER 1991; HOLLAND: FEBRUARY 11-MARCH 24, 1991; FRANCE: APRIL 1991; BELGIUM, DENMARK, FINLAND, ITALY, HOLLAND, NORWAY, SPAIN, SWEDEN, SWITZERLAND: MARCH 1991; SINGAPORE: NOVEMBER 1993; PUERTO RICO: AUGUST 1991. MINT PACKAGING IS DIFFERENT FOR EACH COUNTRY; PREMIUMS ARE IDENTICAL TO USA CIRCUS PARADE HM, 1991 - USA CI9101-04.

CONNECT-A-CARS/SUPER MACS HAPPY MEAL, 1994/1991
- ❑ ❑ GUA CO9110 HM BAG, 1991, RON/PREMIUMS $2-3

    *** IDENTICAL TOYS: GER/JPN/UK CO9101/02/03/04
- ❑ ❑ *** CO9101 **BIRDIE,** 1991, SPORTS COUPE/WAVING IN PINK CAR/2P $4-7
- ❑ ❑ *** CO9102 **GRIMACE,** 1991, SPEEDSTER/WAVING IN WHT CAR/2P $4-7
- ❑ ❑ *** CO9103 **HAMBURG,** 1991, CABRIOLET/WAVING IN YEL CAR/2P $4-7
- ❑ ❑ *** CO9104 **RONALD,** 1991, ROADSTER/WAVING IN RED CAR/2P $4-7

COMMENTS: NATIONAL DISTRIBUTION: UK: OCTOBER/NOVEMBER 1991; IRELAND/SCOTLAND/WALES: OCTOBER 1991. GERMANY: 1991; JAPAN TESTED IN JUNE 1993 AND RAN IN APRIL 1994; HONG KONG: NOVEMBER 1994; PANAMA, GUATEMALA, CHILE, MEXICO, VENEZUELA: FEBRUARY 1993 AND REGIONAL DISTRIBUTION: MAY 1994; NEW ZEALAND: NOVEMBER 1993; TAIWAN: SEPTEMBER 1992; PUERTO RICO, ARGENTINA: MARCH 1993. COST 49p WITH ANY FOOD PURCHASE IN THE UK.

HOL CI9144

UK CI9104   UK CI9101   UK CI9103   UK CI9102

USA CI9165

UK CO9101   UK CO9102   UK CO9103   UK CO9104

USA CI9102   USA CI9103   USA CI9104   USA CI9101

JPN CO94

UK CO9101   UK CO9102   UK CO9103   UK CO9104

HOLLAND

JPN CO9101   JPN CO9102   JPN CO9103   JPN CO9104

USA CR9101   USA CR9102   USA CR9103   USA CR9104

CRAZY VEHICLES HAPPY MEAL, 1992/1991

❑ ❑ ZEA CR9101 **BIRDIE IN AIRPLANE,** 1990, PNK/YEL/PURP
AIRPLANE/3P $2.50-3.50
❑ ❑ ZEA CR9102 **GRIMACE IN CAR,** 1990, GRN/YEL/ORG CAR/
3P $2.50-3.50
❑ ❑ ZEA CR9103 **HAMBURGLAR IN TRAIN,** 1990, YEL/BLU/PUR
TRAIN/3P $2.50-3.50
❑ ❑ ZEA CR9104 **RONALD IN BUGGY CAR,** 1990, RED/YEL/BLU
BUGGY CAR/3P $2.50-3.50

COMMENTS: REGIONAL DISTRIBUTION: NEW ZEALAND:
FEBRUARY 1992; JAPAN: MARCH 1993; PUERTO RICO: MAY
1993; PANAMA: NOVEMBER 1991; VENEZUELA: AUGUST
1991.

FENSTERWIPPER/WINDOW WAVERS JUNIOR TUTE, 1991

❑ ❑ GER WI9101 **WAVER - BIRDIE,** 1991, SYRO/SUCTION CUP/
EXTENDER/STICKER SHEET/3P $3-5
❑ ❑ GER WI9102 **WAVER - FRY GIRL,** 1991, SYRO/SUCTION
CUP/EXTENDER/STICKER SHEET/3P $3-5
❑ ❑ GER WI9103 **WAVER - GRIMACE,** 1991, SYRO/SUCTION
CUP/EXTENDER/STICKER SHEET/3P $3-5
❑ ❑ GER WI9104 **WAVER - HAMBURLGAR,** 1991, SYRO/
SUCTION CUP/EXTENDER/STICKER SHEET/3P $3-5
❑ ❑ GER WI9105 **WAVER - RONALD,** 1991, SYRO/SUCTION CUP/
EXTENDER/STICKER SHEET/3P $3-5

COMMENTS: NATIONAL DISTRIBUTION: GERMANY - OCTOBER-
NOVEMBER 1991.

FRANCE/GENERIC HAPPY MEAL, 1991

❑ ❑ FRA GE9101 **BASKETBALL HOOP/BALL/RON,** 1991, RED
RON/NET W YEL BALL/STRING $4-6
❑ ❑ FRA GE9102 **STRING PIPE/RONALD,** 1991, YEL BLOW
STRING/RED RONALD $4-6

GER WI9105

GER WI9104

GER WI9102

GER WI9101

GER WI9103

USA

FRA GE9101   FRA GE9102

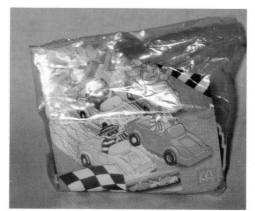

JAPAN

COMMENTS: REGIONAL DISTRIBUTION: FRANCE/HOLLAND - 1991 DURING CLEAN-UP WEEKS. FRA GE9101-02 ARE MARKED "SMI GMBH D-6072 DREIEICH 1" BUT DISTRIBUTED IN PARIS, FRANCE. FRA GE9102 IS SIMILAR TO USA STRING PIPE PROMOTION.

FRY BENDERS HAPPY MEAL, 1992/1991

*** IDENTICAL TOY: COS/MAL/PAN/SIN FB9001/02/03/04
- ❏ ❏ *** FB9001 **FREE STYLE**, 1989, ON ROLLER SKATES/2P $3-4
- ❏ ❏ *** FB9002 **FROGGY**, 1989, W RED SCUBA DIVER TANKS/2P $3-4
- ❏ ❏ *** FB9003 **GRAND SLAM**, 1989, W BASEBALL GLOVE/2P $3-4
- ❏ ❏ *** FB9004 **ROADIE**, 1989, THE BICYCLER/2P $3-4

COMMENTS: REGIONAL DISTRIBUTION: JAPAN: OCTOBER 1991; SINGAPORE: MAY 1992; COSTA RICA: JANUARY 1993; PANAMA: JANUARY 1991; MALAYSIA: OCTOBER-NOVEMBER 1991. See USA FRY BENDERS HAPPY MEAL, 1990 FOR ADDITIONAL U-3 TOY.

GARFIELD DOLLS PROMOTION, 1991

***IDENTICAL DOLLS CAN/MEX DO9101/03/04
- ❏ ❏ *** DO9101 **GARFIELD - SANTA,** 1991, SANTA COSTUME/W BEARD $10-12
- ❏ ❏ *** DO9103 **GARFIELD - ANGEL,** 1991, ANGEL COSTUME/WHT WINGS $10-12
- ❏ ❏ *** DO9104 **ODIE,** 1991, W GRN/RED SCARF $10-12

- ❏ ❏ MEX DO9102 **GARFIELD - ELF,** 1991, ELF COSTUME/RED/GRN HAT $10-12

- ❏ ❏ CAN DO9145 REGISTER TOPPER, 1991, GARFIELD! $2-4
- ❏ ❏ CAN DO9155 TRAYLINER, 1991, PLUSH TOY $1-1.25
- ❏ ❏ MEX DO9155 TRAYLINER, 1991, PLUSH TOY $1-1.25
- ❏ ❏ CAN DO9165 TRANSLITE/LG, 1991 $15-25

COMMENTS: REGIONAL DISTRIBUTION: CANADA - 1991; MEXICO: NOVEMBER/DECEMBER 1991. DOLLS SOLD FOR $2.69 EACH, COLLECT ALL THREE.

GERMANY/EUROPE GENERIC HAPPY MEAL, 1991
- ❏ ❏ DEN GE9110 HM BOX, 1991, MYSTISKE POLSE $3-4

USA FB9001   USA FB9003   USA FB9002   USA FB9004

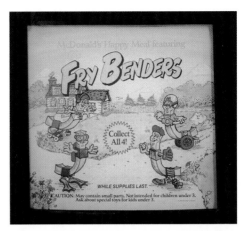

USA FB9065

MEX DO9101   MEX DO9104   MEX DO9102   MEX DO9103

CAN DO9165

Desde Nov. 24 Garfield y Odie en McDonald's. ¡Abrázalos!

MEX DO9155

DEN GE9110

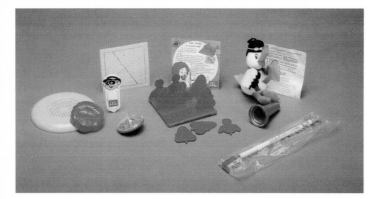

GER GE9104   GER GE9101   GER GE9103   GER GE9107

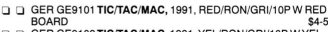

☐ ☐ GER GE9101 **TIC/TAC/MAC**, 1991, RED/RON/GRI/10P W RED BOARD $4-5
☐ ☐ GER GE9102 **TIC/TAC/MAC**, 1991, YEL/RON/GRI/10P W YEL BOARD $4-5
☐ ☐ GER GE9103 **STRAW/BALL/CUP**, 1991, RED CUP/STYRO BALL/STRAW $4-6
☐ ☐ GER GE9104 **SIEVE/MOLD**, 1991, YEL STRAINER/RED RON MOLD/2P $3-5
☐ ☐ GER GE9105 **PAPER CLIP**, 1991, HAMB/WHT $1-2
☐ ☐ GER GE9106 **SPIN TOP**, 1991, RED W ARCHES LOGO $2-3
☐ ☐ GER GE9107 **RULER/PENCIL/SHARPENER**, 1991, CLEAR RULER/RED SHARPENER/RON MCD PENCIL $3-5
☐ ☐ HOL GE9101 **MASK/UNDERSEA**, ND, PASTIC/SNORKEL MASK $1-1.50

COMMENTS: REGIONAL DISTRIBUTION: GERMANY/EUROPE - 1991 DURING CLEAN-UP WEEKS. GER GE9101/02 ARE SIMILAR TO USA TIC TAC MAC GAME.

GOOD MORNING HAPPY MEAL, 1991

*** IDENTICAL PREMIUMS: BEL/DEN/FIN/FRA/ITA/NOR/SWE/SWI/PUE/COS G09150/52
☐ ☐ *** GO9150 **TOOTHBRUSH-RONALD,** 1989, RONALD GETTING OUT OF BED $1-1.50
☐ ☐ *** GO9152 **CUP-RONALD W BUNNY,** 1990, RISING SUN BIRDS/4 OZ. JUICY JUICE $1-1.50

*** IDENTICAL TOYS: PUE/COS GO9151/53
☐ ☐ *** GO9151 **CLOCK-RONALD FLYING,** 1989, CLOCK HANDS PROPELLERS $1-1.50
☐ ☐ *** GO9153 **COMB,** 1990, 5 SECTION FRY KIDS COMB $1-1.50

COMMENTS: REGIONAL DISTRIBUTION: BELGIUM, DENMARK, FINLAND, FRANCE, ITALY, NORWAY, SWEDEN, SWITZER-LAND: JANUARY 1991; PUERTO RICO: JANUARY 1991; COSTA RICA: JULY 1991. See USA GOOD MORNING HAPPY MEAL, 1991.

USA

GER GE9103

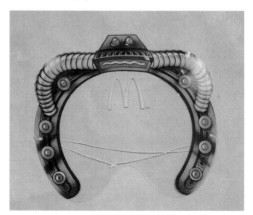

HOL GE9101

GER GE9103

USA GO9164

USA   GO9150   USA GO9151   USA GO9152   USA GO9153

MEX HO9165

HOOK HAPPY MEAL, 1991

❏ ❏ MEX HO9100 **PETER PAN**, 1991, 3P ON PURP RAFT W
   WHEELS (FLOATS) $1.50-2
❏ ❏ MEX HO9101 **MERMAID**, 1991, 1P BLU MERMAID WIND UP
   SWIMS IN WATER $1.50-2
❏ ❏ MEX HO9102 **HOOK**, 1991, 3P CAPT HOOK IN BLU PIRATE
   SHIP $1.50-2
❏ ❏ MEX HO9103 **RUFIO**, 1991, 1P BOY FLOATING ON GRN/
   PURP RUBBER BARRELS-SQUIRTS $1.50-2
❏ ❏ MEX HO9165 TRANSLITE/LG, 1991 $15-25

COMMENTS: REGIONAL DISTRIBUTION: MEXICO: DECEMBER
1991.

HUPH-FROSCH/JUMPING FROGS PROMOTION, 1991

❏ ❏ GER HU9101 **FROG - RED**, 1991, PLASTIC/PRESS BODY/
   JUMPS $1-2
❏ ❏ GER HU9102 **FROG - YEL**, 1991, PLASTIC/PRESS BODY/
   JUMPS $1-2
❏ ❏ GER HU9103 **FROG - BLU**, 1991, PLASTIC/PRESS BODY/
   JUMPS $1-2
❏ ❏ GER HU9104 **FROG - GRN**, 1991, PLASTIC/PRESS BODY/
   JUMPS $1-2

COMMENTS: REGIONAL DISTRIBUTION: GERMANY - 1991.

USA HO9165

USA HO9100   USA HO9101   USA HO9102   USA HO9103

GERMANY

USA HO9126

111

FRA IL9112

UK IL91113   UK IL91112   UK IL91111

HOL IL9101   HOL IL9102   HOL IL9104

I LIKE BIKES/McCYCLE/FIETSPRET II/ FAHRRADZUBEHOR JUNIOR TUTE/HAPPY MEAL, 1994/ 1993/1992/1991

*** IDENTICAL BOXES: GER/UK IL9110/11/12/13

☐ ☐ *** IL9110 HM BOX, 1991, BIRDIE SPINNER $3-4
☐ ☐ *** IL9111 HM BOX, 1991, GRIMACE W REAR VIEW REFLECTOR $3-4
☐ ☐ *** IL9112 HM BOX, 1991, HAMBURGLAR W FRY GUY HORN $3-4
☐ ☐ *** IL9113 HM BOX, 1991, RONALD W BIKE/WATER BOTTLE $3-4
☐ ☐ HOL IL9230 HM BAG, 1991, I LIKE BIKES $3-5

***IDENTICAL TOYS: GER/HOL/UK/USA IL9100/01/02

☐ ☐ *** IL9100 **SPINNER,** 1989, YEL/RED BIRDIE'S SPINNER AIRPLANE W BIRDIE ON TOP/1P/CLAMP/SCREWS $3-5
☐ ☐ *** IL9101 **HORN,** 1989, ORG/BLU FRY GUY'S HORN/F GUY ON FRONT/1P/CLAMP/SCREWS $3-5
☐ ☐ *** IL9102 **MIRROR,** 1990, PURP GRIMACE REARVIEW MIRROR/1P/CLAMP/SCREWS $3-5

☐ ☐ HOL IL9204 **WATER BOTTLE,** 1991, YEL W RONALD'S PIC W BLU BIKE HOLDER/2P/CLAMP/SCREWS $3-5
☐ ☐ JPN IL9105 **HORN,** 1991, BIRDIE W AIR PUMP/TOP W CLAMPS $5-7

☐ ☐ UK IL9141 CEILING DANGLER, 1991 $12-15
☐ ☐ HOL IL9244 POSTER/SM, 1992 $5-8
☐ ☐ UK IL9145 REGISTER TOPPER, 1991 $4-7
☐ ☐ UK IL9164 TRANSLITE/SM, 1991 $8-10
☐ ☐ UK IL9165 TRANSLITE/LG, 1991 $12-15
☐ ☐ GER IL9265 TRANSLITE/LG, 1992 $25-40

COMMENTS: NATIONAL DISTRIBUTION: UK: JUNE 1991; BELGIUM, DENMARK, FINLAND, FRANCE, GREECE, HOLLAND, NORWAY, PORTUGAL, SPAIN, SWEDEN, SWITZERLAND: MAY 28-JULY 8, 1992; SCOTLAND/WALES: JUNE/JULY 1992; GERMANY: (REGIONALLY) MARCH 25-APRIL 14, 1991 AND AGAIN APRIL 1-25, 1993; CHILE: OCTOBER 1994; ARGENTINA: SEPTEMBER 1994; PUERTO RICO: JULY 1991. HOL/ UK PREMIUMS ARE THE SAME AS USA IL9000-02. USA DISTRIBUTED A BIKE BASKET. GERMANY/HOLLAND DISTRIBUTED A WATER BOTTLE IN PLACE OF BIKE BASKET. UK PACKAGING IS DATED 1991. GERMAN PACKAGING IS DATED 1992; CALLED "FAHRRADZUBEHOR" IN GERMANY. See USA I LIKE BIKES HAPPY MEAL, 1990.

GER IL9265

GER IL9101   GER IL9102   GER IL9100

HOL IL9244

JO-JO BALL JUNIOR TUTE, 1991

- ❑ ❑ GER JO9101 **GRIMACE BALLOON/TETHER BALL,** 1991, PURP W ELASTIC $4-6
- ❑ ❑ GER JO9102 **RONALD BALLOON/TETHER BALL,** 1991, YEL W ELASTIC $4-6
- ❑ ❑ GER JO9103 **BIRDIE BALLOON/TETHER BALL,** 1991, PNK W ELASTIC $4-6
- ❑ ❑ GER JO9104 **HAMBUR BALLOON/TETHER BALL,** 1991, RED W ELASTIC $4-6
- ❑ ❑ GER JO9165 TRANSLITE/LG, 1991 $25-40

COMMENTS: NATIONAL DISTRIBUTION: GERMANY: JUNE 13-JULY 7, 1991. INFLATED RUBBER BALLOONS ARE 12-15" ROUND WITH CHARACTERS IMPRINTED.

GER JO9165

KIDS ARE SPECIAL PROMOTION, 1991

- ❑ ❑ SIN SU9101 **SUNGLASSES - BIRDIE,** 1991, WHT/PNK SUNGLASSES $4-5
- ❑ ❑ SIN SU9104 **SUNGLASSES - RONALD,** 1991, YEL/RED SUNGLASSES $4-5
- ❑ ❑ SIN KI9103 **MUG,** 1991 $1-1.25
- ❑ ❑ SIN ON8801 **BLU LUNCH BOX,** 1988, GRIM/RM RAISED SCENE W BULLETIN BOARD $2-3
- ❑ ❑ SIN KI9105 **CUPS/MITT,** 1991 $2-3
- ❑ ❑ SIN RO8900 **HOTCAKES,** 1988, ROBOCAKES/HOTCAKES/ SAUSAGE $2-4
- ❑ ❑ *** BT9072 **BEACH BALL/GRIM BOUNCIN,** 1988, YEL/ INFLATABLE $1-2
- ❑ ❑ SIN KI9108 **FLOATEE,** 1991, GRIMACE $2-3
- ❑ ❑ SIN CM9000 **SET 1 GRIMACE CANTEEN,** 1989, 2P BLU W YEL TOP $1-1.50
- ❑ ❑ SIN CM9001 **SET 2 BIRDIE/MESS KIT,** 1989, 3P GRN W ORG HANDLE $1-1.50
- ❑ ❑ SIN CM9002 **SET 3 FRY KID UTENSILS,** 1989, 3P TURQ FK/ YEL SP/PURP KN W OR W/O 5 BANDAIDS $1-1.50
- ❑ ❑ SIN KI9112 **SPORT BOTTLE/STRAW,** 1991 $1-1.25

COMMENTS: REGIONAL DISTRIBUTION: SINGAPORE: 1991. See USA CAMP McDONALDLAND HAPPY MEAL, 1990; SUMMER TOYS HM, 1990, USA NEW FOOD CHANGEABLES, 1989; USA ON THE GO HM, 1988; USA SUNGLASSES PROMOTION, 1991. THESE TOYS ARE A COMBINATIONS OF PREVIOUSLY ISSUED HAPPY MEAL PROMOTIONAL ITEMS.

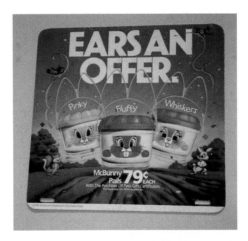

CAN LU9101   CAN LU9102   CAN LU9103

LUNCH BAG PROMOTION, 1991

- ❑ ❑ CAN LU9101 **GIRAFFE,** 1991, GIRAFFE PNK W/BLK CLOTH 9"X6" $5-7
- ❑ ❑ CAN LU9102 **RONALD,** 1991, RON ON BLK/PURP CLOTH 9"X6" $5-7
- ❑ ❑ CAN LU9103 **ROBIN HOOD,** 1991, ROBIN HOOD GRN/BLK CLOTH 9"X6" $5-7

COMMENTS: REGIONAL DISTRIBUTION: CANADA - 1991.

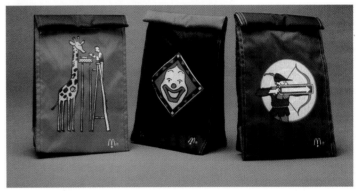

CAN BP9142

MCBUNNY/EARSAN PAILS HAPPY MEAL, 1991

- *** IDENTICAL BUCKETS: CAN/PAN BP9101/02/03
- ❑ ❑ *** BP9101 **FLUFFY,** 1988, PAIL/WHT-BLU W BLU LID/YEL HANDLE $5-8
- ❑ ❑ *** BP9102 **PINKY,** 1988, PAIL/WHT-YEL W YEL LID/YEL HANDLE $5-8
- ❑ ❑ *** BP9103 **WHISKERS,** 1988, PAIL/WHT-GRN GRN LID/YEL HANDLE $5-8

- ❑ ❑ CAN BP9142 COUNTER CARD, 1991 $4-5

USA

CAN. BP9101   CAN BP9102   CAN BP9103

113

GER   MC9202

MCDINOSAURS/MCDINO TRANSFORMABLES/ DINOSAURIER JUNIOR TUTE/HAPPY MEAL, 1992/1991

❑ ❑ UK MC9216 HM BOX, 1992, MCDINOSAURS/JUNGLE $3-4
❑ ❑ UK MC9217 HM BOX, 1992, MCDINOSAURS/EGG NEST/ PURPLE EGGS $3-4
❑ ❑ UK MC9218 HM BOX, 1992, MCDINOSAURUS/SURF BOARD $3-4
❑ ❑ UK MC9219 HM BOX, 1992, MCDINOSAURUS/VOLCANO $3-4
❑ ❑ JPN MC9210 HM BOX, 1992, RON/CHARS WARCHES $3-4

*** IDENTICAL TOYS: JP/MEX/UK MC9200
❑ ❑ ***** MC9200 HAPPY MEAL-O-DON,** 1990, RED HM BOX/RED DINO $2.50-3.50

*** IDENTICAL TOYS: GER/JP/UK/ZEA MC9202
❑ ❑ ***** MC9202 MCNUGGETS-O-SAURUS,** 1991, **YEL BOX W BRN MCD LOGO** $2.50-3.50

❑ ❑ JPN MC9203 **HOT CAKES-O-DACTYL,** 1990, WHT HOT CAKES CONT/PUR DINO $2.50-3.50

*** IDENTICAL TOYS: JP/ZEA MC9201/04
❑ ❑ JPN MC9201 **QUARTER P CHEESE-O-SAUR,** 1990, QP/ TURQ DINO $2.50-3.50
❑ ❑ JPN MC9204 **BIG MAC-O-SAURUS REX,** 1990, BIG MAC/ ORG DINO $2.50-3.50

*** IDENTICAL TOYS: GER/JP/MEX/UK MC9205
❑ ❑ ***** MC9205 FRENCH FRIES,** 1991, RED/YEL BRONTOSAU-RUS $2.50-3.50

*** IDENTICAL TOY: JP/MEX MC9206
❑ ❑ ***** MC9206 MCDINO CONE,** 1990, ICE CREAM CONE/BLU DINO $2.50-3.50

*** IDENTICAL TOY: GER/JP/MEX/UK MC9207
❑ ❑ ***** MC9207 SHAKE,** 1990, PNK MCDINO $2.50-3.50

❑ ❑ JPN MC9244 CREW POSTER, 1992 $8-12
❑ ❑ GER MC9265 TRANSLITE/LG, 1990 $25-40
❑ ❑ UK MC9164 TRANSLITE/SM, 1990 $4-7
❑ ❑ UK MC9165 TRANSLITE/LG, 1990 $8-12

GERMANY   GER MC9207   GER MC9205

MEX MC9200   MEX MC9205   MEX MC9206   MEX MC9207

UK MC9207   UK MC9205   UK MC9202   UK MC9200

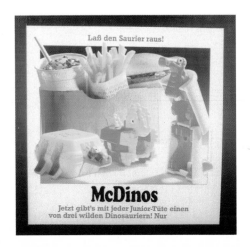

Laß den Saurier raus!

McDinos
Jetzt gibt's mit jeder Junior-Tüte einen
von drei wilden Dinosauriern! Nur

GER MC9265

USA MC9200-07

McDONALDLAND CONNECTIBLES HAPPY MEAL, 1991

- ❑ ❑ ZEA CO9200 **BIRDIE,** 1990, 2P ON A BLU/PNK/YEL TRI-CYCLE $5-7
- ❑ ❑ ZEA CO9201 **GRIMACE,** 1990, 2P IN A RED WAGON $5-7
- ❑ ❑ ZEA CO9202 **HAMBURG,** 1990, 2P IN A GRN/YEL AIRPLANE $5-7
- ❑ ❑ ZEA CO9203 **RONALD,** 1990, 2P IN A YEL/RED SOAPBOX RACER $5-7

COMMENTS: NATIONAL DISTRIBUTION: NEW ZEALAND: OCTOBER-NOVEMBER 1992; SINGAPORE: AUGUST-SEPTEMBER 1991.

McDONALDLAND FIGUREN PROMOTION, 1991

- ❑ ❑ GER FI9101 **RONALD,** 1985, W ONE ARM DOWN/ONE ARM STRAIGHT OUT $7-10
- ❑ ❑ GER FI9102 **SHAKY,** 1985, W BOTH ARMS OUT $7-10
- ❑ ❑ GER FI9103 **MAYOR,** 1985, W ARMS TO SIDE/SASH $7-10
- ❑ ❑ GER FI9104 **HAMBUR,** 1985, W ARMS HOLDING ORG/BLK CAPE OPEN $7-10

COMMENTS: REGIONAL DISTRIBUTION: GERMANY - 1991. FIGURINES ARE DATED 1985.

McDONALDLAND FUNGLASSES/SUNGLASSES PROMOTION, 1991

- *** IDENTICAL SUNGLASSES: JPN/ZEA FG9101/02/03/04
- ❑ ❑ *** FG9101 **SUNGLASSES - BIRDIE,** 1991, WHT/PNK SUNGLASSES $4-5
- ❑ ❑ *** FG9102 **SUNGLASSES - GRIMACE,** 1991, PURP SUNGLASSES $4-5
- ❑ ❑ *** FG9103 **SUNGLASSES - HAMBURGLAR,** 1991, YEL SUNGLASSES $4-5
- ❑ ❑ *** FG9104 **SUNGLASSES - RONALD,** 1991, YEL/RED SUNGLASSES $4-5

COMMENTS: NATIONAL DISTRIBUTION: NEW ZEALAND: DECEMBER 1991; VENEZUELA: JANUARY 1991; JAPAN: SUMMER 1992. SUNGLASSES ARE THE SAME AS - USA SUNGLASSES/McDONALDLAND, 1989; USA SU8901/02/03/04.

ZEA CO9200   ZEA CO9201   ZEA CO9202   ZEA CO9203

GER FI9101

GERMANY

GER FI9102

GER FI9104

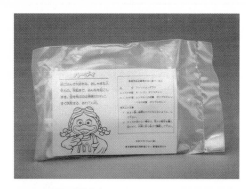

USA SU8901   USA SU8902   USA SU8903

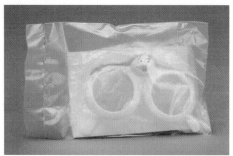

USA SU8964

JPN GL9201

HOL BI9144

McDONALDLAND ON WHEELS/DE FIETSJES EN JE JEBT/MCCHARACTERS ON BIKES/MCWHEELS/ HAPPY MEAL, 1991

❑ ❑ HOL BI9101 **BIRDIE**, 1990, ON PNK BIKE/BLU WHLS
$2.50-3.50

❑ ❑ HOL BI9102 **GRIMACE**, 1990, ON BLU BIKE/GRN WHLS
$2.50-3.50

❑ ❑ HOL BI9103 **HAMBURGLAR**, 1990, ON YEL BIKE/RED WHLS
$2.50-3.50

❑ ❑ HOL BI9104 **RONALD**, 1990, ON RED BIKE/YEL WHLS
$2.50-3.50

❑ ❑ HOL BI9144 POSTER/SM, 1991, DE FIETSJES IN JE JEBT
$5-8

COMMENTS: NATIONAL DISTRIBUTION: BELGIUM, DENMARK, FINLAND, FRANCE, ITALY, HOLLAND, NORWAY, SPAIN, SWEDEN, SWITZERLAND: APRIL 22-JUNE 16, 1992; MALAYSIA AS MCWHEELS: APRIL-MAY 1991. CALLED "McDONALDLAND ON WHEELS" IN HOLLAND; "MCWHEELS" IN MALAYSIA AND SOLD AS A SELF LIQUIDATOR.

HOL BI9103

HOL BI9102

HOL BI9101

HOL BI9104

USA CI9104　　USA CI9101　　USA CI9102　　USA CI9103

MCDRIVE THRU CREW/MCFARMLAND HAPPY MEAL, 1991

- ❑ ❑ PAN MD9000 **FRIES IN POTATO SPEEDSTER,** 1990, PULL BACK FRICTION CAR　$12-15
- ❑ ❑ PAN MD9001 **HAMBURGLAR IN KETCHUP RACER,** 1990, PULL BACK FRICTION CAR　$10-12
- ❑ ❑ PAN MD9002 **MCNUGGET IN EGG ROADSTER,** 1990, PULL BACK FRICTION CAR　$10-12
- ❑ ❑ PAN MD9003 **SHAKE IN MILK CARTON ZOOMER,** 1990, PULL BACK FRICTION CAR　$10-12

COMMENTS: REGIONAL DISTRIBUTION: PANAMA: FEBRUARY 1991; SINGAPORE: 1991. See USA MCDRIVE THRU CREW TEST MARKET HAPPY MEAL, 1990.

*** SA9101

PAN MD9001　　PAN MD9003　　PAN MD9002　　PAN MD9000

MCSAFARI HAPPY MEAL, 1991

- ❑ ❑ *** SA9101 **HAT-CROCODILE DUNDEE,** 1991, VACU-FORM/ BRN/SUEDE　$5-7
- ❑ ❑ USA CM9000 **SET 1 GRIMACE CANTEEN,** 1989, 2P BLU W YEL TOP　$1-1.50
- ❑ ❑ USA CM9001 **SET 2 BIRDIE CAMPER/MESS KIT,** 1989, 3P GRN W ORG HANDLE　$1-1.50
- ❑ ❑ USA CM9003 **SET 4 COLLAPSIBLE CUP/RONALD,** 1989, 2P RED CUP W LID　$1-1.50
- ❑ ❑ UK WA9101 **WAIST POUCH,** ND, HALF CIRCLE/BLU/RED/ PNK/YEL　$1.50-2.50
- ❑ ❑ GER SS9101 **SUNGLASSES/SHADES,** 1991, BLU/PNK/YEL DK SHADES　$3-4

COMMENTS: REGIONAL DISTRIBUTION: BELGIUM, DENMARK, FINLAND, FRANCE, ITALY, NORWAY, SPAIN, SWEDEN, SWITZERLAND: 1991. PREMIUMS ARE A COMBINATION OF PREMIUMS DISTRIBUTED IN VARIOUS COUNTRIES. *** SA9101 IS A CROCODILE DUNDEE HAT WORN BY USA EMPLOYEES DURING CROCODILE PROMOTION OF TAPES SOLD. See USA CAMP McDONALDLAND HM, 1990.

UK WA9101

USA CM9003　　USA CM9000　　USA CM9001

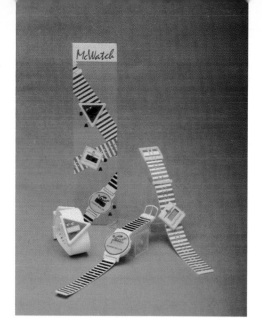

GER WA9101   GER WA9102   GER WA9103

MCWATCH PROMOTION, 1991
❑ ❑ GER WA9101 **WATCH - GRIMACE,** 1991, WHT BAND/
TRIANGLE GRIMACE WATCH $10-15
❑ ❑ GER WA9102 **WATCH - HAMB,** 1991, BLK/WHT BAND/
ROUND YEL/RED WATCH $10-15
❑ ❑ GER WA9103 **WATCH - RONALD,** 1991, RED/WHT BAND/
SQUARE YEL/WHT WATCH $10-15

COMMENTS: REGIONAL DISTRIBUTION: GERMANY 1991.

MIGHTY MINIS 4X4/STARKE MINIS JUNIOR TUTE/HAPPY MEAL, 1993/1991
❑ ❑ GER MI9310 HM BOX, 1993, DESERT SCENE/CANYON $2-3
❑ ❑ GER MI9311 HM BOX, 1993, PARKING GARAGE IN HIGH
RISE $2-3
❑ ❑ GER MI9312 HM BOX, 1993, NORTHERN LOGGING CAMP/
NORDIC $2-3
❑ ❑ GER MI9313 HM BOX, 1993, SNOW/WINTER SCENE/
FROZEN WATER FALL $2-3

   *** IDENTICAL TOYS: GER/MEX/UK MI9300/01/02/03
❑ ❑ GER MI9300 **DUNE BUSTER,** 1993, PNK VW/BEETLE W
CRANK $2-3
❑ ❑ GER MI9301 **LITTLE CLASSIC,** 1993, YEL 57 FORD
THUNDERBIRD W CRANK $2-3
❑ ❑ GER MI9302 **CARGO CLIMBER,** 1993, ORG/YEL VAN W
CRANK $2-3
❑ ❑ GER MI9303 **POCKET PICKUP,** 1993, RED/BLU PICK-UP
TRUCK W CRANK $2-3

❑ ❑ UK MI9326 DISPLAY/PREMIUMS, 1993 $25-40
❑ ❑ UK MI9364 TRANSLITE/SM, 1993 $4-6
❑ ❑ UK MI9365 TRANSLITE/LG, 1993 $7-10
❑ ❑ GER MI9365 TRANSLITE/LG, 1993 $25-40
❑ ❑ UK MI9366 M C CARD/MAGNETIC/SM, 1993 $4-7
❑ ❑ UK MI9367 M C CARD/MAGNETIC/LG, 1993 $8-12

COMMENTS: NATIONAL DISTRIBUTION: GERMANY: MAY 6-26,
1993; UK: FEBRUARY/MARCH 1993; REGIONAL DISTRIBU-
TION: MEXICO: NOVEMBER 1991; BELGIUM, DENMARK,
FINLAND, FRANCE, GREECE, ITALY, NORWAY, PORTUGAL,
SPAIN, SWEDEN, SWITZERLAND, HONG KONG: JANUARY
1993; JAPAN TESTED IN JULY 1991 AND RAN IN MARCH
1992. GER/UK MI9300-03 IDENTICAL TO USA MIGHTY MINI
HAPPY MEAL, 1991; USA MI9100-03 EXCEPT FOR UK
PACKAGING DATED 1993.

REAL GHOSTBUSTERS JUNIOR TUTE/HAPPY MEAL, 1993/1992/1991
❑ ❑ MEX RE9110 HM BOX, 1991, SPANISH GRAPHICS $3-4

   *** IDENTICAL TOYS: CAN/GER/MEX/SPA RE9250/54
❑ ❑ *** RE9250 **ECTO SIREN**/SIRENE ECTO 1, 1984, 1P BLU/
WHT/RED BIKE SIREN/WHT ECTO CAR W ECTO-1 STICK
SHEET $4-5
❑ ❑ *** RE9254 **P.K.E.WATER BOTTLE**/FLASCHE, 1984, 2P YEL
BOTTLE W BLU HOLDER W GB STICKER SHEET $4-5

GER MI9310   GER MI9311   GER MI9312

UK MI9303   UK MI9301   UK MI9302   UK MI9300

GER MI9301   GER MI9302   GER MI9303

GER MI9365

*** IDENTICAL TOYS: CAN/MEX/SPA RE9253/57

❑ ❑ *** RE9253 **EGON SPINNER**/TOURNIQUET EGON, 1984, 3P
GRN BIKE ATTACHMENT/**BLUE SPINNER/YEL MAN** $4-5
❑ ❑ *** RE9157 **SLIMER HORN**/KLAXON SLIMER, 1984, 1P GRN
SLIMER ATTACHED TO BLUE HORN ON BIKE $4-5

❑ ❑ GER RE9253 **EGON SPINNER**/GEIST-WINDRAD, 1984, 3P
GRN BIKE ATTACHMENT/**RED SPINNER/GRN SLIMER** $5-7

❑ ❑ CAN RE8901 **PLACEMAT 1 - GHB,** 1989, LAMINATED $4-5
❑ ❑ CAN RE8902 **PLACEMAT 2 - GHB,** 1989, LAMINATED $4-5
❑ ❑ CAN RE8903 **PLACEMAT 3 - GHB,** 1989, LAMINATED $4-5
❑ ❑ CAN RE8904 **PLACEMAT 4 - GHB,** 1989, LAMINATED $4-5

❑ ❑ CAN RE9160 BUTTON/ENGLISH, 1991 $3-4
❑ ❑ CAN RE9161 BUTTON/FRENCH, 1991 $3-4
❑ ❑ CAN RE9165 TRANSLITE/LG, 1991 $25-40
❑ ❑ GER RE9265 TRANSLITE/LG, 1992 $25-40

COMMENTS: REGIONAL DISTRIBUTION: CANADA: MAY 1991;
MEXICO/SPAIN: JUNE 1991. NATIONAL DISTRIBUTION:
GERMANY: APRIL 1993. CAN RE9050/53/54/57 = USA
RE9250/53/54/57, LOOSE OUT OF PACKAGE (See USA REAL
GHOSTBUSTERS II HAPPY MEAL, 1992).

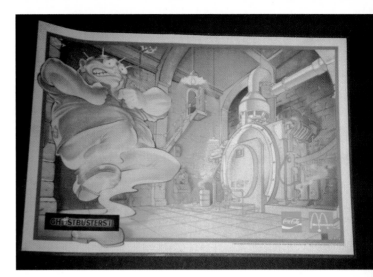

CAN RE8901

MEX RE9153   MEX RE9154   MEX RE9157

CAN RE9150   CAN RE9153   CAN RE9154   CAN RE9157

CAN RE8902

CAN RE8903

119

CAN RE9165

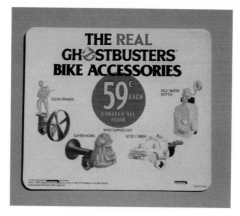

CANADA

GERMANY

CAN RE9161

CAN SO9301   CAN SO9302   CAN SO9303   CAN SO9304

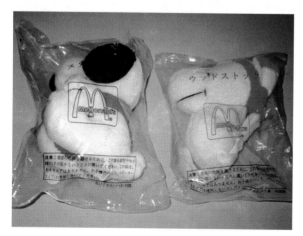

JPN SO9103   JPN SO9104

SCHOOL FUN KIT PROMOTION, 1991
- ❏ ❏ *** SC9101 **TAPE DISPENSER,** 1991, RONALD McDONALD/ FRIENDS $3-4
- ❏ ❏ *** SC9102 **PENCIL SHARPENER/HOLDER,** 1991, GRIMACE $3-4
- ❏ ❏ *** SC9103 **RULER/TEMPLATE,** 1991, RONALD McDONALD $2-3
- ❏ ❏ *** SC9104 **FRIES CLIP,** 1991, YEL $1-1.25
- ❏ ❏ *** SC9105 **PENCIL POUCH,** 1991, BIRDIE $2-3
- ❏ ❏ *** SC9106 **POST-IT NOTES/SHOE,** 1991, RONALD McDONALD $1-1.25

COMMENTS: REGIONAL DISTRIBUTION: EUROPE: 1991.

SNOOPY ET SES AMIS PROMOTION, 1994/1993/1992/ 1991

*** **IDENTICAL TOYS: CAN/JAPAN/ZEA SN9301/02/03/04**
- ❏ ❏ *** SO9101 **STUFFED DOLL - CHARLIE BROWN,** 1991, RED SANTA HAT/GRN SHIRT/10" $7-10
- ❏ ❏ *** SO9102 **STUFFED DOLL - LUCY,** 1991, WHT MUFF/RED DRESS/10" $7-10
- ❏ ❏ *** SO9103 **STUFFED DOLL - SNOOPY,** 1991, RED/GRN SCARF/5" $7-10
- ❏ ❏ *** SO9104 **STUFFED DOLL - WOODSTOCK,** 1991, RED/ WHT SCARF/4" $7-10

COMMENTS: REGIONAL DISTRIBUTION: MEXICO: DECEMBER 1991; JAPAN: NOVEMBER 1993 AND DECEMBER 1994; QUEBEC, CANADA - DECEMBER 1993; JAPAN - 1993; NEW ZEALAND - DECEMBER 1994. IN NEW ZEALAND, PRO-CEEDS FROM THIS PROMOTION WERE DONATED TO NEW ZEALAND'S RONALD McDONALD CHILDREN'S CHARITIES (RMCC). RMCC OPERATES AS A CHARITABLE TRUST TO HELP RAISE FUNDS FOR THE RONALD McDONALD HOUSES IN EACH COUNTRY; IN THIS PROMOTION SPECIFICALLY AUCKLAND AND WELLINGTON RMCC HOUSES.

SUNGLASSES/SHADES/SONNENBRILLEN PROMOTION, 1991

*** **IDENTICAL SUNGLASSES GER/UK SS9101/02/03**
- ❏ ❏ *** SS9101 **SUNGLASSES/SHADES - BLU,** 1991, BLU DK SHADES $3-4
- ❏ ❏ *** SS9102 **SUNGLASSES/SHADES - PNK,** 1991, PNK DK SHADES $3-4
- ❏ ❏ *** SS9103 **SUNGLASSES/SHADES - YEL,** 1991, YEL DK SHADES $3-4

COMMENTS: REGIONAL DISTRIBUTION: GERMANY: APRIL-MAY 1991; UK - 1991. UK SHADES COST 59p WITH ANY FOOD PURCHASE.

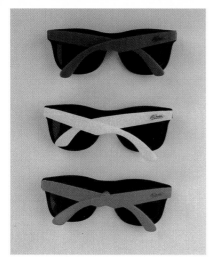

GER SS9101

UK SS9101

GER SS9103

GER SS9102

GERMANY

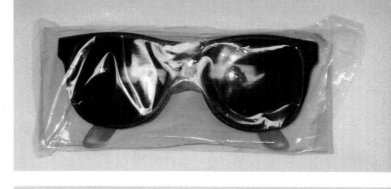

SHOE TAGS PROMOTION, 1991

    *** **IDENTICAL TAGS: FRA/GER/HOL SH9101**
❏ ❏ *** SH9101 **SHOE TAG - FRY GIRL/FRY GUY,** 1991, 2P WHT
    TAGS $3-4

COMMENTS: REGIONAL DISTRIBUTION: FRANCE/GERMANY/
    NETHERLANDS - 1991.

SPACE PATROL/MYSTERY OF THE LOST ARCHES PROMOTION, 1991

❏ ❏ *** SP9101 **ALIEN EYE/CAMERA,** 1991, CLICKS/TURNS
                                        $1-1.25
❏ ❏ *** MY9203 **PHONE/PERISCOPE,** 1991, ORG PHONE $1-1.25
❏ ❏ *** SP9102 **SPACE TELESCOPE,** 1991, RED/BLU $1-1.25
❏ ❏ *** SP9103 **MAGNIFIER,** 1991, MOON ROCK MAG/HIDDEN
    COMPARTMENT/GRN $1-1.25

COMMENTS: REGIONAL DISTRIBUTION: EUROPE: AUGUST
    1991. See USA MYSTERY OF THE LOST ARCHES HAPPY
    MEAL, 1992.

FRA SH9101

SUPER BALL/FLUMMIES JUNIOR TUTE, 1991

❏ ❏ GER FL9130 HM BAG, 1991, BRN JUNIOR TUTE $1-2

❏ ❏ GER FL9101 **BIRDIE FLUMMIE,** 1991, YEL W BIRDIE FACE
    INSIDE $4-6
❏ ❏ GER FL9102 **FRY GIRL FLUMMIE,** 1991, GRN W F GIRL
    INSIDE $4-6
❏ ❏ GER FL9103 **GRIMACE FLUMMIE,** 1991, BLU W SHAKY
    FACE INSIDE $4-6
❏ ❏ GER FL9104 **HAMBURGLAR FLUMMIE,** 1991, CLEAR W
    HAMB FACE INSIDE $4-6
❏ ❏ GER FL9105 **RONALD FLUMMIE,** 1991, PNK W RON FACE
    INSIDE $4-6

❏ ❏ GER FL9165 TRANSLITE/LG, 1991,T $25-40

COMMENTS: NATIONAL DISTRIBUTION: GERMANY - SEPTEM-
    BER 5-29, 1991.

USA

GER FL9104   GER FL9101   GER FL9103   GER FL9105   GER FL9102

GER FL9165

Laßt mal was springen!

Flummis

Mit jeder Junior-Tüte gibt's jetzt einen von fünf Springbällen. Nur

UK SU9102

UK SU9101   UK SU9104   UK SU9103

CAN SU9150   CAN SU9151

CAN SU9164

USA

SUPER MARIO 3 HAPPY MEAL, 1991

*** IDENTICAL BOXES: GER/UK SU9110/11/12/13
- ❑ ❑ *** SU9110 HM BOX, 1991, DESERT LAND $3-4
- ❑ ❑ *** SU9111 HM BOX, 1991, ISLAND WORLD $3-4
- ❑ ❑ *** SU9112 HM BOX, 1991, PIPE LAND $3-4
- ❑ ❑ *** SU9113 HM BOX, 1991, SKY LAND $3-4

*** IDENTICAL TOYS: CAN/UK/ZEA SU9001/02/03/04
- ❑ ❑ *** SU9001 **KOOPA PARATROOPER,** 1991, STANDING/PUMP ACTION $3-5
- ❑ ❑ *** SU9002 **LITTLE GOOMBA,** 1991, W RED PUMP/CORD/ FLIP OVER $3-5
- ❑ ❑ *** SU9003 **LUIGI,** 1991, ON A CLOUD/1P/PULL BACK $3-5
- ❑ ❑ *** SU9004 **MARIO,** 1991, SITTING ON SPRING $3-5

- ❑ ❑ CAN SU9150 BUTTON/ENGLISH, 1991, SUPER MARIO 3 $3-4
- ❑ ❑ CAN SU9151 BUTTON/FRENCH, 1991, SUPER MARIO 3 $3-4
- ❑ ❑ CAN SU9164 TRANSLITE/SM, 1991 $5-7
- ❑ ❑ UK SU9164 TRANSLITE/SM, 1991 $5-7
- ❑ ❑ UK SU9165 TRANSLITE/LG, 1991 $8-12
- ❑ ❑ UK SU9168 EXTENSION PACK, 1991 $6-8

COMMENTS: NATIONAL DISTRIBUTION: UK: SEPTEMBER 1991; NEW ZEALAND: JUNE 26, 1993; JAPAN: OCTOBER 1990. PREMIUMS: UK SU9001-04 ARE THE SAME AS USA SU9001-04. UK PACKAGING IS DATED 1991.

TEENAGE MUTANT NINJA TURTLES HAPPY MEAL, 1991
- ❑ ❑ MEX TE9101 **SCOOP,** 1991, GREEN HANDLE SCOOP/PALA PARA AGUA Y ARENA/1P/MR W MIRAGE STUDIOS $4-5
- ❑ ❑ MEX TE9102 **DIRIGIBLE,** 1991, GREEN DIRIGIBLE/BLIMP/ RUBBER/1P/MR W MIRAGE STUDIOS $4-5
- ❑ ❑ MEX TE9103 **FRISBEE,** 1991, GREEN DISC FRISBEE W PAPER PIC INSERT/6 1/2"/1P/MR W MIRAGE STUDIOS $4-5
- ❑ ❑ MEX TE9104 **SAND BUCKET,** 1991, GREEN/WHT W NINJA GRAPHICS $4-5

COMMENTS: REGIONAL DISTRIBUTION: MEXICO - AUGUST 1991.

MEX TE9101   MEX TE9102   MEX TE9103

WAIST POUCHES/SUMMER TIME PROMOTION, 1991

❑ ❑ UK WA9101 **WAIST POUCH - BLU,** ND, HALF CIRCLE W
   BELT $1.50-2.50
❑ ❑ UK WA9102 **WAIST POUCH - RED/PNK,** ND, HALF CIRCLE W
   BELT $1.50-2.50
❑ ❑ UK WA9103 **WAIST POUCH - YEL,** ND, HALF CIRCLE W BELT
                                                 $1.50-2.50

COMMENTS: REGIONAL DISTRIBUTION: UK: JULY-AUGUST 1991.
COST 59p WITH ANY FOOD PURCHASE. WAIST POUCHES
CAME IN "HOT NEON" COLORS ALSO. POUCHES WERE
MADE BY SIMON MARKETING, GERMANY.

1992

BACK TO THE FUTURE HAPPY MEAL, 1992

❑ ❑ PAN BK9201 **DOC'S DELOREAN/CAR,** 1991, GREY/BLU CAR
   W DOC HANGING OUT WINDOW $1-1.50
❑ ❑ PAN BK9202 **MARTY'S HOVERBOARD,** 1991, MARTY ON
   PINK HVBRD $1-1.50
❑ ❑ PAN BK9203 **VERNE'S JUNKMOBILE,** 1991, VERNE ON PNK/
   RED/GRN/BLUE WHEELS $1-1.50
❑ ❑ PAN BK9204 **EINSTEIN'S TRAVELING TRAIN,** 1991, BLU
   TRAIN W RED WHEELS $1-1.50

COMMENTS: NATIONAL DISTRIBUTION: PANAMA: NOVEMBER
1992. DISTRIBUTION OF DOC'S DELOREAN CARS WAS
RESTRICTED DUE TO PROBLEMS WITH THE TIRES. A
PARENT'S ADVISORY WAS ISSUED STATING, "SMALL
CHILDREN HAVE BEEN ABLE TO REMOVE REAR
TIRES...WE STRONGLY RECOMMEND THAT THOSE
CHILDREN WHO MIGHT PUT THESE TOYS IN THEIR
MOUTH NOT BE ALLOWED TO DO SO." See USA BACK TO
THE FUTURE HAPPY MEAL, 1992.

BARBIE/CORGI RACERS HAPPY MEAL, 1992

❑ ❑ UK BA9210 HM BOX, 1991, BARBIE/CATWALKS/WEEKEND-
   FANTASY BARBIE $3-4
❑ ❑ UK BA9211 HM BOX, 1991, BARBIE/CATWALKS/HAWAII-
   WEDDING FANTASY BARBIE $3-4
❑ ❑ UK BA9212 HM BOX, 1991, CORGI/RACE "START" TRACK 1
                                                 $3-4
❑ ❑ UK BA9213 HM BOX, 1991, CORGI/RACE "FINISH" TRACK 2
                                                 $3-4

❑ ❑ UK CO9209 **BMW,** 1991, BLUE BMW $8-12
❑ ❑ UK CO9210 **PORCHE,** 1991, **NEON GRN PORCHE** $8-12
❑ ❑ UK CO9211 **FERRARI,** 1991, **NEON ORG FERRARI** $8-12
❑ ❑ UK CO9212 **MERCEDES,** 1991, PINK MERCEDES $8-12

UK WA9102

USA BK9201   USA BK9202   USA BK9203

USA BK9204

USA BK9264

UK CO9209   UK CO9211   UK CO9210   UK CO9212

UK CO9209   UK CO9210   UK CO9211   UK CO9212

UK CO9211   UK CO9210

MEX BA9210   MEX HW9211

GERMANY

❏ ❏ UK BA9205 **FANTASY BARBIE,** 1991, PINK GOWN/PURP MASK $3-5
❏ ❏ UK BA9206 **HAWAIIAN FUN BARBIE,** 1991, PINK TOP W PINK SARONG SKIRT $3-5
❏ ❏ UK BA9207 **WEEKEND BARBIE,** 1991, W SUITCASE $3-5
❏ ❏ UK BA9208 **WEDDING FANTASY,** 1991, WHT WEDDING GOWN W PINK BOUQUET/LILAC RIBBON $3-5
❏ ❏ UK BA9264 TRANSLITE/SM, 1991 $7-10
❏ ❏ UK BA9265 TRANSLITE/LG, 1991 $10-15
❏ ❏ UK BA9215 EXTENSION PACK, 1991 $5-8

COMMENTS: NATIONAL DISTRIBUTION: UK: JANUARY 31-FEBRUARY 1992. UK CO9210 PICTURE APPEARS YELLOW, COLOR OF PORCHE CAR IS NEON GREEN; UK CO9211 PICTURE APPEARS RED, COLOR OF FERRARI CAR IS NEON ORANGE.

BARBIE/HOT WHEELS HAPPY MEAL, 1992
❏ ❏ MEX BA9210 HM BOX, 1992, VACACIONES HAWAIIANAS $3-4
❏ ❏ MEX HW9211 HM BOX, 1992, EQUIPOS CON EL AUTO $3-4

*** IDENTICAL BARBIE DOLLS: GER/HOL/UK BA9140/41/44/45
❏ ❏ *** BA9140 **ALL AMERICAN/WEEKEND,** 1990, BLU JUMPER W REEBOK TENNIS SHOES $3-5
❏ ❏ *** BA9141 **COSTUME BALL,** 1990, PINK GOWN W PURP MASK IN RIGHT HAND $3-5
❏ ❏ *** BA9144 **HAWAIIAN FUN,** 1990, PINK TOP W PINK SARONG SKIRT $3-5
❏ ❏ *** BA9145 **WEDDING DAY MIDGE,** 1990, WHITE WEDDING GOWN W PINK BOUQUET $3-5

*** IDENTICAL HOT WHEEL CARS: FRA/HOL HW9151/55/60/62
❏ ❏ *** HW9151 **57 T-BIRD,** 1990, RED 1957 T-BIRD $3-5
❏ ❏ *** HW9155 **55 CHEVY,** 1990, YEL 1955 CHEVROLET $3-5
❏ ❏ *** HW9160 **63 CORVETTE,** 1990, BLK 63 CORVETTE $3-5
❏ ❏ *** HW9162 **CAMARO Z-28,** 1990, ORG Z-28 CAMARO $3-5

❏ ❏ FRA BA9244 POSTER/LG, 1992 $20-25
❏ ❏ HOL BA9244 POSTER/SM, 1992 $15-20

UK   BA9140   *** BA9145   *** BA9141   *** BA9144

FRA BA9244

124

COMMENTS: NATIONAL DISTRIBUTION: BELGIUM, DENMARK, FINLAND, FRANCE, GREECE, ITALY, HOLLAND, NORWAY, PORTUGAL, SPAIN, SWEDEN, SWITZERLAND, MEXICO, LATIN AMERICA: - JANUARY 9-FEBRUARY 19, 1992; PANAMA, PUERTO RICO: AUGUST 1991. LOOSE, OUT OF PACKAGE: HOL BA9140/41/44/45 = USA BA9140/41/44/45; HOL HW9151/55/60/62 = USA HW9151/55/60/62. REGIONAL DISTRIBUTION IN MEXICO/LATIN AMERICA - 1992; HOL BA9240/41/44/45 WERE PACKAGED: MADE IN GERMANY WITH NETHERLANDS PAPER INSERTS.

BATMAN HAPPY MEAL, 1992

   *** **IDENTICAL TOYS: CAN/ZEA BT9201/02/03/04**

❑ ❑ *** BT9201 **BATMAN,** 1991, BATMAN PRESS AND GO BLK CAR/1P $2.50-4

❑ ❑ *** BT9202 **BATMOBILE,** 1991, BATMAN W BLK BATMISSILE/ 2P $2.50-4

❑ ❑ *** BT9203 **CATWOMAN CAT COUPE,** 1991, FEMME-CHAT/ BATWOMAN IN PURP COUPE/1P $2.50-4

❑ ❑ *** BT9204 **PENGUIN/ROTO-ROADSTER,** 1991, PENGUIN IN YEL ROADSTER/1P $2.50-4

❑ ❑ *** BT9295 PIN, 1992, SQUARE/BLK/WHT BATMAN RE-TURNS MCD $4-5

❑ ❑ *** BT9296 PIN, 1992, BATMAN'S FACE/McDONALD'S $4-5

❑ ❑ CAN BT9255 TRAYLINER, 1992, BATMAN RETURNS $1-1.50

❑ ❑ CAN BT9257 TRAYLINER, 1992, BATMAN RETURNS CUPS $1-1.50

❑ ❑ CAN BT9265 TRANSLITE/LG, 1992, BATMAN RETURNS $15-25

COMMENTS: NATIONAL DISTRIBUTION: CANADA: JUNE 12-JULY 9, 1992; NEW ZEALAND: AUGUST 1992. PREMIUMS: CAN/ ZEA BT9201-04 = USA BT9201-04, LOOSE OUT OF PACK-AGE. See USA BATMAN HAPPY MEAL, 1992.

HOL BA9244

CAN BT9255

CAN BT9257

CAN BT9202   CAN BT9201   CAN BT9203   CAN BT9204

CAN BT9265

USA BT9203

USA BT9201   BT9202   BT9204

USA BT9295   USA BT9296

AUS BT9245

**BATMAN MASK
HAPPY MEAL NOW AVAILABLE**

This weeks mask is:

BATMAN............. WEEK 1
PENGUIN .... WEEK 2
CATWOMAN.......... WEEK 3
PENGUIN WARRIOR... WEEK 4

Free with a Cheeseburger or Junior Burger
Happy Meal...all yours for $3.50

Back,

AUS BT9205

BATMAN MASK HAPPY MEAL, 1992

- ❏ ❏ AUS BT9201 **BATMAN,** 1992, BLACK MASK/PLASTIC W ELASTIC $15-20
- ❏ ❏ AUS BT9202 **CATWOMAN,** 1992, BLACK MASK/PLASTIC W ELASTIC $15-20
- ❏ ❏ AUS BT9203 **PENGUIN,** 1992, BLACK MASK/PLASTIC W ELASTIC $15-20
- ❏ ❏ AUS BT9204 **JOKER,** 1992, BLACK MASK/PLASTIC W ELASTIC $15-20
- ❏ ❏ AUS BT9245 REGISTER TOPPER, 1992 $7-10

COMMENTS: REGIONAL DISTRIBUTION: AUSTRALIA - FALL 1992.

BEAD/BALL/RING TOSS PROMOTION, 1992

*** IDENTICAL GAMES: CAN/GER/UK RI9201/02/03/04/05/06
- ❏ ❏ *** RI9201 **CAPTAIN,** 1992, TRIPPLE BALL TOSS/ORG or YEL BASE $3-4
- ❏ ❏ *** RI9202 **RONALD,** 1992, DOUBLE RING TOSS/ORG or YEL BASE $3-4
- ❏ ❏ *** RI9203 **BIG MAC,** 1992, DOUBLE RING TOSS/2 BALLS/ ORG or YEL BASE $3-4
- ❏ ❏ *** RI9204 **MAYOR,** 1992, SINGLE RING TOSS/2 BALLS/ORG or YEL BASE $3-4
- ❏ ❏ *** RI9205 **HAMBURGLAR,** 1992, DOUBLE RING TOSS/ORG or YEL BASE $3-4
- ❏ ❏ *** RI9206 **FRY GUY,** 1992, 2 BALLS IN GLASSES/ORG or YEL BASE $3-5

COMMENTS: REGIONAL DISTRIBUTION: CANADA, GERMANY, UK: 1992.

AUS BT9201   AUS BT9203

AUS BT9202   AUS BT9204

UK SET   UK RI9202

UK RI9202   UK RI9206

BEAUTY N' THE BEAST/BELLE EN HET BEEST HAPPY MEAL, 1992

GERMANY

MEX BE9210

*** IDENTICAL BOXES: GER/UK BE9210/11/12/13

❏ ❏ *** BE9210 HM BOX, 1992, CASTLE BALLROOM/FOR BEAST
$3-4

❏ ❏ *** BE9211 HM BOX, 1992, CASTLE/COTTAGE/FATHER'S HOUSE/TO HOLD BEAUTY $3-4

❏ ❏ *** BE9212 HM BOX, 1992, DINING HALL KITCHEN/TO HOLD TEA CUP $3-4

❏ ❏ *** BE9213 HM BOX, 1992, VILLAGE STREET/DOUBLE DOORS/TO HOLD CLOCK $3-4

❏ ❏ MEX BE9210 HM BOX, 1992, BEAUTY/BEAST/LA BELLA Y LA BESTIA $3-4

❏ ❏ MEX BE9211 HM BOX, 1992, CASTLE/COTTAGE/FATHER'S HOUSE/TO HOLD BEAUTY $3-4

*** IDENTICAL TOYS: FRA/HOL/NED/UK BE9201/02/03/04

❏ ❏ UK BE9201 **BEAUTY,** 1992, BEAUTY W CHANGEABLE DRESS/YEL AND BLU DRESS/3P $7-10

❏ ❏ UK BE9202 **BEAST,** 1992, BEAST/4" W 2P/PUR CLOTH CAPE/ARMS AND LEGS MOVE $10-15

❏ ❏ UK BE9203 **CLOCK,** 1992, COGSWORTH/1P BRN/YEL CLOCK/SPINS BACK AND FORTH 5-8

❏ ❏ UK BE9204 **TEA POT,** 1992, MRS. POTTS/1P TEA POT W YEL HANDLE/PURP LID $5-8

❏ ❏ UK BE9226 DISPLAY/PREMIUMS, 1992 $200-250
❏ ❏ FRA BE9265 TRANSLITE/LG, 1992 $40-50
❏ ❏ UK BE9264 TRANSLITE/SM, 1992 $35-40
❏ ❏ UK BE9265 TRANSLITE/LG, 1992 $40-50
❏ ❏ UK BE9266 M C CARD/MAGNETIC/LG, 1992 12-15
❏ ❏ UK BE9267 M C CARD/MAGNETIC/SM, 1992 $10-12

UK BE9201-04

COMMENTS: NATIONAL DISTRIBUTION: GERMANY: NOVEMBER 26-DECEMBER 20, 1992; UK: OCTOBER 2, 1992; BELGIUM, DENMARK, FINLAND, GREECE, NORWAY, SPAIN: DECEMBER 1992; GUATEMALA: NOV/DEC 1992. UK AND HOL PREMIUMS ARE THE SAME EXCEPT FOR PACKAGING. RELEASE OF HM COINCIDED WITH RELEASE OF DISNEY MOVIE.

HOL BE9244

UK BE9210   UK BE9211   UK BE9212   UK BE9213

FRA BE9244

FRA BE9465

UK BE9205

MEX BE9211

BEAUTY N' THE BEAST/DIE SCHONE & DAS BIEST PROMOTION, 1992

❑ ❑ UK BE9205 **BEAUTY/BEAST DOLLS,** 1992, BEAUTY W YEL CLOTH DRESS/BEAST W BLU CAPE $25-40

❑ ❑ FRA BE9244 POSTER/LOBBY/LG, 1992 $40-50

COMMENTS: REGIONAL DISTRIBUTION: GERMANY - DECEMBER 1992: FRANCE: OCTOBER 1992. DOLLS WERE SOLD AS A SET DURING A SELF LIQUIDATING PROMTION. PROMOTION WAS A TIE-IN WITH THE INTERNATIONAL MOVIE BY DISNEY, BEAUTY N THE BEAST.

BUGS BUNNY & SUS AMIGOS/LOONEY TUNES/FESTIVE FRIENDS DOLLS PROMOTION, 1993/1992

❑ ❑ MEX DO9201 **BUGS BUNNY,** 1992, W RED/GRN SCARF ON NECK $8-12

❑ ❑ MEX DO9202 **TAZMANIAN DEVIL,** 1992, **TAZ W/O BEARD** $8-12

❑ ❑ MEX DO9203 **SYLVESTER,** 1992, **SYL W/O NIGHTSHIRT** $8-12

❑ ❑ MEX DO9204 **TWEETY,** 1992, YEL CHICK W/GREEN ELF OUTFIT/GRN HAT $8-12

   *** **IDENTICAL STUFFED DOLLS CAN/FRA LO9201/02/03/04**

❑ ❑ *** LO9201 **BUGS BUNNY,** 1992, BUGS W RED/GRN SCARF AROUND EARS $8-12

❑ ❑ *** LO9202 **TAZMANIAN DEVIL,** 1992, **TAZ W BEARD** $8-12

❑ ❑ *** LO9203 **SYLVESTOR,** 1992, **SYL W RED/WHT NIGHT-SHIRT** $8-12

❑ ❑ *** LO9204 **TWEETY,** 1992, W GRN HAT/SHIRT/BOOTS $8-12

❑ ❑ CAN LO9245 REGISTER TOPPER/EACH CHARACTER, 1992, SYLVESTER/TASMANIAN/TWEETY/BUGS $4-5

❑ ❑ CAN LO9255 TRAYLINER, 1992, CHARS W CHRISTMAS TREE $2-3

GER BE9244

MEXICO

128

CANADA

CANADA

CANADA

CAN LO9245

FRA LO9204

COMMENTS: REGIONAL DISTRIBUTION: MEXICO, GUATEMALA, QUEBEC, CANADA - NOV/DEC 1992; FRANCE: 1993. STUFFED ANIMALS SOLD FOR $2.89 EACH WITH A FOOD PURCHASE. MEX DO9201 BUGS BUNNY IS DIFFERENT FROM THE CAN LO9201.

CAN LO9255

FRA DO9201

FRA DO9202

FRA DO9203

FRA DO9201

FRA DO9204

130

CAMERA FUNSHOTS PROMOTION, 1992

❏ ❏ CAN CA9201 **CAMERA/CONCORD,** 1992, GRN $5-6
❏ ❏ CAN CA9202 **CAMERA/CONCORD,** 1992, PNK $5-6
❏ ❏ CAN CA9203 **CAMERA/CONCORD,** 1992, ORG $5-6
❏ ❏ CAN CA9245 REGISTER TOPPER, 1992, FUNSHOTS
          CAMERA $1.50-3
❏ ❏ CAN CA9255 TRAYLINER, 1992, FUNSHOTS $1-1.25

COMMENTS: REGIONAL DISTRIBUTION: CANADA - 1992.

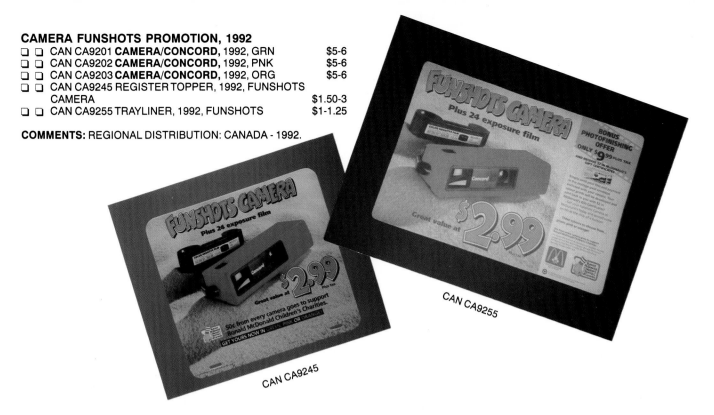

CAN CA9255

CAN CA9245

CANADA/GENERIC PROMOTION, 1992

❏ ❏ CAN GE9201 **RING-DISQUE ORBITAL,** 1992, RED/4P/
          ORBITAL RING $3-4
❏ ❏ CAN GE9202 **MCCLACKER'S,** 1992, ORG/3P/CLACKERS $3-4
❏ ❏ CAN GE9203 **SPINNING TOP,** 1992, GRN DISC W STRING
                                                       $2-3
❏ ❏ CAN GE9204 **SHOELACE PURSE,** 1992, YEL/RONALD/OVAL
                                                       $2-3
❏ ❏ CAN GE9205 **HOCKEY MAZE,** 1992, BEAD GAME $2-3
❏ ❏ CAN GE9206 **BLIMP BALLOON/GLOBAL PIZZA LIGHTSHIP,**
          1992, RED/RON/GRI/HAMB/PIZZA $4-6
❏ ❏ CAN GE9207 **BLIMP BALLOON/GLOBAL PIZZA LIGHTSHIP,**
          1992, BLU/RON/GRI/BIRDIE/PIZZA $4-6
❏ ❏ CAN GE9208 **PIZZA LACES,** 1992, ORG $1-1.50
❏ ❏ CAN GE9209 **PIZZA LACES,** 1992, WHT $1-1.50
❏ ❏ CAN GE9215 **BOOKLET/BANDADES,** 1992, COMFORTING
          YOUR CHILD/2 BANDADES $1-1.50
❏ ❏ CAN GE9216 **MCPASSPORT BOOKLET,** 1992, RED/25
          ANNIVERSARY MCD IN CANADA $2-3
❏ ❏ CAN GE9217 **WALLET/RONALD FACE,** 1992, BLU or GRN or
          ORG or RED $1.50-2.50
❏ ❏ CAN GE9218 **LEARN TO DRAW,** 1991, RONALD or HAMB/
          ENGLISH $1-1.25
❏ ❏ CAN GE9219 **LEARN TO DRAW,** 1991, BIRDIE or GRIMACE/
          FRENCH $1-1.25
❏ ❏ CAN GE9220 **MCSPINNER/YO YO,** 1992, RED $1-1.50
❏ ❏ CAN GE9221 **STICKERS/GLOW,** 1992, RON W FLYING
          HAMB
                                                       $2-3
❏ ❏ CAN GE9222 **HAT/RON IN SPACE,** 1992, PAPER $1-1.50

COMMENTS: REGIONAL DISTRIBUTION: CANADA - 1992 DURING
          CLEAN-UP WEEK AND/OR AS TREAT-OF-THE-WEEK.

CAN GE9202   CAN GE9201

CANADA

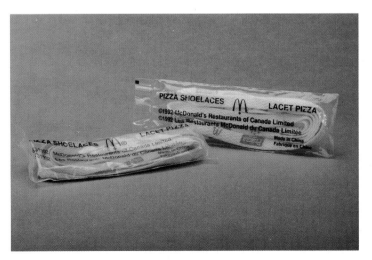

CAN GE9208

131

CAN GE9205

CAN GE9206

CAN GE9207

CAN GE9218

WITH A SPECIAL OKANAGAN SECTION!

Kid's Passport

ONLY $2.00 EACH

WORTH UP TO $5,000.00 IN VALUE

WIN a trip to WONDERWORLD

It's a Book Full of Value
It's a Book Full of Fun

McDonald's

CAN GE9216

CAN GE9219

CAN GE9215

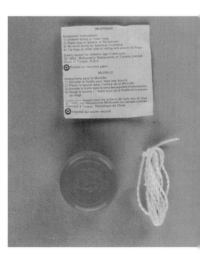

CAN GE9220

Glow-In-The-Dark Stickers
Autocollants phosphorescents

CAN GE9222

CAN GE9221

CHINESE BALL PROMOTION, 1992

❏ ❏ GER CH9201 **CHINESE BALL/RONALD,** 1992, PAPER
PARCHMENT BALL W LOGO $2-3

COMMENTS: REGIONAL DISTRIBUTION: GERMANY 1992 DURING
MCNUGGET PROMOTION. SEE CAN GE9305 CANADA
GENERIC PARCHMENT BALL.

GER CH9201

CHRISTMAS CLIPS PROMOTION, 1992

❏ ❏ GER CL9203 **SNOWMAN,** 1992, CLIP/SNOWMAN W ARCHES
ON BLK STOVE TOP HAT/1P $4-6
❏ ❏ GER CL9204 **SANTA,** 1992, CLIP/SANTA'S FACE W ARCHES
ON HAT/1P $4-6

COMMENTS: REGIONAL DISTRIBUTION: GERMANY - DECEMBER
1992 DURING CLEAN-UP WEEKS.

GER CL9204   GER CL9203

CONNECTIBLE BOATS PROMOTION, 1992

❏ ❏ JPN BO9201 **PADDLEBOAT,** 1992 $4-5
❏ ❏ JPN BO9202 **BI-PLANE,** 1992 $4-5
❏ ❏ JPN BO9203 **FIREBOAT,** 1992, WHISTLING $4-5
❏ ❏ JPN BO9204 **FIREBOAT,** 1992, SQUIRTING $4-5
❏ ❏ JPN BO9205 **DOCK,** 1992 $4-5

COMMENTS: REGIONAL DISTRIBUTION: JAPAN: 1992.

JAPAN

133

HOL DR9201   HOL DR9202   HOL DR9203   HOL DR9204

JPN DR9301   JPN DR9302   JPN DR9303   JPN DR9304

JPN DR9301   UK DR9301

JAPAN   GERMANY   HOLLAND

UK DR9302 UK DR9304 UK DR9303 UK DR9301

DRAGONETTES/DRACHEN/CHINESE DRAAKJES JUNIOR TUTE/HAPPY MEAL, 1993/1992

❏ ❏ GER DR9310 HM BOX, 1993, CHINESE FAMILIES AT GATE/ WALL/LANTERN $2-3
❏ ❏ GER DR9311 HM BOX, 1993, TWO DRAGONS/JUNK/ $2-3
❏ ❏ GER DR9312 HM BOX, 1993, PAGOTA/CHINESE HOUSE $2-3
❏ ❏ GER DR9313 HM BOX, 1993, STREET SCENE/CHILDREN AT PALACE $2-3
❏ ❏ JPN DR9310 HM BOX, 1993, DRAGON $2-3

   *** IDENTICAL TOYS: HOL/GER/UK DR9201/02/03/04
❏ ❏ *** DR9201 **GIGI,** 1988, PUR DRAGON **W BLK/WHT BATON** $3-5
❏ ❏ *** DR9202 **LUCKY,** 1988, YEL DRAGON **W RED BOOKS** $3-5
❏ ❏ *** DR9203 **PUFF,** 1988, GRN DRAGON **W RED BOTTLE** $3-5
❏ ❏ *** DR9204 **RITCHIE,** 1988, BLU DRAGON **W RED BALL W/ FOOT PEG** $3-5

❏ ❏ JPN DR9301 **GIGI,** 1988, PUR DRAGON **W YEL CANDLE** $4-6
❏ ❏ JPN DR9302 **LUCKY,** 1988, YEL DRAGON **W RED FF CONTAINERS** $4-6
❏ ❏ JPN DR9303 **PUFF,** 1988, GRN DRAGON **W RED CONTAINER** $4-6
❏ ❏ JPN DR9304 **RITCHIE,** 1988, BLU DRAGON **W/RED BALL W/ NO DOUBLE FOOT PEG** $4-6

❏ ❏ UK DR9326 DISPLAY W PREMS, 1992 $75-100
❏ ❏ HOL DR9344 POSTER, 1992 $5-7
❏ ❏ HOL DR9355 TRAYLINER, 1992, CHINESE DRAAKJES $1-1.25
❏ ❏ UK DR9364 TRANSLITE/SM, 1992 $10-20
❏ ❏ GER DR9365 TRANSLITE/LG, 1993 $25-40
❏ ❏ UK DR9365 TRANSLITE/LG, 1992 $15-25
❏ ❏ UK DR9366 M C/MAGNETIC/SM, 1992 $3-5
❏ ❏ UK DR9367 M C/MAGNETIC/LG, 1992 $4-6

COMMENTS: NATIONAL DISTRIBUTION: GERMANY: AUGUST 27-SEPTEMBER 20, 1992 AND REGIONAL DISTRIBUTION IN 1993 WITH 4 BOXES; UK: JANUARY 29, 1993 IN CONJUNCTION WITH "TASTES OF THE ORIENT PROMO." NETHERLANDS/HOLLAND: MARCH 18-APRIL 28, 1993. GER DR9203 AND JPN DR9303 ARE VARIATIONS/DIFFERENT. REGIONAL DISTRIBUTION IN GERMANY/JAPAN - 1993. NOTE DIFFERENCES IN CANDLE/BATON COLORS ON DR9301 AND WITH/ WITHOUT FOOT PEG ON DR9304, BETWEEN THE VARIOUS COUNTRIES. IT IS CONCEIVABLE THAT ALL COMBINATIONS WERE DISTRIBUTED WITHIN THE VARIOUS COUNTRIES, BASED ON SUPPLY AND DEMAND.

GER DR9313

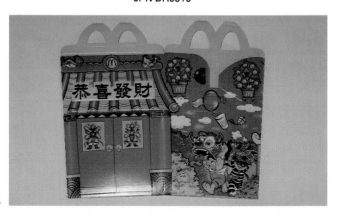

JPN DR9310

HOL DR9344   HOL DR9355   GER DR9365

EURO DISNEY RESORT HAPPY MEAL, 1992

❏ ❏ GER EU9210 HM BOX, 1992, MAIN STREET $3-4
❏ ❏ GER EU9211 HM BOX, 1992, PETER PAN FLYING $3-4
❏ ❏ GER EU9212 HM BOX, 1992, THUNDER MOUNTAIN $3-4
❏ ❏ GER EU9213 HM BOX, 1992, TIGGER/WINNIE AT THE FAIR
$3-4

      *** **IDENTICAL TOYS: HOL/UK EU9201/02/03/04**
❏ ❏ *** **EU9201 FIRE ENGINE/PONGO,** 1992, 101 DALMATION IN
RED FIRE ENGINE/1P $5-7
❏ ❏ *** **EU9202 TRAIN ENGINE/KNABBEL EN BABBEL,** 1992,
CHIP N' DALE TOP OF RED ENGINE/1P $5-7
❏ ❏ *** **EU9203 PIRATE'S SHIP/KAPIT EIN HAAK,** 1992, CAPT
HOOK IN PIRATE SHIP/WHT MAST/2P $5-7
❏ ❏ *** **EU9204 TEA CUP/TEIGETJE,** 1992, TIGER IN WHT TEA
CUP/SPINS/1P $5-7

❏ ❏ HOL EU9244 POSTER, 1992 $15-20
❏ ❏ UK EU9264 TRANSLITE/SM, 1992 $15-20
❏ ❏ UK EU9265 TRANSLITE/LG, 1992 $25-45
❏ ❏ UK EU9267 M C CARD/MAGNETIC/LG, 1992 $10-15

COMMENTS: NATIONAL DISTRIBUTION: UK: AUGUST 21, 1992 TO
COMMEMORATE THE OPENING OF EURO DISNEY IN
PARIS, FRANCE. REGIONAL DISTRIBUTION IN BELGIUM,
DENMARK, FINLAND, FRANCE, ITALY, HOLLAND, NORWAY,
PORTUGAL, SPAIN, SWEDEN, SWITZERLAND, SCOTLAND,
WALES: AUGUST 13-SEPTEMBER 23, 1992.

GERMANY

GER EU9210   GER EU9213   GER EU9212   GER EU9211

HOL EU9201   HOL EU9203   HOL EU9204   HOL EU9202

HOL EU9244

135

FOOD CARD PROMOTION, 1994/1993/1992

❏ ❏	FRA FO9201	**CARD - MCFAC**, 1992		$4-6
❏ ❏	FRA FO9202	**CARD - BIG MAC**, 1992		$4-6
❏ ❏	FRA FO9203	**CARD - HAPPY MEAL**, 1992		$4-6
❏ ❏	FRA FO9204	**CARD - 4 HM**, 1992		$4-6
❏ ❏	BEL FO9401	**CARD -DAARGEBEURT**, 1994		$4-6
❏ ❏	BEL FO9402	**CARD -EENHEDEN**, 1994		$4-6

COMMENTS: REGIONAL DISTRIBUTION: PARIS, FRANCE: 1992. CARDS WERE PRESOLD ITEMS; PUNCH OUTS AS FOOD ITEMS REDEEMED. IN JAPAN, THESE CARDS ARE CALLED U CARDS, W MAGNETIC STRIPE AND PUNCHED AT EDGE WHEN USED.

FRA FO9201   FRA FO9203
FRA FO9202

BEL FO9402

FRA FO9204

BEL FO9401

FRANCE/GENERIC PROMOTION, 1994/1993/1992

❏ ❏	FRA GE9230 HM BAG, 1992, RON ON SKIS		$2-3
❏ ❏	FRA GE9201 **BADGE/STICKERS**, 1992, ROUND DISC/ STICKERS		$2-3
❏ ❏	FRA GE9202 **POST CARD - CASTLE**, 1992, RON		$1-1.25
❏ ❏	FRA GE9203 **HEADBAND**, 1992, INDIAN HEADDRESS		$1-1.25
❏ ❏	FRA GE9204 **POSTCARD - RONALD**, 1992, RONALD McDONALD ARRIVE!		$1-1.25
❏ ❏	FRA GE9205 **MOBILE - RONALD**, 1992, SPACE		$1-1.25
❏ ❏	FRA GE9206 **BEAD GAME - RONALD**, 1992, RON ON SURF BOARD		$5-7
❏ ❏	FRA GE9207 **WINDOW CHAR - GRI**, 1992, GRIMACE W SUCTION CUPS		$3-4
❏ ❏	FRA GE9208 **PAPER CLIP**, 1992, GRIMACE/PURP		$1.50-2
❏ ❏	FRA GE9209 **FLAGS/PAPER**, 1992, CHARACTERS/PAPER		$2.50-4
❏ ❏	FRA GE9210 **GAME/WATERWAYS**, 1992, PAPER		$1-1.25
❏ ❏	FRA GE9211 **CARD/PAINT**, 1992, GRIMACE		$1-1.25
❏ ❏	FRA GE9212 **MAGIC WINDOW**, 1992, WINTER		$1-1.25
❏ ❏	FRA GE9213 **POST CARD - SPACE**, 1992, RONALD		$1-1.25
❏ ❏	FRA GE9214 **CARD/GAMES**, 1994, PAPER/PAINT		$1-1.25
❏ ❏	FRA GE9215 **POST CARD - SUB**, 1992, RONALD		$1-1.25
❏ ❏	FRA GE9216 **BADGE**, 1994, GRIM RIDING BIKE		$1-1.25
❏ ❏	FRA GE9217 **MONEY POUCH**, 1994, RON/ROCKET SHIP		$1-1.25
❏ ❏	FRA GE9218 **KEY HOLDER**, 1994, BIRDIE or RON/METAL LOOP		$1-1.25
❏ ❏	FRA GE9219 **HAT**, 1994, BIG MAC/MCD		$3-5
❏ ❏	FRA GE9220 **MONEY POUCH**, 1994, MONEY WALLETS/BLU/ GRN		$2-3
❏ ❏	FRA GE9221 **MASK/UNDERSEA**, 1994, PAPER		$1-1.25
❏ ❏	FRA GE9222 **BADGE**, 1994, MCBACON/LE ROYAL		$3-4
❏ ❏	FRA GE9223 **LABELS/CHARS**, 1994, PAPER		$1-1.25

COMMENTS: REGIONAL DISTRIBUTION: FRANCE/TAIWAN - 1992/ 1993/1994/1995. FRA GE9209 CHARACTER FLAGS WERE MADE IN GERMANY AND DISTRIBUTED IN SEVERAL COUNTRIES. VARIOUS ITEMS WERE GIVEN AT BIRTHDAY PARTIES, WITHIN BIRTHDAY PARTY PACKS. THESE ARE A SAMPLING OF GENERIC PREMIUMS GIVEN DURING HOLIDAY, BIRTHDAY PARTY, SPECIAL OCCASIONS AND CLEAN-UP WEEKS. FRA GE9207 WAS DISTRIBUTED: 1995/ 1994/1993/1992 AND DURING THE DECEMBER TIME PERIODS.

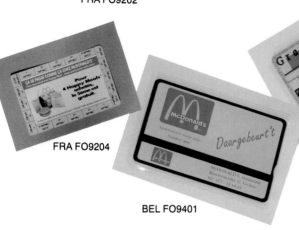

FRA GE9230

FRA GE9201

FRA GE9203

FRA GE9202

FRA GE9207

FRA GE9208

FRA GE9204

FRA GE9205

FRA GE9206

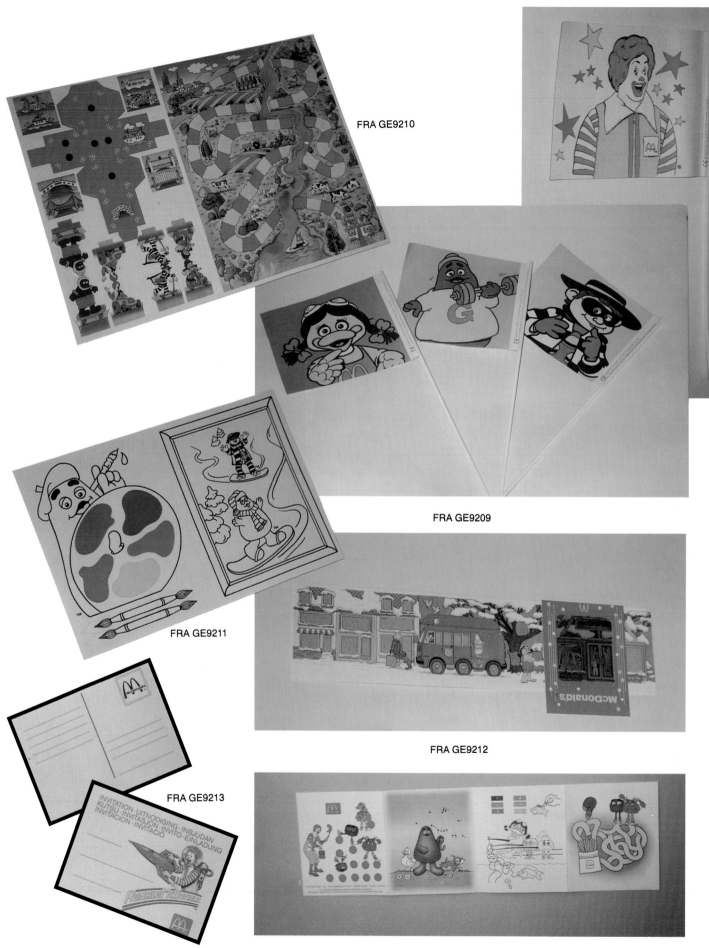

FRA GE9210

FRA GE9209

FRA GE9211

FRA GE9212

FRA GE9213

FRA GE9214

138

FRA GE9215

FRA GE9216

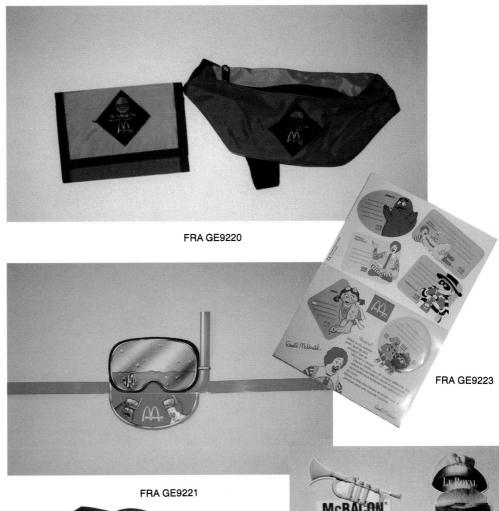

FRA GE9220

FRA GE9221

FRA GE9223

FRA GE9222

FRA GE9217

FRA GE9219

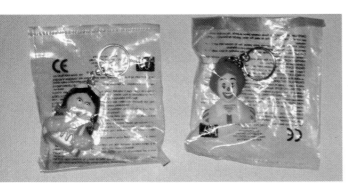

FRA GE9218

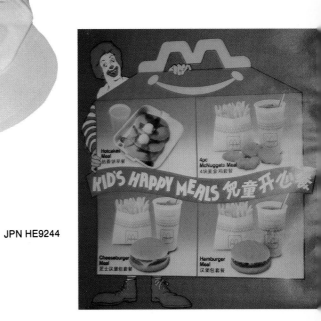

JPN HE9244

GER GE9210

GERMANY

FUN AROUND CUPS/FUNKY NEON CUPS PROMOTION, 1992

❑ ❑ JPN CU9201 **CUP-SPACE,** 1992, RONALD McDONALD $2-3
❑ ❑ JPN CU9202 **CUP-CARNIVAL,** 1992, BIRDIE $2-3
❑ ❑ JPN CU9203 **CUP-UNDERSEA,** 1992, GRIMACE $2-3
❑ ❑ JPN CU9204 **CUP-SNOWMOBILE,** 1992, HAMBURGLAR $2-3

❑ ❑ UK CU9201 **CUP-IT'S BAD,** 1992, NEON COLORS $1-1.25
❑ ❑ UK CU9202 **CUP-IT'S WET,** 1992, NEON COLORS $1-1.25
❑ ❑ UK CU9203 **CUP-GO,GO,GO,** 1992, NEON COLORS $1-1.25
❑ ❑ UK CU9204 **CUP-IT'S CHOICE,** 1992, NEON COLORS $1-1.25
❑ ❑ UK CU9205 **CUP-CHILL OUT,** 1992, NEON COLORS $1-1.25
❑ ❑ UK CU9206 **CUP-IT'S BOSS,** 1992, NEON COLORS $1-1.25
❑ ❑ UK CU9207 **CUP-IT'S COOL,** 1992, NEON COLORS $1-1.25
❑ ❑ UK CU9208 **CUP-IT'S XCELLENT,** 1992, NEON COLORS
$1-1.25

COMMENTS: REGIONAL DISTRIBUTION: JAPAN (FUN AROUND CUPS): 1992; UK (FUNKY NEON): 1992.

GERMANY/EUROPE/GENERIC HAPPY MEAL, 1992

❑ ❑ GER GE9210 HM BOX, 1992, RON/CHARS AT THE BEACH
$2-3
❑ ❑ GER GE9211 HM BOX, 1992, RON/CHARS UNDER THE ARCHES $2-3
❑ ❑ GER GE9230 HM BAG, ND, #1 - 10/BRN BAG $2-3
❑ ❑ GER GE9231 HM BAG, ND, #11 -20/BRN BAG $2-3
❑ ❑ GER GE9232 HM BAG, ND, #21-30/BRN BAG $2-3
❑ ❑ GER GE9233 HM BAG, ND, #31-40/BRN BAG $2-3
❑ ❑ GER GE9234 HM BAG, ND, #41-50/BRN BAG $2-3
❑ ❑ GER GE9201 **PAPER CLIP/GRIMACE,** 1992, PURP/CENTER PRESS $4-5
❑ ❑ GER GE9202 **COMPASS/BIRDIE,** 1992, YEL/CIRCLE $3-5
❑ ❑ GER GE9203 **COMPASS/RONALD,** 1992, RED/CIRCLE $3-5
❑ ❑ GER GE9204 **BEAD GAME/BIR/RON,** 1992, 2 SIDED BEAD GAME $4-6
❑ ❑ GER GE9205 **MAGNIFYING GLASS,** 1992, HAMBURGLAR
$1-2
❑ ❑ GER GE9206 **PAINT BOOK,** 1992, MALBUCH/MCD CHARAC-TERS $1-1.25
❑ ❑ GER GE9207 **STICKER SHEET,** 1992, CHARACTERS $1-1.50
❑ ❑ GER GE9208 **RULER/ERASER/SHARP,** 1992, YEL RULER/ RON ERASER/CHAR PENCIL/RED SHARPENER $4-6
❑ ❑ GER GE9209 **PUZZLE,** 1992, RON ON THE MOON $4-6
❑ ❑ NOR GE9201 **BEAD GAME/RON,** 1992, RONALD $3-4
❑ ❑ UK GE9201 **ORNAMENT,** 1992, CHRISTMAS TREE $2.50-3

COMMENTS: REGIONAL DISTRIBUTION: GERMANY/EUROPE - 1992 DURING CLEAN-UP WEEKS. GER GE9130/31/32/33/34 LIST THE 50 HAPPY MEAL BAGS GIVEN OUT PRIOR TO THE GENERIC WHITE JUNIOR TUTE HAPPY MEAL BAG. PRIOR TO THE BROWN BAGS, WHITE BAGS WERE GIVEN. THE FIFTY BROWN BAGS ARE NUMBERED AND APPEAR TO HAVE 3-D TYPE GRAPHICS WITH NUMBERS IN THE BOTTOM LEFT CORNER. NOTE, RONALD & CO. BROWN BAG LISTS THE NEW CHARACTERS, SHAKY/GERMAN NAME (GRIMACE/USA NAME), BIRDIE AND HAMBURGLAR. GER GE9206 PAINT BOOK WAS GIVEN OUT OVER A PERIOD OF YEARS (1990-1995)

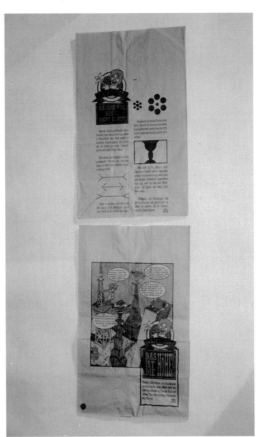

GERMANY

GER GE9203   GER GE9202

GER GE9204

GER GE9205

GER GE9206   GER GE9207

GER GE9208   GER GE9201   GER GE9208

GER GE9209

NOR GE9201

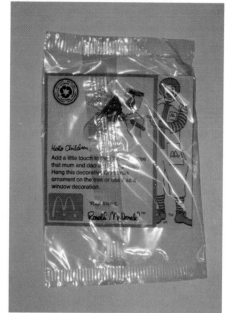

UK GE9201

GUA HA9201   GUA HA9202   GUA HA9203

GUA HA9202

USA

HALLOWEEN '92 HAPPY MEAL, 1992

- ❏ ❏ GUA HA9201 **GHOST,** 1986, 3P WHT W COOKIE CUTTER
  LID/BLK HANDLE $1-1.25
- ❏ ❏ GUA HA9202 **PUMPKIN,** 1986, 3P ORG COOKIE CUTTER
  LID/BLK HANDLE $1-1.25
- ❏ ❏ GUA HA9203 **WITCH,** 1986, 3P GRN COOKIE CUTTER
  INSERT W BLK HANDLE $1-1.25

COMMENTS: NATIONAL DISTRIBUTION: GUATEMALA: OCTOBER
9-29, 1992.

HAPPY MEAL/FUN FAIR HAPPY MEAL, 1993/1992

- ❏ ❏ UK HM9210 HM BOX, 1992, RON/FRIENDS AT THE BEACH
                                                              $2-3
- ❏ ❏ UK HM9211 HM BOX, 1992, RON/FRIENDS ON A TRICYCLE
                                                              $2-3
- ❏ ❏ JPN HM9201 **BUBBLE BLOWER,** 1992, YEL CIRCLE/PURP
  CIRCLE/RED TRAY/3P $4-6
- ❏ ❏ UK HM9201 **BUBBLE BLOWER,** 1992, YEL CIRCLE W HOLES
  W RED TRAY/2P $3-4
- ❏ ❏ UK HM9202 **GLIDER/AIRPLANE,** 1992, RED BODY/2P YEL
  WINGS W STICKERS/3P $3-4
- ❏ ❏ UK HM9203 **MARKERS/4,** 1992, RED/YEL/BLU/GRN $2-3
- ❏ ❏ UK HM9204 **JUMP ROPE,** 1992, NEON GRN ROPE/PURP
  HANDLES $2-3
- ❏ ❏ UK HM9226 DISPLAY W BOXES, 1992 $15-25
- ❏ ❏ UK HM9265 TRANSLITE/SM, 1992 $4-7

COMMENTS: REGIONAL DISTRIBUTION: JAPAN/UK - 1993/1992;
BELGIUM, DENMARK, FINLAND, FRANCE, GREECE, ITALY,
NORWAY, PORTUGAL, SPAIN, SWEDEN, SWITZERLAND:
JUNE-JULY 1992. PREMIUMS/BOXES USED DURING
CLEAN-UP WEEKS IN JAPAN/UK DURING 1993/1992.
BUBBLE BLOWER MADE IN ITALY. JAPAN ADDED A SEC-
OND RING TO BUBBLE BLOWER FOR LARGER BUBBLES.
JPN HM9201 WAS ALSO GIVEN AS GENERIC PREMIUM IN
JAPAN.

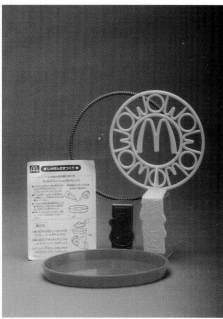

UK HM9201   UK HM9204   UK HM9202

JPN HM9201

USA

HEADSTARTERS HAPPY MEAL, 1992
- ❏ ❏ JPN HE9201 **DOGHOUSE - BIRDIE,** 1992, ON BLU/YEL DOGHOUSE/PUSH CAR $5-$8
- ❏ ❏ JPN HE9202 **TRAIN - GRIMACE,** 1992, ON GRN/PURP/PUSH DOWN TRAIN $5-8
- ❏ ❏ JPN HE9203 **AUTO - HAMBURGLAR,** 1992, ON ORG/PUSH DOWN PEANUTS AUTO $5-8
- ❏ ❏ JPN HE9204 **FIRE ENGINE - RONALD,** 1992, ON RED/YEL FIRE ENGINE/PUSH DOWN $5-8
- ❏ ❏ JPN HE9244 CREW POSTER, 1992, KID'S HAPPY MEALS $7-10

COMMENTS: REGIONAL DISTRIBUTION: JAPAN: 1992. VEHICLES ARE SOMEWHAT SIMILAR TO GERMANY'S PEANUTS JUNION TUTE SELF LIQUIDATOR, 1991.

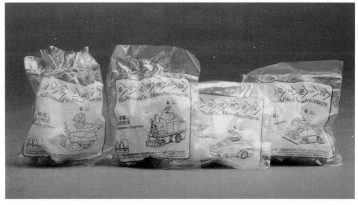

JPN HE9201   JPN HE9202   JPN HE9203   JPN HE9204

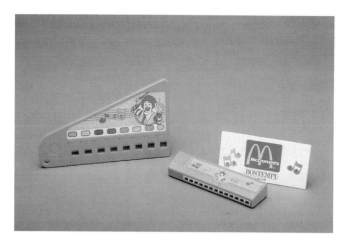

GER MU9203   GER MU9202

GER MU9265

INSTRUMENT/MUSIC IS OUR WORLD/BONTEMPI/ MUSIKINSTRUMENTE JUNIOR TUTE, 1992
- ❑ ❑ GER MU9230 HM BAG, 1992, BRN BAG/JT/INSTUMENTS $3-4
- ❑ ❑ GER MU9201 **MARRACA**/RUMBA RASSEL, 1992, BLU W
  RON PIC $5-7
- ❑ ❑ GER MU9202 **HARMONICA**/MUNDHARMONIKA, 1992, BLU W
  RON PIC $5-7
- ❑ ❑ GER MU9203 **PAN PIPES**/PANFLOTE, 1992, BLU W RON PIC
                                                       $5-7
- ❑ ❑ GER MU9265 TRANSLITE/LG, 1992 $25-40

COMMENTS: NATIONAL DISTRIBUTION: GERMANY: APRIL 9-MAY
  3, 1992.

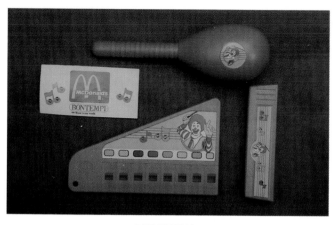

GER MU9201

JAPAN/GENERIC PROMOTION, 1992
- ❑ ❑ JPN GE9210 HM BOX, 1992, CHARS/ROUND TOP $4-5
- ❑ ❑ JPN GE9211 HM BOX, 1992, CHARS/APPLE TREE $4-5
- ❑ ❑ JPN GE9201 **SPIN BALL/RONALD,** 1992, RED TOP/3 GRN
  RINGS/PAPER RON $5-6
- ❑ ❑ JPN GE9202 **MAGNIFIER,** 1992, RED/BLK PAPER $4-5
- ❑ ❑ JPN GE9203 **SQUIRT GUN/BIRDIE,** 1992, YEL $4-6
- ❑ ❑ JPN GE9204 **PICNIC BASKET,** 1992, PNK W UTENSILS/
  PAPER/CUPS $15-20
- ❑ ❑ JPN GE9205 **PLACE MAT,** 1992, RON/CHARS W ARCHES
                                                       $4-6
- ❑ ❑ JPN GE9206 **COLORING BOOK,** 1992, RON AT TREE $3-4
- ❑ ❑ JPN GE9207 **BOAT,** 1992, ORG W STRING $3-4

COMMENTS: REGIONAL DISTRIBUTION: JAPAN: 1992. JPN
  GE9204 IS SIMILAR IN CONCEPT TO AN EARLIER USA
  McDONALD'S ADVERTISEMENT WHICH ENCOURAGES
  FAMILY VALUES AND SHARING TIME TOGETHER.

JPN GE9210

JPN GE9211

JPN GE9202

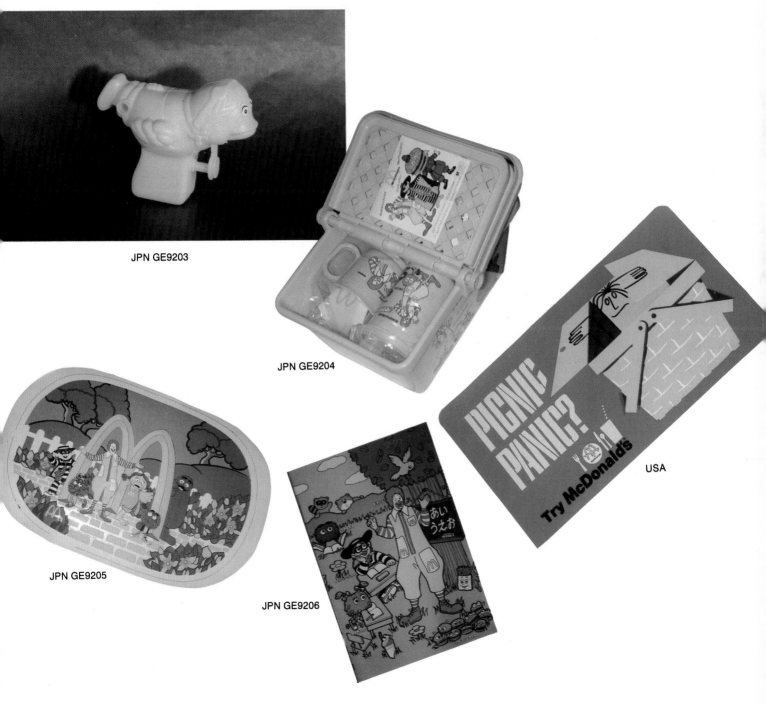

JPN GE9201

JPN GE9207

JPN GE9203

JPN GE9204

USA

JPN GE9205

JPN GE9206

CAN ZO9301-06

JUNGLE ANIMALS HAPPY MEAL, 1992

- ❏ ❏ CAN ZO9301 **ELK,** 1992, GRN 4P ELK $1.50-2.50
- ❏ ❏ CAN ZO9302 **ELEPHANT,** 1992, PURP 4P ELEPHANT
  $1.50-2.50
- ❏ ❏ CAN ZO9303 **GIRAFFE,** 1992, YEL 3P GIRAFFE $1.50-2.50
- ❏ ❏ CAN ZO9304 **MONKEY,** 1992, RED 4P MONKEY $1.50-2.50
- ❏ ❏ CAN ZO9305 **MOOSE,** 1993, BLU 4P MOOSE $1.50-2.50
- ❏ ❏ CAN ZO9306 **OSTRICH,** 1993, PNK 5P OSTRICH $1.50-2.50

COMMENTS: NATIONAL DISTRIBUTION: CANADA: 1992.

MAGIC COLORS/MARKERS/ZAUBERSTIFTE JUNIOR TUTE, 1992

- ❏ ❏ GER ZA9230 HM BAG, 1991, JUNIOR TUTE/MARKERS $3-4
- ❏ ❏ GER ZA9201 **SET 1 MARKERS/4,** 1991, BLK/RED/YEL/WHT
  $4-6
- ❏ ❏ GER ZA9202 **SET 2 MARKERS/4,** 1991, GRN/GRN/YEL/WHT
  $4-6
- ❏ ❏ GER ZA9203 **SET 3 MARKERS/4,** 1991, BRN/BLU/RED/WHT
  $4-6
- ❏ ❏ GER ZA9265 TRANSLITE/LG, 1991 $25-40

COMMENTS: NATIONAL DISTRIBUTION: GERMANY: FEBRUARY 20-MARCH 15, 1992.

MAGNETS HAPPY MEAL, 1992

- ❏ ❏ GER CL9201 **RONALD/BIRDIE,** 1992, SET OF TWO 2"
  MAGNETS W RONALD'S FACE/BIRDIE'S FACE $4-7
- ❏ ❏ GER CL9202 **SHAKY/HAMBURGLAR,** 1992, SET OF TWO 2"
  MAGNETS W SHAKY'S FACE/HAMB'S FACE $4-7

COMMENTS: REGIONAL DISTRIBUTION: GERMANY: 1992 DURING CLEAN-UP WEEKS.

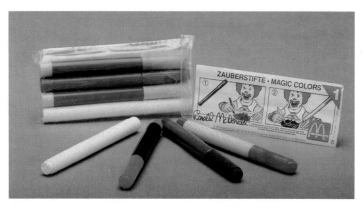

GER ZA9203   GER ZA9201

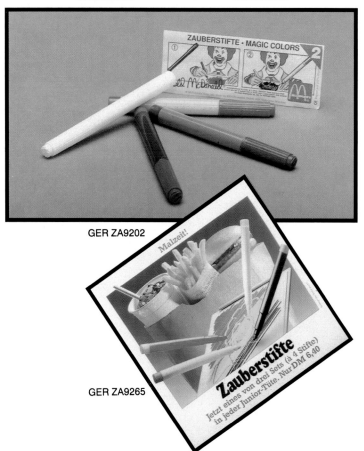

GER ZA9202

GER ZA9265

GER CL9201   GER CL9202

MCBOO BAGS HAPPY MEAL, 1992

- ❏ ❏ USA HA9100 **MCBOO WITCH BAG,** 1991, GRN VINYL BAG
  W ORG HANDLE $1-1.50
- ❏ ❏ USA HA9101 **MCBOO GHOST BAG,** 1991, PUR VINYL BAG
  W YEL HANDLES $1-1.50

COMMENTS: REGIONAL DISTRIBUTION: PANAMA: 1992.

USA HA9100

USA HA9101

TAKE OFF WITH A HAPPY MEAL TODAY!

USA HA9141

MCCHARACTERS ON STRAWS/FIGUREN TRINKHALME PROMOTION, 1992

❑ ❑ GER ST9210 HM BAG, 1992, JUNIOR TUTE/MCD CHARS $3-4
❑ ❑ GER ST9201 **BIRDIE,** 1992, W ORG PULL OUT CENTER $2-3
❑ ❑ GER ST9202 **GRIMACE,** 1992, W PURP PULL CENTER
$2-3
❑ ❑ GER ST9203 **HAMB,** 1992, W YEL PULL OUT CENTER $2-3
❑ ❑ GER ST9204 **RONALD,** 1992, W RED PULL CENTER $2-3

COMMENTS: NATIONAL DISTRIBUTION: GERMANY: 1992.

GERMANY

USA HA9165

GER ST9204

GER ST9201

GER ST9203

GER ST9202

USA MY9265

MCDETECTIVE/MYSTERY/MYSTERY OF THE LOST ARCHES HAPPY MEAL, 1992

❏ ❏ JPN MY9201 **MAGIC LENS CAMERA,** 1991, W SILVER "SEARCH TEAM" DECAL $1-1.25

*** **IDENTICAL TOYS: GUA/JPN MY9202/03/05**
❏ ❏ *** MY9202 **MICRO-CASSETTE/MAGNIFIER,** 1991, GRN W SLIDE OUT MAGNIFIER $1-1.25
❏ ❏ *** MY9203 **PHONE/PERISCOPE,** 1991, ORG PHONE $1-1.25
❏ ❏ *** MY9205 **TELESCOPE,** 1991, RED/YELLOW $1-1.25

COMMENTS: REGIONAL DISTRIBUTION: GUATEMALA: 1992. GUA MY9202/03/05 = USA MY9202/03/05. See USA MYSTERY OF THE LOST ARCHES HAPPY MEAL, 1992.

McDONALDLAND FIGURINES PROMOTION/HAPPY MEAL, 1992

❏ ❏ CAN FI9209 **BIRDIE,** 1992, PNK/STANDING W ARMS FOLDED IN FRONT $2-3
❏ ❏ CAN FI9210 **FRY GIRL,** 1992, BLU/STANDING $2-3
❏ ❏ CAN FI9211 **FRY GUY,** 1992, ORG/STANDING $2-3
❏ ❏ CAN FI9212 **GRIMACE,** 1992, PURP/STANDING $2-3

COMMENTS: REGIONAL DISTRIBUTION: CANADA - 1992.

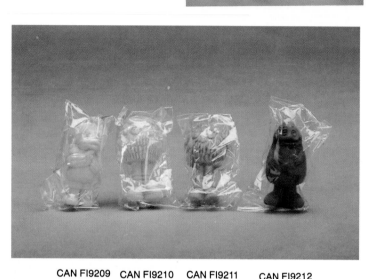

CAN FI9209   CAN FI9210   CAN FI9211   CAN FI9212

McDONALDLAND MAGIC/MAGIA HAPPY MEAL, 1992

*** **IDENTICAL TOYS: MEX/ZEA MA9201/02/03/04**
❏ ❏ *** MA9201 **RONALD W HAT,** 1991, W STRING/FLIPS $5-7
❏ ❏ *** MA9202 **GRIMACE IN MILKSHAKE,** 1991, HIDDEN MILKSHAKE $5-7
❏ ❏ *** MA9203 **BIRDIE W SLIDE OUT FOOD,** 1991, PULL OUT HAMBURGLAR $5-7
❏ ❏ *** MA9204 **FRY GUY ON BOX,** 1991, YEL/RED BOX/4 FRIENDS APPEAR $5-7

COMMENTS: REGIONAL DISTRIBUTION: MEXICO: DECEMBER 1992 AND APRIL 1993; PANAMA: DECEMBER 1992; MALAYSIA, TAIWAN, NEW ZEALAND: MARCH-APRIL 1992; ARGENTINA: MAY 1993; JAPAN TESTED IN OCTOBER 1991 AND RAN IN OCTOBER 1992.

McDONALDLAND PLACEMATS HAPPY MEAL, 1993/1992
*** **IDENTICAL PLACEMATS: AUS/ZEA PL9301/02/03/04**
❏ ❏ *** PL9301 **PLACEMAT - RONALD,** 1992, VINYL/RONALD W BIRDIE/FUN TIMES TWO AT MCD $5-7
❏ ❏ *** PL9302 **PLACEMAT - MCD BAND,** 1992, VINYL/ROCK N ROLL W MCD BAND $5-7
❏ ❏ *** PL9303 **PLACEMAT - SPORTS,** 1992, VINYL/RON/HAMB/ GRI W SPORT ACTIVITIES $5-7
❏ ❏ *** PL9304 **PLACEMAT - ZOO,** 1992, VINYL/RON/HAMB W WHO DO YOU KNOW AT THE ZOO? $5-7

❏ ❏ AUS PL9342 COUNTER CARD, 1992 $4-6

COMMENTS: REGIONAL DISTRIBUTION: NEW ZEALAND: OCTOBER-DECEMBER 1992. REGIONAL DISTRIBUTION: AUSTRALIA: SUMMER 1993.

*** MA9204

AUSTRALIA

AUS PL9342

AUS PL9303

AUS PL9304

AUSTRALIA

AUS PL9301   AUSTRALIA

AUS PL9302

MCROCKIN' FOODS/RAP MACS/HAPPY ROCKERS/ ROCKOMIDA DIVERTIDA/MCMECHANICAL JUNIOR TUTE/HAPPY MEAL, 1993/1992

☐ ☐ GER MC9310 HM BOX, 1992, ON STAGE/4 MCROCKIN' FOODS BAND $2-3
☐ ☐ GER MC9311 HM BOX, 1992, ON TOUR/MCROCKIN' FOODS TOUR BUS $2-3
☐ ☐ FRA BE9030 HM BAG, 1990, RON W SNORKEL $2-3
☐ ☐ HOL MC9330 HM BAG, 1992, 4 HM PREMIUMS $2-3

*** IDENTICAL TOYS: GER/HOL/UK MC9301/02/03/04
☐ ☐ *** MC9301 **CHEESEBURGER,** 1991, CHEESEBURGER HOPS $2-3
☐ ☐ *** MC9302 **FILET-O-FISH,** 1991, FISH "SWIMS W FINS" $2-3
☐ ☐ *** MC9303 **FRIES,** 1991, FRIES MARCHES ALONG $2-3
☐ ☐ *** MC9304 **SHAKE,** 1991, SHAKE DOES THE TWIST $2-3

☐ ☐ UK MC9326 DISPLAY/PREMIUMS, 1992 $75-100
☐ ☐ HOL MC9344 POSTER/SM, 1993 $5-8
☐ ☐ UK MC9364 TRANSLITE/SM, 1992 $4-7
☐ ☐ UK MC9365 TRANSLITE/LG, 1992 $7-10
☐ ☐ GER MC9365 TRANSLITE/LG, 1993 $25-40
☐ ☐ UK MC9366 MESSAGE CENTER CARD/SM, 1992 $3-5
☐ ☐ UK MC9367 MESSAGE CENTER CARD/LG, 1992 $3-5

COMMENTS: NATIONAL DISTRIBUTION: UK: NOVEMBER 27-DECEMBER 1992; GERMANY: SEPTEMBER 2-29, 1993; BELGIUM, DENMARK, FINLAND, FRANCE, GREECE, ITALY, HOLLAND, NORWAY, PORTUGAL, SPAIN, SWEDEN, SWITZERLAND: APRIL 16-MAY 27, 1992; PANAMA: 1992. HOLLAND DISTRIBUTED FRA BE9001 HM BAG, 1990 (RON W SNORKEL) WITH THE HAPPY ROCKERS HAPPY MEAL TOO. CALLED "ROCKOMIDA DIVERTIDA HM" IN SOUTH AMERICA/PANAMA; REGIONAL DISTRIBUTION: HONG KONG: AUGUST 1992; MALAYSIA: OCTOBER-NOVEMBER 1992 AS "MCMECHANICAL"; SINGAPORE: JUNE 1992; TAIWAN: JULY 1992; JAPAN TESTED IN DECEMBER 1991 AND RAN IN DECEMBER- JANUARY 1993.

GER MC9310   GER MC9311

FRA BE9030

HOLLAND

HOL MC9330

HOL MC9301

HOL MC9302   HOL MC9304   HOL MC9303

UK MC9204   UK MC9302   UK ME9301   UK ME9303

HOL MC9344

MCWEATHERMAN KIT/WEERSTATION/METEO HAPPY MEAL, 1993/1992

❏ ❏ HOL WE9230 HM BAG, 1993, RON W WINDMILL/2 X 0 $3-4

    *** IDENTICAL TOYS: HOL/JP/SPA WE9201/02/03/04

❏ ❏ ***** WE9201 RAINGAUGE - BIRDIE,** 1992, REGENMETER
                                  $10-15

❏ ❏ ***** WE9202 THERMOMETER - GRIM,** 1992, TREE/
    TEMPERATUURMETER $10-15

❏ ❏ ***** WE9203 WINDGAUGE - HAMBURGLAR,** 1992,
    WINDMETER $10-15

❏ ❏ ***** WE9204 WEATHER RECORDER - RON,** 1992,
    WEERSTATION $10-15

❏ ❏ HOL WE9255 TRAYLINER, 1992 $1-1.25
❏ ❏ SPA WE9255 TRAYLINER, 1992 $1-1.25

COMMENTS: REGIONAL DISTRIBUTION: JAPAN: 1992; BELGIUM, DENMARK, FINLAND, FRANCE, HOLLAND, ITALY, NORWAY, PORTUGAL, SWITZERLAND: OCTOBER 20-NOVEMBER 30, 1993; SPAIN - 1992; JAPAN: APRIL-MAY 1993; HONG KONG: MAY 1992; SINGAPORE: MAY-JUNE 1993; GUATEMALA: APRIL 1993.

*** WE9201   *** WE9202   *** WE9203   *** WE9204

HOL WE9255

HOL WE9244

SPA WE9255

HOL WE9201

HOL WE9204

MEXICO/GENERIC HAPPY MEAL, 1993/1992
❑ ❑ MEX GE9201 HM BOX, 1992, RONALD ON PHOTO SAFARI
$2-3
❑ ❑ MEX GE9202 HM BOX, 1992, RONALD MOUNTAIN CLIMBING
$2-3
❑ ❑ MEX GE9301 HM BOX, 1993, RONALD IN RED BUMPER CAR
$2-3

COMMENTS: REGIONAL DISTRIBUTION: MEXICO - 1992/1993.
GENERIC HM BOXES USED DURING CLEAN-UP WEEKS.

HOL WE9201   HOL WE9203   HOL WE9204   HOL WE9202

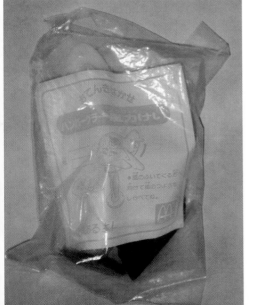

JPN WE9203

HOL WE9202   HOL WE9203

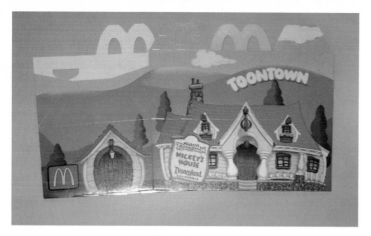

AUS MI9210

JPN MI9210

MICKEY'S/DISNEY TOONTOWN HAPPY MEAL, 1993/1992

❑ ❑ AUS MI9210 HM BOX, 1992, MICKEY'S HOUSE $2-3
❑ ❑ JPN MI9210 HM BOX, 1992, JOLLY TROLLEY $2-3

❑ ❑ AUS MI9201 **FINGER PUPPET - MICKEY,** 1992, WAVING $4-6
❑ ❑ AUS MI9202 **FINGER PUPPET - MINNIE,** 1992, WAVING $4-6
❑ ❑ AUS MI9203 **FINGER PUPPET - GOOFY,** 1992, WAVING $4-6
❑ ❑ AUS MI9204 **FINGER PUPPET - DONALD,** 1992, WAVING $4-6

❑ ❑ MEX MI9301 **MICKEY AS SANTA,** 1993, GRN SHIRT/RED PANTS/STUFFFED DOLL/HARD FACE $10-12
❑ ❑ MEX MI9302 **MINNIE W SANTA HAT,** 1993, RED SANTA HAT/ GRN/WHT DRESS/STUFFED DOLL/HARD FACE $10-12
❑ ❑ MEX MI9303 **GOOFY AS SANTA,** 1993, SANTA COSTUME/ STUFFED FIGURE/HARD FACE $10-12
❑ ❑ MEX MI9304 **DONALD DUCK W SCARF,** 1993, RED/GRN SCARF/STUFFED DOLL/HARD FACE $10-12

COMMENTS: REGIONAL DISTRIBUTION: MEXICO (STUFFED DOLLS): DECEMBER 1993; FINGER PUPPETS: AUSTRALIA: OCTOBER 1994; MALAYSIA: JULY 1992; SINGAPORE: NOVEMBER 1994; GUATEMALA: DECEMBER 1993; EUROPE: 1994; JAPAN: 1992; TAIWAN: MARCH 1994; FINGER PUPPET SET WAS REGIONALLY DISTRIBUTED IN MALAYSIA AND SINGAPORE.

AUS MI9204   AUS MI9203   AUS MI9202   AUS MI9201

MEX MI9303   MEX MI9302   MEX MI9301   MEX MI9304

MUSICAL INSTRUMENTS HAPPY MEAL, 1992

❑ ❑ SIN MU9201 **WHISTLE - BIRDIE,** 1992, PNK/YEL BRID WHISTLE $5-7
❑ ❑ SIN MU9202 **ACCORDIAN - GRIMACE,** 1992, PNK/PURP/ GRN/ACCORDIAN $5-7
❑ ❑ SIN MU9203 **WHISTLE - FRY KID,** 1992, YEL F KID ON STRING $5-7
❑ ❑ SIN MU9204 **PAN PIPES - RONALD,** 1992, WHT W MULTICOLORS $5-7

COMMENTS: REGIONAL DISTRIBUTION: SINGAPORE, JAPAN: 1992.

MEX GE9301

SIN MU9201   SIN MU9203   SIN MU9202

SIN MU9204   SIN MU9203

SIN MU9204

NATURE'S WATCH HAPPY MEAL, 1992

❏ ❏ SIN NA9201 **BIRD FEEDER,** 1991, 3P ORG LID/CLEAR CONT/
YEL BOTTOM $1-1.25
❏ ❏ SIN NA9202 **DOUBLE SHOVEL-RAKE,** 1991, 2P RED
SHOVEL/1P PURP RAKE $1-1.25
❏ ❏ SIN NA9203 **GREENHOUSE,** 1991, 2P CLEAR DOME TOP/
GRN BOT W PKG MARIGOLD SEEDS $1-1.25
❏ ❏ SIN NA9204 **SPRINKLER,** 1991, 1P GRN SPRINKLER CAN W
YEL NOZZLE $1-1.25

COMMENTS: NATIONAL DISTRIBUTION: MARCH: 1993. BIRD
FEEDER SIN NA9201 CAME PACKAGED WITH AND WITH-
OUT 2 CURAD HAPPY STRIP BANDADES. SIN NA9202 =
USA NA9205, LOOSE OUT OF PACKAGE. See USA
NATURE'S WATCH HAPPY MEAL, 1992.

USA NA9226

GER SC9204

USA NA9201   USA NA9202   USA NA9203   USA NA9204

NOISE MAKER/SCHNARREN PROMOTION, 1992

❏ ❏ GER SC9201 **BIRDIE,** 1992, YEL CANISTER W YEL STICK
$3-4
❏ ❏ GER SC9202 **SHAKY,** 1992, PURP CANISTER W YEL STICK
$3-4
❏ ❏ GER SC9203 **HAMBURGLAR,** 1992, BLK CANISTER W YEL
PLAS STICK $3-4
❏ ❏ GER SC9204 **RONALD,** 1992, RED CANISTER W YEL PLAS
STICK $3-4

COMMENTS: REGIONAL DISTRIBUTION: GERMANY: 1992.

NOTE TRAY/NOTE PAPER PROMOTION, 1992

❏ ❏ GER NO9201 **NOTE TRAY - RONALD,** 1992, YEL W NOTE
PAPER 2P $4-7
❏ ❏ GER NO9202 **NOTE TRAY - RONALD,** 1992, RED W NOTE
PAPER 2P $4-7

COMMENTS: REGIONAL PROMOTION: GERMANY/EUROPE: 1992.

GER NO9202   GER NO9201

*** PA9201 *** PA9202   *** PA9204   *** PA9203

PAPER MARK/PAPIER MAKEN HAPPY MEAL, 1992

*** IDENTICAL TOYS: GER/UK PA9201/02/03/04
- ❑ ❑ *** PA9201 **PAPER MARK - RONALD,** 1992, RED/IMPRINTS RONALD'S FACE $5-8
- ❑ ❑ *** PA9202 **PAPER MARK - SHAKY,** 1992, PURP/IMPRINTS SHAKY'S FACE $5-8
- ❑ ❑ *** PA9203 **PAPER MARK - BIRDIE,** 1992, PNK/IMPRINTS BIRDIE'S FACE $5-8
- ❑ ❑ *** PA9204 **PAPER MARK - HAMB,** 1992, WHT/IMPRINTS HAMB'S FACE $5-8

COMMENTS: REGIONAL DISTRIBUTION: UK/EUROPE: 1992. DISTRIBUTED DURING CLEAN-UP WEEKS. NOTE: COUNTRY DESIGNATION (INITIAL(S)) ON BOTTOM LEFT HAND CORNER OF PAPER INSERT OF UNDER PICTURE OF RONALD'S FOOT—i.e. UK - ENGLAND; F - FRANCE; NL - NETHERLANDS.

PARACHUTE/FALLSCHIRMSPRINGER PROMOTION, 1992
- ❑ ❑ GER PC9201 **RONALD,** 1992, FIGURINE W RED PARACHUTE/STRING/2P $7-10
- ❑ ❑ GER PC9202 **BIRDIE,** 1992, FIGURINE W YEL PARACHUTE/STRING/2P $7-10

COMMENTS: REGIONAL DISTRIBUTION: GERMANY: 1992.

PLAY-DOH JUNIOR TUTE, 1992
- ❑ ❑ GER PL9201 **BLUE PLAY-DOH,** 1992, YEL CONT/BLU LID/ 2 OZ $4-5
- ❑ ❑ GER PL9202 **PINK PLAY-DOH,** 1992, YEL CONT/PINK LID/ 2 OZ $4-5
- ❑ ❑ GER PL9203 **YELLOW PLAY-DOH,** 1992, YEL CONT/YEL LID/ 2 OZ $4-5
- ❑ ❑ GER PL9204 **WHITE PLAY-DOH,** 1992, YEL CONT/WHT LID/ 2 OZ $4-5
- ❑ ❑ GER PL9265 TRANSLITE/LG, 1992 $25-40

COMMENTS: NATIONAL DISTRIBUTION: GERMANY: OCTOBER 15-NOVEMBER 8, 1992; BELGIUM, DENMARK, FINLAND, FRANCE, ITALY, HOLLAND, NORWAY, SPAIN, SWEDEN, SWITZERLAND: 1992.

POTATO HEAD KIDS II HAPPY MEAL, 1992
- ❑ ❑ GUA PO9201 **DIMPLES,** 1986, W BLU/YEL HAT/PURP SHOES/3P $2.50-3.50
- ❑ ❑ GUA PO9204 **SLUGGER,** 1986, W BASEBALL GLOVE/BLU HAT/YEL SHOES/3P $2.50-3.50
- ❑ ❑ GUA PO9206 **TULIP,** 1986, W PNK HAT/BLU SHOES/3P $2.50-3.50
- ❑ ❑ GUA PO9207 **POTATO PUFF,** 1986, W PNK HAT/PURP SHOES/3P $2.50-3.50

COMMENTS: REGIONAL DISTRIBUTION: GUATEMALA: 1992.

GER PC9201   GER PC9202

Play-Doh Spielknete
Jetzt eine Dose in jeder Junior-Tüte! Nur

GER PL9201

GER PL9202

GER PL9203

USA PO9206

USA PO9201

USA PO9204

USA PO9207

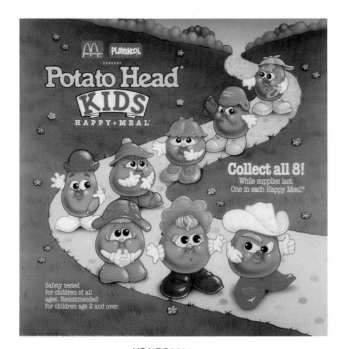

USA PO9265

AUS RE9201   AUS RE9202   AUS RE9205
          AUS RE9204   AUS RE9203

RESCUE RANGERS/DISNEY CHARACTERS PROMO-TION, 1994/1993/1992

❑ ❑ AUS RE9201 **ARMOUR DUCK,** 1992, 1" BLU FIGURINE $3-4
❑ ❑ AUS RE9202 **SCROOGE,** 1992, 1" BLU FIGURINE $3-4
❑ ❑ AUS RE9203 **WEBBY,** 1992, 1" YEL FIGURINE $3-4
❑ ❑ AUS RE9204 **NEPHEW,** 1992, 1" ORG FIGURINE $3-4
❑ ❑ AUS RE9205 **MONTERAY JACK,** 1992, 1" BLU FIGURINE $3-4

COMMENTS: REGIONAL DISTRIBUTION: AUSTRALIA: APRIL/MAY 1992 AND AGAIN IN 1993; SINGAPORE: OCTOBER 1991. FIGURINES ARE SAME AS USA CEREAL BOX PREMIUMS EXCEPT LOGO ON BOTTOM IS BLANKED OUT. OTHER VARIATIONS/SIZES OF THESE FIGURINES MAY EXIST.

JPN SC9201

SCHOOL DAYS HAPPY MEAL, 1992

❑ ❑ JPN SC9201 **PROTRACTOR - RONALD,** 1992, W MOVING FOOD SELECTION $8-12

COMMENTS: REGIONAL DISTRIBUTION: JAPAN - 1992.

SEARCH & WIN/GRATIEZ & GAGNEZ/EURO DISNEY SCRATCH CARD PROMOTION, 1992

*** IDENTICAL CARDS: FRA/UK CA9201/02/03/04
❑ ❑ *** CA9201 **ADVENTURE LAND,** 1992, RED SCRATCH CARD
$1-1.25
❑ ❑ *** CA9202 **DISCOVERY LAND,** 1992, PURP SCRATCH CARD
$1-1.25
❑ ❑ *** CA9203 **FANTASY LAND,** 1992, BLU SCRATCH CARD
$1-1.25
❑ ❑ *** CA9204 **FRONTIER LAND,** 1992, GRN SCRATCH CARD
$1-1.25

❑ ❑ UK CA9242 COUNTER CARD, 1992 $3-4
❑ ❑ UK CA9251 MUG, 1992, BLK W DISNEY LOGO $5-7

COMMENTS: REGIONAL DISTRIBUTION: UK - 1992. FREE WITH A VISIT.

UK CA9201

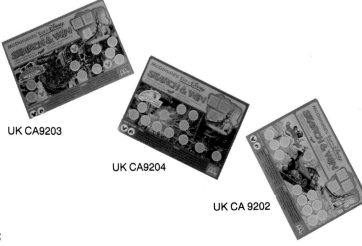

UK CA9203

UK CA9204

UK CA 9202

FRA CA9242

❏ ❏ GER SE9201 **BIRDIE**, 1992, IN PNK AUTO $5-7
❏ ❏ GER SE9202 **RONALD**, 1992, IN RED AUTO $5-7

COMMENTS: REGIONAL DISTRIBUTION: GERMANY/HONG
KONG/USA - 1992. PACKAGE SAYS, "MADE IN CHINA...FOR
WEDO PROM...GERMANY. MELROSE PARK,
IL...USA...KOWLOON HONG KONG".

SOMMERSPIELE/SUMMER GAMES JUNIOR TUTE, 1992

❏ ❏ GER SO9210 HM BAG, 1992, JUNIOR TUTE/SPORTS $2-3
❏ ❏ GER SO9201 **PADDLE/BALL**, 1992, BLU PING PONG
PADDLE W YEL BALL $3-5
❏ ❏ GER SO9202 **FRISBEE**, 1992, PNK/BLK W LOGO $3-5
❏ ❏ GER SO9204 **FEATHER DART**, 1992, STUFFED/WHT-BLK W
5 RED FEATHERS $3-5
❏ ❏ GER SO9265 TRANSLITE/LG, 1992 $25-40

COMMENTS: NATIONAL DISTRIBUTION: GERMANY: JUNE 4-28,
1992.

FRA SE9201   FRA SE9202

GER SO9265

GER SO9202

UK SP9210   UK SP9211   UK SP9212   UK SP9213

**SPACE LAUNCHERS/ASTRO MACS/MCD/DE
ASTRONAUTJES/MCCOPTERS/MCSPACE LAUNCHERS
JUNIOR TUTE/HAPPY MEAL, 1994/1993/1992**

*** **IDENTICAL BOXES: GER/UK SP9210/11/12/13**
❏ ❏ *** SP9210 HM BOX, 1993, ROCKET LAUNCH PAD/VOLCANO
W "FOLD BACK" TABS/BLAST OFF $2-3
❏ ❏ *** SP9211 HM BOX, 1993, ROCKETSHIP/MOON BUGGY $2-3
❏ ❏ *** SP9212 HM BOX, 1993, ETV/LANDING/DOCKING BAY $2-
❏ ❏ *** SP9213 HM BOX, 1993, SPACE STATION BRIDGE $2-3

*** **IDENTICAL TOYS: FRA/GER/HOL/JPN/UK SP9301/02/03/04
04**
❏ ❏ *** SP9201 **BIRDIE/LAUNCH**, 1992, IN RED SPACE SUIT W
BLU LAUNCHER/2P $3-4
❏ ❏ *** SP9202 **FRY GIRL/LAUNCH**, 1992, IN RED CAPSUL W
YEL LAUNCHER/2P $3-4
❏ ❏ *** SP9203 **GRIMACE/LAUNCH**, 1992, IN PURP SPACE SUIT
W YEL ROCKET/YEL LAUNCHER/3P $3-4
❏ ❏ *** SP9204 **RONALD/LAUNCH**, 1992, IN WHT SPACE
CAPSUL W RED LAUNCHER/3P $3-4

		UK SP9226 DISPLAY/PREMIUMS, 1993	$75-100
☐	☐	UK SP9226 DISPLAY/PREMIUMS, 1993	$75-100
☐	☐	FRA SP9244 POSTER, 1993	$12-20
☐	☐	HOL SP9244 POSTER, 1993	$12-20
☐	☐	UK SP9264 TRANSLITE/SM, 1993	$5-8
☐	☐	UK SP9265 TRANSLITE/LG, 1993	$12-20
☐	☐	GER SP9265 TRANSLITE/LG, 1993	$25-40

COMMENTS: NATIONAL DISTRIBUTION: UK, ARGENTINA: AUGUST 13, 1993; FRANCE: NOVEMBER 1992; GERMANY: MAY 1994; BELGIUM, DENMARK, FINLAND, GREECE, HOLLAND, NORWAY, PORTUGAL, SPAIN, SWEDEN, SWITZERLAND: NOVEMBER 5-DECEMBER 16, 1992; KOREA: APRIL 1994; JAPAN: TESTED IN APRIL 1993 AND RAN IN MARCH 1994; MEXICO - FEBRUARY 1994; INDONESIA: SEPTEMBER 1994; HONG KONG: DECEMBER 1992; SINGAPORE: AUGUST 1993; NEW ZEALAND: OCTOBER 1993; GUATEMALA: 1994; GERMANY: MAY 1994; CHILE, VENEZUELA: MAY 1993. CALLED "SPACE LAUNCHERS HM" IN UK; "McDONALD'S HM/ASTRO MACS" IN GERMANY; "DE ASTRONAUTJES HM" IN HOLLAND; "MCCOPTERS" IN FRANCE; "MCSPACE LAUNCHERS" IN JAPAN.

GER SP9210

HOL SP9201   HOL SP9202   HOL SP9203   HOL SP9204

GER SP9201

FRA SP9244

UK

HOL SP9244

157

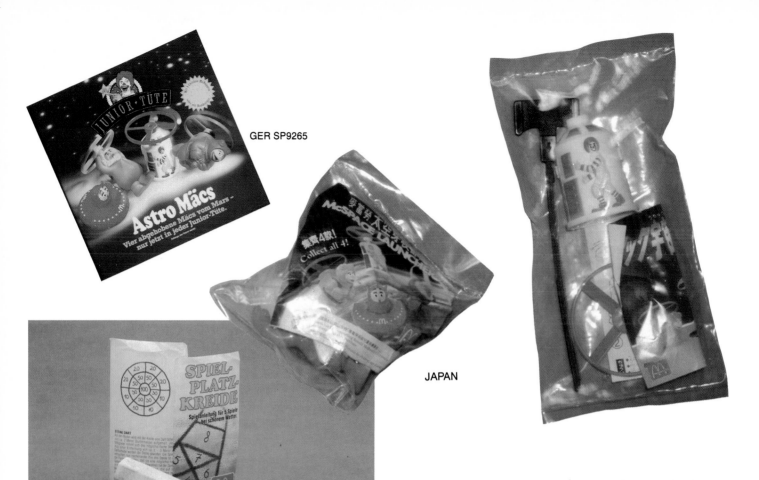

GER SP9265

JAPAN

GER CH9202

SPIEL-PLATZ-KREIDE/SPIELANLEITUNG PROMOTION, 1992
❑ ❑ GER CH9202 **CHALK,** 1992, PURP AND WHT CHALK FOR
SIDEWALK GAMES/2P $3-4

COMMENTS: REGIONAL DISTRIBUTION: GERMANY - 1992
DURING CLEAN-UP WEEKS.

SPIN TOPS/KREISEL PROMOTION, 1994/1993/1992
❑ ❑ AUS SP9301 **SPIN TOP - BIRDIE,** ND, FLAT TOP/THIN $1.50-2
❑ ❑ AUS SP9302 **SPIN TOP - GRIMACE,** ND, FLAT TOP/THIN
$1.50-2
❑ ❑ AUS SP9303 **SPIN TOP - HAMBUR,** ND, FLAT TOP/THIN
$1.50-2
❑ ❑ AUS SP9304 **SPIN TOP - RONALD,** ND, FLAT TOP/THIN
$1.50-2

*** IDENTICAL TOPS: AUS/FRA/GER SP9305/06/07/08/09
❑ ❑ *** SP9205 **SPIN TOP - BIRDIE,** 1992, BUBBLE TOP/THICK
$1.50-2
❑ ❑ *** SP9206 **SPIN TOP - GRIMACE,** 1992, BUBBLE TOP/THICK
$1.50-2
❑ ❑ *** SP9207 **SPIN TOP - HAMBUR,** 1992, BUBBLE TOP/THICK
$1.50-2
❑ ❑ *** SP9208 **SPIN TOP - RONALD,** 1992, BUBBLE TOP/THICK
$1.50-2
❑ ❑ *** SP9209 **SPIN TOP - FRY KID,** 1992, BUBBLE TOP/THICK
$1.50-2

COMMENTS: REGIONAL DISTRIBUTION: AUSTRALIA, FRANCE,
GERMANY: 1992/1993/1994. GIVEN AS CLEAN-UP PREMI-
UMS AND FOR U-5 CHILREN.

AUS SP9301   AUS SP9304   AUS SP9302
AUS SP9303

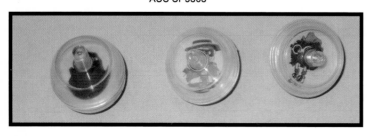

*** SP9206   *** SP9207   *** SP9209

SPORTS BALL HAPPY MEAL, 1992

*** IDENTICAL TOYS: AUS/ZEA SP9201/02/04
- ❏ ❏ *** SB9201 **CRICKET BALL,** 1992, RED W YEL STRIPES/ LOGO $2.50-3
- ❏ ❏ *** SB9202 **BASKETBALL,** 1992, ORG W BLK STRIPES/ LOGO $2.50-3
- ❏ ❏ *** SB9204 **SOCCER BALL,** 1992, BLK/WHT W YEL LOGO $2.50-3

- ❏ ❏ AUS SB9203 **RUGBY BALL,** 1992, **YEL W WHT TIES**/RED LOGO $2.50-3
- ❏ ❏ ZEA SB9203 **RUGBY BALL,** 1992, **RED W WHT TIES**/GOLD LOGO $2.50-3

COMMENTS: NATIONAL DISTRIBUTION: AUSTRALIA - JANUARY/ FEBRUARY 1992; NEW ZEALAND - JANUARY/APRIL 1992; REGIONAL DISTRIBUTION: MEXICO: APRIL 1991. BALLS WERE DISTRIBUTED WITHOUT A WHITE TAG IDENTIFICATION MARKING. DIFFERENT RUGBY BALLS (USA FOOTBALLS) WERE DISTRIBUTED IN DIFFERENT COUNTRIES. DIFFERENT MONTHS OF DISTRIBUTION IN DIFFERENT COUNTRIES DUE TO REPETITIVE DISTRIBUTION IN SOME COUNTRIES.

SPORTS BUDDIES HAPPY MEAL, 1992
- ❏ ❏ UK BU9210 HM BOX, 1992, HAMMER THROWER/COMPETITION AREA $2-3
- ❏ ❏ UK BU9211 HM BOX, 1992, JAVELIN THROWER/STADIUM ENTRANCE $2-3
- ❏ ❏ UK BU9212 HM BOX, 1992, TRACK/RELAY RUNNER AND FINISHING TAPE $2-3
- ❏ ❏ UK BU9213 HM BOX, 1992, WEIGHT LIFTER/WEIGHT LIFTER'S CHAMPIONSHIP $2-3

- ❏ ❏ UK BU9201 **HAMMER THROWER,** 1991, BLK HAIR/YEL ROPE/GRN HEADBAND/3P $2-4
- ❏ ❏ UK BU9202 **JAVELIN THROWER,** 1991, BRN HAIR/BLU SHOES/ORG HEADBAND/PNK SHORTS/3P $2-4
- ❏ ❏ UK BU9203 **TRACK/RELAY RUNNER,** 1991, RED HAIR/PINK SHORTS/WHT SHOES/3P $2-4
- ❏ ❏ UK BU9204 **WEIGHT LIFTER,** 1991, YEL HAIR W BLU WEIGHTS/PINK-MAGENTA BELT/3P $2-4

- ❏ ❏ UK BU9264 TRANSLITE/SM, 1991, $4-7
- ❏ ❏ UK BU9265 TRANSLITE/LG, 1991 $8-12
- ❏ ❏ UK BU9266 MAGNETIC C CARD, 1991 $4-5

COMMENTS: NATIONAL DISTRIBUTION: UK: JUNE 12, 1992; SCOTLAND/WALES: JUNE/JULY 1992' SINGAPORE: JULY 1992; JAPAN: JULY 1992.

AUS SB9204   AUS SB9202   AUS SB9201   AUS SB9203

ZEA SB9203

NEW ZEALAND

UK BU9210

UK BU9213

UK BU9201   UK BU9202   UK BU9203   UK BU9204

UK BU9212

159

SQUIRT BALLS/AQUA BALLS PROMOTION, 1992

- ❏ ❏ GER SQ9201 **CROCODILE,** 1992, GRN $2-3
- ❏ ❏ GER SQ9202 **PIG,** 1992, PINK $2-3
- ❏ ❏ GER SQ9203 **POLAR BEAR,** 1992, WHT $2-3
- ❏ ❏ GER SQ9204 **HORSE,** 1992, YEL $2-3
- ❏ ❏ GER SQ9205 **SHEEP,** 1992, WHT $2-3
- ❏ ❏ GER SQ9206 **LION,** 1992, YEL $2-3
- ❏ ❏ GER SQ9207 **SHARK,** 1992, PURP $2-3
- ❏ ❏ GER SQ9208 **TURTLE,** 1992, GRN $2-3
- ❏ ❏ GER SQ9209 **WHALE,** 1992, BLU $2-3
- ❏ ❏ GER SQ9210 **ELEPHANT,** 1992, PINK $2-3
- ❏ ❏ GER SQ9211 **HIPPO,** 1992, PURPLE $2-3
- ❏ ❏ GER SQ9212 **COW,** 1992, BLK/WHT $2-3
- ❏ ❏ GER SQ9213 **CHICKEN,** 1992, YEL $2-3
- ❏ ❏ GER SQ9214 **RABBIT,** 1992, WHT $2-3
- ❏ ❏ GER SQ9215 **FISH,** 1992, GRN $2-3
- ❏ ❏ GER SQ9216 **DINOSAUR,** 1992, PURP $2-3

COMMENTS: NATIONAL DISTRIBUTION: GERMANY: 1992. AT LEAST 16 DIFFERENT WATER SQUIRT BALL FIGURINES WERE GIVEN OUT. PREMIUMS ARE ALL APPROXIMATELY 2" RUBBER SQUIRT AQUABALLS.

GER SQ9206   GER SQ9215   GER SQ9202

GER SQ9213   GER SQ9205   GER SQ9201   GER SQ9210

STAMP PAD PROMOTION, 1992

- ❏ ❏ AUS ST9201 **STAMP PAD - BIRDIE,** 1992, FACE ON TRIANGLE STAMP PAD/2P $5-7
- ❏ ❏ AUS ST9202 **STAMP PAD - GRIMACE,** 1992, FACE ON TRIANGLE STAMP PAD/2P $5-7
- ❏ ❏ AUS ST9203 **STAMP PAD - HAMBURGLAR,** 1992, FACE ON TRIANGLE STAMP PAD/2P $5-7
- ❏ ❏ AUS ST9204 **STAMP PAD - RONALD,** 1992, FACE ON TRIANGLE STAMP PAD/2P $5-7

COMMENTS: REGIONAL DISTRIBUTION: AUSTRALIA - JUNE 1992.

GER SQ9212   GER SQ9208   GER SQ9209   GER SQ9211

AUS ST9204

GER SQ9204   GEh SQ9203

*** ST9202   *** ST9203

STENCIL/ZAUBERSCHREIBER PROMOTION, 1992

*** IDENTICAL TOYS: EUROPE

- ❏ ❏ *** ST9201 **STENCIL/RONALD,** 1992, YEL STENCIL/ORG DISC/2P $3-5
- ❏ ❏ *** ST9202 **STENCIL/RONALD,** 1992, RED/RON CUTOUT/ PENCIL HOLDER $3-5
- ❏ ❏ *** ST9203 **STENCIL/RONALD,** 1992, YEL/RON CUTOUT/ PENCIL HOLDER $3-5

COMMENTS: REGIONAL DISTRIBUTION: GERMANY/ CESKOSLOVENSKY/FRANCAIS/MAGYAR/POLSKI/ PYCCKNN/SRPSKOHRVATSKI LANGUAGES - 1992. HOLLAND PAPER INSERT IS MARKED, "NL" FOR NETHERLANDS.

SUPER BALOO/TALE SPIN/RESCUE RANGERS/KAPT'N BALU/BALOO EN Z'N VRIENDJES HAPPY MEAL, 1993/1992

*** IDENTICAL BOXES: GER/HOL/UK TA/SU9210/11/12/13
- ❏ ❏ *** SU9210 HM BOX, 1992, BARN/AIRPLANE HANGAR $2-3
- ❏ ❏ *** SU9211 HM BOX, 1992, WATER FALLS/CLIFF/SEA SHORE $2-3
- ❏ ❏ *** SU9212 HM BOX, 1992, AIRPLANE/COCKPIT/CONTROLS $2-3
- ❏ ❏ *** SU9213 HM BOX, 1992, GRASS HUT/JUNGLE BAR/THATCH HUT FOR LOUIS $2-3

*** IDENTICAL TOY: GER/HOL/ZEA/UK TA9201
- ❏ ❏ *** TA9201 **KAPT'N BALU,** 1992, YEL SHIRT/BALOO BEAR STANDING $2-3

*** IDENTICAL TOYS: GER/HOL/ZEA/UK TA9202/03
- ❏ ❏ *** TA9202 **KIT IN RACING PLANE**, 1992, IN RED/BLU PLASTIC RACING PLANE $2-3
- ❏ ❏ *** TA9203 **LOUIE,** 1992, ORG ORANGUTAN/GRN SHIRT $2-3

*** IDENTICAL TOYS: HOL/ZEA/UK TA9304
- ❏ ❏ *** TA9204 **MOLLY IN BI-PLANE,** 1992, IN RED/YEL/ORG BI-PLANE $2-3

- ❏ ❏ UK TA9226 DISPLAY W PREMIUMS, 1992 $20-35
- ❏ ❏ UK TA9244 CREW POSTER, 1992 $4-7
- ❏ ❏ UK TA9264 TRANSLITE/TALE SPIN/SM, 1992 $15-20
- ❏ ❏ UK TA9265 TRANSLITE/TALE SPIN/LG, 1992 $25-35
- ❏ ❏ GER TA9265 TRANSLITE/KAPT'N BALU/LG, 1992 $25-40
- ❏ ❏ UK TA9266 M C CARD/MAGNETIC/SM, 1992 $4-7
- ❏ ❏ UK TA9267 M C CARD/MAGNETIC/LG, 1992 $8-12

COMMENTS: NATIONAL DISTRIBUTION: GERMANY: AUGUST 6-26, 1992; UK: JANUARY 1, 1993; BELGIUM, DENMARK, FINLAND, FRANCE, ITALY, HOLLAND, NORWAY, PORTUGAL, SPAIN, SWEDEN, SWITZERLAND: SEPTEMBER 24-NOVEMBER 4, 1992. AUSTRALIA REGIONAL DISTRIBUTION: MAY-JUNE 1993; REGIONAL DISTRIBUTION: EUROPE: OCTOBER 1992. NATIONAL DISTRIBUTION: NEW ZEALAND: JUNE-JULY 1992. CALLED "KAPT'N BALLU" IN GERMANY AND SUPER BALOO; CALLED TALESPIN IN UNITED KINGDOM; CALLED SUPER BALOO IN HOLLAND. SU = SUPER BALOO = TALESPIN . THIS HAPPY MEAL HAD DIFFERENT NAMES IN DIFFERENT COUNTRIES; DIFFERENT PACKAGING. TA9201-04 AND SU9201-04 ARE SIMILAR TO USA TA9001-04. GER SU9210/11/12/13 AND GER TA9310 HM BOXES WERE NOT DISTRIBUTED IN GERMANY; THEY WERE MADE IN GERMANY, DISTRIBUTED IN OTHER EUROPEAN COUNTRIES.

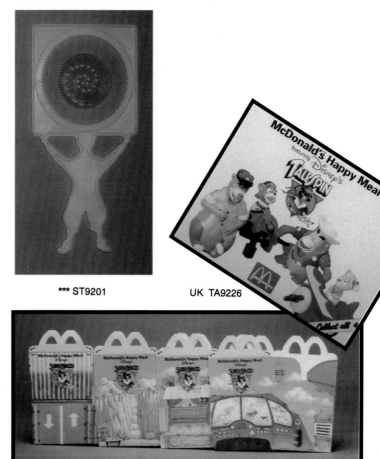

*** ST9201   UK TA9226

UK SU9210   UK SU9211   UK SU9212   UK SU9213

UK TA9201   UK TA9203   UK TA9202   UK TA9204

GER TA9265

HOLLAND

GER TA9201   GER TA9203   GER TA9202

CAN TI9202 CAN TI9204 CAN TI9217

CAN TI9201 CAN TI9203 CAN TI9215 CAN TI9216 CAN TI9218

USA TI9264

AUS TU9245

TINY TOON ADVENTURES HAPPY MEAL, 1994/1992

❑ ❑ CAN TI9210 HM BOX, 1992, ARCTIC $1-2
❑ ❑ CAN TI9211 HM BOX, 1992, CAFE/WACKYLAND $1-2
❑ ❑ CAN TI9212 HM BOX, 1992, FOREST/REDWOOD $1-2
❑ ❑ CAN TI9213 HM BOX, 1992, JUNGLE $1-2

❑ ❑ CAN TI9201 **BABS BUNNY,** 1992, PINK BUNNY W TINY
TOONS RECORD PLAYER IN BUBBLE $1-2
❑ ❑ CAN TI9202 **BUSTER BUNNY,** 1992, BLU BUNNY IN RED
BUMPER CAR/BASKETBALL BUBBLE $1-2
❑ ❑ CAN TI9203 **DIZZY DEVIL,** 1992, PUR DIZZY DEVIL IN
BUBBLE CAR $4-5
❑ ❑ CAN TI9204 **ELMYRA,** 1992, GIRL W YEL HAT IN GRN CAR W
BUNNY IN BUBBLE $4-5
❑ ❑ CAN TI9215 **GOGO DODO,** 1992, GRN GOGO DODO ON YEL
3 WHEEL ROLLER $4-5
❑ ❑ CAN TI9216 **MONTANA MAX,** 1992, MAX IN GRN CASH
REGISTER CAR $4-5
❑ ❑ CAN TI9217 **PLUCKY DUCK,** 1992, PLUCKY IN BLU STEAM
ROLLER CAR $4-5
❑ ❑ CAN TI9218 **SWEETIE,** 1992, PINK BUNNY ON PAVEMENT
ROLLER $4-5

COMMENTS: NATIONAL DISTRIBUTION: CANADA: OCTOBER-
NOVEMBER 1992; MEXICO, COSTA RICA: JANUARY 1992;
PUERTO RICO: FEBRUARY 1991. See USA TINY TOON
ADVENTURES II HAPPY MEAL, 1992.

TUMBLER HAPPY MEAL, 1992

❑ ❑ AUS TU9201 **CUP - RON AT THE BEACH,** 1992, RON/GRI AT
BEACH $3-5
❑ ❑ AUS TU9202 **CUP - RON CAMPING,** 1992, RON/BIRDIE/
HAMB PUTTING UP TENT $3-5
❑ ❑ AUS TU9203 **CUP - RON WITH A KITE,** 1992, RON/FRY GIRL
FLYING A KITE $3-5
❑ ❑ AUS TU9245 REGISTER TOPPER, 1992 $8-12

COMMENTS: REGIONAL DISTRIBUTION: AUSTRALIA: 1992.

WALL PLAQUES/CHARACTERS PROMOTION, 1992

❑ ❑ AUS WP9201 **BIRDIE,** 1992, VACUFORM/BIRDIE FLYING/LG
$8-10
❑ ❑ AUS WP9202 **GRIMACE,** 1992, VACUFORM/GRI BATTING/LG
$8-10
❑ ❑ AUS WP9203 **HAMB,** 1992, VACUFORM/HAMB/LG $8-10
❑ ❑ AUS WP9204 **RONALD,** 1992, VACUFORM/RONALD/LG $8-10
❑ ❑ ZEA WP9201 **BIRDIE,** 1992, VACUFORM/BIRDIE FLYING/SM
$8-10
❑ ❑ ZEA WP9202 **GRIMACE,** 1992, VACUFORM/GRI BATTING/SM
$8-10
❑ ❑ ZEA WP9203 **HAMB,** 1992, VACUFORM/HAMB/SM $8-10
❑ ❑ ZEA WP9204 **RONALD,** 1992, VACUFORM/RONALD/SM $8-10

COMMENTS: REGIONAL DISTRIBUTION: AUSTRALIA: 1992; NEW
ZEALAND: FEBRUARY 1992. WALL PLAQUES VARY IN
SIZES IN THE DIFFERENT COUNTRIES DISTRIBUTED.

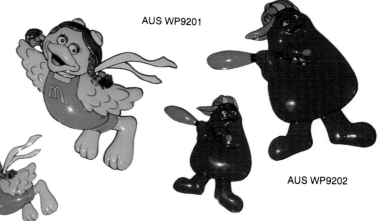

AUS WP9201

AUS WP9202

AUS WP9201

AUS WP9202

WATER CIRCUS/LOS MACUATICOS HAPPY MEAL, 1993/1992

    *** **IDENTICAL TOYS: JPN/LATIN AMERICA WA9201/02/03/ 04**

❏ ❏ *** WA9201 **BOAT/WHISTLE,** 1992, BIRDIE/SQUIRTER $3-4

❏ ❏ *** WA9202 **SQUIRT/SPIN,** 1992, GRIMACE/SQUIRTER $3-4

❏ ❏ *** WA9203 **SQUIRT/TURN/POUR,** 1992, HAMBURGLAR/ SQUIRTER $3-4

❏ ❏ *** WA9204 **HOLDING UMBRELLA,** 1992, RONALD/ SQUIRTER $3-4

COMMENTS: REGIONAL DISTRIBUTION: JAPAN: 1992; LATIN AMERICA: 1993, CALLED "LOS MACUATICOS".

YO, YOGI! HAPPY MEAL, 1992

❏ ❏ CAN YO9201 **LAF 1 - YO, YOGI,** 1992, ON GRN/ORG SCOOTER $3-4

❏ ❏ CAN YO9202 **LAF 2 - CINDY BEAR/CINDY,** 1992, ON GRN SCOOTER $3-4

❏ ❏ CAN YO9203 **LAF 3 - HUCKLEBERRY HOUND,** 1992, ON SOAP BOX DERBY CAR $3-4

❏ ❏ CAN YO9204 **LAF 4 - BOO BOO,** 1992, ON BLU/YEL SKATE BOARD $3-4

❏ ❏ CAN YO9240 TRAYLINER, 1992, COLLECT ALL FOUR!/59 CENTS $1-1.50

❏ ❏ CAN YO9252 REGISTER TOPPER, 1992, YO, YOGI!/REV-UP ACTION TOYS/59 CENTS $2-4

COMMENTS: NATIONAL DISTRIBUTION: CANADA: 1992.

AUS WP9204   AUS WP9203

CAN YO9201   CAN YO9203   CAN YO9202   CAN YO9204

CAN YO9240

CANADA

CANADA

USA   HOLLAND

GER AL9310

GER AL9311

GER AL9312

GER AL9313

AUS AL9310

ALADDIN/SAGENHAFTEN TRINKBECHERN/STRAW GRIPPERS JUNIOR TUTE/HAPPY MEAL, 1994/1993

❑	❑	AUS AL9310 HM BOX, 1993, ALADDIN/JASMINE ON MAGIC CARPET	$2-3
❑	❑	GER AL9310 HM BOX, 1993, PALACE	$2-3
❑	❑	GER AL9311 HM BOX, 1993, GOLD/TIGER MOUTH	$2-3
❑	❑	GER AL9312 HM BOX, 1993, DANCING GIRLS	$2-3
❑	❑	GER AL9313 HM BOX, 1993, TREASURE	$2-3
❑	❑	*** AL9310 HM BOX, 1993, SPANISH	$2-3
❑	❑	GER AL9330 HM BAG, 1993, MOVIE SCENE	$1-1.25

*** IDENTICAL TOYS: DEN/UK AL9301/02/03/04

❑	❑	*** AL9301 **ALADDIN/JASMINE,** 1993, ON MAGIC RUG	$4-7
❑	❑	*** AL9302 **GENIE,** 1993, IN MAGIC BOTTLE	$4-7
❑	❑	*** AL9303 **JAFAR,** 1993, BLK CAPE/STANDING	$4-7
❑	❑	*** AL9304 **SULTAN,** 1993, SITTING/FOLDED ARMS	$4-7

❑	❑	AUS AL9401 **ALADDIN,** 1993, 2.5"/W RT ARM RAISED/WHT PANTS	$5-7
❑	❑	AUS AL9402 **JASMINE,** 1993, 2"/W RT ARM RAISED/TURQ PANTS	$5-7
❑	❑	AUS AL9403 **JAFAR,** 1993, 3"/W BLK PANTS/HAT/SHIRT	$5-7
❑	❑	AUS AL9404 **ABU,** 1993, 1 1/2"/MONKEY	$5-7

❑	❑	GER AL9301 **CUP-ALADDIN,** 1993, BEIGE LID/STRAW/3P	$4-7
❑	❑	GER AL9302 **CUP-GENIE,** 1993, BLU LID/STRAW/3P	$4-7
❑	❑	GER AL9303 **CUP-JAFAR,** 1993, RED LID/STRAW/3P	$4-7
❑	❑	GER AL9304 **CUP-JASMINE,** 1993, TURQ LID/STRAW/3P	$4-7

❑	❑	PAN AL9305 **LUNCH BOX,** 1993, W STICKERS	$3-5
❑	❑	PAN AL9306 **SANDWICH BOX,** 1993, TRIANGLE SHAPE W GENIE GRAPHICS	$3-5
❑	❑	PAN AL9307 **CUP/STRAW,** 1993, W GENIE FLYING ON RUG	$3-5
❑	❑	PAN AL9308 **PLACEMAT,** 1993, GENIE GRAPHICS	$3-5

❑	❑	ZEA AL9301 **ALADDIN,** 1993, IN ABU/MONKEY VEHICLE	$7-10
❑	❑	ZEA AL9302 **JAFAR,** 1993, IN THE IAGO/BIRD VEHICLE	$7-10
❑	❑	ZEA AL9303 **JASMINE,** 1993, IN THE RAJAH/TIGER VEHICLE	$7-10
❑	❑	ZEA AL9304 **GENIE,** 1993, IN THE LAMP VEHICLE	$7-10

❑	❑	UK AL9326 DISPLAY W PREM, 1993	$65-90
❑	❑	DEN AL9344 POSTER, 1993, MCD HM ALADDIN	$12-20
❑	❑	HOL AL9355 TRAYLINER, 1993, ALADDIN SFEERVOL KERST HM	$1-1.50
❑	❑	UK AL9364 TRANSLITE/SM, 1993	$15-20
❑	❑	UK AL9365 TRANSLITE/LG, 1993	$30-45
❑	❑	GER AL9365 TRANSLITE/LG, 1993	$35-50

COMMENTS: NATIONAL DISTRIBUTION: AUSTRALIA: JULY/AUGUST 1994; NETHERLANDS: DECEMBER 8-JANUARY 11, 1994; GERMANY: NOVEMBER/DECEMBER 1993; UK: OCTOBER-NOVEMBER 19, 1993; NEW ZEALAND: JULY/AUGUST 1993. MEXICO/PANAMA/ARGENTINA/COSTA RICA/VENEZUELA/HOLLAND: JULY/AUGUST 1993. AUSTRALIAN HAPPY MEAL WAS CALLLED, "ALADDIN STRAW GRIPPERS; AUS AL9401/02/03/04. NO MCD LOGO ON AUSTRALIAN SET; MARKINGS: "DISNEY CHINA." ZEA AL9301-04 ARE DIFFERENT FROM THE UK/GER/PAN SETS.

DEN AL9301   DEN AL9302   DEN AL9304   DEN AL9303

ZEA AL9301   ZEA AL9302   ZEA AL9303   ZEA AL9304

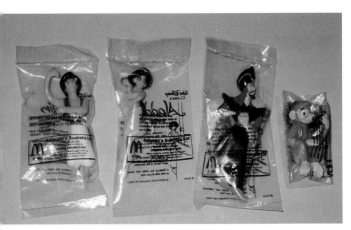

AUS AL9401   AUS AL9402   AUS AL9403   AUS AL9404

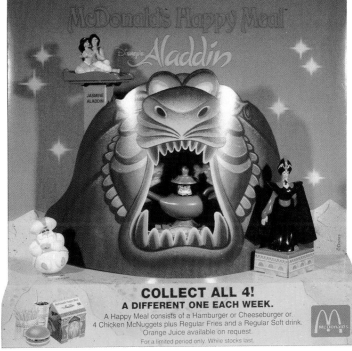

UK AL9326

GER AL9301

GER AL9302

GER AL9303

GER AL9304

DEN AL9344

165

HOL AL9355

NEW ZEALAND

WEEK 1 ALADDIN IN THE ABU VEHICLE
WEEK 2 JAFAR IN THE IAGO VEHICLE
WEEK 3 JASMINE IN THE RAJAH VEHICLE
WEEK 4 GENIE IN THE LAMP VEHICLE

GER AL9365

WEEK 3 JASMINE IN THE RAJAH VEHICLE

McDonald's Happy Meal Featuring

Disney's Aladdin

Safety tested for children age 3 and over.
CAUTION: May contain small parts.
Not intended for children under 3.

© 1993 McDonald's New Zealand
Contents made in China. Printed in Hong Kong.
© DISNEY

COLLECT ALL 4 while stocks last.

NEW ZEALAND

GER AR9303   GER AR9302

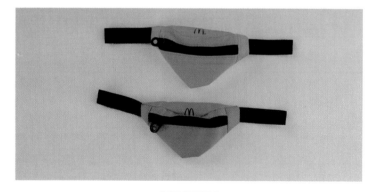

GER AR9304
GER AR9305

AUS GE9310

ARMBAND/FLUSSIGKEITS JUNIOR TUTE, 1993

❑ ❑ GER AR9301 **ARMBAND - PNK,** 1992, FISH/CRAB/SNAIL W
    VELCRO $4-6
❑ ❑ GER AR9302 **ARMBAND - GRN,** 1992, FISH/CRAB/SNAIL W
    VELCRO $4-6
❑ ❑ GER AR9303 **ARMBAND - YEL,** 1992, FISH/CRAB/SNAIL W
    VELCRO $4-6

COMMENTS: REGIONAL DISTRIBUTION: GERMANY - 1993.
WRISTBANDS WITH LIQUID INSIDE ARE SEE THROUGH
PLASTIC.

ARMBAND/WRIST WALLET/TASCHE PROMOTION, 1993

❑ ❑ GER AR9304 **ARMBAND - PNK,** ND, TRIANGLE SHAPED/
    ZIPPER/W VELCRO $4-6
❑ ❑ GER AR9305 **ARMBAND - GRN,** ND, TRIANGLE SHAPED/
    ZIPPER/W VELCRO $4-6

COMMENTS: REGIONAL DISTRIBUTION: GERMANY - 1993.
WRISTBANDS HAVE MCD LOGO ON FRONT.

AUSTRALIA/GENERIC PROMOTION, 1993

❑ ❑ AUS GE9310 HM BOX, 1993, FIND THE HIDDEN ANIMALS
                                               $2-3
❑ ❑ AUS GE9311 HM BOX, 1993, RON/BIRDIE PAINTING GRIM
                                             $2-3
❑ ❑ AUS GE9312 HM BOX, 1993, CHARS ON TRAIN $2-3
❑ ❑ AUS GE9313 HM BOX, 1993, CHARS W ARCHES/GRN $2-3
❑ ❑ AUS GE9314 HM BOX, 1993, BRIDIE/HAMB/PNK $2-3

❑ ❑ AUS GE9301 **FRISBEE,** 1993, 3" YEL DISC/RONALD $1-1.25
❑ ❑ AUS GE9302 **MAGNET,** ND, RONALD/FACE/PLASTIC $1-1.25
❑ ❑ AUS GE9303 **COMB,** 1993, RONALD/RED $1-1.25
❑ ❑ AUS GE9304 **PAPER CLIP.** ND. GRIMACE/PLASTIC $1-1.25
❑ ❑ AUS GE9305 **FRISBEE,** ND, NUTSY SUNDAE SAILER $1-1.50
❑ ❑ AUS GE9306 **MCLUNCH MONEY PURSE,** 1993 $2-3
❑ ❑ AUS GE9307 **STAMP PAD,** 1993, ARCHES/RONALD $4-5

□ □ AUS GE9309 **JACK,** 1993, YEL or GRN $1-1.25
□ □ AUS GE9315 **FINGER PUPPET/RON,** 1993, W TOP HAT
                                                    $1-1.50
□ □ AUS GE9316 **ERASER,** ND, GOOFY/DISNEY CHARS $2-2.50
□ □ AUS GE9317 **BIRTHDAY HAT,** ND, PAPER/CHARS $1-1.25

COMMENTS: REGIONAL DISTRIBUTION: AUSTRALIA: 1993.
AUSTRALIAN HAPPY MEAL BOXES ARE SMALLER THAN
EUROPEAN/GERMAN/UK/USA BOXES. THEY ARE NOT
IDENTICAL TO BOXES FROM OTHER COUNTRIES.

AUS GE9314

AUS GE9311

AUS GE9301   AUS GE9307

AUS GE9312

AUS GE9302

AUS GE9313

AUS GE9303

AUS GE9317

AUS GE9304

AUS GE9306

AUS GE9309

AUS GE9315

AUS GE9316

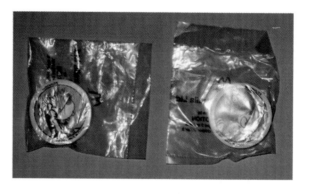

AUS GE9305

AUS BA8811

AUS BA8813

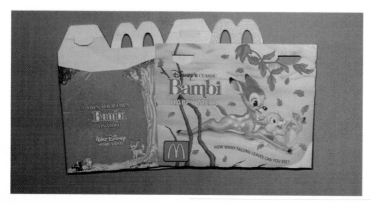

BAMBI/WALT DISNEY CLASSIC HAPPY MEAL, 1994/1993

❏	❏	AUS BA8810 HM BOX, 1993, FALL/SM BOX	$3-4
❏	❏	AUS BA8811 HM BOX, 1993, SPRING/SM BOX	$3-4
❏	❏	AUS BA8812 HM BOX, 1993, SUMMER/SM BOX	$3-4
❏	❏	AUS BA8813 HM BOX, 1993, WINTER/SM BOX	$3-4
❏	❏	GER BA8810 HM BOX, 1993, FALL	$3-4
❏	❏	GER BA8811 HM BOX, 1993, SPRING	$3-4
❏	❏	GER BA8812 HM BOX, 1993, SUMMER	$3-4
❏	❏	GER BA8813 HM BOX, 1993, WINTER	$3-4

*** IDENTICAL TOYS: BEL/FRA/UK BA8803/04/07/08

❏	❏	*** BA8807 **BAMBI,** 1993, W BUTTERFLY ON TAIL/WHT NOSE/GOLDEN BRN	$2-3
❏	❏	*** BA8808 **FLOWER,** 1993, SKUNK W FLOWER W MOSTLY BLK/WHT TAIL	$2-3
❏	❏	*** BA8803 **FRIEND OWL,** 1993, OWL	$2-3
❏	❏	*** BA8804 **THUMPER,** 1993, RABBIT W CARROT	$2-3

❏	❏	AUS BA8821 **BAMBI,** 1994, BAMBI/SM ON FLAT GRN STAND	$4-6
❏	❏	AUS BA8822 **FLOWER,** 1994, SKUNK/SM W FLOWER	$2-3
❏	❏	AUS BA8823 **HOOT,** 1994, OWL/SM	$2-3
❏	❏	AUS BA8824 **THUMPER,** 1994, RABBIT/SM W CARROT	$2-3

❏	❏	AUS BA8842 COUNTER CARD, 1994	$5-7
❏	❏	FRA BA8844 POSTER, 1993	$15-20
❏	❏	HOL BA8844 POSTER, 1993	$15-20

COMMENTS: REGIONAL DISTRIBUTION: UK: 1993; BELGIUM, DENMARK, FINLAND, FRANCE, GREECE, ITALY, HOLLAND, NORWAY, PORTUGAL, SPAIN, SWEDEN, SWITZERLAND: JULY 1993; AUSTRALIA: MAY 1994; BRAZIL: APRIL 1993. TOYS/BOXES ARE SIMILAR/NOT THE SAME AS USA BA8801-04 AND USA BA8810-13. NATIONAL DISTRIBUTION: AUSTRALIA - APRIL 29, 1994; BELGIUM - 1993. NOTE: BEL/FRA/UK BA8807 BAMBI IS A GOLDEN COLOR, NOT SAME

AS USA. BEL/FRA/UK BA8808 HAS A TAIL OUTLINED IN
BLACK WITH WHT ACCENTS, NOT LIKE USA BA8802
WHICH HAS WHITE TAIL W BLACK ACCENTS. ***BA8803/04
= USA BA8803/04 (See USA BAMBI HAPPY MEAL, 1988).
AUSTRALIA FIGURINES ARE SIMILAR TO USA BA8802-04
EXCEPT AUS BA8821 - BAMBI HAS A GREEN STAND AND
ALL AUSTRALIAN BAMBI FIGURINES ARE ABOUT ONE-
HALF THE SIZE OF USA BAMBI FIGURINES. AUSTRALIAN
BOXES ARE ALL ABOUT ONE-HALF THE SIZE OF OLDER/
LARGER USA BOXES. PLEASE NOTE: BAMBI IS LISTED AS
DISTRIBUTED IN 1988 (BA88) BECAUSE OF CONFLICT IN
SUCCEEDING YEAR PROMOTIONS, BARBIE (BA90XX-
BA95XX). YEARS OF DISTRIBUTION VARY BY THE COUN-
TRIES LISTED IN COMMENTS.

GER BA8810

AUSTRALIA

AUS BA8821   AUS BA8823   AUS BA8824   AUS BA8822

BEL BA8807   BEL BA8808

USA   AUSTRALIA

169

HOL BA8844

FRA BA8844

AUS BA8842

HOL BA9310   HOL BA9311   HOL BA9312   HOL BA9313

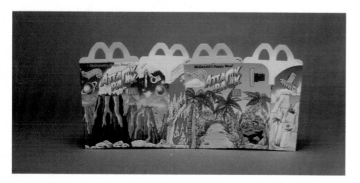

UK HW9313   UK HW9314

BARBIE/HOT WHEELS ATTACK PACK JUNIOR TUTE/ HAPPY MEAL, 1994/1993

- ❑ ❑ HOL BA9310 HM BOX, 1993, BALLERINA/MY FIRST BARBIE'S STAGE $2-3
- ❑ ❑ HOL BA9311 HM BOX, 1993, CRYSTAL HEART BARBIE'S CAR $2-3
- ❑ ❑ HOL BA9312 HM BOX, 1993, HOLLYWOOD HAIR IN BEAUTY SALON $2-3
- ❑ ❑ HOL BA9313 HM BOX, 1993, KEN ON SHIP $2-3
- ❑ ❑ UK BA9310 HM BOX, 1993, CRYSTAL HEART BARBIE'S CAR $2-3
- ❑ ❑ UK BA9311 HM BOX, 1993, KEN ON SHIP WAITING FOR SEA HOLIDAY BARBIE $2-3
- ❑ ❑ UK HW9313 HM BOX, 1993, JUNGLE/CAVE $2-3
- ❑ ❑ UK HW9314 HM BOX, 1993, GREEN VOLCANO $2-3
- ❑ ❑ CAN BA9330 HM BAG, 1993, BARBIE/ENGLISH/FRENCH $1-1.25

*** IDENTICAL BARBIE FIGURINES: CAN/ZEA BA9301/04/ 05/08

- ❑ ❑ *** BA9301 **HAPPY BIRTHDAY PARTY**, 1993, **WHT DOLL/** CAKE/WHT/PNK/BLU DRESS/**BLONDE HAIR** $3-4
- ❑ ❑ *** BA9304 **PAINT'N DAZZLE**, 1993, PNK DRESS/**BRUNETTE HAIR** $2-3
- ❑ ❑ *** BA9305 **ROMANTIC BRIDE**, 1993, WHT DRESS/PEACH BOUQUET/BLDE HAIR $2-3
- ❑ ❑ *** BA9308 **WESTERN STAMPIN**, 1993, BLU COUNTRY DRESS/BLU BOOTS $2-3

*** IDENTICAL BARBIE FIGURINES: GER/FRA/HOL/JP/UK BA9302/03

❏ ❏ *** BA9302 **HOLLYWOOD HAIR BARBIE,** 1993, GOLD SHORT
DRESS/**PNK STAR BASE** $3-4
❏ ❏ *** BA9303 **MY FIRST BALLERINA,** 1993, PURP BALLERINA
DRESS/BRN LONG SYN HAIR $1.50-2.50

❏ ❏ JPN BA9306 **SECRET HEART,** 1993, WHT/ROSE LONG
GOWN/HOLDING RED HEART/LONG BLOND HAIR $1.50-2.50
❏ ❏ JPN BA9307 **TWINKLE LIGHTS,** 1993, PINK/WHT GOWN/
WHT PURSE/LONG BLONDE SYN HAIR $1.50-2.50

*** **IDENTICAL BARBIE FIGURINES: GER/FRA/HOL/UK
BA9322/23**
❏ ❏ *** BA9322 **SEA HOLIDAY BARBIE,** 1993, BLONDE HAIR/
DARK BLU CLOTH DRESS $4-6
❏ ❏ *** BA9323 **CRYSTAL HEART BARBIE,** 1993, YEL HAIR/
PURP/WHT/PINK DRESS W HEARTS $4-6

❏ ❏ GUA BA9315 **NIGHT CLUB DRESS,** 1993, GO GO DANCE
DRESS/MOLDED HAIR $5-7
❏ ❏ GUA BA9316 **CASUAL DRESSED,** 1993, SHORTS/BALLOON
SLEEVE BLOUSE/MOLDED HAIR $5-7
❏ ❏ GUA BA9317 **FORMAL DRESS,** 1993, LONG RUFFLED
DRESS/MOLDED HAIR $5-7
❏ ❏ GUA BA9318 **COCKTAIL DRESS,** 1993, SHORT PARTY
DRESS/MOLDED HAIR $5-7

*** **IDENTICAL ATTACK PACK CARS: CAN/FRA/GER/HOL/
JP/UK AP9301/02/03/04**
❏ ❏ *** AP9301 **SAND STINGER,** 1993, ORG/BLK RACER/4
WHLS/ORG HOOK $2-3
❏ ❏ *** AP9302 **SLASH CAT,** 1993, GRN/ORG STRIPES/4 WHLS/
RED HOOK $2-3
❏ ❏ *** AP9303 **SLAUGHTER JAWS,** 1993, YEL/BLU JEEP/4
WHLS/RED HOOK $2-3
❏ ❏ *** AP9304 **TARAN CHEWA,** 1993, RED/GREEN/6 WHLS/BLK
HOOK $2-3

❏ ❏ UK BA9326 DISPLAY/PREMIUMS, 1993 $140-175
❏ ❏ FRA BA9342 COUNTER CARDS/4 SETS, 1993 $15-20
❏ ❏ HOL BA9344 POSTER, 1993 $15-20
❏ ❏ JPN BA9344 CREW POSTER, 1993 $15-20
❏ ❏ CAN BA9345 REGISTER TOPPER, 1993, BARBIE/HOT
WHEELS ATTACK PACK $4-5
❏ ❏ CAN BA9355 TRAYLINER, 1993, BARBIE/HOT WHEELS
$1.50-2.50
❏ ❏ UK BA9364 TRANSLITE/SM, 1993 $15-25
❏ ❏ UK BA9365 TRANSLITE/LG, 1993 $25-40

COMMENTS: NATIONAL DISTRIBUTION: CANADA: AUGUST 13-
SEPTEMBER 1993 AS A PROMOTION; UK: JULY 16, 1993;
NETHERLANDS/HOLLAND: SEPTEMBER 9-OCTOBER 10,
1993; FRANCE: 1993; GERMANY: SEPTEMBER 30-NOVEM-
BER 24, 1993; GUATEMALA, COSTA RICA, PANAMA:
NOVEMBER 1993; JAPAN: TESTED IN 1994; SINGAPORE
TESTED: MARCH/APRIL 1994; ARGENTINA: AUGUST 1994;
NEW ZEALAND: OCTOBER 1994; MEXICO, VENEZUELA:
NOVEMBER 1993. NEW ZEALAND BA9301/04/05/08 = CAN
BA9301/04/05/08. CAN BA9301 AND CAN BA9301/04 HAVE
DIFFERENT COLOR HAIR FROM USA BA9301/04. CAN
BA9305/08 = USA BA9305/08. GER BA9302/03/22/23 = HOL
BA9302/03/22/23 = UK BA9302/03/22/23, LOOSE OUT OF
PACKAGE. HOLLYWOOD HAIR BARBIE IN THE USA IS ON A
BLUE BASE, NOT PINK. SEE USA BARBIE /HOT WHEELS IV
HAPPY MEAL, 1993.

UK BA9323   UK BA9302   UK BA9303   UK BA9322

HOL BA9302   HOL BA9303   HOL BA9322   HOL BA9323

HOLLAND

HOLLAND

CAN AP9302   CAN AP9303   CAN AP9301   CAN AP9304

CAN BA9304   CAN BA9305   CAN BA9308   CAN BA9301

FRA AP9303   FRA AP9301   FRA AP9302   FRA AP9304

UK BA9326

GERMANY

CAN BA9355

JPN BA9344

HOL BA9344

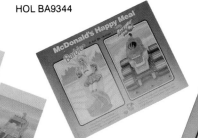

FRA BA9342

FRA BA9342

BARBIE / X-MEN HAPPY MEAL, 1993

- ❏ ❏ AUS BA9310 HM BOX, 1993, RON ON SKATEBOARD W GRIM ON ROLLER BLADES W/BIRDIE $2-3
- ❏ ❏ AUS BA9311 HM BOX, 1993, RON/BIRDIE/GRI/HAMB W ARCHES/BLUE BOX $2-3
- ❏ ❏ AUS BA9312 HM BOX, 1993, RON/HAMB/BIRDIE AS MCD BAND/NAME THE MUSICAL INSTRUMENTS $2-3

- ❏ ❏ AUS BA9301 **BARBIE BRIDE,** 1993, WHT WEDDING DRESS/ LONG WHT VEIL/LONG PNK BOUQUET(NOT SM ROSES) $9-12
- ❏ ❏ AUS BA9302 **BARBIE GLITTER BEACH,** 1993, LAVENDER/ SILVER BATHING SUIT W SEA SHELL/STAR FISH/1P $9-12
- ❏ ❏ AUS BA9303 **BARBIE SECRET HEARTS,** 1993, LAVENDER DRESS W LAVENDER/PINK HEARTS ON WHITE DRESS TRIM/1P $9-12
- ❏ ❏ AUS BA9304 **BARBIE TEEN TALK,** 1993, BLUE DRESS/BLUE HAT/PINK PURSE W FLOWERS/1P $9-12
- ❏ ❏ AUS XM9301 **X-MEN - WOLVERINE,** 1993, WEEK 1 YEL/BLK MASKED X-MEN IN RED/BLU CAR/2 WHEELS/1P $10-12
- ❏ ❏ AUS XM9302 **X-MEN - STORM,** 1993, WEEK 2 WHT HAIRED/ DRESSED X-MEN IN WHT/PURP/YEL CAR/2 WHEELS/1P $10-12
- ❏ ❏ AUS XM9303 **X-MEN - CYCLOPS,** 1993, WEEK 3 BLUE X-MEN IN BLUE/YEL CAR/2 WHEELS/1P $10-12
- ❏ ❏ AUS XM9304 **X-MEN - MAGNETS,** 1993, WEEK 4 RED X-MEN IN PURP/YEL CAR/2 WHEELS/1P $10-12

- ❏ ❏ AUS BA9341 CEILING DANGLER/LG, 1993 $35-50
- ❏ ❏ AUS BA9342 COUNTER CARD/BARBIE, 1993 $15-20
- ❏ ❏ AUS XM9342 COUNTER CARD/X-MEN, 1993 $15-20

COMMENTS: NATIONAL DISTRIBUTION: AUSTRALIA - JUNE/JULY, 1993.

AUS BA9312

AUS BA9310

AUS BA9311

AUS BA9301   AUS BA9302   AUS BA9303   AUS BA9304

AUSTRALIA

AUS BA9341

AUS XM9301   AUS XM9302   AUS XM9304   AUS XM9303

AUS BA9342

AUS XM9342

AUS XM9341

AUS BT9301
AUS BT9302
AUS BT9303
AUS BT9304

AUSTRALIA

BATMAN PENS HAPPY MEAL, 1993

❑ ❑ AUS BT9301 **PEN - BATMAN,** 1993, BLACK W CORD $10-13
❑ ❑ AUS BT9302 **PEN - CATWOMAN,** 1993, BLACK W CORD
                                                          $10-13
❑ ❑ AUS BT9303 **PEN - PENGUIN,** 1993, GREY W CORD $10-13
❑ ❑ AUS BT9304 **PEN - BATMOBILE,** 1993, RED W CORD $10-13

COMMENTS: REGIONAL DISTRIBUTION: AUSTRALIA - 1993.

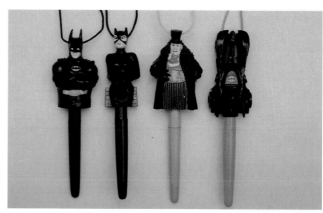

AUS BT9301   AUS BT9302   AUS BT9303   AUS BT9304

BIG BUDDIES HAPPY MEAL, 1993

❏ ❏ ZEA BU9301 **BIRDIE**, 1993, LARGE 3 1/2" FIGURINE $8-10
❏ ❏ ZEA BU9302 **GRIMACE**, 1993, LARGE 4" FIGURINE $8-10
❏ ❏ ZEA BU9303 **HAMBURGLAR**, 1993, LARGE 3 3/4"FIGURINE $8-10
❏ ❏ ZEA BU9304 **RONALD**, 1993, LARGE 5" FIGURINE $8-10

COMMENTS: REGIONAL DISTRIBUTION: NEW ZEALAND - NOVEMBER 6-30, 1993. THESE HAVE BEEN GIVEN OUT DURING CLEAN-UP PERIODS; CONSEQUENTLY CAUSING COLLECTORS TO CONFUSE DATES ON INITIAL RELEASE.

CABBAGE PATCH KIDS/TONKA HAPPY MEAL, 1993

❏ ❏ CAN CP9310 HM BOX, 1993, CP BIRTHDAY/TONKA CEMENT MIXER $2-3
❏ ❏ CAN CP9311 HM BOX, 1993, CP SLUMBER PARTY/TONKA FIRE TRUCK $2-3
❏ ❏ CAN CP9305 **U-3 MELANIE MERRILL/RIBBONS/BOWS**, 1992, WHT BUNNET/PURP BEAR $2.50-4
❏ ❏ CAN TK9305 **U-3 DUMP TRUCK**, 1992, BLU/YEL PLASTIC $2-3

*** IDENTICAL TOYS: CAN/PHI/SIN/ZEA CP9301/02/03/04
❏ ❏ *** CP9301 **JENNIFER RITA**/TINY DANCER, 1993, PURP/WHT BALLET DRESS $3-4
❏ ❏ *** CP9302 **CHRISTINA MARIA**/HAPPY BIRTHDAY, 1992, PNK DRESS/GRN GIFT/**NO TEDDY BEAR** $3-4
❏ ❏ *** CP9303 **JAIME CHRISTINE**/FUN ON ICE, 1992, **WHT DOLL**/WHT MUFF/**NO HOLLY**/TURQ DRESS/WHT SKATES $3-4
❏ ❏ *** CP9304 **EMILY ELIZABETH**/SWEET DREAMER, 1992, PNK NIGHT GOWN/TEDDY BEAR/**NO STOCKING** $3-4

*** IDENTICAL TOYS: CAN/PHI/SIN/ZEA TK9301/02/03/04
❏ ❏ *** TK9301 **LOADER**, 1992, YEL/BLK $1-1.50
❏ ❏ *** TK9302 **CEMENT MIXER**, 1992, ORG/BLK $1-1.50
❏ ❏ *** TK9303 **DUMP TRUCK**, 1992, YEL/BLK $1-1.50
❏ ❏ *** TK9304 **FIRE TRUCK**, 1992, RED/BLK $1-1.50

❏ ❏ CAN CP9342 COUNTER CARD/CPK, 1993 $3-5
❏ ❏ CAN TK9342 COUNTER CARD/TONKA, 1993 $3-5
❏ ❏ CAN CP9355 TRAYLINER, 1993, HAPPY MEALS ARE HERE! $2-3
❏ ❏ CAN CP9364 TRANSLITE/SM, 1993 $7-10

COMMENTS: NATIONAL DISTRIBUTION: CANADA: DECEMBER 1993; NEW ZEALAND: MAY 7, 1993; PHILLIPINES: OCTOBER 1994; PANAMA: 1993; SINGAPORE: OCTOBER 1994. THIS HAPPY MEAL WAS "CANADA'S FIRST OFFICIAL HAPPY MEAL" - DECEMBER 1993. PRIOR TO DECEMBER 1993, TOYS WERE "SURPRISE OF THE WEEK" AND PRICED INDIVIDUALLY, SEPARATE FROM FOOD PURCHASE; OTHER TOYS WERE DISTRIBUTED AS "TREAT-OF-THE-WEEK" PROMOTIONS; SOME TOYS WERE SOLD AS SELF-LIQUIDATOR PROMOTIONS. CAN/ZEA CP9301 = USA CP9201; CAN/ZEA TK9301-04 = USA TK9201-04 (See USA CABBAGE PATCH KIDS/TONKA HAPPY MEAL, 1992). NEW ZEALAND CP9301/02/03/04 = CAN CP9301/02/03/04.

ZEA BU9302

ZEA BU9303

ZEA BU9304

ZEA BU9301

CAN CP9305

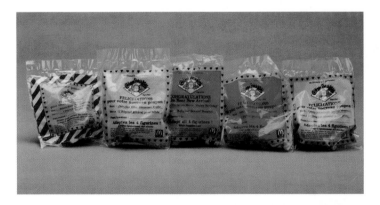

CAN CP9310   CAN CP9311

CAN TK9305   *** TK9301   *** TK9302   *** TK9303   *** TK9304

CAN CP9342

CAN TK9342

CAN CP9355

CAN GE9301   CAN GE9302   CAN GE9303   CAN GE9304

CAN GE9305

CANADA/GENERIC PROMOTION, 1993

- ❏ ❏ CAN GE9301 **STENCIL,** 1993, RON ON DINOSAUR $1-1.50
- ❏ ❏ CAN GE9302 **FRISBEE,** 1993, RON/RED $1-1.50
- ❏ ❏ CAN GE9303 **FREEZE POP,** 1993, BIRDIE STICK W WHT CONTAINER $1-1.50
- ❏ ❏ CAN GE9304 **FREEZE POP,** 1993, GRIMACE STICK W WHT CONTAINER $1-1.50
- ❏ ❏ CAN GE9305 **BALL/BLOW-UP,** 1993, PARCHMENT/PAPER $1-1.50
- ❏ ❏ CAN GE9306 **POCKET ATLAS,** 1993, RONALD McDONALD'S/ 4" X 3"/YEL or BLU/PAPER $1-1.25
- ❏ ❏ CAN GE9307 **MCPLANETES,** 1993, SPACELAND POP-UP/ PAPER $1-1.25
- ❏ ❏ CAN GE9308 **TOOTHBRUSH,** 1993, GRIMACE/PURP $1.50-2
- ❏ ❏ CAN GE9309 **KID'S FLOSS,** 1993, YEL AND PURP FLOSS/2P $1-1.25
- ❏ ❏ CAN GE9310 **PAPER CLIP,** 1993, FRENCH FRIES/YEL $1-1.25
- ❏ ❏ CAN GE9311 **COMIC #1,** 1993, MISSING MCNUGGET $1-1.25
- ❏ ❏ CAN GE9312 **COMIC #2,** 1993, SEA ISLAND TREASURE $1-1.25
- ❏ ❏ CAN GE9313 **CAP/SPORTS,** 1993, TORONTO BLUE JAYS $4-5

COMMENTS: REGIONAL DISTRIBUTION: CANADA : 1993 DURING CLEAN-UP WEEKS AND AS TREAT-OF-THE WEEK PROMOTIONAL ITEMS. CAN GE9305 PARCHMENT PAPER BALL WAS DISTRIBUTED IN SEVERAL EUROPEAN COUNTRIES, INCLUDING FRANCE AND GERMANY (CHINESE BALL, 1994).

CAN GE9306

CAN GE9307   CAN GE9311

CAN GE9313

CAN GE9312

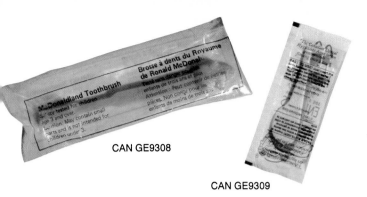

CAN GE9308

CAN GE9309

CHARACTER/FIGURENKREIDE/FINGER CRAYONS
JUNIOR TUTE, 1993

- ❏ ❏ GER CH9301 **SET 1 - FRY GIRL**, 1993, SITTING ON STEP/
  BLUE $2-3
- ❏ ❏ GER CH9302 **SET 2 - BIRDIE**, 1993, STANDING/YEL $2-3
- ❏ ❏ GER CH9303 **SET 3 - FRY GUY**, 1993, SITTING ON STEP/
  GRN $2-3
- ❏ ❏ GER CH9304 **SET 4 - GRIMACE**, 1993, STANDING/PURP $2-3

COMMENTS: REGIONAL DISTRIBUTION: GERMANY - 1993.
CRAYONS FOR THE FINGERS CAME PACKAGED.

GERMANY

GER CH9301   GER CH9302   GER CH9303   GER CH9304

CHARLIE BROWN HAPPY MEAL, 1993

- ❏ ❏ JPN CB9301 **SNOOPY/BALL**, 1993, ON GRN PEDESTAL W
  BALL $5-7
- ❏ ❏ JPN CB9302 **LUCY**, 1993, ARMS OUTSTRETCHED $5-7
- ❏ ❏ JPN CB9303 **WOODSTOCK**, 1993, FIELDING/STANDING $5-7
- ❏ ❏ JPN CB9304 **CHARLIE BROWN**, 1993, GOAL POST POSI-
  TION $5-7
- ❏ ❏ JPN CB9355 TRAYLINER, 1993, CB $1-2

COMMENTS: REGIONAL DISTRIBUTION: JAPAN - 1993.

JPN CB9301-04

JPN CB9344

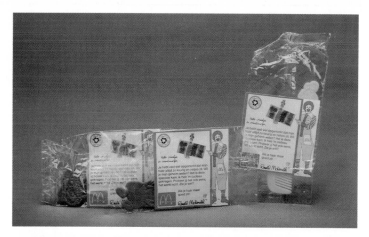

COMBS PROMOTION, 1993

❏ ❏ GER CO9301 **RONALD,** 1993, YEL 5" COMB W RONALD
STANDING WAVING LEFT HAND $3-4
❏ ❏ GER CO9302 **SHAKY,** 1993, PUR 5" COMB W SHAKY
STANDING $3-4
❏ ❏ GER CO9303 **HAMBURGLAR,** 1993, RED 5" COMB W HAMB
BUST $3-4
❏ ❏ GER CO9304 **FRY KIDS,** 1993, GRN 5" COMB W FRY KIDS
STANDING $3-4

COMMENTS: REGIONAL DISTRIBUTION: GERMANY/HOLLAND -
1993. COMBS WERE MADE IN GERMANY AND DISTRIB-
UTED THROUGHOUT EUROPE. PREMIUMS WERE GIVEN
TO U-5 CHILDREN AND DURING CLEAN-UP WEEK PROMO-
TION.

CRAZY STRAW HAPPY MEAL, 1993

❏ ❏ AUS CR9301 **BIRDIE,** 1993, 2P/BIRDIE SNAPS ONTO BENT
STRAW $5-7
❏ ❏ AUS CR9302 **GRIMACE,** 1993, 2P/GRIMACE SNAPS ONTO
BENT STRAW $5-7
❏ ❏ AUS CR9303 **HAMBURG,** 1993, 2P/HAMBURGLAR SNAPS
ONTO BENT STRAW $5-7
❏ ❏ AUS CR9304 **RONALD,** 1993, 2P/RONALD SNAPS ONTO
BENT STRAW $5-7

COMMENTS: REGIONAL DISTRIBUTION: AUSTRALIA: JANUARY
1993. THE CHARACTER CLIP-ONS WERE DISTRIBUTED BY
THEMSELVES IN ANOTHER PROMOTION IN AUSTRALIA.

DARKWING DUCK I & II/DISNEY ADVENTURES HAPPY MEAL, 1994/1993

❏ ❏ AUS DA9310 HM BOX, 1993, DARKWING DUCK $2-3

DARKWING DUCK I
*** IDENTICAL TOYS: AUS/ZEA DA9301/02/03/04
❏ ❏ *** DA9301 **DARKWING DUCK,** 1993, IN A 3 WHEEL
DUCKPLANE $4-6
❏ ❏ *** DA9302 **HONKER MUDDLE FOOT,** 1993, IN A CAN $4-6
❏ ❏ *** DA9303 **LAUNCHPAD MCQUACK,** 1993, IN A 2-WHEEL
DUCKPLANE $4-6
❏ ❏ *** DA9304 **GOSALYN,** 1993, IN A 2-WHEEL CAR $4-6

❏ ❏ AUS DA9442 COUNTER CARD, 1994 $3-5

DARKWING DUCK II
❏ ❏ AUS DA9401 **DARKWING DUCK,** 1994, W PURP HAT/CAPE $3-4
❏ ❏ AUS DA9402 **LAUNCHPAD/MCQUACK,** 1994, W FLIGHT
JACKET/THUMBS UP $3-4
❏ ❏ AUS DA9403 **GOSALYN,** 1994, W RED HAIR/PURP SHIRT $3-4
❏ ❏ AUS DA9404 **MEGAWOLF/VOLT,** 1994, W RED HAT/TURQ
GLOVES/SHOES $3-4

COMMENTS: REGIONAL DISTRIBUTION: NEW ZEALAND - MAY/
JUNE 24, 1993; AUSTRALIA - JUNE/JULY 1994.

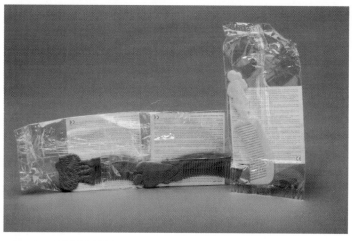

GER CO9301　　GER CO9302　　GER CO9303

AUS CR9301　AUS CR9302　AUS CR9303　AUS CR9304

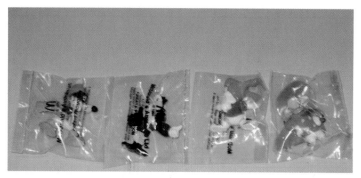

AUS DA9404　AUS DA9402　AUS DA9403　AUS DA9401

AUS DA9442

AUS DA9404

AUS DA9401

AUS DA9403

AUS DA9301   AUS DA9302   AUS DA9303   AUS DA9304

DINO MOTION/DINOSAURS/DINOSAURES DINO PULSION HAPPY MEAL, 1993

*** **IDENTICAL TOYS: CAN/ZEA DI9301/02/03/04/05/06**

❏ ❏ *** DI9301 **BABY SINCLAIR/BEBE,** 1992, 1P YEL BABY DINO
   HOLDING POT $1-1.50
❏ ❏ *** DI9302 **CHARLENE SINCLAIR,** 1992, 1P GRN MOTHER W
   PHONE $1-1.50
❏ ❏ *** DI9303 **EARL SINCLAIR,** 1992, 1P BLY/GRN POP W
   LUNCH BOX $1-1.50
❏ ❏ *** DI9304 **FRAN SINCLAIR,** 1992, 2P PNK/GRN HOLDING
   SPOON $1-1.50
❏ ❏ *** DI9305 **ETHYL/GRANDMA ETHYL,** 1992, 1P PNK/PUR IN
   CHAIR $1-1.50
❏ ❏ *** DI9306 **ROBBIE SINCLAIR,** 1992, 1P RED/GRN W GUITAR
                                                         $1-1.50

❏ ❏ CAN DI9355 TRAYLINER, 1992, DINO-MOTION/69 CENTS
                                                         $1-1.25
❏ ❏ CAN DI9357 TRAYLINER, 1992, DINO-MOTION TOYS W
   DISNEY RESORT $1.50-2.50
❏ ❏ CAN DI9342 COUNTER CARD, 1993, DINO-MOTION
   DINOSAURS $3-4
❏ ❏ CAN DI9345 REGISTER TOPPER, 1993, DINO-MOTION
   DINOSAURS $3-4

COMMENTS: NATIONAL DISTRIBUTION: CANADA - APRIL/MAY
   1993; NEW ZEALAND - MAY 1993. CAN/ZEA DI9301-06 =
   USA DI9301-06, LOOSE OUT OF PACKAGE. See USA DINO-
   MOTION DINOSAURS HAPPY MEAL, 1993.

CAN DI9301   CAN DI9302   CAN DI9303   CAN DI9305 CAN DI9306
              CAN DI9304

CAN DI9342

CAN DI9357

CAN DI9355

CAN DI9345

179

DINO-PUZZLE-KREIDE HAPPY MEAL, 1993

- ❑ ❑ GER PU9301 **DINO - GRN HEAD,** 1991, W PEAK MOUTH/
  GRN/RED/BLU/YEL/4P $4-6
- ❑ ❑ GER PU9302 **DINO - RED RED,** 1991, FLYING DINO/RED/
  YEL/PURP/GRN/5P $4-6
- ❑ ❑ GER PU9303 **DINO - BLU HEAD,** 1991, W SAW TOOTH
  MOUTH/YEL/PURP/RED/GRN/4P $4-6
- ❑ ❑ GER PU9304 **DINO - YEL HEAD,** 1991, W HORNS/YEL/RED/
  GRN/PURP/4P $4-6

COMMENTS: REGIONAL DISTRIBUTION - GERMANY: 1993.
DINOSAUR CRAYONS CAME IN SEVERAL COLOR VARIA-
TIONS.

GERMANY

GER PU9301

AUS FA9342

DISNEY FUNRIDES HAPPY MEAL, 1993

- ❑ ❑ ZEA DI9305 **DONALD-PIRATE'S SHIP/BOAT,** 1992, IN WHT
  BOAT/SHIP $4-6
- ❑ ❑ ZEA DI9306 **GOOFY-TRAIN ENGINE,** 1992, ON TOP OF RED
  ENGINE/1P $4-6
- ❑ ❑ ZEA DI9307 **MICKEY-FIRE ENGINE,** 1992, IN RED FIRE
  ENGINE/1P $4-6
- ❑ ❑ ZEA DI9308 **MINNIE-TEA CUP,** 1992, IN YEL TEA CUP/
  SPINS/1P $4-6

COMMENTS: NATIONAL DISTRIBUTION: NEW ZEALAND: DECEM-
BER 11, 1993; JAPAN: AUGUST 1993; SINGAPORE: OCTO-
BER-NOVEMBER 1994. VEHICLES ARE SIMILAR TO EURO
DISNEY VEHICLES.

ZEA DI9305   ZEA DI9308   ZEA DI9307   ZEA DI9306

DUCK TALES II PROMOTION, 1993

- ❑ ❑ AUS DU9301 **SCROOGE,** 1993, HARD RUBBER 2" BLU/WHT
  DUCK HOLDING $ BAG $3-4
- ❑ ❑ AUS DU9302 **NEPHEW,** 1993, HARD RUBBER 2" GRN/WHT
  DUCK HOLDING BATON $3-4
- ❑ ❑ AUS DU9303 **ARMOUR DUCK,** 1993, HARD RUBBER 2 1/2"
  ORG/WHT DUCK W SPACE COSTUME $3-4
- ❑ ❑ AUS DU9304 **WEBBY,** 1993, HARD RUBBER 2" YEL/WHT
  WEBBY W PNK RIBBON/DOLL $3-4

COMMENTS: REGIONAL DISTRIBUTION: AUSTRALIA: MARCH/
APRIL, 1993. NO McDONALD'S IDENTIFICATION ON THE
FIGURINES.

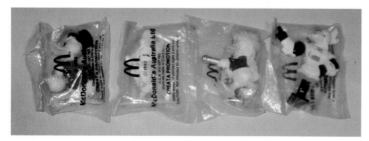

AUS DU9301   AUS DU9304   AUS DU9302   AUS DU9303

FACE GRIPPERS HAPPY MEAL, 1993

- ❑ ❑ AUS FA9301 **BIRDIE,** 1993, FACE/2X3" $5-8
- ❑ ❑ AUS FA9302 **GRIMACE,** 1993, FACE/2X3" $5-8
- ❑ ❑ AUS FA9303 **HAMBURG,** 1993, FACE/2X3" $5-8
- ❑ ❑ AUS FA9304 **RONALD,** 1993, FACE/2X3" $5-8
- ❑ ❑ AUS FA9342 COUNTER CARD, 1993 $3-5

COMMENTS: NATIONAL DISTRIBUTION: AUSTRALIA: NOVEMBER
12-DECEMBER 9, 1993. EACH CAME PACKAGED WITH A
SUCTION CUP. FACES WERE DESIGNED TO HOLD A
PENCIL/PEN.

AUS FA9301   AUS FA9302   AUS FA9303   AUS FA9304

FARM ANIMALS HAPPY MEAL, 1993

❑ ❑ CAN AN9301 **GOAT,** 1993, GRN/3P $1.50-2.50
❑ ❑ CAN AN9302 **ROOSTER,** 1993, RED/3P $1.50-2.50
❑ ❑ CAN AN9303 **COW,** 1993, GRN/3P $1.50-2.50
❑ ❑ CAN AN9304 **PIG,** 1993, PNK/3P $1.50-2.50
❑ ❑ CAN AN9305 **TRACTOR,** 1993, ORG/4P $1.50-2.50
❑ ❑ CAN AN9306 **FARMER,** 1993, YEL/5P $1.50-2.50
❑ ❑ CAN AN9307 **HORSE,** 1993, BLU/3P $1.50-2.50
❑ ❑ CAN AN9308 **BULL,** 1993, PUR/3P $1.50-2.50

COMMENTS: NATIONAL DISTRIBUTION: CANADA: 1993.

CAN AN9301   CAN AN9302   CAN AN9303   CAN AN9304

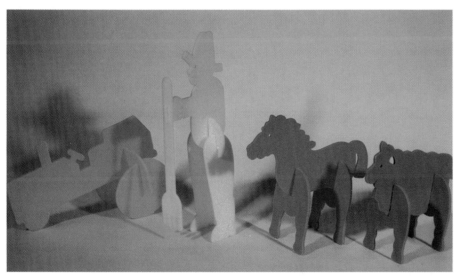

CAN AN9305   CAN AN9306   CAN AN9307   CAN AN9308

FIGUREN/McDONALDLAND HAPPY MEAL, 1993

❑ ❑ GER FI9301 **BIRDIE,** 1992, W WINGS SPREAD OUT/2" $5-8
❑ ❑ GER FI9302 **GRIMACE/SHAKY,** 1992, W ARMS OUTREACH-
ING/PURP/2 1/2" $5-8
❑ ❑ GER FI9303 **HAMBURGLAR,** 1992, W ARMS SPREAD DOWN/
2" $5-8
❑ ❑ GER FI9304 **RONALD,** 1992, W ARMS SPREAD DOWN/3 "
                                              $5-8

COMMENTS: REGIONAL DISTRIBUTION: GERMANY: 1993.
FIGURINES ARE MARKED, "McDONALD'S 1992" AND
PACKAGING "1993."

GER FI9301   GER FI9302   GER FI9303   GER FI9304

GER MA9302   GER MA9303   GER MA9304

MEX FL9310

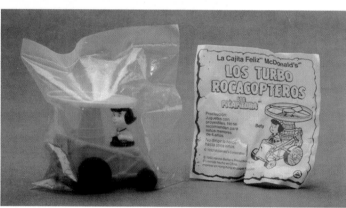

MEX FL9304

MEX FL9302   MEX FL9305   MEX FL9303   MEX FL9304

USA FO9364

FINGER KREIDE/ANIMAL CRAYONS PROMOTION, 1993

❑ ❑ GER MA9301 **APE,** 1993, GRN or YEL or BLU or RED $2-3
❑ ❑ GER MA9302 **ELEPHANT,** 1993, GRN or YEL or BLU or RED
            $2-3
❑ ❑ GER MA9303 **LION,** 1993, GRN or YEL or BLU or RED $2-3
❑ ❑ GER MA9304 **HIPPOPOTAMUS,** 1993, GRN or YEL or BLU or
RED $2-3

COMMENTS: REGIONAL DISTRIBUTION: GERMANY: 1993.
FINGER CRAYONS CAME IN ASSORTED COLORS. THESE
WERE GIVEN OUT TO THE U-5 CHILDREN AND/OR CLEAN-
UP PERIODS. ALSO DISTRIBUTED IN USA IN NON
McDONALD'S FAST FOOD RESTAURANTS, 1993. NO
SPECIFIC COUNTRY MARKINGS.

FLINTSTONE FLYERS/LOS TURBO ROCACOPTEROS HAPPY MEAL, 1993

❑ ❑ GUA FL9330 HM BAG, ND, GENERIC HM BAG $1-1.25
❑ ❑ MEX FL9310 HM BOX, 1992, LOS TURBO ROCACOPTEROS
            $2-3
❑ ❑ MEX FL9302 **FRED,** 1992, IN VEHICLE W HELICOPTER
SPINNER/3P $5-7
❑ ❑ MEX FL9303 **BARNEY,** 1992, IN LOG TYPE VEHICLE W
HELICOPTER SPINNER/3P $5-7
❑ ❑ MEX FL9304 **BETTY/BETY,** 1992, IN VEHICLE W HELICOP-
TER SPINNER/3P $5-7
❑ ❑ MEX FL9305 **WILMA,** 1992, IN VEHICLE W HELICOPTER
SPINNER/3P $5-7

COMMENTS: REGIONAL DISTRIBUTION: MEXICO, PANAMA,
VENEZUELA: JANUARY 1993; GUATEMALA, COSTA RICA,
VENEZUELA FEBRUARY 1993.

FOOD FUNDAMENTALS HAPPY MEAL, 1994/1993

❑ ❑ MEX FO9310 HM BAG, 1992, RON/4 PREMIUMS $1-1.25
❑ ❑ MEX FO9301 **MILLY,** 1992, 2P WHT MILK CARTON W MILK
CARTON SHAPED NOTE PAD $1-1.50
❑ ❑ MEX FO9302 **OTIS,** 1992, 2P BRN/BLU SANDWICH W
HELMET W SANDWICH NOTE PAD $1-1.50
❑ ❑ MEX FO9303 **RUBY,** 1992, 2P RED APPLE W APPLE SHAPED
NOTE PAD $1-1.50
❑ ❑ MEX FO9304 **SLUGGER,** 1992, 2P BRN/GRN STEAK W
STEAK SHAPED NOTE PAD $1-1.50

COMMENTS: REGIONAL DISTRIBUTION: MEXICO/PANAMA: APRIL
1994; PUERTO RICO: AUGUST 1994; VENEZUELA: OCTO-
BER 1994; ARGENTINA: NOVEMBER 1994; SINGAPORE:
APRIL 26-MAY 26, 1993. MEX FO9401-04 = USA FO9301-04.
See USA FOOD FUNDAMENTALS HAPPY MEAL, 1993.

FLOPPY PUPPETS/GLIEDERTIERE HAPPY MEAL, 1993

❑ ❑ GER GL9301 **DOG**, 1993, ORG/RED BASE $5-7
❑ ❑ GER GL9302 **DONKEY**, 1993, RED/BLK BASE $5-7
❑ ❑ GER GL9303 **ELEPHANT**, 1993, BLU/YEL BASE $5-7
❑ ❑ GER GL9304 **LION**, 1993, YEL/BRN BASE $5-7

COMMENTS: REGIONAL DISTRIBUTION: GERMANY - DECEMBER 1993.

FRANCE/GENERIC PROMOTION, 1993

❑ ❑ FRA GE9301 **TOOTHBRUSH**, 1993, GRIMACE/PURP $3-4
❑ ❑ FRA GE9302 **REFLECTOR**, 1993, YEL/RON $3-4

COMMENTS: REGIONAL DISTRIBUTION: FRANCE/HOLLAND - 1993 DURING CLEAN-UP WEEKS.

GERMANY/EUROPE GENERIC HAPPY MEAL, 1993

❑ ❑ BEL GE9310 HM BOX, 1993, ADVENT CALENDAR/WINDOWS $2-3
❑ ❑ GER GE9310 HM BOX, 1993, RR STATION $2-3
❑ ❑ GER GE9311 HM BOX, 1993, HOUSE/FIRE TRUCKS $2-3
❑ ❑ GER GE9312 HM BOX, 1993, FARM/COW/PIGS $2-3
❑ ❑ GER GE9301 **RONALD W RINGS**, 1993, RED RONALD/3 YEL RINGS $3-5
❑ ❑ GER GE9302 **RONALD W RINGS**, 1993, YEL RONALD/3 RED RINGS $3-5
❑ ❑ GER GE9303 **GAME/WINKS/RON**, 1993, ORG TRAY/BLU/GR/RED/YEL DISC/5P $4-6
❑ ❑ GER GE9304 **BIRTHD CALENDAR**, 1993, PAPER/FOLD OUT $1-2
❑ ❑ GER GE9305 **FLOOR PUZZLE**, 1993, RON W MCD CHAR/15P $10-15
❑ ❑ GER GE9306 **PREHISTORIC**, 1993, DINOSAUR PLAYBOARD/STICKERS/2P $5-8
❑ ❑ GER GE9307 **SPACE**, 1993, SPACE PLAYBOARD/STICKERS/2P $5-8
❑ ❑ GER GE9308 **PUZZLE**, 1993, RON/GRI/CAPT/MAYOR BICYCLING $3-4
❑ ❑ GER GE9309 **SLINKY**, 1993, MULTI-COLOR/REGENBOGEN SPIRALE $2.50-4
❑ ❑ GER GE9314 **TRACE/DRAW**, 1993, PAPER/BOOKLET $1-1.25
❑ ❑ GER GE9315 **CUBE**, 1993, FOLD-UP/PAPER $1-1.25
❑ ❑ GER GE9316 **TRACE**, 1993, RONALD/RED or YEL $2-3
❑ ❑ *** GE9317 **LUNCH BOX**, 1993, YEL/ARCHES HANDLE $——

COMMENTS: REGIONAL DISTTRIBUTION: FRANCE/GERMANY: 1993. TOYS WERE DISTRIBUTED IN SEVERAL EUROPEAN COUNTRIES WITH DIFFERENT PAPER. GER GE9306/07 ARE PICTURE MAKING PREMIUMS PACKAGED BY SIMON MARKETING, DISTRIBUTED IN EUROPE. *** GE9317 LUNCH BOX IS UNDETERMINED ORIGIN. IN GERMANY, THE BROWN AND WHITE UNNUMBERED BAGS PRECEEDED THE NUMBERED BROWN BAGS (UP TO #60) WHICH LED INTO THE NUMBERED WHITE BAGS #61-XXX.

GERMANY

GER FL9201   GER FL9202   GER FL9203   GER FL9204

FRA FL9201   FRA FL9202   FRA FL9203   FRA FL9204

FRA GE9302

FRA GE9301

GER GE9304   GER GE9301   GER GE9302

GER GE9305

GER GE9308

BEL GE9310

Regenbogen Spirale
Rainbow Spring

GER GE9315

GER GE9314

GER GE9309

GER GE9316

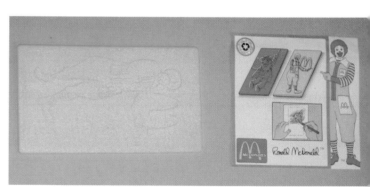

GER GE9317

GER

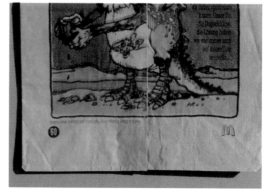

GERMANY

GROWING FIGURES PROMOTION, 1993

❑ ❑ CAN GR9301 **SPONGE - BIRDIE,** 1993, RED BIRDIE $1-2
❑ ❑ CAN GR9302 **SPONGE - GRIMACE,** 1993, PURP GRIMACE
           $1-2
❑ ❑ CAN GR9303 **SPONGE - RONALD,** 1993, RED RONALD $1-2

COMMENTS: REGIONAL DISTRIBUTION: CANADA - 1993.
PREMIUMS GIVEN AS TREAT-OF-THE WEEK PROMOTION.

CAN GR9301   CAN GR9302   CAN GR9303

HAPPY MEAL BAND/ROCK 'N ROLL BAND/MCTWIST HAPPY MEAL, 1994/1993

     *** **IDENTICAL BOXES: GER/UK HM9310/11/12/13**
❑ ❑ *** HM9310 HM BOX, 1993, CONCERT STAGE/GRIMACE W
     HORN $2-3
❑ ❑ *** HM9311 HM BOX, 1993, DRESSING ROOM/BIRDIE W
     MIKE $2-3
❑ ❑ *** HM9312 HM BOX, 1993, THE BAND/RONALD W GUITAR
           $2-3
❑ ❑ *** HM9313 HM BOX, 1993, RECORDING ROOM/BAND
     SOUND ROOM $2-3
❑ ❑ MEX HM9410 HM BOX, 1994, BAND $2-3

     *** **IDENTICAL TOYS: BEL/DEN/GER/FRA/HOL/MEX/NED/UK
HM9301/02/03/04**
❑ ❑ *** HM9301 **BIRDIE W MIKE,** 1993, THE SINGER W MIKE $3-5
❑ ❑ *** HM9302 **GRIMACE W SAX,** 1993, W BLK SUNGLASSES W
     YEL HRN $3-5
❑ ❑ *** HM9303 **HAMBURGLAR W DRUMS,** 1993, W DRUMS $3-5
❑ ❑ *** HM9304 **RONALD W GUITAR,** 1993, W BLK SUNGLASSES
     ON KNEES $3-5

❑ ❑ UK HM9364 TRANSLITE/SM, 1993 $4-6
❑ ❑ UK HM9365 TRANSLITE/LG, 1993 $7-10
❑ ❑ UK HM9326 DISPLAY/PREMIUMS, 1993 $75-100
❑ ❑ FRA HM9341 DANGLER/EACH, 1993 $5-8
❑ ❑ FRA HM9344 POSTER/SM, 1993 $5-8
❑ ❑ HOL HM9344 POSTER/SM, 1993 $5-8
❑ ❑ DEN HM9344 POSTER/LG, 1993, MCTWIST $15-20

COMMENTS: NATIONAL DISTRIBUTION: UK: JUNE 4, 1993;
BELGIUM, FINLAND, FRANCE, GREECE, HOLLAND,
NORWAY, PORTUGAL, SPAIN, SWEDEN, SWITZERLAND,
ITALY, DENMARK: JUNE 17-JULY 21, 1993; ARGENTINA,
COSTA RICA, GUATEMALA, CHILE: MAY 1994; PANAMA:
FEBRUARY 1994; VENEZUELA, PUERTO RICO: APRIL 1994;
MEXICO: SEPTEMBER 1994; JAPAN TESTED IN AUGUST
1993; AUSTRALIA (REGIONALLY): 1993. PREMIUMS WERE
MARKED SIMON MARKETING, GERMANY. CALLED
"MCTWIST HM" IN DENMARK AND "ROCK & ROLL" IN
NETHERLANDS. UK HM BOXES HAVE WORD, "BAND" IN
TITLE, GER HM BOXES HAVE SAME GRAPHICS WITHOUT
THE WORD, "BAND" IN TITLE.

GER HM9311

GER HM9313

UK HM9310-13

UK

GER HM9312

185

UK HM9301   HM9302   HM9303   HM9304

UK HM9326

DEN HM9344

HOL HM9344

MEX HM9301

FRA HM9341

JAPAN/GENERIC PROMOTION, 1993

☐ ☐ JPN MS9310 HM BOX, 1993, GRIM IN TENT $2-3
☐ ☐ JPN GE9312 HM BOX, 1993, FARM/COW/PIGS $2-3
☐ ☐ JPN GE9330 HM BAG, 1993, RON W ARCHES $1-1.25
☐ ☐ JPN GE9301 **BIRDIE/GRI/HAMB/RON/TRAYLINER**, 1993,
        FINGER PUPPETS/PUNCH-OUTS/PAPER $3-4
☐ ☐ JPN GE9302 **AIRPLANE/TRAYLINER**, 1993, 2 PUNCH-OUT
        AIRPLANES/CHARS $3-4

❑ ❑ JPN GE9303 **FARM SCENE/RONALD,** 1993, PAPER $1-1.25
❑ ❑ JPN GE9304 **KALEIDOSCOPE,** 1993, BLU W RON/CHARS
$5-7
❑ ❑ JPN GE9305 **SCOPE,** 1993, W HAMB PIC $2.50-4
❑ ❑ JPN GE9306 **MOUNTAIN SCENE,** 1993, PAPER/BIRDIE
$1-1.25
❑ ❑ JPN GE9307 **SPONGE - GRIMACE,** 1993, PURP/
CUTOUT(BATH SET) $1-2
❑ ❑ JPN GE9308 **PUZZLE - DUMBO,** 1993, DUMBO/7" X 10" $7-10
❑ ❑ JPN GE9310 **BATH SET,** 1993, YEL TOWEL/3 SOAP CRAY-
ONS/SPONGE/BAG $7-10
❑ ❑ JPN GE9311 **FOOD COUPON,** 1993 $1-1.25
❑ ❑ JPN GE9313 **SHOE GAME/CATCH,** 1993, RED SHOE W
STRING/BALL $4-6
❑ ❑ JPN GE9314 **FRY KID GAME/CATCH,** 1993, BLU W STRING/
BALL $4-6
❑ ❑ JPN GE9315 **ERASER - CONE,** 1993, SUNDAE/2P $4-6
❑ ❑ JPN GE9316 **GAME/START/GOAL,** 1993, PAPER/W MAGNET
$4-6
❑ ❑ JPN GE9317 **KLEENEX/SOCCER,** 1993, PAPER $1-1.25
❑ ❑ JPN GE9318 **KLEENEX/BASEBALL,** 1993, PAPER $1-1.25
❑ ❑ JPN GE9319 **BALL/BLOW UP,** 1993, CHARS/BLU or WHT
$1-1.25
❑ ❑ JPN GE9350 BUTTON/AIRSHIP, 1993 $8-12
❑ ❑ JPN GE9351 BUTTON/FOOD, 1993 $3-4
❑ ❑ JPN GE9352 BUTTON/BIG MAC, 1993 $3-4
❑ ❑ JPN GE9353 BUTTON/88 SERVICE CAMPAIGN, 1993 $3-4

COMMENTS: REGIONAL DISTRIBUTION: JAPAN: 1993 WITH
CHARACTERS ON TRAYLINERS PROMOTION. JAPANESE
TRAYLINERS HAVE McDONALD'S INFORMATION ON ONE
HALF AND ADVERTISING ON THE OTHER HALF. JPN
GE9312 = ZEA BI9102, BIG MAC & COMPANY HAPPY MEAL,
1991. JPN DT8803 WAS THE SAME SCOPE USED WITH THE
DUCK TALES PROMOTION, INTERNATIONALLY; IT WAS
REDISTRIBUTED SEVERAL TIMES IN SEVERAL DIFFERENT
COUNTRIES. JPN HM BOXES ARE THE SAME AS GERMANY
BOXES - GER MS9310 AND GER GE9312.

JPN GE9304   JPN GE9305

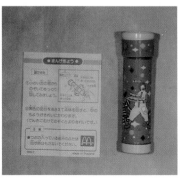

JPN MS9310
JPN GE9312

JPN GE9330

JPN GE9317   JPN GE9318

JPN GE9302

JPN GE9301

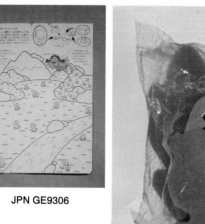

JPN GE9303

JPN GE9306

JPN GE9307

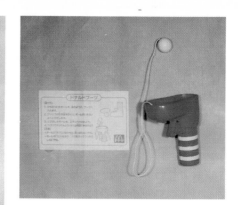

JPN GE9313

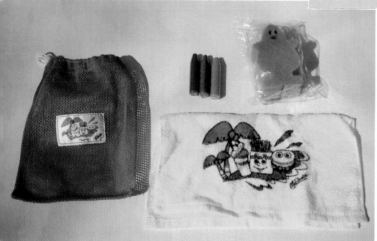

JPN GE9310

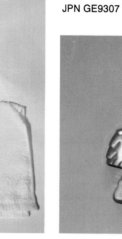

JPN GE9314

JPN GE9311

JPN GE9315

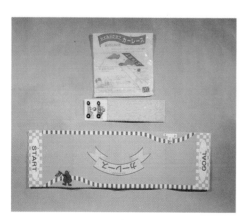

JPN GE9316

JPN GE9319

JPN GE9351   JPN GE9352   JPN GE9353

USA

JPN GE9311

JUNGLE BOOK/JUNGLEBOEK HAPPY MEAL, 1993

*** IDENTICAL BOXES: GER/HOL/FRA/UK JU9310/11/12/13

❏ ❏ *** JU9310 HM BOX, 1993, HOLDING UP STONE BRIDGE/ BALOO W KING LOUIE $2-3
❏ ❏ *** JU9311 HM BOX, 1993, ARMY OF ELEPHANTS $2-3
❏ ❏ *** JU9312 HM BOX, 1993, TIGER CHASES MOWGLI IN JUNGLE $2-3
❏ ❏ *** JU9313 HM BOX, 1993, MONKEY IN TREE/JUNGLE TREE $2-3

*** IDENTICAL TOYS: GER/HOL/NED/UK JU9001/02/03/04

❏ ❏ *** JU9001 **KING LOUIE,** 1993, ORG APE HOLDING BANANA $1.50-2.50
❏ ❏ *** JU9002 **KAA,** 1993, GRN SNAKE $1.50-2.50
❏ ❏ *** JU9003 **SHERE KAHN,** 1993, ORANGE TIGER $1.50-2.50
❏ ❏ *** JU9005 **MOWGLI BOY,** 1993, BOY/MAN CUB IN GRN POT/W WHEELS $2-3

❏ ❏ UK JU9326 DISPLAY W PREMIUMS, 1993 $35-50
❏ ❏ FRA JU9342 COUNTER CARD, 1993 $5-8
❏ ❏ HOL JU9344 POSTER/SM, 1993 $5-8
❏ ❏ HOL JU9355 TRAYLINER, 1993, JUNGLEBOEK $1-1.25
❏ ❏ UK JU9364 TRANSLITE/SM, 1993 $5-8
❏ ❏ UK JU9365 TRANSLITE/LG, 1993 $10-15

COMMENTS: NATIONAL DISTRIBUTION: UK: MARCH 26-APRIL 1993; GERMANY: MARCH/APRIL 1993; DENMARK, FINLAND, FRANCE, GREECE, ITALY, HOLLAND, NORWAY, PORTUGAL, SPAIN, SWEDEN, SWITZERLAND: APRIL 29 - JUNE 02, 1993. UK/HOL JU9301-03 ARE IDENTICAL TO USA JU9001-03. GERMANY/HOLLAND/UK JU9305 MOWGI BOY HAS WHEELS. USA JU9005 DOES NOT HAVE WHEELS; WAS THE U-3 (UNDER AGE 3) PREMIUM IN THE USA (See USA JUNGLE BOOK HAPPY MEAL, 1990). NAMES ON BOXES VARY ACCORDING TO LANGUAGE OF THE COUNTRY OF DISTRIBUTION.

GERMANY

HOL JU9312   *** JU9311   *** JU9313   *** JU9310

UK JU9313   UK JU9312   UK JU9311   UK JU9310

FRA JU9312

USA

UK JU9003   *** JU9005   *** JU9002   *** JU9001

GER JU9001   GER JU9002   GER JU9003   GER JU9005

FRA JU9342

HOL JU9344

HOL JU9355

USA

USA

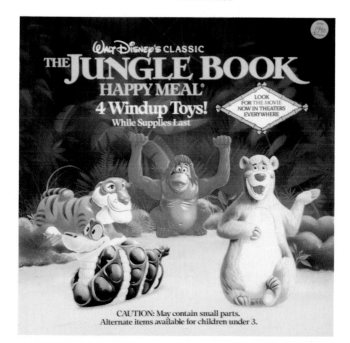

JUNIOR MEAL HAPPY MEAL, 1993

- ❑ ❑ HUN JU9301 **TOOTHBRUSH-APPLE,** 1993, NEON GRN $3-5
- ❑ ❑ HUN JU9302 **TOOTHBRUSH-BANANA,** 1993, NEON YEL $3-5
- ❑ ❑ HUN JU9303 **TOOTHBRUSH-ORANGE,** 1993, NEON ORANGE $3-5
- ❑ ❑ HUN JU9304 **TOOTHBRUSH-STRAWBERRY,** 1993, NEON PNK $3-5

COMMENTS: REGIONAL DISTRIBUTION: HUNGARY: 1993. TOOTHBRUSHES WERE "REACH" BRAND BY JOHNSON & JOHNSON IN NEON COLORS.

KNOTENBEISSER/SHOE LACE TIES JUNIOR TUTE, 1993

- ❑ ❑ GER KN9310 HM BAG, 1993, JUNIOR TUTE/ KNOTENBEISSER $2-3
- ❑ ❑ GER KN9301 **BIRDIE FASTENER,** 1993, SET 2/HOLDS SHOW LACES $3-5
- ❑ ❑ GER KN9302 **HAMB FASTENER,** 1993, SET 2/HOLDS SHOW LACES $3-5
- ❑ ❑ GER KN9303 **RONALD FASTENER,** 1993, SET 2/HOLDS SHOW LACES $3-5
- ❑ ❑ GER SH9365 TRANSLITE/LG, 1992 $25-40

COMMENTS: NATIONAL DISTRIBUTION: GERMANY: MARCH 4-28, 1993.

LITTLE LIBRARY BOOKS HAPPY MEAL, 1993

PENGUIN BOOKS

- ❑ ❑ ZEA LI9301 **BOOK - BOW DOWN SHADRACH,** 1992, BY JOY COWLEY $5-8
- ❑ ❑ ZEA LI9302 **BOOK - DOWNHILL CROCODILE WHIZZ,** 1992, BY MARGARET MAHY $5-8
- ❑ ❑ ZEA LI9303 **BOOK - RAGING ROBOTS & UNRULY UNCLES,** 1992, BY MARGARET MAHY $5-8
- ❑ ❑ ZEA LI9304 **BOOK - UNDER THE MOUNTAIN,** 1992, BY MAURICE GEE $5-8

FAMILY LIBRARY BOOKS

- ❑ ❑ ZEA LI9305 **BOOK - WHOSE BEHIND THE DOOR AT MY HOUSE,** 1992 $5-8
- ❑ ❑ ZEA LI9306 **BOOK - WHOSE BEHIND THE DOOR IN THE CITY,** 1992 $5-8
- ❑ ❑ ZEA LI9307 **BOOK - WHOSE BEHIND THE DOOR AT MY HOUSE,** 1992 $5-8
- ❑ ❑ ZEA LI9308 **BOOK - WHOSE BEHIND THE DOOR AT MY SCHOOL,** 1992 $5-8

COMMENTS: NATIONAL DISTRIBUTION: NEW ZEALAND: MARCH 1993. FOUR BOOKS WERE INTENDED FOR THE YOUNG CHILDREN, FOUR BOOKS FOR THE OLDER CHILDREN. THESE BOOKS WERE WRITTEN BY NEW ZEALAND AUTHORS, PRINTED IN AUSTRALIA; HAVE THE MCD KIWI LOGO ON THE BACK.

GERMANY

GER KN9365

GER KN9301   GER KN9302   GER KN9303

ZEA LI9308

ZEA LI9307

ZEA LI9306

ZEA LI9305

ZEA LI9301   ZEA LI9302   ZEA LI9303   ZEA LI9304

GERMANY

LOONEY TUNES/SUPER LOONEY TUNES/CLIP-ON CLOTHES JUNIOR TUTE/HAPPY MEAL, 1994/1993

❑ ❑ UK SU9310 HM BOX, 1993, CAVE $2-3
❑ ❑ UK SU9311 HM BOX, 1993, COTTAGE $2-3
❑ ❑ UK SU9312 HM BOX, 1993, RAILWAY TRAIN $2-3
❑ ❑ UK SU9313 HM BOX, 1993, TELEPHONE BOOTH/BOX $2-3

    *** IDENTICAL TOYS: GER/UK SU9101/02/03/04
❑ ❑ ***** SU9101 SUPER BUGS/BUGS BUNNY,** 1991, 3 1/2" W RED SUIT/SUPER MAN BUGS/3P $2-3
❑ ❑ ***** SU9102 TASMANIAN DEVIL/TAZ-FLASH,** 1991, RED DEVIL SUIT/TAZ DEVIL/3P $2-3
❑ ❑ ***** SU9103 PETUNIA PIG/WONDER PIG,** 1991, PINK COSTUME/WONDER WOMAN PIG/3P $2-3
❑ ❑ ***** SU9104 DAFFY DUCK/BAT DUCK,** 1991, 3" W BLU/GRY OUTFIT/BAT DUCK MAN/3P $2-3

❑ ❑ UK SU9326 DISPLAY/PREMIUMS, 1991 $25-40
❑ ❑ UK SU9364 TRANSLITE/SM, 1991 $4-8
❑ ❑ UK SU9365 TRANSLITE/LG, 1991 $8-12
❑ ❑ GER SU9365 TRANSLITE/LG, 1993 $25-40

COMMENTS: NATIONAL DISTRIBUTION: UK, PANAMA: DECEMBER 17-JANUARY 6, 1994; GERMANY: JULY 1994; GUATEMALA: FEBRUARY 1994; VENEZUELA: MARCH 1994; JAPAN: TESTED IN OCTOBER 1994. UK SU9101-04 ARE THE SAME AS USA SU9101-04 (See SUPER LOONEY TUNES HAPPY MEAL, 1991). CALLED "LOONEY TUNES HM" IN THE GERMANY/UK AND "SUPER LOONEY TUNES HM" IN THE USA.

UK SU9310   UK SU9311   UK SU9312   UK SU9313

GER SU9101   GER SU9102   GER SU9103   GER SU9104

GER SU9365

UK SN9101-04

UK SN9101   UK SN9102   UK SN9103   UK SN9104

M SQUAD/MISSION UNDERCOVER/MCSPY/MYSTERY II/ MCAGENT 008 HAPPY MEAL, 1993

❑ ❑ GER MS9310 HM BOX, 1993, GRIM IN TENT $2-3
❑ ❑ GER MS9311 HM BOX, 1993, GRIM/FRY KID DRIVING RED TRUCK $2-3
❑ ❑ GER ON8801 **BLUE LUNCH BOX,** 1988, GRIM/RM RAISED SCENE W BULLETIN BOARD $2-3
❑ ❑ GER MY9203 **PHONE/PERISCOPE,** 1991, ORG PHONE/1P $2-3

❑ ❑ GER MS9302 **SPY-NOCULARS,** 1992, RED/BLU VIDEO CAM THAT TURNS INTO BINOCULARS/1P $2-3
❑ ❑ GER MS9304 **DECODER/2 PENS,** 1992, RED/YEL DECODER W YEL/WHT PENS/BLU HOLDER/5P $4-5
❑ ❑ JPN MS9303 **SPY-STAMPER PAD,** 1992, STAMPER W INK PAD TURNS INTO A CALCULATOR/2P $1-1.50

COMMENTS: REGIONAL DISTRIBUTION: BELGIUM, DENMARK, FINLAND, FRANCE, GREECE, ITALY, NORWAY, PORTUGAL, SPAIN, SWEDEN, SWITZERLAND: JUNE 1993; JAPAN: DECEMBER 1993; PUERTO RICO: DECEMBER 1993. CALLED, "MISSION UNDERCOVER" IN BELGIUM; "MCSPY" IN JAPAN; "MYSTERY II" IN PUERTO RICO. TOYS PACKAGED IN GERMANY/NOT SPECIFICALLY DISTRIBUTED IN GERMANY; W EUROPEAN LANGUAGES PRINTED ON INSERT CARD. GER MS9302/03, GER ON8801, AND GER MY9203 WERE ISSUED PREVIOUSLY IN THE USA. GER ON8801 WAS ISSUED IN RED AND GRN IN THE USA, NOT BLUE.

GER MS9302

GER MS9310   GER MS9311

GER MS9304

MAGIC WINDOW/PICTURE PROMOTION, 1993

❏ ❏ UK MA9301 **MAGIC WINDOW - RONALD/BAND,** 1992, PURP/
   MCD BAND/PAPER $3-4
❏ ❏ UK MA9302 **MAGIC WINDOW - GRIMACE,** 1992, YEL/RIDING
   BICYCLE/PAPER $3-4
❏ ❏ UK MA9303 **MAGIC WINDOW - CHARS EXERCISING,** 1992,
   GRN/ON PLATFORM/PAPER $3-4
❏ ❏ UK MA9304 **MAGIC WINDOW - CHARS/GRIM,** 1992, ORG/ON
   TRAIN/PAPER $3-4

COMMENTS: REGIONAL DISTRIBUTION: UK: 1992. MADE BY
   SIMON MARKETING INT. GMBH.D-6072 DREIEICH. PRINTED
   IN THE NETHERLANDS.

MALKREISEL/SPIN TOPS JUNIOR TUTE, 1993

❏ ❏ GER SP9301 **TOP - RED,** 1993, W GRN OR BLU OR YEL
   SPINNER $2-3
❏ ❏ GER SP9302 **TOP - YEL,** 1993, W PURP OR PNK OR RED
   SPINNER $2-3

COMMENTS: NATIONAL DISTRIBUTION: GERMANY - AUGUST
   1993.

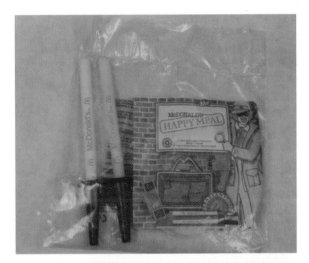

UK MA9301

JPN MS9303

GER SP9301

AUS CH9304   AUS CH9303   AUS CH9302   AUS CH9301

McDONALDLAND CHARACTERS PROMOTION, 1993

❑ ❑ AUS CH9301 **BIG MAC,** 1993, 2" FIGURINE $6-8
❑ ❑ AUS CH9302 **HAMBURGLAR,** 1993, 2" FIGURINE $6-8
❑ ❑ AUS CH9303 **MAYOR MCCHEESE,** 1993, 2" FIGURINE $6-8
❑ ❑ AUS CH9304 **RONALD,** 1993, 2" FIGURINE $6-8

COMMENTS: REGIONAL DISTRIBUTION:AUSTRALIA/NEW
ZEALAND - 1993.

McDONALDLAND VILLAGE HAPPY MEAL, 1994/1993

*** IDENTICAL BOX: MEX/JPN VI9310
❑ ❑ *** VI9310 HM BOX, 1993, VILLAGE $2-3

❑ ❑ GER VI9310 HM BOX, 1993, CITY HOUSE $2-3
❑ ❑ GER VI9311 HM BOX, 1993, COUNTRY SCENE $2-3
❑ ❑ GER VI9312 HM BOX, 1993, FIREHOUSE $2-3
❑ ❑ GER VI9313 HM BOX, 1993, RESTAURANT $2-3

*** IDENTICAL TOYS: CAN/CHN/FRA/JP/ZEA VI9301/02/03/04
❑ ❑ *** VI9301 **VILLAGE HOUSE/BLU ROOF,** 1993, BIRDIE IN
BLU JEEP/STICKER SHEET $5-8
❑ ❑ *** VI9302 **VILLAGE HOUSE/GRN ROOF,** 1993, FRY KIDS IN
RED FIRE TRUCK/STICKER SH $5-8
❑ ❑ *** VI9303 **VILLAGE HOUSE/RED ROOF,** 1993, RON IN RED
SHOE CAR/STICKER SHEET $5-8
❑ ❑ *** VI9304 **VILLAGE HOUSE/YEL ROOF,** 1993, GRIMACE IN
GRN ENGINE/STICKER SHEET $5-8

❑ ❑ CHN VI9302 **VILLAGE HOUSE/PURP ROOF,** 1993, FRY KIDS
IN RED FIRE TRUCK/STICKER SH $5-8
❑ ❑ CHN VI9304 **VILLAGE HOUSE/PNK ROOF,** 1993, GRIMACE
IN GRN ENGINE/STICKER SHEET $5-8

COMMENTS: REGIONAL DISTRIBUTION: EUROPE/UK: NOVEM-
BER-DECEMBER 1993; CHILE: MAY 1994; JAPAN: JUNE
1994; QUEBEC, CANADA, VENEZUELA, NEW ZEALAND:
MARCH 1994;ARGENTINA: OCTOBER 1994. HAPPY MEAL
SET IN JAPAN IS CALLED, "OKOSAMA SET." NOTE: ROOF
COLORS VARY ACCORDING TO THE COUNTRIES DISTRIB-
UTED: RED or BLU or GRN or YEL or PURPLE OR PINK.
CHINA'S SET HAS LIGHTER COLORS ON ROOF, i.e. PINK
INSTEAD OF RED; PURPLE INSTEAD OF GREEN. VILLAGE
HOUSES WERE PACKAGED IN GERMANY AND CHINA; NOT
SPECIFICALLY DISTRIBUTED IN GERMANY.

JPN VI9310

*** VI9304
NEW ZEALAND

*** VI9301   GERMANY

NEW ZEALAND
*** VI9302

NEW ZEALAND
*** VI9303

GERMANY

CHN VI9304   CHN VI9302

CHN VI9304   CHN VI9302

MCJUEGOS HAPPY MEAL, 1993

- ❑ ❑ MEX JU9301 **BEAD GAME - BIRDIE,** 1993, PNK $4-7
- ❑ ❑ MEX JU9302 **BEAD GAME - GRIMACE,** 1993, GRN $4-7
- ❑ ❑ MEX JU9303 **BEAD GAME - HAMBURGLAR,** 1993, ORG $4-7
- ❑ ❑ MEX JU9304 **BEAD GAME - RONALD,** 1993, YEL $4-7

COMMENTS: REGIONAL DISTRIBUTION: MEXICO, COSTA RICO: MAY 1993; PUERTO RICO: JUNE 1993.

MEGAFUN FEST HAPPY MEAL, 1993

- ❑ ❑ SIN MA9201 **HAT - RONALD,** 1993, IN HAT TRICK $10-15
- ❑ ❑ SIN CI9101 **CAR - RONALD,** 1993, IN BOB CAR $10-15
- ❑ ❑ SIN RE9404 **CAR - RONALD,** 1993, IN GRN SOAP BOX/REV-UP CAR $10-15
- ❑ ❑ SIN ME9304 **YO YO - RONALD,** 1993, BLU $10-15
- ❑ ❑ SIN ME9355 TRAYLINER, 1993, THE RONALD McDONALD MEGAFUN FEST $1-1.50

COMMENTS: REGIONAL DISTRIBUTION: JAPAN/SINGAPORE - MARCH 1993. SIN (ME9301) MA9201 = McDONALDLAND MAGIA *** MA9201; SIN (ME9302) = SIN CI9101, CIRCUS PARADE HAPPY MEAL, 1991; SIN (ME9303) = UK RE9404, REV-UP HAPPY MEAL, 1994. THE FIRST THREE PREMIUMS WERE PREVIOUSLY ISSUED IN DIFFERENT HAPPY MEAL PROMOTIONS.

MEX JU9301   MEX JU9302   MEX JU9303   MEX JU9304

SIN ME9304

SIN ME9355

MEX MU9310

MEX MU9302   MEX MU9301

MUPPET BABIES (MEXICO) HAPPY MEAL, 1993

❑ ❑ MEX MU9310 HM BOX, 1993, MUPPET BABIES CHARAC ON YO YOGI $2-3
❑ ❑ MEX MU9301 **GONZO,** 1992, RED GONZO ON GRN/YEL SQUAD $5-7
❑ ❑ MEX MU9302 **MS. PIGGY,** 1992, WAVING ON TUR-PNK MOPED $5-7
❑ ❑ MEX MU9303 **KERMIT,** 1992, ON ORG/BLU JET SKI $5-7
❑ ❑ MEX MU9304 **FOSSIE,** 1992, ON GRN/PUR RACE CAR SKATEBOARD $5-7

COMMENTS: REGIONAL DISTRIBUTION: MEXICO, PANAMA, GUATEMALA: MARCH 1993 - COLLECT ALL 4; PUERTO RICO, COSTA RICA, VENEZUELA: APRIL 1993.

MUSIC CASSETTES HAPPY MEAL, 1993

❑ ❑ ZEA MU9301 **CASSETTE-THE WIGGLES,** 1993, 4 SONGS $4-5
❑ ❑ ZEA MU9302 **CASSETTE-INSECTS/BUGS,** 1993, 4 SONGS $4-5
❑ ❑ ZEA MU9303 **CASSETTE-ROCK/ROLL,** 1993, 4 SONGS $4-5
❑ ❑ ZEA MU9304 **CASSETTE-WALKING,** 1993, 4 SONGS $4-5

COMMENTS: NATIONAL DISTRIBUTION: NEW ZEALAND: OCTOBER 1993.

MYSTERY RIDERS HAPPY MEAL, 1993

❑ ❑ ZEA MY9301 **#1 HELICOPTER,** 1992, GRN HELICOPTER $5-7
❑ ❑ ZEA MY9302 **#2 TRAIN,** 1992, RED CHOO CHOO TRAIN $5-7
❑ ❑ ZEA MY9303 **#3 STEAMBOAT,** 1992, BLU STEAMBOAT $5-7
❑ ❑ ZEA MY9304 **#4 BUGGY/JEEP,** 1992, PNK/PURP BUGGY $5-7

COMMENTS: NATIONAL DISTRIBUTION: NEW ZEALAND - JANUARY 1993 AND SEPTEMBER 27, 1993. BY SPINNING THE RECTANGLE, DIFFERENT CHARACTER FACES APPEAR.

ZEA MY9303

ZEA MY9302

ZEA MY9301

ZEA MY9304

NICKELODEON GAME GADGETS/MCMOVERS/SOUNDS OF McDONALDLAND HAPPY MEAL, 1993

❑ ❑ *** NI9301 **APPLAUSE PAWS,** 1992, YEL CLAPPING HANDS/
PNK BASE $1-1.25
❑ ❑ *** NI9302 **BLIMP GAME,** 1992, GRN BLIMP W WHISTLES/
SPINS $1-1.25
❑ ❑ *** NI9303 **GOTCHA GUSHER,** 1992, FLY SPRAY CAN
SQUIRTER $1-1.25
❑ ❑ *** NI9304 **LOUD-MOUTH MIKE,** 1992, PNK/GRN MICRO-
PHONE $1-1.25

COMMENTS: REGIONAL DISTRIBUTION: LATIN AMERICA: 1993;
UK: NOVEMBER-DECEMBER 1994. CALLED, "MCMOVERS"
IN THE UK AND "SOUNDS OF McDONALDLAND" IN RE-
GIONAL DISTRIBUTIONS.

PHONECARD/BT PROMOTION, 1993

❑ ❑ UK PH9301 **BACON & EGG MCMUFFIN CARD,** 1993, BT
PHONE CARD $8-12
❑ ❑ UK PH9302 **BIG BREAKFAST CARD,** 1993, BT PHONE CARD
$8-12
❑ ❑ UK PH9303 **McDONALD'S BREAKFAST CARD,** 1993, BT
PHONE CARD $8-12
❑ ❑ UK PH9304 **SAUSAGE & EGG MCMUFFIN CARD,** 1993, BT
PHONE CARD $8-12
❑ ❑ UK PH9355 TRAYLINER, 1993, BT PHONECARD $1-1.25

COMMENTS: REGIONAL DISTRIBUTION: UK: OCTOBER 1993.
FREE £1.00 BT PHONE CARD WITH 3 VOUCHERS. EACH
VOUCHER EQUALED ONE BREAKFAST VISIT.

PINBALL PROMOTION, 1993

❑ ❑ AUS PI9301 **PINBALL - BIRDIE,** 1993, BLU/BIRDIE FLYING
$4-5
❑ ❑ AUS PI9302 **PINBALL - GRIM,** 1993, ORG/GRIM RUNNING
$4-5
❑ ❑ AUS PI9303 **PINBALL - HAMB,** 1993, GRN/HAMB WAVING
$4-5
❑ ❑ AUS PI9304 **PINBALL - RON,** 1993, RED/RON WAVING $4-5

COMMENTS: REGIONAL DISTRIBUTION: AUSTRALIA: 1993.

POST CARDS/McDONALDLAND PROMOTION, 1993

*** IDENTICAL POST CARDS: GER/FRA/UK PO9301/02/03/04
❑ ❑ *** PO9301 **POST CARD - HAPPY BIRTHDAY,** 1993, RON/
CHARS W BIRTHDAY CAKE/PAPER $1-2
❑ ❑ *** PO9302 **POST CARD - PLANTING A GARDEN,** 1993,
RON/CHARS PLANTING/PAPER $1-2
❑ ❑ *** PO9303 **POST CARD - PLAYING/BAND,** 1993, RON/
CHARS ON STAGE/PAPER $1-2
❑ ❑ *** PO9304 **POST CARD - PLAYING SOCCER,** 1993, RON/
CHARS SCORING/PAPER $1-2

COMMENTS: REGIONAL DISTRIBUTION: EUROPE: 1993. PACK-
AGED BY SIMON MARKETING IN GERMANY; DISTRIBUTED
IN EUROPE. NOTE: COUNTRY OF DISTRIBUTION IS
MARKED ON THE PAPER INSERT: F = FRANCE; UK =
ENGLAND; HOL = HOLLAND.

UK PH9303   UK PH9304

UK PH9302   UK PH9301

UK PH9355

AUS PI9301   AUS PI9303   AUS PI9302

FRANCE

FRA PO9301   FRA PO9302

FRA PO9303   FRA PO9304

GERMANY

GER CU9301   GER CU9303

PUZZELWURFEL/HAPPY CUBES JUNIOR TUTE, 1993

❏ ❏ GER CU9310 HM BAG, 1993, JUNIOR TUTE/PUZZLE $2-3
❏ ❏ GER CU9301 **CUBE PUZZLE,** 1993, GRN/6P $5-7
❏ ❏ GER CU9302 **CUBE PUZZLE,** 1993, RED/6P $5-7
❏ ❏ GER CU9303 **CUBE PUZZLE,** 1993, YEL/6P $5-7
❏ ❏ GER CU9365 TRANSLITE/LG, 1993 $25-40

COMMENTS: NATIONAL DISTRIBUTION: GERMANY: FEBRUARY 4-28, 1993.

REV-UPS/VROOMERS HAPPY MEAL, 1993

*** IDENTICAL BOXES: GER/UK RE9310/11/12/13
❏ ❏ *** RE9310 HM BOX, 1993, BEACH SCENE/THE BEACH $2-3
❏ ❏ *** RE9311 HM BOX, 1993, CITY SCENE/VILLAGE/SHOPPING UNDER ARCHES $2-3
❏ ❏ *** RE9312 HM BOX, 1993, GRAND STANDS/SKATEBOARD PARK W RONALD $2-3
❏ ❏ *** RE9313 HM BOX, 1993, HORSE FARM/COUNTRY LANE $2-3

*** IDENTICAL TOYS: DEN/UK RE9301/02/03/04
❏ ❏ *** RE9301 **BIRDIE ON MOPED,** 1992, TURQ MOPED $3-4
❏ ❏ *** RE9302 **GRIMACE ON SKATEBOARD,** 1992, GRN SKATEBOARD $3-4
❏ ❏ *** RE9303 **HAMBURGLAR ON JET SKI,** 1991, ORG WATER JET SKI $3-4
❏ ❏ *** RE9304 **RONALD ON RACER,** 1992, ON GREEN SOAP BOX DERBY RACER $3-4

❏ ❏ UK RE9326 DISPLAY/PREMIUMS, 1993 $75-100
❏ ❏ DEN RE9344 POSTER/SM, 1993, VROOMERS $15-20
❏ ❏ UK RE9364 TRANSLITE/SM, 1993 $4-6
❏ ❏ UK RE9365 TRANSLITE/LG, 1993 $7-10

COMMENTS: NATIONAL DISTRIBUTION: UK: MAY 7, 1993; BELGIUM, DENMARK, FINLAND, FRANCE, GREECE, ITALY, HOLLAND, NORWAY, PORTUGAL, SPAIN, SWEDEN, SWITZERLAND, GUATEMALA, MEXICO, PANAMA, VENEZUELA: FEBRUARY 1993; TAIWAN: FEBRUARY 1994; COSTA RICA: JANUARY 1993; PUERTO RICO, SINGAPORE: APRIL-MAY 1993; JAPAN: 1994.

GER CU9365

UK RE9312   *** RE9313   *** RE9311   *** RE9310

UK RE9301   UK RE9302   UK RE9303   UK RE9304

UK RE9326

DEN RE9344

RONALD SCHOOL KIT HAPPY MEAL, 1994/1993

❏ ❏ GUA SC9301 **RULER/SCORE CARD,** 1993, GRIM SCORE
CARD/RULER $2-4
❏ ❏ GUA SC9302 **ERASER-FF BOX,** 1993, RED FF BOX/ERASER
$2-4
❏ ❏ GUA SC9303 **STAMP PAD/RON,** 1993 $3-5
❏ ❏ GUA SC9304 **SCISSORS/RON,** 1993, YEL $1-2

COMMENTS: REGIONAL DISTRIBUTION: GUATEMALA - 1993 AND
1994.

SNOW DOME/SCHNEEKUGELN JUNIOR TUTE, 1993

❏ ❏ GER SN9301 **SNOW DOME - RONALD,** 1993, W ICE SKATES
W HOUSE/SNOW $7-10
❏ ❏ GER SN9302 **SNOW DOME - SNOWMAN,** 1993, IN FRONT
OF McDONALD'S RESTAURANT $7-10
❏ ❏ GER SN9303 **SNOW DOME - RON/SNOWMAN,** 1993, W
SNOWMAN IN FOREST $7-10
❏ ❏ GER SN9365 TRANSLITE/LG, 1993 $25-40

COMMENTS: NATIONAL DISTRIBUTION: GERMANY - NOVEMBER
4-28, 1993.

GER SN9301   GER SN9302   GER SN9303

TALE SPIN PROMOTION, 1993

❏ ❏ AUS TA9301 **BALOO,** 1993, STANDING W LEFT ARM RAISED
TO HAT $3-4
❏ ❏ AUS TA9302 **FOX,** 1993, STANDING W BLU/SHIRT/PANTS W
SWORD $3-4
❏ ❏ AUS TA9303 **KIT,** 1993, ON SURF BOARD/STANDING W GRN
SHIRT/BLU BALL CAP ON BACKWARDS $3-4
❏ ❏ AUS TA9304 **MOLLY,** 1993, GIRL STANDING W PINK/PURP
OUTFIT/ARMS EXTENDED OUT/BLU BOWS IN HAIR $3-4

COMMENTS: REGIONAL DISTRIBUTION: AUSTRALIA: SUMMER
1993. FIGURINES ARE SIMILAR TO USA CEREAL PREMI-
UMS, EXCEPT A MOLDED BLANK LABEL COVERS INFOR-
MATION ON BOTTOM OF FIGURINES.

TANGRAM PUZZLE PROMOTION, 1993

❏ ❏ GER GR9301 **SET 1 PUZZLE - RED,** 1993, 7P SPONGE/
SQUARE $3-4
❏ ❏ GER GR9302 **SET 2 PUZZLE - YEL,** 1993, 7P SPONGE/
SQUARE $3-4

GERMANY

GER SN9365

AUS TA9301   AUS TA9303

AUS TA9302   AUS TA9304

GER GR9301

GER GR9303

GER TE9365

UK TW9301   UK TW9302   UK TW9303   UK TW9304

❏ ❏ GER GR9303 **SET 3 PUZZLE - BLU,** 1993, 7P SPONGE/
SQUARE $3-4

❏ ❏ GER GR9304 **SET 4 PUZZLE - GRN,** 1993, 7P SPONGE/
SQUARE $3-4

COMMENTS: REGIONAL DISTRIBUTION: GERMANY 1993 AND
1994. TWO DIFFERENT PACKAGED SETS MAY EXISTS.

TEAM NFL CAPS PROMOTION, 1993

❏ ❏ GER TE9301 **HAT - MIAMI DOLPHINS,** 1993, GRN W TEAM
LOGO/MCD LOGO $5-7

❏ ❏ GER TE9302 **HAT - SAN FRAN 49ERS,** 1993, RED W TEAM
LOGO/MCD LOGO $5-7

❏ ❏ GER TE9303 **HAT - L A RAIDERS,** 1993, BLK W TEAM LOGO/
MCD LOGO $5-7

❏ ❏ GER TE9304 **HAT - MINN VIKINGS,** 1993, PURP W TEAM
LOGO/MCD LOGO $5-7

COMMENTS: NATIONAL DISTRIBUTION: GERMANY - JUNE 1993.
McDONALD'S LOGO PRINTED ON THE BACK OF CAP.

TWISTING SPORTS/SPORT PARADE HAPPY MEAL, 1993

    *** IDENTICAL BOXES: BEL/UK TW9310/11/12/13

❏ ❏ *** TW9310 HM BOX, 1993, BADMITON CLUB/BIRDIE $2-3

❏ ❏ *** TW9311 HM BOX, 1993, FITNESS CENTER $2-3

❏ ❏ *** TW9312 HM BOX, 1993, GYMNASTIC ARENA $2-3

❏ ❏ *** TW9313 HM BOX, 1993, SOCCER FIELD $2-3

❏ ❏ MEX TW9310 HM BOX, 1993, CHARS/SPORTS $2-3

    *** IDENTICAL TOYS: DEN/FRA/UK TW9301/02/03/04

❏ ❏ *** TW9301 **BIRDIE PLAYING BADMINTON,** 1993, ON GRN
PEDESTAL/1P $3-5

❏ ❏ *** TW9302 **GRIMACE W SOCCER BALL,** 1993, ON YEL
PEDESTAL/1P $3-5

❏ ❏ *** TW9303 **HAMBURGLAR LIFTING WEIGHTS,** 1993, ON
ORG PEDESTAL/1P $3-5

❏ ❏ *** TW9304 **RONALD ON TRAMPOLINE,** 1993, ON PURP
PEDESTAL/1P $3-5

❏ ❏ UK TW9326 DISPLAY/PREMS, 1993,T $100-150

❏ ❏ DEN TW9345 REGISTER TOPPER, 1993 $8-12

❏ ❏ UK TW9364 TRANSLITE/SM, 1993,T $15-20

❏ ❏ UK TW9365 TRANSLITE/LG, 1993,T $25-35

COMMENTS: NATIONAL DISTRIBUTION: UK: SEPTEMBER 10-
OCTOBER 1993; FRANCE, PUERTO RICO, ARGENTINA,
VENEZUELA: 1993. CALLED "SPORT PARADE HM" IN
FRANCE AND "TWISTING SPORTS HM" IN UK; "TWISTENDE
SPORTSSTJERNER" IN DEMARK.

WACKY WAVERS HAPPY MEAL, 1993

❏ ❏ AUS WA9301 **BIRDIE/I LIKE BREAKFAST,** 1993, W STICK/
SUCTION CUP/3P $7-10

❏ ❏ AUS WA9302 **GRIMACE/I LIKE THICKSHAKES,** 1993, W
STICK/SUCTION CUP/3P $7-10

UK TW9326

DEN TW9345

□ □ AUS WA9303 **HAMB/I LIKE CHEESE-BURGERS,** 1993, W
 STICK/SUCTION CUP/3P $7-10
□ □ AUS WA9304 **RONALD/WAVE IF YOU LIKE MCD,** 1993, W
 STICK/SUCTION CUP/3P $7-10
□ □ AUS WA9345 REGISTER TOPPER, 1993 $5-8

COMMENTS: REGIONAL DISTRIBUTION: AUSTRALIA: MARCH-
 APRIL 1993.

WATER SQUIRTERS/SPRITZTIERE JUNIOR TUTE/HAPPY MEAL, 1993
□ □ GER WA9301 **SEA DRAGON SQUIRT GUN,** 1993, PINK $4-6
□ □ GER WA9302 **FISH SQUIRT GUN,** 1993, ORANGE $4-6
□ □ GER WA9303 **CROCODILE SQUIRT GUN,** 1993, GREEN $4-6
□ □ GER WA9304 **ELEPHANT SQUIRT GUN,** 1993, BLUE $4-6
□ □ GER WA9365 TRANSLITE/LG, 1993 $25-40

COMMENTS: NATIONAL DISTRIBUTION: GERMANY: JULY 1-25,
 1993; HOLLAND: 1993.

WORLD OF DINOSAURS/DINOSAURIER JUNIOR TUTE/ HAPPY MEAL, 1993
□ □ UK WD9310 HM BOX, 1993, DIPLODOKUS $2-3
□ □ UK WD9311 HM BOX, 1993, STEGOSAURUS/WATERFALL
 $2-3
□ □ UK WD9312 HM BOX, 1993, TRICERATOPS/VOLCANO $2-3
□ □ UK WD9313 HM BOX, 1993, TYRANNOSAURUS REX $2-3

GER WA9301   GER WA9302   GER WA9303   GER WA9304

GER WA9365

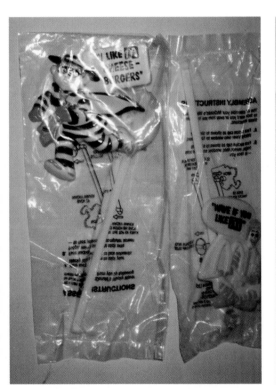

AUS WA9303   AUS WA9304

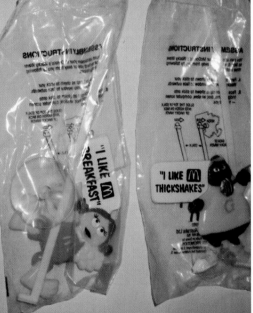

AUS WA9301   AUS WA9302

UK WD9311

AUS WA9345

UK WD9312

201

UK WD9302   UK WD9301   UK WD9303   UK WD9304

GER WD9301

UK WD9326

GER WD9465

*** IDENTICAL TOYS: GER/UK WD9301/02/03/04

❏ ❏ *** WD9301 **DIPLODOKUS**, 1993, 8" LONG/RED/BLU $3-4
❏ ❏ *** WD9302 **STEGOSAURUS**, 1993, 8" LONG/YEL/BRN $3-4
❏ ❏ *** WD9303 **TRICERATOPS**, 1993, 8" LONG/RED/BLK $3-4
❏ ❏ *** WD9304 **TYRANNOSAURUS REX**, 1993, 9" LONG/GRN
$3-4

❏ ❏ AUS WD9305 **PTERANODON**, 1993, 3" LONG $5-7
❏ ❏ AUS WD9306 **STEGOSAURUS**, 1993, 3" LONG $5-7
❏ ❏ AUS WD9307 **TRICERATOPS**, 1993, 3" LONG $5-7
❏ ❏ AUS WD9308 **TYRANNO REX**, 1993, 3" LONG $5-7

❏ ❏ UK WD9326 DISPLAY/PREMIUMS, 1993 $75-100
❏ ❏ UK WD9341 CEILING DANGLER/TERADACTYL, 1993 $7-10
❏ ❏ UK WD9364 TRANSLITE/SM, 1993 $6 -10
❏ ❏ UK WD9365 TRANSLITE/LG, 1993 $10-15
❏ ❏ GER WD9465 TRANSLITE/LG, 1994 $25-40

COMMENTS: NATIONAL DISTRIBUTION: UK: OCTOBER 2-
NOVEMBER 1993; AUSTRALIA, NEW ZEALAND: MAY 1992;
COSTA RICA: MARCH 1993; GERMANY: MARCH 1994.
CALLED, "WORLD OF DINOSAURS" IN THE UK.

YEAR OF THE ROOSTER PROMOTION, 1995/1993

❏ ❏ SIN RO9401 **HAPPY HARRY**, 1993, ROOSTER W VIOLET
SLACKS $3-4
❏ ❏ SIN RO9402 **HEALTHY HENRY**, 1993, ROOSTER W PURP
SLACKS $3-4
❏ ❏ SIN RO9403 **LUCKY LARRY**, 1993, ROOSTER W BLU COAT
$3-4
❏ ❏ SIN RO9404 **WEALTHY WILLY**, 1993, ROOSTER W GRN
SHIRT $3-4

COMMENTS: REGIONAL DISTRIBUTION: HONG KONG,
SINGAPORE: 1993 AND AGAIN IN 1995. COULD HAVE BEEN
A SELF LIQUIDATING PROMOTION.

YO YO/McDONALDLAND JO JO PROMOTION, 1993

❏ ❏ HOL YO9301 **YO YO - BIRDIE/GRIMACE**, 1993, PLAS 2"
DISC/PNK/PURP/2P $3-5
❏ ❏ HOL YO9302 **YO YO - GRIMACE/HAMB**, 1993, PLAS 2" DISC/
PURP/PURP/2P $3-5
❏ ❏ HOL YO9303 **YO YO - HAMBURGLAR/RONALD**, 1993, PLAS
2" DISC/YEL/RED/2P $3-5
❏ ❏ HOL YO9304 **YO YO - RONALD/GRIMACE**, 1993, PLAS 2"
DISC/RED/PURP/2P $3-5

COMMENTS: REGIONAL DISTRIBUTION: GERMANY, BELGIUM,
HOLLAND, NETHERLANDS: 1993. USED AS CLEAN-UP
WEEK GIVE AWAYS. PREMIUMS MARKED MADE IN
GERMANY. PREMIUMS WERE DISTRIBUTED IN EUROPE.

GER YO9302   GER YO9303   GER YO9304

1994

AKROBATS/AKROBATEN/SPIELZEUG JUNIOR TUTE, 1994

- ❏ ❏ USA AS9205 **U-3 RONALD IN LUNAR ROVER,** 1991, RED RUBBER ROVER/YEL SPACESUIT RON $2-2.50
- ❏ ❏ USA BT9306 **BATMAN,** 1993, GRY/BLK BATMAN W BLK REMOVABLE CAPE/2P $1-1.50
- ❏ ❏ USA FI9301 **NATURE VIEWER,** 1993, MAGNIFIER BOTTLE/ 2P $1-1.25
- ❏ ❏ USA LO9305 **U-3 SWINGIN' SEDAN,** 1992, BUGS BUNNY IN RED CAR/RUBBER $2.50-3
- ❏ ❏ USA MS9304 **SPY-TRACKER WATCH,** 1992, WATCH BECOMES A COMPASS/OPENS/1P $1-1.50
- ❏ ❏ USA SN9309 **U-3 DOPEY/SNEEZY SPIN,** 1992, IN BLU COAT ON A PUR RUG $2.50-3.50

- ❏ ❏ GER AK9401 **BIRDIE,** 1994, HAIR UP/STICKY HANDS $5-7
- ❏ ❏ GER AK9402 **HAMBURGLAR,** 1994, ARMS UP/STICKY HANDS $5-7
- ❏ ❏ GER AK9403 **RONALD,** 1994, ARMS UP/STICKY HANDS/ FEET $5-7

- ❏ ❏ GER AK9465 TRANSLITE/LG, 1994 $20-30

COMMENTS: NATIONAL DISTRIBUTION: GERMANY: JANUARY/ FEBRUARY 1994. PREMIUMS WERE DESIGNED TO BE WINDOW/WALL CLIMBERS. U-5 PREMIUMS WERE USA ISSUED (IN ORIGINAL USA PACKAGING) PREMIUMS. USA U-3 TOYS WERE DESIGNED FOR CHILDREN UNDER THE AGE OF 3.

GER AK9401   GER AK9402   GER AK9403

ANIMANIACS HAPPY MEAL, 1995/1994

- ❏ ❏ UK AN9510 HM BOX, 1995 $2-3
- ❏ ❏ UK AN9511 HM BOX, 1995 $2-3
- ❏ ❏ UK AN9512 HM BOX, 1995 $2-3
- ❏ ❏ UK AN9513 HM BOX, 1995 $2-3
- ❏ ❏ CAN AN9409 **U-3 BICYCLE BUILT FOR TRIO,** 1993, PURP BIKE W 3 RED WHLS/3 CHARS RIDING $1.50-2

  *** IDENTICAL TOYS: CAN/GER/UK AN9401/02/03/07
- ❏ ❏ *** AN9401 **BICYCLE BUILT FOR TRIO,** 1993, PURP BIKE W 3 RED WHEELS/3 CHARS RIDING $1-1.50
- ❏ ❏ *** AN9402 **DOT'S ICE CREAM MACHINE,** 1993, ICE CREAM TRUCK W & W/O WORDS "ICE CREAM" $1-1.50
- ❏ ❏ *** AN9403 **GOODSKATE GOODFEATHERS,** 1993, YEL SKATEBOARD/BLU WHEELS/3 BIRDLIKE CHARS RIDING $1-1.50
- ❏ ❏ *** AN9407 **UPSIDE-DOWN WAKKO,** 1993, GRN TRICYCLE/ PUR WHEELS W CHAR RIDING UP SIDE DOWN $1-1.50

- ❏ ❏ CAN AN9404 **MINDY/BUTTONS' WILD RIDE,** 1993, TURQ AUTO/BOY AND ANIMAL RIDING $1-1.50
- ❏ ❏ CAN AN9405 **PINKY AND THE BRAIN MOBILE,** 1993, ORG TRICYCLE W CHAR RIDING IN FRONT WHEEL $1-1.50
- ❏ ❏ CAN AN9406 **SLAPPY/SKIPPY'S CHOPPER,** 1993, PNK/GRN CYCLE W SIDE CAR/2 CHARS RIDING $1-1.50
- ❏ ❏ CAN AN9408 **YAKKO RIDIN' RALPH,** 1993, CHAR RIDING RALPH AS A TRICYCLE $1-1.50
- ❏ ❏ CAN AN9410 ACTIVITY STICKERS, 1994, STICKER SHEET/ BACKING BOARD $.50-1
- ❏ ❏ CAN AN9442 COUNTER CARD, 1994 $3-5
- ❏ ❏ CAN AN9446 PROMTIONAL HM SHEET, 1994, ANIMANIACS HM $1.50-3
- ❏ ❏ UK AN9426 DISPLAY, 1995 $15-25

GER AK9465

GERMANY

GER AN9402

CAN AN9446

CAN AN9442

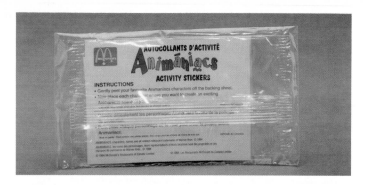

CAN AN9410

USA AN9464

BEL AR9411

COMMENTS: NATIONAL DISTRIBUTION: UK: SEPTEMBER 1995; CANADA, PUERTO RICO: MAY 6-JUNE 2, 1994; NEW ZEALAND: DECEMBER 1994; GERMANY: JUNE 1995: AUSTRALIA: MARCH 1995. UK AN9401/03/07 = USA AN9401/03/07 (See USA ANIMANIACS HAPPY MEAL, 1994). THE USA VERSION ISSUED 8 PREMIUMS, UK ISSUED 4 PREMIUMS. PREMIUM MARKINGS "1993 WARNER BROS". CAN AN9401-09 = USA AN9401-09, LOOSE OUT OF PACKAGE. GERMAN VERSION - GERAN9402 CAME W/O WORDS "ICE CREAM" ON TRUNK.

ARISTOCATS/ARISTOGATOS/ARISTOCHATS HAPPY MEAL, 1994

*** IDENTICAL BOXES: BEL/GER/UK AR9410/11/12/13
- ❏ ❏ *** AR9410 HM BOX, 1993, CATS IN ATTIC $2-3
- ❏ ❏ *** AR9411 HM BOX, 1993, CATS ON RAILROAD TRACKS $2-3
- ❏ ❏ *** AR9412 HM BOX, 1993, PARLOR/LOUNGE $2-3
- ❏ ❏ *** AR9413 HM BOX, 1993, VICTORIAN STREET/PARIS $2-3

*** IDENTICAL TOYS: DEN/UK AR9401/02/03/04
- ❏ ❏ *** AR9401 **DUCHESS,** 1993, WHT CAT ON PURP PILLOW $4-5
- ❏ ❏ *** AR9402 **EDGAR,** 1993, BUTLER ON RED MOTOR CYCLE $4-5
- ❏ ❏ *** AR9403 **KITTENS,** 1993, 3 KITTENS IN BLU SIDE CAR $4-5
- ❏ ❏ *** AR9404 **O'MALLEY,** 1993, GINGER CAT RESTING $4-5

- ❏ ❏ UK AR9426 DISPLAY W PREMIUMS, 1993 $125-175
- ❏ ❏ DEN AR9444 POSTER, 1993, ARISTOCATS $10-15
- ❏ ❏ DEN AR9445 REGISTER TOPPER, 1993, DUCHESS $5-8
- ❏ ❏ DEN AR9446 REGISTER TOPPER, 1993, EDGAR $5-8
- ❏ ❏ DEN AR9447 REGISTER TOPPER, 1993, KITTENS $5-8
- ❏ ❏ DEN AR9448 REGISTER TOPPER, 1993, O'MALLEY $5-8
- ❏ ❏ FRA AR9445 REGISTER TOPPER, 1993, DUCHESS $5-8
- ❏ ❏ FRA AR9446 REGISTER TOPPER, 1993, EDGAR $5-8
- ❏ ❏ FRA AR9447 REGISTER TOPPER, 1993, KITTENS $5-8
- ❏ ❏ FRA AR9448 REGISTER TOPPER, 1993, O'MALLEY $5-8
- ❏ ❏ UK AR9464 TRANSLITE/SM, 1993 $7-10
- ❏ ❏ FRA AR9465 TRANSLITE/LG, 1993 $10-15
- ❏ ❏ UK AR9465 TRANSLITE/LG, 1993 $10-15

COMMENTS: NATIONAL DISTRIBUTION: UK: MARCH 25-APRIL 21, 1994; HOLLAND/NETHERLANDS: JUNE 29-AUGUST 2, 1994; HUNGARY/SCANDANAVIA/SWITZERLAND - APRIL 1994; BELGIUM/FRANCE - JULY 1994. GER AR9410-13 WAS DISTRIBUTED IN SPAIN USING THE NAME, "ARISTOGATOS HM"; CALLED "ARISTOCHATS HM" IN FRANCE/GERMANY. UK HM PROMOTION COINCIDED WITH RELEASE OF DISNEY MOVIE. BELGIUM MADE BOXES WERE DISTRIBUTED IN SPAIN. CALLED, "WALT DISNEY'S CLASSIC" ARISTOCATS. DIFFERING DATES OF DISTRIBUTION INDICATE RESURFACING OF PREMIUMS BEING GIVEN OUT, BASED ON SUPPLY AND DEMAND.

UK AR9413   UK AR9412   UK AR9411   UK AR9410

UK AR9401   UK AR9402   UK AR9403   UK AR9404

UK AR9426

DEN AR9444

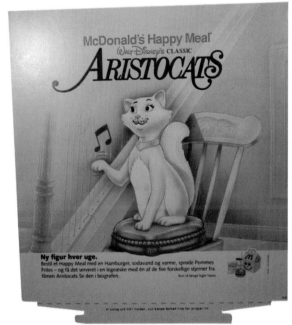

FRA AR9446

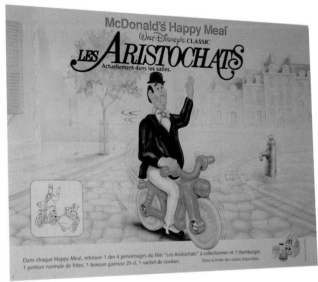

DEN AR9445

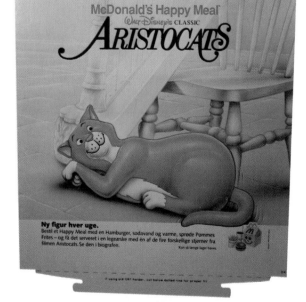

FRA AR9447   DEN AR9448

205

FRA AR9465

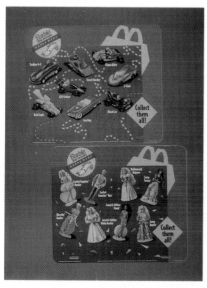

GERMANY

ASTERIX JUNIOR TUTE/HAPPY MEAL, 1994

❑ ❑ BEL AS9410 HM BOX, 1994, SHORE $2-3
❑ ❑ BEL AS9411 HM BOX, 1994, FOREST $2-3
❑ ❑ BEL AS9412 HM BOX, 1994, BIRD HOUSE/VILLAGE $2-3
❑ ❑ BEL AS9413 HM BOX, 1994, OBELIX IN BOAT $2-3

    *** **IDENTICAL TOYS: GER/FRA/NED AS9401/02/03/04**
❑ ❑ *** AS9401 **DELPHIN**, 1994, GREY DOLPHIN $3-5
❑ ❑ *** AS9402 **IDEFIX**, 1994, WHT/BLK DOG $3-5
❑ ❑ *** AS9403 **ASTERIX**, 1994, IN BRN BOAT W SAIL $3-5
❑ ❑ *** AS9404 **OBELIX**, 1994, LG MAN W BLU/WHT BARREL PANTS $3-5

❑ ❑ GER AS9465 TRANSLITE/LG, 1994 $25-40

COMMENTS: NATIONAL DISTRIBUTION: GERMANY: SEPTEMBER 28-OCTOBER 1994; NETHERLANDS: OCTOBER 12-NOVEMBER 15, 1994; FRANCE: OCTOBER 1994. PACKAGING DIFFERENT FOR EACH PREMIUM WITHIN EACH COUNTRY.

BARBIE & FRIENDS / WORLD OF HOT WHEELS HAPPY MEAL, 1994

❑ ❑ MEX BA9410 HM BOX, 1994, BICYCLIN BARBIE $2-3
❑ ❑ CAN BA9430 HM BAG, 1994, BARBIE AND FRIENDS/WORLD OF HOT WHEELS $1-1.25

❑ ❑ CAN BA9417 **U-3 BARBIE BALL**, 1994, LILAC BALL W BARBIE PICTURE $1-1.50
❑ ❑ CAN SX9418 **U-3 FAST FORWARD**, 1991, GRN/PURPLE MINI-STREEX W WHEELS $1-1.50

    *** **IDENTICAL TOYS: CAN/MEX BA9401/03/05/08**
❑ ❑ *** BA9401 **#1 BICYCLIN BARBIE**, 1994, GRN/PNK BARBIE ON PNK BIKE $1-1.50
❑ ❑ CAN BA9402 **#2 JEWEL/GLITTER SHANI**, 1994, BLACK BARBIE W ORG DRESS $1-1.50
❑ ❑ *** BA9403 **#3 CAMP BARBIE**, 1994, PNK JACKET/BLONDE HAIR/BLU SHORTS/GRN BASE $1-1.50
❑ ❑ CAN BA9404 **#4 CAMP TERESA**, 1994, BLU SHIRT/PNK SUNGLASSES/BRN HAIR/YEL PANTS $1-1.50
❑ ❑ CAN BA9419 **#4 CAMP TERESA**, 1994, BLU SHIRT/BLU SUNGLASSES/BLU FISHING PATCH ON YEL PANTS $2.50-4
❑ ❑ *** BA9405 **#5 LOCKET SURPRISE BARBIE**, 1994, WHT BARBIE/PNK PARTY DRESS/BLONDE HAIR/PNK HEELS $1-1.50
❑ ❑ CAN BA9406 **#6 LOCKET SURPRISE KEN**, 1994, WHT KEN W GOLD JACKET/TURQ SLACKS $1-1.50
❑ ❑ CAN BA9407 **#7 JEWEL/GLITTER BRIDE**, 1994, WHT LONG DRESS/BLONDE HAIR/PNK FLOWERS $1-1.50

GER AS9404   GER AS9403   GER AS9402   GER AS9401

MEX BA9410

CAN BA9443

GER AS9465

CAN BA9442

CAN BA9446

JPN BA9455

MEX HW9416   MEX HW9409   MEX HW9413

❑ ❑ *** BA9408 **#8 BRIDESMAID SKIPPER,** 1994, LILAC DRESS/
BLONDE HAIR $1-1.50

    *** **IDENTICAL HOT WHEELS: CAN/MEX HW9409/11/13/14/16**
❑ ❑ CAN HW9409 **#9 BOLD EAGLE,** 1994, YEL/SILVER HOT
ROD

                                                           $1-1.50
❑ ❑ CAN HW9410 **#10 BLACK,** 1994, BLACK HOT ROD $1-1.50
❑ ❑ *** **HW9411 #11 FLAME RIDER,** 1994, BLK/RED HOT ROD W
MCD LOGO $1-1.50
❑ ❑ CAN HW9412 **#12 GAS HOG,** 1994, RED CONVERTIBLE
                                                         $1-1.50
❑ ❑ *** **HW9413 #13 TURBINE 4-2,** 1994, BLU TURBINE/JET CAR
                                                         $1-1.50
❑ ❑ *** **HW9414 #14 2-COOL,** 1994, PURP/SIL SPORTS CAR
                                                         $1-1.50
❑ ❑ CAN HW9415 **#15 STREET SHOCKER,** 1994, GRN SPORTS
CAR $1-1.50
❑ ❑ *** **HW9416 #16 X21J CRUISER,** 1994, BLU/SIL FORMULA 1
CAR $1-1.50

❑ ❑ CAN BA9426 DISPLAY/PREMIUMS, 1994 $50-75
❑ ❑ CAN BA9442 COUNTER CARD/BARBIE/FRIEN, 1994 $3-5
❑ ❑ CAN BA9443 COUNTER CARD/HOT WHEELS, 1994 $3-5
❑ ❑ CAN BA9446 PROMO CARD, 1994, COLOR PIC TOYS $2-4
❑ ❑ JPN BA9455 TRAYLINER, 1994, PICTURE 16 TOYS $1-1.25
❑ ❑ CAN BA9464 TRANSLITE/SM, 1994 $4-6

COMMENTS: NATIONAL DISTRIBUTION: CANADA: AUGUST 5-
SEPTEMBER 8, 1994; JAPAN: 1994; MEXICO, COSTA RICA,
GUATEMALA, PANAMA, VENEZUELA: 1994; NEW ZEALAND:
OCTOBER 1994; SINGAPORE, PANAMA: 1994. NOTE:
CANADA AND JAPAN'S HAPPY MEAL TOYS DISTRIBUTED
ARE THE SAME AS USA'S BARBIE/HOT WHEEL HAPPY
MEAL PREMIUMS, 1994. CAN BA9417 IS SHOWN ON THE
PROMOTIONAL/ADVERTISING CARD SENT TO THE
STORES. CAN BA9404 WAS DISTRIBUTED IN CANADA AND
IN JAPAN WITH INTERNATIONAL PACKAGING.

BASEBALL HATS/BUBBLE BLOWER HAPPY MEAL, 1994
❑ ❑ JPN HA9401 **BIRDIE,** 1994, WEARING YEL BASEBALL HAT W
RED ARCHES $4-7
❑ ❑ JPN HA9402 **GRIMACE,** 1994, WEARING PURP HAT W YEL
ARCHES $4-7

JPN HA9401   JPN HA9402   JPN HA9403   JPN HA9404

JPN HA9455

❑ ❑ JPN HA9403 **HAMB,** 1994, WEARING BLK HAT W YEL
ARCHES $4-7
❑ ❑ JPN HA9404 **RONALD,** 1994, WEARING RED HAT W YEL
ARCHES $4-7
❑ ❑ JPN HA9455 TRAYLINER, 1994, T $1-1.25

COMMENTS: REGIONAL DISTRIBUTION: JAPAN - 1994.

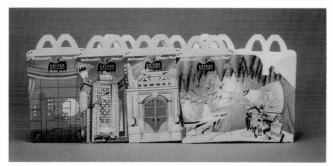

UK BT9413   UK BT9412   UK BT9411   UK BT9410

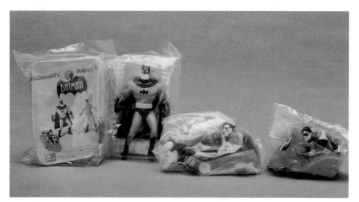

UK BT9407   UK BT9406   UK BT9401   UK BT9403

BATMAN THE ANIMATED SERIES JUNIOR TUTE/HAPPY MEAL, 1994

*** IDENTICAL BOXES: GER/UK BT9410/11/12/13
❑ ❑ *** BT9410 HM BOX, 1994, BAT CAVE $2-3
❑ ❑ *** BT9411 HM BOX, 1994, CITY MUSEUM $2-3
❑ ❑ *** BT9412 HM BOX, 1994, GOTHAM CITY/PENGUIN $2-3
❑ ❑ *** BT9413 HM BOX, 1994, PENTHOUSE SUITE/CATWOMAN
$2-3

*** IDENTICAL TOYS: GER/NED/UK BT9401/03/06/07
❑ ❑ *** BT9401 **JOKER**, 1993, IN PURP CAR/1P $3-4
❑ ❑ *** BT9403 **ROBIN**, 1993, IN RED BATMOBILE/1P $3-4
❑ ❑ *** BT9406 **BATMAN**, 1993, W BLK CAPE/2P $3-4
❑ ❑ *** BT9407 **CATWOMAN**, 1993, W YEL LEOPARD/2P $3-4

❑ ❑ GER BT9420 COMIC BOOK -**COMICGEN**, 1993, 6" X 8" $1-2
❑ ❑ UK BT9426 DISPLAY/PREMIUMS, 1993 $125-175
❑ ❑ FRA BT9442 COUNTER CARD, 1994 $5-8
❑ ❑ DEN BT9444 POSTER/SM, 1993 $8-12
❑ ❑ DEN BT9447 POSTER/LG, 1993 $15-25
❑ ❑ UK BT9464 TRANSLITE/SM, 1993 $15-20
❑ ❑ UK BT9465 TRANSLITE/LG, 1993 $30-45
❑ ❑ GER BT9465 TRANSLITE/LG, 1993 $30-45

COMMENTS: NATIONAL DISTRIBUTION: UK: JANUARY 28-FEBRUARY 24, 1994; HOLLAND, BELGIUM, SWITZERLAND, NETHERLANDS: MARCH 30-MAY 3, 1994; GERMANY: SEPTEMBER 1994. GER/NED/UK BT9401/03/06/07 = USA BT9301/03/06/07 (See USA BATMAN THE ANIMATED SERIES HAPPY MEAL, 1993). THE UK ISSUED 4 PREMIUMS (1994), THE USA ISSUED 8 PREMIUMS (1993). GERMANY ALSO ISSUED A 10 PAGE COMIC/6" X 8" PROMOTING BATMAN FIGURES/VIDEOS. GERMANY BATMAN JUNIOR TUTE BOXES WERE THE ONLY SET OF BOXES MADE BY SIMON MARKETING THAT WAS DISTRIBUTED IN GERMANY. ALL OTHER JUNIOR TUTE CAME WITH BAGS.

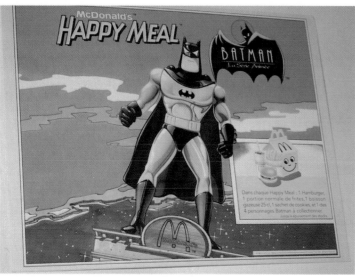

FRA BT9442

FRANCE

GER BT9465

GER BT9420

FRA BT9444

USA

USA BT9364

DEN BT9444

DEN BT9447

USA BT9301   USA BT9303   USA BT9306   USA BT9307

USA BO9465

BOBBY'S WORLD HAPPY MEAL, 1994

❑ ❑ CAN BO9410 HM BOX, 1993, CHEAP SKATES/BOBBY
SKATING $2-3
❑ ❑ CAN BO9411 HM BOX, 1993, DRAG/BOBBY IN WAGON $2-3
❑ ❑ CAN BO9412 HM BOX, 1993, PLAN(ET)/BOBBY ON BIG
WHEELS $2-3
❑ ❑ CAN BO9413 HM BOX, 1993, WAVE/BOBBY IN POOL $2-3
❑ ❑ CAN BO9405 **U-3 BOBBY/INNER TUBE,** 1993, BOBBY IN
INNER TUBE/RUBBER $1.50-2
❑ ❑ CAN BO9401 **3-WHEELER/SPACESHIP,** 1993, YEL 3-
WHEELER/RED SPACESHIP/3P $1-1.50
❑ ❑ CAN BO9402 **INNERTUBE/SUBMARINE,** 1993, GRN
INNERTUBE/ORG SUBMARINE/3P $1-1.50
❑ ❑ CAN BO9403 **SKATES/ROLLER COASTER,** 1993, BLU
SKATES/GRN ROLLER COASTER/3P $1- 1.50
❑ ❑ CAN BO9404 **WAGON/RACE CAR,** 1993, RED WAGON/BLU
RACE CAR/3P $1-1.50
❑ ❑ CAN BO9426 DISPLAY, 1994 $15-25

COMMENTS: NATIONAL DISTRIBUTION: CANADA - MARCH 1994;
PUERTO RICO: 1994.

CABBAGE PATCH KIDS/TONKA (CANADA) HAPPY MEAL, 1994

❑ ❑ CAN CP9430 HM BAG, 1994, CABBAGE PATCH KIDS/TONKA
$1-1.25
❑ ❑ CAN CP9409 **U-3 SARAJANE,** 1994, CPK DOLL/RUBBER
$1.50-2
❑ ❑ CAN TK9410 **U-3 DUMP TRUCK,** 1994, YEL/BLU RUBBER
$1.50-2
❑ ❑ CAN CP9401 **WK 1 MIMI KRISTINA,** 1994, ANGEL/GOLD
HORN $1-1.50
❑ ❑ CAN CP9402 **WK 2 KIMBERLY KATHERINE,** 1994, SANTA'S
HELPER/WHT APRON $1-1.50
❑ ❑ CAN CP9403 **WK 3 ABIGAIL LYNN,** 1994, TOY SOLDIER/BLU
TOP HAT/CANDY CANE/BLK DOLL $1-1.50
❑ ❑ CAN CP9404 **WK 4 MICHELLE ELYSE,** 1994, SNOW FAIRY/
WHT DRESS/SNOWFLAKE/WHT DOLL $1-1.50
❑ ❑ CAN TK9405 **WK 1 LOADER,** 1994, ORG W BLK LIFT $1-1.50
❑ ❑ CAN TK9406 **WK 2 CRANE,** 1994, GRN W BLK HOOK $1-1.50
❑ ❑ CAN TK9407 **WK 3 GRADER,** 1994, YEL W YEL BLADE
$1-1.50
❑ ❑ CAN TK9408 **WK 4 BULLDOZER,** 1994, YEL W BLK BLADE
$1-1.50
❑ ❑ CAN CP9426 DISPLAY, 1994 $40-60

COMMENTS: NATIONAL DISTRIBUTION: CANADA, PUERTO RICO:
DECEMBER 1994. PREMIUMS ARE THE SAME AS: USA
CABBAGE PATCH / TONKA HAPPY MEAL, 1994.

USA BO9405

USA TK9410   USA CP9409

USA CP9401   USA CP9402   USA CP9403   USA CP9404

USA TK9405   USA TK9406   USA TK9407   USA TK9408

CANADA/GENERIC PROMOTION, 1994

❏ ❏ CAN GE9430 HM BAG, 1994, JOYEUX FESTIN/C'EST
l'HEURE D'ALLER CHEZ MCD $1-2
❏ ❏ CAN GE9401 **STICKER BLOCKS,** 1994, 30 STICKERS/PAPER
      $1-1.25
❏ ❏ CAN GE9402 **MYSTERY PUZZLE/BARBIE,** 1994, 6 IMAGES/
PAPER $1-1.25
❏ ❏ CAN GE9403 **DISAPPEARING PIZZA,** 1994, 3P PAPER GAME
      $1-1.25
❏ ❏ CAN GE9404 **PUZZLE-BIRDIE/RONALD/GRI/HAMB,** 1994, 7"
X 4"/PAPER $1-1.25
❏ ❏ CAN GE9405 **CARD-YOU'RE TOTALLY COOL,** 1994, PAPER
      $1-1.25
❏ ❏ CAN GE9406 **CARD-FRIENDS LIKE YOU,** 1994, PAPER
      $1-1.25
❏ ❏ CAN GE9407 **3-D GLASSES,** 1994, 3D GLASSES W HALLOW-
EEN PARTY BOOKLET/2P $1.50-2
❏ ❏ CAN GE9408 **3-D GLASSES,** 1994, GRN DINOSAUR/PAPER
      $1-1.25
❏ ❏ CAN GE9409 **3-D GLASSES,** 1994, RED DINOSAUR/PAPER
      $1-1.25
❏ ❏ CAN GE9410 **3-D GLASSES,** 1994, ORG DINOSAUR/PAPER
      $1-1.25
❏ ❏ CAN GE9411 **3-D GLASSES,** 1994, PURP DINOSAUR/PAPER
      $1-1.25
❏ ❏ CAN GE9412 **COMIC - DEEP SEA DANG,** 1994 $1-1.25
❏ ❏ CAN GE9413 **THUMBELINA/STICKERS,** 1994 $1-1.25
❏ ❏ CAN GE9414 **PUZZLE-RON ON SKATES,** 1994 $1-1.25

COMMENTS: REGIONAL DISTRIBUTION: CANADA: 1994 DURING
CLEAN-UP WEEKS AND AS TREAT-OF-THE WEEK PROMO-
TIONAL ITEMS.

CAN GE9401

CAN GE9430

CAN GE9402

CAN GE9408

CAN GE9409

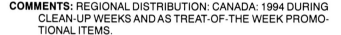

CAN GE9405   CAN GE9406

CAN GE9410

CAN GE9411

CAN GE9407

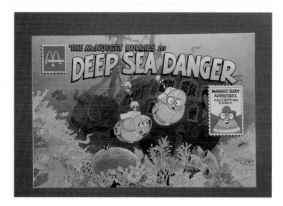

CAN GE9412

CAN GE9413

CAN GE9414

GER SI9465

CRAZY CLAY/SILLY PUTTY/VERRUCKTE KNETE JUNIOR TUTE MEAL, 1994

- ❑ ❑ GER SI9401 **GRN PUTTY,** 1993, 2P PNK FACE MOLD/GRN PUTTY $4-6
- ❑ ❑ GER SI9402 **BLU PUTTY,** 1993, 2P YEL FACE MOLD/BLU PUTTY $4-6
- ❑ ❑ GER SI9403 **YEL PUTTY,** 1993, 2P GRN FACE MOLD/YEL PUTTY $4-6
- ❑ ❑ GER SI9404 **PNK PUTTY,** 1993, 2P BLU FACE MOLD/PNK PUTTY $4-6
- ❑ ❑ GER SI9465 TRANSLITE/LG, 1993 $25-40

COMMENTS: REGIONAL DISTRIBUTION: GERMANY: DECEMBER-JANUARY 1994. DISTRIBUTED IN FRANCE; MARKED "MADE IN GERMANY" DURING 1993.

GER SI9402   GER SI9403   GER SI9401   GER SI9404

GER SI9403   GER SI9404

CRAZY VEHICLES HAPPY MEAL, 1994

❑ ❑ JPN CR9101 **BIRDIE/AIRPLANE,** 1990, IN 3P PNK/YEL/PURP
    AIRPLANE $2.50-3.50
❑ ❑ JPN CR9102 **GRIMACE/CAR,** 1990, IN 3P GRN/YEL/ORG
    CAR $2.50-3.50
❑ ❑ JPN CR9103 **HAMBURGLAR/TRAIN,** 1990, IN 3P YEL/BLU/
    PUR TRAIN $2.50-3.50
❑ ❑ JPN CR9104 **RONALD/CAR,** 1990, IN 3P RED/YEL/BLU
    BUGGY CAR $2.50-3.50

COMMENTS: LIMITED REGIONAL DISTRIBUTION: JAPAN: 1994.
    See USA CRAZY VEHICLES HAPPY MEAL, 1991.

DINO KINO PROMOTION, 1994

❑ ❑ AUS DI9410 HM BOX, 1994 $2-3

    *** IDENTICAL BOOKLETS: AUS/GER DI9401/02/03/04
❑ ❑ *** DI9401 **CARTOON BOOKLET #1,** 1994, PAPER W
    STICKERS $2-3
❑ ❑ *** DI9402 **CARTOON BOOKLET #2,** 1994, PAPER W
    STICKERS $2-3
❑ ❑ *** DI9403 **CARTOON BOOKLET #3,** 1994, PAPER W
    STICKERS $2-3
❑ ❑ *** DI9404 **CARTOON BOOKLET #4,** 1994, PAPER W
    STICKERS $2-3

COMMENTS: REGIONAL DISTRIBUTION: AUSTRALIA, GERMANY:
    1994.

JPN CR9102

AUS DI9410

GER DI9401

GER DI9402

GER DI9403   GER DI9404

GER ME9401　　GER ME9402　　GER ME9403　　GER ME9404

DINOSAURIER DINO MEMORY CARD GAME JUNIOR TUTE, 1994

❏ ❏ GER ME9430 HM BAG, 1993, JUNIOR TUTE BAG　　$2-3
❏ ❏ GER ME9401 **BOX 1-TYRANNOSAURUS**, 1993, 16 CARDS
　　　　　　　　　　　　　　　　　　　　　　$3-5
❏ ❏ GER ME9402 **BOX 2-TRICERATOPS**, 1993, 16 CARDS　$3-5
❏ ❏ GER ME9403 **BOX 3-DIPLODOKUS**, 1993, 16 CARDS　$3-5
❏ ❏ GER ME9404 **BOX 4-STEGOSAURUS**, 1993, 16 CARDS　$3-5
❏ ❏ GER ME9441 DANGLER/EACH DINO, 1993, SET of 4　$10-12

COMMENTS: NATIONAL DISTRIBUTION: GERMANY: APRIL 1994. PACKAGED IN CARD BOX WITH CARDS.

DISNEY PLUSH/MICKEY & FRIENDS/LOS CAMPEONES DISNEY, 1995/1994

　　*** **IDENTICAL STUFFED DOLLS: SIN/LAM: MI9401/02/03/04**
❏ ❏ *** MI9401 **MICKEY-FOOTBALL**, 1994, PLUSH/STUFFED DOLL　　　　　　　　　　　　　　　　　$10-12
❏ ❏ *** MI9402 **MINNIE-TENNIS**, 1994, PLUSH/STUFFED DOLL
　　　　　　　　　　　　　　　　　　　　　　$10-12
❏ ❏ *** MI9403 **GOOFY-BASKETBALL**, 1994, PLUSH/STUFFED DOLL　　　　　　　　　　　　　　　　$10-12
❏ ❏ *** MI9404 **DONALD DUCK-BASEBALL**, 1994, PLUSH/STUFFED DOLL　　　　　　　　　　　　$10-12

COMMENTS: REGIONAL DISTRIBUTION: LATIN AMERICA, SINGAPORE: DECEMBER-JANUARY 1995. STUFFED DOLLS ARE CALLED, "LOS CAMPEONES DISNEY" IN MEXICO; THEY ARE DRESSED IN SPORTS OUTFITS LISTED.

GER ME9441

CAN EA9446

CAN EA9421

JPN DO9401　　JPN DO9402　　JPN DO9403　　JPN DO9404

DOLL PROMOTION, 1994

❏ ❏ JPN DO9401 **DOLL - BIRDIE**, 1994, 4"/STUFFED　　$5-7
❏ ❏ JPN DO9402 **DOLL - GRIMACE**, 1994, 4"/STUFFED　$5-7
❏ ❏ JPN DO9403 **DOLL - HAMBUR**, 1994, 3"/STUFFED　$5-7
❏ ❏ JPN DO9404 **DOLL - RONALD**, 1994, 5"/STUFFED　$5-7

COMMENTS: REGIONAL DISTRIBUTION: JAPAN 1994 AS SELF-LIQUIDATOR.

EARTH DAYS/JOURS DE LA TERRE HAPPY MEAL, 1994

❏ ❏ CAN EA9430 HM BAG, 1993, EARTH DAYS/OWL　$1-1.25
❏ ❏ CAN EA9405 **U-3 TOOL CARRIER**, 1993, BLU W RED SHOVEL W YEL STRAP　　　　　　$1.25-1.50
❏ ❏ CAN EA9401 **BINOCULARS**, 1993, 1P HINGE OPEN EARTH SHAPED/GRN　　　　　　　　$1-1.25
❏ ❏ CAN EA9402 **BIRDFEEDER**, 1993, BIRD HOUSE SHAPED BIRDFEEDER　　　　　　　　　$1-1.25
❏ ❏ CAN EA9403 **TERRARIUM/GLOBE**, 1993, CLEAR CYCLINDER TOP W BOTTOM　　　　$1-1.25
❏ ❏ CAN EA9404 **TOOL CARRIER**, 1993, BLU W RED SHOVEL W YEL STRAP/3P　　　　　$1-1.25
❏ ❏ CAN EA9426 DISPLAY, 1994　　　　　　　$10-20
❏ ❏ CAN EA9442 COUNTER CARD, 1993　　　　$4-5
❏ ❏ CAN EA9446 PROMOTIONAL HM SHEET, 1993, EARTH DAY HM　　　　　　　　　　　$1.50-3

COMMENTS: NATIONAL DISTRIBUTION: CANADA: APRIL 8-MAY 5, 1994. CAN EA9401-05 = USA EA9401-05, LOOSE OUT OF PACKAGE. CANADA'S U-3 IS THE TOOL CARRIER WITH SHOVEL IN DIFFERENT PACKAGING.

FACE MASKS HAPPY MEAL, 1994

- ❏ ❏ AUS MA9401 **MASK - BIRDIE,** 1993, 6" X 8" PLAS $7-10
- ❏ ❏ AUS MA9402 **MASK - GRIMACE,** 1993, 6" X 8" PLAS $7-10
- ❏ ❏ AUS MA9403 **MASK - HAMBURGLAR,** 1993, 6" X 8" PLAS
        $7-10
- ❏ ❏ AUS MA9404 **MASK - RONALD,** 1993, 6" X 8" PLAS $7-10

COMMENTS: NATIONAL DISTRIBUTION: AUSTRALIA - FEBRUARY 8 - MARCH 1994. EACH MASK HAD A STICKER ON BACK WHICH SAID: "McDONALD'S AUSTRALIA LTD".

JPN FI9430

AUS MA9401   AUS MA9403

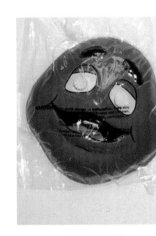

AUS MA9404   AUS MA9402

JPN FI9444

FIVE LUCKY STARS/YEAR OF THE DOG HAPPY MEAL, 1994

- ❏ ❏ JPN FI9430 HM BAG, 1993, FIVE LUCKY STARS/BRN $1-1.50
- ❏ ❏ JPN FI9401 **BUCKS,** 1994, BRN DOG SITTING ON FIRE CRACKERS $5-7
- ❏ ❏ JPN FI9402 **HAPPY,** 1994, GREY DOG W BRN BARREL $5-7
- ❏ ❏ JPN FI9403 **LUCKY,** 1994, SPOTTED WHT DOG W FF CHEST
    $5-7
- ❏ ❏ JPN FI9404 **PRECIOUS,** 1994, BRN/WHT DOG W RED SLED
    $5-7
- ❏ ❏ JPN FI9405 **RICHIE,** 1994, BRN/BEIGE DOG W FISH BOWL
    $5-7
- ❏ ❏ JPN FI9444 CREW POSTER, 1994 $12-15

COMMENTS: NATIONAL DISTRIBUTION: JAPAN, HONG KONG, SINGAPORE: FEBRUARY 1994.

JPN FI9401   JPN FI9402   JPN FI9403   JPN FI9404   JPN FI9405

AUS FL9401

AUS FL9402

AUS FL9403

FLACHMAGNETE/MAGNETS PROMOTION, 1994
- ❏ ❏ AUS FL9421 **MAGNET - BIRDIE,** 1994, WAVING $1-1.50
- ❏ ❏ AUS FL9422 **MAGNET - GRIMACE,** 1994, WAVING $1-1.50
- ❏ ❏ AUS FL9423 **MAGNET - RONALD,** 1994, WAVING $1-1.50
- ❏ ❏ GER FL9422 **MAGNET - GRIMACE,** 1994, WAVING $1-1.50
- ❏ ❏ GER FL9423 **MAGNET - RONALD,** 1994, WAVING $1-1.50
- ❏ ❏ GER FL9424 **MAGNET - BIRDIE,** 1994, WAVING $1-1.50

COMMENTS: REGIONAL DISTRIBUTION: AUSTRALIA, GERMANY: 1994. TWO SETS APPEAR TO BE FROM SAME MOLD, DIFFERENT FOCAL POINTS.

FLINTSTONES GADGETS (AUSTRALIA) HAPPY MEAL, 1995/1994
- ❏ ❏ AUS FL9505 **MASTODON,** 1994, SQUIRT/BRN $4-6
- ❏ ❏ AUS FL9506 **DICTABIRD,** 1994, W ONE WING SPREAD OUT/ WHT $4-6
- ❏ ❏ AUS FL9507 **PIGASAURUS,** 1994, SITTING/GRN $4-6
- ❏ ❏ AUS FL9508 **LOBSTER,** 1994, W 2 WHEELS/ORG $4-6
- ❏ ❏ AUS FL9442 COUNTER CARD, 1994 $5-8

COMMENTS: NATIONAL DISTRIBUTION: AUSTRALIA: DECEMBER 1994.

FLINTSTONES JUNIOR TUTE/HAPPY MEAL, 1994
- ❏ ❏ MEX FL9430 HM BAG, 1994, SPANISH GRAPHICS/ FLINTSTONES $1-1.25

*** IDENTICAL BOXES: BEL/UK FL9410/11/12/13
- ❏ ❏ *** FL9410 HM BOX, 1994, BARNEY RUBBLE'S HOUSE $2-3
- ❏ ❏ *** FL9411 HM BOX, 1994, BEDROCK BOWL-O-RAMA $2-3
- ❏ ❏ *** FL9412 HM BOX, 1994, FRED FLINTSTONE'S HOUSE $2-3
- ❏ ❏ *** FL9413 HM BOX, 1994, TOWN OF BEDROCK $2-3

*** IDENTICAL TOYS: GER/NET FL9401/02/03/04
- ❏ ❏ *** FL9401 **ROC DONALD'S BLDG,** 1993, YEL BLDG/4 DOORS/STICKERS/5P $4-5
- ❏ ❏ *** FL9402 **BEDROCK RTD BUS,** 1993, GRN BUS W STICKERS $4-5
- ❏ ❏ *** FL9403 **FRED QUARRY CRANE/DINO,** 1993, FRED RIDING BRN DINO $4-5
- ❏ ❏ *** FL9404 **WILMA FLINTMOBILE/DINO,** 1993, PURP DINO IN VEHICLE W WILMA $4-5

- ❏ ❏ FRA FL9444 CREW POSTER/SM, 1994 $5-8
- ❏ ❏ FRA FL9464 TRANSLITE/SM, 1994 $10-15
- ❏ ❏ GER FL9465 TRANSLITE/LG, 1994 $15-25

COMMENTS: NATIONAL DISTRIBUTION: HOLLAND, SWITZERLAND: JULY/AUGUST 1994; NETHERLANDS: AUGUST 3-SEPTEMBER 6, 1994; GERMANY: AUGUST 1994; UK: JULY 1994; MEXICO, COSTA RICO, PANAMA, CHILE, GUATEMALA: AUGUST 1994. UK DISTRIBUTED PREMIUMS WHICH WERE MADE IN GERMANY.

GER FL9424 GER FL9422 GER FL9423

AUS FL9507 AUS FL9505 AUS FL9506 AUS FL9508

AUS FL9442

UK FL9410 UK FL9411 UK FL9412 UK FL9413

GERMANY

GER FL9401 GER FL9402 GER FL9403 GER FL9404

FRA FL9503   FRA FL9502   FRA FL9504   FRA FL9501

GERMANY

GER FL9465

JAPAN

FRA FL9464

FLINTSTONES (CANADA) HAPPY MEAL, 1994

❑ ❑ CAN FL9410 HM BAG, 1994, FLINTSTONES $1-1.25
❑ ❑ CAN FL9406 **U-3 ROCKING DINO,** 1993, PURP DINO/
RUBBER $1.50-2
❑ ❑ CAN FL9401 **BARNEY/FOSSIL FILL-UP/BLDG,** 1993, GRY
BLDG/DOOR/BARNEY IN CAR/STICKERS/3P $1-1.25
❑ ❑ CAN FL9402 **BETTY/BAMM BAMM/ROC D/BLDG,** 1993, YEL
BLDG/DOOR/BETTY IN BRN-LOG CAR/STICKERS/3P $1-1.25
❑ ❑ CAN FL9403 **FRED/BEDR BOWL-O-RAMA/BLDG,** 1993, GRN
BLDG/DOOR/FRED IN RED CAR/STICKERS/3P $1-1.25
❑ ❑ CAN FL9404 **PEBBLES/DINO/TOYS-S-A/BLDG,** 1993, RED
BLDG/DOOR/PEBBLES IN BLU CYCLE/STICKERS/3P $1-1.25
❑ ❑ CAN FL9405 **WILMA/FLINTSTONES HOUSE/BLDG,** 1993,
PEACH BLDG/DOOR/WILMA IN GRY CAR/STICKERS/3P
$1-1.25

CAN FL9429

FRA FL9444

217

CAN FL9442

CAN FL9427   CAN FL9428

❑ ❑ CAN FL9420 **CUP-FRED FLINSTONE,** 1994, NEWLY PRO-
MOTED, FRED/PLASTIC $1-1.25
❑ ❑ CAN FL9421 **CUP-BETTY/BARNEY,** 1994, ONLY CHORES
FOR BETTY AND BARNEY/PLASTIC $1-1.25
❑ ❑ CAN FL9422 **CUP-FRED,** 1994, ITS QUITTING TIME, FRED/
PLASTIC $1-1.25
❑ ❑ CAN FL9423 **CUP-ROC DONALD'S,** 1994, THE
FLINTSTONES AND RUBBLE ENJOY/PLASTIC $1-1.25
❑ ❑ CAN FL9424 **CUP-FRED BOWLING,** 1994, FRED "TWINKLE
TOES"/PLASTIC $1-1.25
❑ ❑ CAN FL9425 **CUP-BARNEY,** 1994, BARNEY IS CATAPULTED/
PLASTIC $1-1.25

❑ ❑ CAN FL9427 PROFILE/RUBBLE, 1994, POP-UP/PAPER
                                                       $1-1.50
❑ ❑ CAN FL9428 PROFILE/FLINTSTONE, 1994, POP-UP/PAPER
                                                       $1-1.50
❑ ❑ CAN FL9429 PROMO HM SHEET, 1994, LES PIERRAFEU
                                                       $1.50-3
❑ ❑ CAN FL9442 COUNTER CARD, 1994 $3-5
❑ ❑ CAN FL9450 BUTTON, 1994, I LOVE ROC DONALD'S $2-3
❑ ❑ JPN FL9455 TRAYLINER, 1994, BEDROCK VILLAGE $1-1.50
❑ ❑ CAN FL9495 PIN, 1994, THE FLINTSTONES/ROC DONALD'S
SUMMER '94 $3-4
❑ ❑ CAN FL9496 PIN, 1994, GRAND POOBAH MEALS $2.50-3

COMMENTS: NATIONAL DISTRIBUTION: CANADA, MALAYSIA:
JUNE 3-JULY 7, 1994. SUPPLEMENTAL PLASTIC CUP
PROMOTION WAS THE SAME TIME AS CANADA'S
FLINTSTONES HM. CAN FL9401-06 = USA FL9401-06,
LOOSE OUT OF PACKAGE.

FLINTSTONES STATIONERY VEHICLES (AUSTRALIA) PROMOTION, 1994

❑ ❑ AUS FL9401 **FRED'S FLINTMOBILE,** 1994, HOLDS ERASER
ON TOP/BRN/TAN/GREY $4-6
❑ ❑ AUS FL9402 **BAMM BAMM'S BEDROCK MEMO HOLDER,**
1994, HOLDS NOTEPAD/RED/TAN $4-6
❑ ❑ AUS FL9403 **PEBBLES TRIKE EMBOSSER,** 1994, W
CUTOUT LOGO/RED/ORG $4-6
❑ ❑ AUS FL9404 **BARNEY'S RUBBLEMOBILE,** 1994, PENCIL
SHARPENER/LOG VEHICLE/BRN/TAN $4-6

COMMENTS: REGIONAL DISTRIBUTION: AUSTRALIA - AUGUST-
SEPTEMBER 1994. PREMIUMS SOLD FOR $.95 EACH.

CAN FL9455

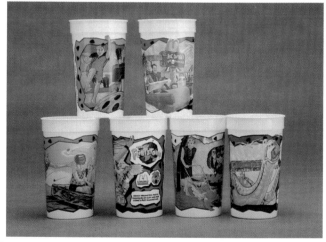

CAN FL9421   CAN FL9423
CAN FL9420   CAN FL9422   CAN FL9424   CAN FL9425

AUS FL9404   AUS FL9403   AUS FL9402   AUS FL9401

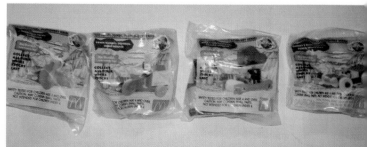

FRED FLINTSTONES (GERMANY) PROMOTION, 1994

❑ ❑ GER FR9401 **STENCIL - FRED,** 1994, GRN or YEL or RED or BLU $1.50-2

COMMENTS: REGIONAL DISTRIBUTION: GERMANY - 1994.

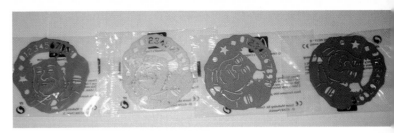

GERMANY/GENERIC PROMOTION, 1994

❑ ❑ GER GE9401 **GAME - DOMINO,** 1994, PAPER/28P $1-1.50
❑ ❑ GER GE9402 **MAGIC PICTURE - SPACE,** 1994, PAPER/RED CELLO WINDOW $1-1.50
❑ ❑ GER GE9403 **BANDAID,** 1994, RONALD $1-1.25
❑ ❑ GER GE9404 **STICKER BOOK,** 1994, RAUMFAHRT/RONALD/ PAPER $2-3
❑ ❑ GER GE9405 **STICKER BOOK,** 1994, KIRMES/BIRDIE/ PAPER

$2-3
❑ ❑ GER GE9406 **CANDY-GUMMIE BEARS,** 1994, HARIBO GOLDBAREN $———
❑ ❑ GER GE9407 **MASK,** 1994, CHARS/PAPER $1.50-2
❑ ❑ GER GE9408 **POST CARD - BIRDIE,** 1994, FOOT PRINTS $1-1.25
❑ ❑ GER GE9409 **POST CARD - RONALD,** 1994, BIRTHDAY PARTY INVIT $1-1.25
❑ ❑ GER GE9410 **MEMBER CARD,** 1994, ID CARD $1-1.25

COMMENTS: REGIONAL DISTRIBUTION: GERMANY: 1994.

GER FR9401

GER GE9402

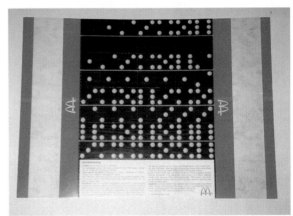

GER GE9401

GER GE9403

GER GE9404

GER GE9405

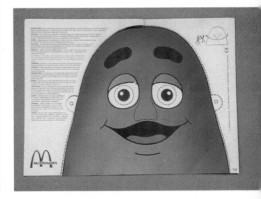

GER GE9407

GER GE9406

GER GE9408

GER GE9409

GER GE9410

GOOF TROOP HAPPY MEAL, 1995/1994

❑ ❑ AUS GO9401 **GOOFY,** 1993, STANDING W GRN SKATE-
BOARD $4-5
❑ ❑ AUS GO9402 **MAX,** 1993, ON ROLLERBLADES $4-5
❑ ❑ AUS GO9403 **PJ,** 1993, MON GRN SKATEBOARD $4-5
❑ ❑ AUS GO9404 **PETE,** 1993, STANDING W HANDS ON HIP $4-5

❑ ❑ AUS GO9505 **GOOF TROOP #1,** 1993, RUBBER FACE/
WATER SQUIRT $3-4
❑ ❑ AUS GO9506 **GOOF TROOP #2,** 1993, RUBBER FACE/
WATER SQUIRT $3-4
❑ ❑ AUS GO9507 **GOOF TROOP #3,** 1993, RUBBER FACE/
WATER SQUIRT $3-4

COMMENTS: NATIONAL DISTRIBUTION: AUSTRALIA (FIGU-
RINES): JANUARY 9-FEBRUARY 7, 1994; AUSTRALIA
(SQUIRTERS): FEBRUARY 1995. AUS GO9405/06/07 WERE
GIVEN TO CHILDREN UNDER THE AGE OF 3; SIMILAR TO
USA CEREAL PREMIUMS, LOOSE OUT OF PACKAGE.

AUS GO9401   AUS GO9404   AUS GO9403   AUS GO9402

GUMMI BEARS HAPPY MEAL, 1994

❑ ❑ AUS GU9401 **CUBBI,** 1994, 2" PNK FIGURINE $2-3
❑ ❑ AUS GU9402 **GRUFFI,** 1994, 2" TAN FIGURINE $2-3
❑ ❑ AUS GU9403 **SUNNI,** 1994, 2" YEL GIRL FIRURINE $2-3
❑ ❑ AUS GU9404 **TUMMI,** 1994, 2" BLU FIGURINE $2-3

COMMENTS: NATIONAL DISTRIBUTION: AUSTRALIA: MARCH
1994. FIGURINES ARE VERY SIMILAR TO USA CEREAL
PREMIUMS.

HALLOWEEN '94 HAPPY MEAL, 1994

❑ ❑ CAN HA9401 **GHOST,** 1986, 3P WHT GHOST W COOKIE
CUTTER INSERT W BLK HANDLE $1-1.50
❑ ❑ CAN HA9402 **PUMPKIN,** 1986, 3P ORG PUMPKIN W COOKIE
CUTTER INSERT W BLK HANDLE $1-1.50
❑ ❑ CAN HA9403 **WITCH,** 1986, 3P PURP WITCH W COOKIE
CUTTER INSERT W BLK HANDLE $1-1.50
❑ ❑ CAN HA9442 COUNTER CARD, 1994 $4-5

COMMENTS: NATIONAL DISTRIBUTION: CANADA, COSTA RICO,
GUATEMALA, PANAMA, PUERTO RICO: OCTOBER 1994.

HALLOWEEN MCNUGGET BUDDIES/MONSTER
MCNUGGETS JUNIOR TUTE, 1995/1994.

❑ ❑ PAN HA9410 HM BOX, 1994, SPANISH $2-3

*** IDENTICAL TOYS: GER/MEX/ZEA/UK HA9401/02/04/06
❑ ❑ *** HA9401 **MCBOO MCNUGGET,** 1992, WHT GHOST/2P
$1.50-2
❑ ❑ *** HA9402 **MONSTER MCNUGGET,** 1992, GRN HAT/PUR
PANTS/GRN HANDS/3P $1.50-2
❑ ❑ *** HA9404 **MCNUGGLA,** 1992, BLK HAT/BAT/BLK CAPE/3P
$1.50-2
❑ ❑ *** HA9406 **WITCHIE MCNUGGET,** 1992, BLK WITCH HAT/
PUR CAPE/BROOM/3P $1.50-2

*** IDENTICAL TOY: GER/ZEA HA9403
❑ ❑ *** HA9403 **MUMMY MCNUGGET,** 1992, WHT HAT/SPIDER/
WHT PANTS/3P $1.50-2

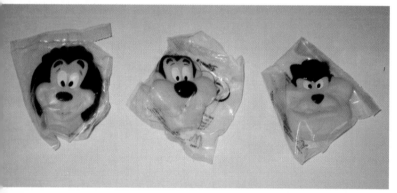

AUS GO9505   AUS GO9506   AUS GO9507

AUS GU9401   AUS GU9404   AUS GU9402   AUS GU9403

☐ ☐ ZEA HA9405 **PUMPKIN MCNUGGET,** 1992, ORG PUMP HAT/
PUMP BASE/3P $1.50-2

☐ ☐ FRA HA9426 DISPLAY, 1992, RED SIGN/PUMPKIN/5 PAPER
BUDDIES $25-40

COMMENTS: REGIONAL DISTRIBUTION: NEW ZEALAND (6
HALLOWEEN MCNUGGETS): AUGUST 10, 1994 DURING
CLEAN-UP WEEK; GERMANY (5 HALLOWEEN
MCNUGGETS): FEBRUARY 1995; MEXICO (4 HALLOWEEN
MCNUGGETS): 1995; UK: OCTOBER 1995; GUATEMALA:
1993. GER/MEX/UK/ZEA HA9401-06 = USA HA9301-06,
LOOSE OUT OF PACKAGE. See USA HALLOWEEN '93
MCNUGGET BUDDIES HM, 1993.

USA HA9464

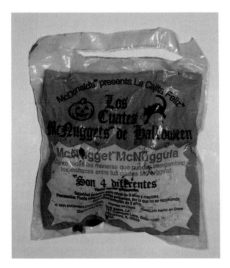

MEX HA9406

USA HA9402   USA HA9401   USA HA9403

USA

USA HA9364

*** HA9426

221

GER HA9465

JAPAN

JAPAN/GENERIC PROMOTION, 1994

❏ ❏ JPN GE9401 **NECKLACE/SOCCER BALL,** 1994, GOLDTONE
$4-6
❏ ❏ JPN GE9402 **COASTER - CHRISTMAS,** 1994, SANTA/RED or GRN
$1-1.50
❏ ❏ JPN GE9403 **COASTER - CHILDREN,** 1994, GRN or YEL
$1-1.50
❏ ❏ JPN GE9404 **COASTER - F FRIES,** 1994, W SHAKE/B MAC/ SET 3
$3-4
❏ ❏ JPN GE9405 **STICKERS,** 1994, W CHARS $1-1.25
❏ ❏ JPN GE9406 **STICKERS,** 1994, W MUSICAL CHILDREN
$1-1.25
❏ ❏ JPN GE9407 **COLORING BOOK,** 1994, CHARS $1.50-2.50
❏ ❏ JPN GE9408 **CARD - CHRISTMAS,** 1994, W TREE/CHILDREN
$1-1.25
❏ ❏ JPN GE9409 **SCARFS,** 1994, SANTA/LOGO/MCD $1.50-2.50
❏ ❏ JPN GE9410 **BARREL,** 1994, TURQ/CHAR/2P $3-4
❏ ❏ JPN GE9411 **BANK,** 1994, RED W STICKERS $4-5
❏ ❏ JPN GE9412 **PUZZLE/BLOCKS,** 1994, ROCKET/RON $4-5
❏ ❏ JPN GE9413 **LAP TRAY,** 1994, YEL/BLOW UP $4-5
❏ ❏ JPN GE9414 **GROWTH CHART,** 1994, GRN/PAPER $1-1.25
❏ ❏ JPN GE9415 **CARD GAME,** 1994, YEL BOX/CARDS $4-5
❏ ❏ JPN GE9416 **CARD GAME,** 1994, RED BOX/CARDS $4-5
❏ ❏ JPN GE9417 **LEGO TRUCK,** 1994, PASTEL SERIES $15-20
❏ ❏ JPN GE9418 **WATCH - RONALD,** 1994, YEL/RON SITTING
$4-5
❏ ❏ JPN GE9419 **RESTAURANT,** 1994, W SIGN $4-6
❏ ❏ JPN GE9420 **RESTAURANT,** 1994, W/O SIGN $4-6

COMMENTS: REGIONAL DISTRIBUTION: JAPAN: 1994.

JAPAN

JPN GE9401

JAPAN

JAPAN

JPN GE9402

JPN GE9403

JPN GE9404

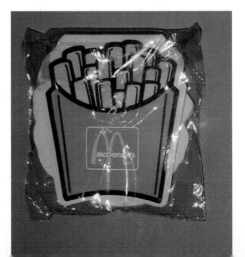

222

JPN GE9405

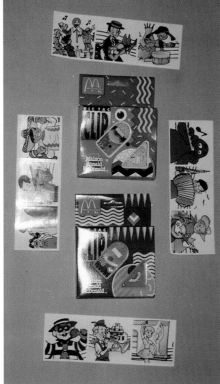

JPN GE9406

JPN GE9407

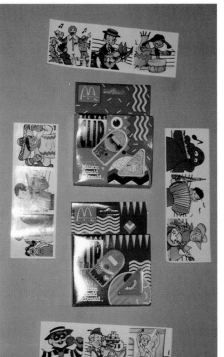

JPN GE9408

JPN GE9409

JPN GE9410

JPN GE9411

JPN GE9412

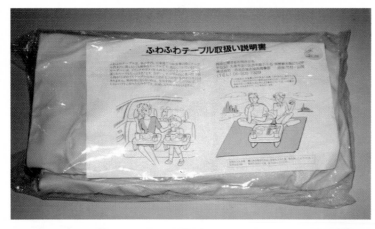

JPN GE9415

JPN GE9416

JPN GE9413

JPN GE9417

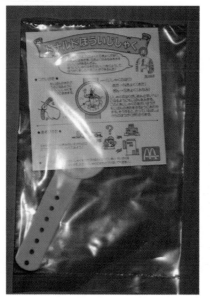

JPN GE9418

JPN GE9414

JPN GE9419

JURASSIC PARK PROMOTION, 1994

		***IDENTICAL CUPS: CAN/FRA JU9401/02/03/04/05/06			
❑	❑	*** JU9401 **CUP - TYRANNOSAURUS REX**, 1994			$1-1.25
❑	❑	*** JU9402 **CUP - GALLIMIMUS**, 1994			$1-1.25
❑	❑	*** JU9403 **CUP - DILOPHOSAURUS**, 1994			$1-1.25
❑	❑	*** JU9404 **CUP - TRICERATOPS**, 1994			$1-1.25
❑	❑	*** JU9405 **CUP - VELOCIRAPTOR**, 1994			$1-1.25
❑	❑	*** JU9406 **CUP - BRACHIOSAURUS**, 1994			$1-1.25
❑	❑	FRA JU9444 POSTER, 1994			$2-3
❑	❑	CAN JU9455 TRAYLINER, 1994			$1-1.25

COMMENTS: REGIONAL DISTRIBUTION: CANADA/FRANCE: 1994.
SIZES OF CUPS VARY SLIGHTLY, BASED ON COUNTRY OF
DISTRIBUTION (LITERS VS. OUNCES). USA DID A SIMILAR
PROMOTION.

JPN GE9420

THANK YOU
FOR COMING TO McDONALD'S

FRA JU9401   FRA JU9402

FRA JU9403   FRA JU9404   FRA JU9405   FRA JU9406

FRA JU9444

CAN JU9455

KAMPUNG FUN HAPPY MEAL, 1994

☐	☐	SIN KA9410 HM BOX, 1994, SMILING GRAPHICS/YOU COLOR	$2-3
☐	☐	JPN KA9430 HM BAG, 1994, KAMPUNG BURGER	$1-1.25
☐	☐	JPN KA9431 HM BAG, 1994, KAMPUNG FUN/SM#4	$1-1.25
☐	☐	JPN KA9432 HM BAG, 1994, KAMPUNG FUN/LG#8	$1-1.25
☐	☐	JPN KA9433 HM BAG, 1994, KAMPUNG FUN/JAPANESE CASTLE	$1-1.25
☐	☐	SIN KA9401 **LAYANG-LAYANG**, 1994	$4-6
☐	☐	SIN KA9402 **YOYO**, 1994, RED	$4-6
☐	☐	SIN KA9403 **JUMP ROPE**, 1994, PURP	$2-3
☐	☐	SIN CI9101 **CAR - RONALD**, 1989, RINGMASTER IN CAR	$2-3
☐	☐	SIN KA9455 TRAYLINER, 1994	$1-1.25

COMMENTS: REGIONAL DISTRIBUTION: SINGAPORE: SUMMER 1994.

SIN KA9410

JPN KA9430

JPN KA9431   JPN KA9432

JPN KA9433

SIN KA9455

SIN KA9402

LEGO SYSTEM HAPPY MEAL, 1994

❑	❑	UK LE9410 HM BOX, 1994, BIRDIE/HELICOPTER	$2-3
❑	❑	UK LE9411 HM BOX, 1994, GRIMACE/AIRPLANE	$2-3
❑	❑	UK LE9412 HM BOX, 1994, HAMB/MOON VEHICLE	$2-3
❑	❑	UK LE9413 HM BOX, 1994, RONALD/SEA SKIMMER	$2-3

*** IDENTICAL TOYS: HOL/UK LE9401/02/03/04/05

❑	❑	*** LE9405 **U-5 GIDDY THE GATOR,** 1994, DUPLO/4 GRN/2 YEL	$4-5
❑	❑	*** LE9401 **LASER VEHICLE,** 1994	$3-4
❑	❑	*** LE9402 **SEA EAGLE AIRPLANE,** 1994	$3-4
❑	❑	*** LE9403 **SEA SKIMMER HOVERCRAFT,** 1994	$3-4
❑	❑	*** LE9404 **WIND WHIRLER HELICOPTER,** 1994	$3-4

❑	❑	BEL LE9426 DISPLAY/DANGLER, 1994	$40-50
❑	❑	FRA LE9442 COUNTER CARD, 1994	$5-8
❑	❑	BEL LE9444 POSTER/LG, 1994	$15-20
❑	❑	HOL LE9455 TRAYLINER, 1994	$1-1.25
❑	❑	UK LE9464 TRANSLITE/SM, 1994	$5-8
❑	❑	UK LE9465 TRANSLITE/LG, 1994	$8-12
❑	❑	UK LE9417 DISPLAY, 1994	$40-50

COMMENTS: NATIONAL DISTRIBUTION: UK/BELGIUM/FRANCE/ HOLLAND - SEPTEMBER 1994; NETHERLANDS - SEPTEM- BER 7-OCTOBER 11, 1994; SINGAPORE: AUGUST 1992. IN THE UK, PACKAGED WITH LOGO FOR AGES 3-12; U-5 IS PACKAGED FOR CHILDREN 1-5 YEARS OF AGE.

UK LE9413   UK LE9411   UK LE9412   UK LE9410

UK LE9405   UK LE9401   UK LE9402   UK LE9403   UK LE9404

JAPAN

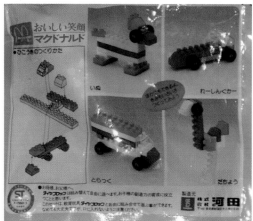

BEL LE9426

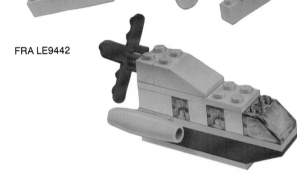

4 jouets LEGO SYSTEM à collectionner.
Réunis les quatre modèles pour en créer des douzaines d'autres. Dans chaque Happy Meal : 1 Hamburger, 1 portion normale de frites, 1 boisson gazeuse 25 cl, 1 sachet de cookies et un des 4 jouets LEGO SYSTEM à collectionner.
Dans la limite des stocks disponibles.

FRA LE9442

HOL LE9455

HOLLAND

BEL LE9444

GERMANY

LION KING/LE REY LION/LEEUWEKONING JUNIOR TUTE/HAPPY MEAL, 1994

- ❑ ❑ GER LI9430 HM BAG, 1994, LION KING $2-3
- ❑ ❑ MEX LI9410 HM BOX, 1994, EL REY LION $2-3

*** IDENTICAL BOXES: BEL/UK LI9410/11/12/13
- ❑ ❑ *** LI9410 HM BOX, 1994, ELEPHANT GRAVEYARD/CAVE $2-3
- ❑ ❑ *** LI9411 HM BOX, 1994, JUNGLE/ELEPHANTS/GIRAFFES $2-3
- ❑ ❑ *** LI9412 HM BOX, 1994, RAFIKI PRESENTS SIMBA/ON THE ROCKS $2-3
- ❑ ❑ *** LI9413 HM BOX, 1994, ANIMALS ON SAVANNAH/WATERFALL $2-3

- ❑ ❑ MEX LI9414 **LUNCH BAG,** 1994, VINYL/PORTA EQUIPO DE EXPLORADORES/L KING $3-5
- ❑ ❑ MEX LI9415 **BINOCULARS,** 1994, GRN FOLD UP/ BINOCULARES EXPLORADORES $3-5
- ❑ ❑ MEX LI9416 **FOOD CONTAINER,** 1994, ROUND/PULL BACK LID/PORTAVIANDA SIMBA/2P $3-5
- ❑ ❑ MEX LI9417 **CANTEEN,** 1994, CANTIMPLORA DE LA JUNGLA $3-5
- ❑ ❑ MEX LI9418 **PLACEMAT,** 1994, PLASTIC/NALA/SIMBA $3-4

*** IDENTICAL TOYS: NET/UK LI9401/02/03/04
- ❑ ❑ *** LI9401 **PUMBAA,** 1994, TIMON/WART HOG $4-6
- ❑ ❑ *** LI9402 **SCAR,** 1994, LION $4-6
- ❑ ❑ *** LI9403 **SIMBA,** 1994, SMALL LION $4-6
- ❑ ❑ *** LI9404 **ZASU,** 1994, BIRD $4-6

- ❑ ❑ GER LI9401 **ERASER - SIMBA,** 1994, YEL $2-3
- ❑ ❑ GER LI9402 **ERASER - ZASU,** 1994, BLU $2-3
- ❑ ❑ GER LI9403 **ERASER - SCAR,** 1994, ORG $2-3
- ❑ ❑ GER LI9404 **ERASER - HYENA,** 1994, PURP $2-3

- ❑ ❑ UK LI9405 **PUZZLE 1 - NALA/SIMBA/W LION CUBS,** 1994 $5-7
- ❑ ❑ UK LI9406 **PUZZLE 2 - RAFIKI,** 1994 $5-7
- ❑ ❑ UK LI9407 **PUZZLE 3 - MUSAFA W SIMBA,** 1994 $5-7
- ❑ ❑ UK LI9408 **PUZZLE 4 - MUSAFA W SIMBA/SCARAT,** 1994 $5-7

- ❑ ❑ FRA LI9441 DANGLER/DISP, 1994 $40-50
- ❑ ❑ FRA LI9442 COUNTER CARD, 1994 $5-8
- ❑ ❑ UK LI9464 TRANSLITE/SM, 1994 $5-8
- ❑ ❑ UK LI9465 TRANSLITE/LG, 1994 $5-8
- ❑ ❑ UK LI9426 DISPLAY, 1994 $40-50

COMMENTS: REGIONAL DISTRIBUTION: GERMANY: DECEMBER 1994; EUROPE: NOVEMBER 1994; ARGENTINA/CHILE/ MEXICO/GUATEMALA/COSTA RICA/PANAMA/VENEZUELA: JULY 1994; VENEZUELA - JULY/AUGUST 1994. NATIONAL DISTRIBUTION: UK - OCTOBER 1994; NETHERLANDS - NOVEMBER 30-JANUARY 3, 1995;

BEL LI9410

BEL LI9411

BEL LI9412

BEL LI9414

UK LI9413   UK LI9412
UK LI9410   UK LI9411

UK LI9402   UK LI9403   UK LI9404   UK LI9401

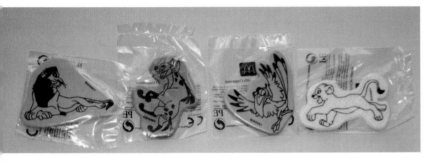

GER LI9403   GER LI9404   GER LI9402   GER LI9401

UK LI9405   UK LI9407
UK LI9406   UK LI9408

FRA LI9441

229

FRA LI9442

FRA LI9442

FRA LI9441

USA LO9365

LOONEY TUNES QUACK UP CAR CHASE HAPPY MEAL, 1994

❑ ❑ COS LO9301 **BUGS SUPER STRETCH LIMO,** 1992, **RED CAR STRETCHES**/SPORTS CAR $1-1.50

❑ ❑ COS LO9302 **DAFFY SPLITTIN SPORTS,** 1992, **YEL CAR SPLITS** OPEN $1-1.50

❑ ❑ COS LO9303 **PORKY GHOST CATCHER,** 1992, **GRN CAR GHOST POPS OUT** $1-1.50

❑ ❑ COS LO9304 **TAZ TORNADO TRACKER,** 1992, **TURQ CAR TAZ SPINS** $1-1.50

COMMENTS: NATIONAL DISTRIBUTION: COSTA RICO: 1994. IN THE USA, AN ORANGE U-3 AND ORANGE STRETCH LIMO WERE DISTRIBUTED IN THE SOUTHEAST. See USA LOONEY TUNES QUACK UP CAR CHASE HAPPY MEAL, 1993.

LUCKY GOLDEN STRAW PROMOTION, 1994

❑ ❑ UK LU9401 **GOLDEN STRAW,** 1994 $1-1.25

❑ ❑ UK LU9455 TRAYLINER, 1994, JOIN IN THE QUEST $1-1.25

❑ ❑ UK LU9457 DECAL/LG, 1994, JOIN THE THE QUEST $3-5

COMMENTS: REGIONAL DISTRIBUTION: UK JANUARY-FEBRUARY 13, 1994.

UK LU9401

UK LU9455

MAGIC SCHOOL BUS HAPPY MEAL, 1994

❏ ❏ CAN MA9430 HM BAG, 1994, THE MAGIC SCHOOL BUS/
WAHOO! $1-1.25

❏ ❏ CAN MA9405 **U-3 UNDERSEA ADVENTURE GAME,** 1994,
GRN BEAD GAME WITHOUT TAB/1P $1-1.50
❏ ❏ CAN MA9401 **COLLECTOR CARD KIT,** 1994, YEL SCHOOL
BUS/10 CARDS/STICKER SHEET $1-1.25
❏ ❏ CAN MA9402 **GEO FOSSIL FINDER,** 1994, FOSSIL TRACE W
PENCIL/4P $1-1.25
❏ ❏ CAN MA9403 **SPACE TRACER,** 1994, BLU TRACING
PROTRACTOR/PLANETS/1P $1-1.25
❏ ❏ CAN MA9404 **UNDERSEA ADVENTURE GAME,** 1994, GRN
BEAD GAME W YEL TAB/1P $1-1.25

❏ ❏ CAN MA9442 COUNTER CARD, 1994 $3-5
❏ ❏ CAN MA9450 PIN, 1994 $3-4

COMMENTS: NATIONAL DISTRIBUTION: CANADA - SEPTEMBER-
OCTOBER 1994.

MAZE/MCMAZE GAME HAPPY MEAL, 1994

❏ ❏ AUS MA9405 **MAZE - BIRDIE,** 1993, BLUE PLASTIC MAZE W
FLIPPER/2" X 3 1/4" $5-7
❏ ❏ AUS MA9406 **MAZE - GRIMACE,** 1993, ORANGE PLASTIC
MAZE W FLIPPER/2" X 3 1/4" $5-7
❏ ❏ AUS MA9407 **MAZE - HAMB,** 1993, GREEN PLASTIC MAZE W
FLIPPER/2" X 3 1/4" $5-7
❏ ❏ AUS MA9408 **MAZE - RONALD,** 1993, BLU/GREEN PLASTIC
MAZE W FLIPPER/2" X 3 1/4" $5-7

COMMENTS: NATIONAL DISTRIBUTION: AUSTRALIA: DECEMBER
10-JANUARY 8, 1994. JAPAN COULD HAVE RUN THESE
FOUR MAZES IN MAY OF 1988; COULD HAVE BEEN
CALLED, "MCMAZE".

MCCHARACTERS/FLAG PROMOTION, 1993/1994

❏ ❏ GER FL9301 **FLAG - BIRDIE,** 1993, PAPER FLAG/5" X 6"
$1-1.50
❏ ❏ GER FL9302 **FLAG - GRIMACE,** 1993, PAPER FLAG/5" X 6"
$1-1.50
❏ ❏ GER FL9303 **FLAG - HAMBURGLAR,** 1993, PAPER FLAG/5"
X 6" $1-1.50
❏ ❏ GER FL9304 **FLAG - RONALD,** 1993, PAPER FLAG/5" X 6"
$1-1.50

COMMENTS: REGIONAL DISTRIBUTION: EUROPE - 1993/1994.

MCFILM/MOVIES/MAKIN' MOVIES HAPPY MEAL, 1994

❏ ❏ CAN MM9410 HM BOX, 1993, MAKING PRINTS $2-3
❏ ❏ CAN MM9411 HM BOX, 1993, POPCORN $2-3
❏ ❏ CAN MM9412 HM BOX, 1993, SCOREBOARD $2-3
❏ ❏ CAN MM9413 HM BOX, 1993, TICKETS $2-3
❏ ❏ UK FI9410 HM BOX, 1994, GRIMACE ON PIRATE SHIP $2-3
❏ ❏ UK FI9411 HM BOX, 1994, RON IN PRINT SHOP/EDITING
FILM $2-3
❏ ❏ UK FI9412 HM BOX, 1994, McDONALD'S HOTEL/WILD WEST
$2-3
❏ ❏ UK FI9413 HM BOX, 1994, RON MAGIC ACT ON STAGE/GRI
FILMING $2-3
❏ ❏ MEX FI9410 HM BOX, 1994, SPANISH $2-3

❏ ❏ CAN MM9405 **U-3 SOUND MACHINE,** 1993, PURP/TURQ/BLK
$1-1.50

***** IDENTICAL TOYS: HOL/JP/UK MM9401/02 and BE9201
and NI9301**
❏ ❏ *** MM9401 **CLAPBOARD,** 1993, BLK CHALK BOARD W
CHALK/2P $1-1.50
❏ ❏ *** MM9402 **MEGAPHONE/DIRECTOR'S,** 1993, RED/YEL
MEGAPHONE/1P $1-1.50
❏ ❏ *** BE9201 **ANIMATION WHEEL,** 1992, BLK/BLU W 4
CARTOON STRIPS/BOOKLET/2P $1.50-2.50
❏ ❏ *** NI9301 **APPLAUSE PAWS,** 1992, YEL CLAPPING HANDS/
PNK BASE/1P $2-2.50

UK LU9457

CAN MA9450

UK FI9410

UK FI9411

UK FI9412

HOLLAND   HOL NI9301   USA

USA MM9401   USA MM9402   USA MM9403   USA MM9404

BEL FI9444

❑	❑	BEL FI9444 POSTER/LG, 1994	$15-20
❑	❑	CAN MM9426 DISPLAY W PREMIUMS, 1993	$15-25
❑	❑	CAN MM9464 TRANSLITE/SM, 1993	$3-5
❑	❑	DEN FI9444 POSTER/LG, 1992,	$15-20
❑	❑	HOL FI9455 TRAYLINER, 1994	$1-1.50

COMMENTS: NATIONAL DISTRIBUTION: CANADA: JANUARY-FEBRUARY 1994; HOLLAND/NETHERLANDS/BELGIUM: FEBRUARY 23-MARCH 29, 1994; PUERTO RICO: JANUARY 1994; PANAMA: MARCH 1994; JAPAN TESTED IN JUNE 1994 AND RAN IN 1995 USING CLAPBOARD AND NICKELODEON TOY: LOUD MIKE MIKE; SINGAPORE: AUGUST 1994; FRANCE: APRIL 1994; UK: NOVEMBER 1994. CALLED, "MAKING MOVIES IN SINGAPORE AND "MCFILM" IN THE UK. HOL MM9401/02 = USA MM9401/02-MAKIN MOVIES HM, 1994. USA NI9301 HAS A BLUE BASE WHEREAS HOL/UK NI9301 HAVE A PINK BASE (SEE USA NICKELODEON GAME GADGETS HAPPY MEAL, 1993). HOL BE9201 = USA BE9201-BEHIND THE SCENES HM, 1992. HOL NI9301 = USA NI9301-NICKELODEON GAME GADGETS HM, 1993. REGIONAL DISTRIBUTION: JAPAN - JUNE 1994; SINGAPORE - AUGUST 1994; FRANCE - APRIL 1994. JPN MM9401 CHALK CAME WRAPPED IN PAPER WITH MCD LOGO ON ALL SIDES.

HOL FI9455

MCMUSIC HAPPY MEAL, 1994

*** IDENTICAL BOXES: BEL/UK MU9410/11/12/13

❑	❑	*** MU9410 HM BOX, 1994, BAND GAZEBO/IN PARK	$2-3
❑	❑	*** MU9411 HM BOX, 1994, SCHOOL ROOM/RON AT BLACKBOARD	$2-3
❑	❑	*** MU9412 HM BOX, 1994, THEATER	$2-3
❑	❑	*** MU9413 HM BOX, 1994, WILD WEST/MCD/HORSE TIED OUTSIDE	$2-3
❑		MEX MU9410 HM BOX, 1993,	$2-3

*** IDENTICAL TOYS: GER/UK MU9401/02/03/04

❑	❑	*** MU9401 **ORGAN - BIRDIE,** 1994, BLU/MOUTH ORGAN	$4-5
❑	❑	*** MU9402 **PAN PIPES - GRIMACE,** 1994, GRN	$4-5
❑	❑	*** MU9403 **FLUTE - HAMBURGLAR,** 1994, RED/SLIDE FLUTE	$4-5
❑	❑	*** MU9404 **KAZOO - RONALD,** 1994, ORG	$4-5
❑	❑	UK MU9426 DISPLAY W 4 PREMS, 1994	$75-100

COMMENTS: REGIONAL DISTRIBUTION: UK: AUGUST 1994; EUROPE: MAY 1994; GERMANY: FEBRUARY 1995.

UK MU9412   UK MU9413   UK MU9411   UK MU9410

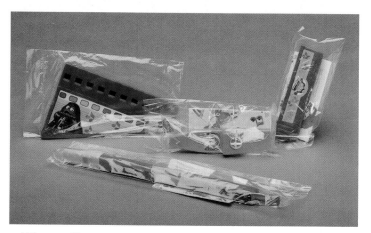

UK MU9402   UK MU9403   UK MU9404   UK MU9401

MCPUZZLE/MC I. Q. CHALLENGERS PROMOTION, 1994

❏ ❏ SIN PU9401 **BIG MAC GENIUS PUZZLE,** 1993, 8P PLASTIC
BIG MAC $8-12
❏ ❏ SIN PU9402 **COKE MCPUZZLE,** 1993, 12P PLASTIC COKE
CUP/SODA/STRAW $8-12
❏ ❏ SIN PU9403 **FRENCH FRIES MCPUZZLE,** 1993, 12P PLASTIC
FRENCH FRIES $8-12
❏ ❏ SIN PU9404 **SMART SUNDAE PUZZLE,** 1993, 12P PLASTIC
STRAWBERRY SUNDAE $8-12

❏ ❏ SIN PU9455 TRAYLINER, 1993, MCPUZZLE $2-3

COMMENTS: REGIONAL DISTRIBUTION: JAPAN, HONG KONG,
SINGAPORE: 1994. SIN PU9401-02-03 WERE DISTRIBUTED
AT OWNERS/OPERATORS CONVENTION - LAS VEGAS,
NEVADA IN USA, APRIL 1994. IN LAS VEGAS, NEVADA/USA;
IT WAS CALLED "MC I.Q. CHALLENGERS."

UK MU9426

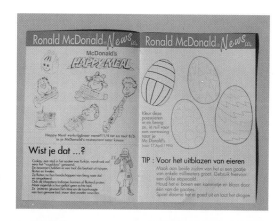

HOLLAND

SIN PU9403   SIN PU9401   SIN PU9402

SIN PU9403

Only $1 each with every Combo meal

SIN PU9455

SIN PU9404

233 SIN PU9401   SIN PU9402   SIN PU9403   SIN PU9404

UK WO9455

UK WO9407

MCSOCCER PROMOTION, 1994

❏ ❏ *** WO9407 **SOCCER BALL,** 1994, RED OR WHT OR YEL WORLD CUP SOCCER BALL $6-8

COMMENTS: REGIONAL DISTRIBUTION: UK, GERMANY: JUNE 1994. SOLD AS SELF LIQUIDATING PROMOTION IN CONJUNCTION WITH WORLD CUP SOCCER GAMES.

MICKEY & FRIENDS EPCOT ADVENTURE HAPPY MEAL, 1994

❏ ❏ CAN MI9410 HM BOX, 1994, CHIP IN CHINA/DALE IN MOROCCO $2-3
❏ ❏ CAN MI9411 HM BOX, 1994, DAISY IN GERMANY/DONALD IN MEXICO $2-3
❏ ❏ CAN MI9412 HM BOX, 1994, MICKEY IN USA/MINNIE IN JAPAN $2-3
❏ ❏ CAN MI9413 HM BOX, 1994, PLUTO IN FRANCE/GOOFY IN NORWAY $2-3

❏ ❏ CAN MI9409 **U-3 MICKEY IN U.S.A.,** 1994, MICKEY W ARMS EXTENDED $1.50-2
❏ ❏ CAN MI9401 **CHIP IN CHINA,** 1994, W CHINESE HAT $1-1.50
❏ ❏ CAN MI9402 **DAISY IN GERMANY,** 1994, DAISY DUCK $1-1.50
❏ ❏ CAN MI9414 **DALE IN CANADA,** 1994, AS CANADIAN MOUNTIE/HAT $3-4
❏ ❏ CAN MI9404 **DONALD IN MEXICO,** 1994, $1-1.50
❏ ❏ CAN MI9405 **GOOFY IN NORWAY,** 1994, GOOFY $1-1.50
❏ ❏ CAN MI9406 **MICKEY MOUSE,** 1994, MICKEY WITH ARMS EXTENDED $1-1.50
❏ ❏ CAN MI9407 **MINNIE IN JAPAN,** 1994, MINNIE $1-1.50
❏ ❏ CAN MI9408 **PLUTO IN FRANCE,** 1994, PLUTO $1-1.50

❏ ❏ CAN MI9426 DISPLAY/PREMIUMS, 1994 $50-65
❏ ❏ CAN MI9442 COUNTER CARD, 1994 $4-6
❏ ❏ CAN MI9464 TRANSLITE/SM, 1994 $5-10

COMMENTS: NATIONAL DISTRIBUTION: CANADA: JULY-AUGUST 1994; SCANDINAVIA/HOLLAND/BELGIUM/FRANCE/SPAIN/ ITALY/SWITZERLAND - JULY 1994; PUERTO RICO: JULY 1994. PREMIUMS ARE THE SAME AS MICKEY & FRIENDS, 1994 USA MI9401-08; CANADA MI9414 REPLACED USA MI9408. INTERNATIONAL DISTRIBUTION SETS ARE THE SAME AS USA MI9401-08. REGIONAL DISTRIBUTION: JAPAN/PUERTO RICO - JULY 1994.

USA MI9404   CAN MI9414

USA MI9407   USA MI9402   USA MI9403   USA MI9404

CAN MI9442

JPN KI9455

234

MR. KIASU ACTION FIGURES PROMOTION, 1994

❑ ❑ JPN KI9401 **MR. KIASU HOLDING A CONE W SHAKE,** 1994
$4-5

❑ ❑ JPN KI9402 **MR. KIASU W SYMBOLS,** 1994 $4-5
❑ ❑ JPN KI9403 **MR. KIASU W HAMB/FRIES/SODA,** 1994 $4-5
❑ ❑ JPN KI9404 **MR. KIASU W MCD FOOD BAG/PURCHASE,**
1994 $4-5
❑ ❑ JPN KI9455 TRAYLINER, 1994, MR. KIASU ACTION FIGURES
$1-1.50

COMMENTS: REGIONAL DISTRIBUTION: JAPAN: 1994. FIGU-
RINES ARE ADVERTISED AS A PAPER WEIGHT, A DOOR
STOPPER, A COCKROACH CRUSHER AND/OR A CHILI
POUNDER OR A WEDDING PRESENT.

NETHERLANDS/NEW ZEALAND/KOREA GENERIC PROMOTION, 1995/1994

❑ ❑ NED GE9401 **SOCCER GAME,** 1994, PAPER W STANDUP
FIGURES $1-1.25
❑ ❑ ZEA GE9402 **STENCIL,** 1994, YEL DISC $3-4
❑ ❑ KOR GE9403 **PEN,** 1994, WHT W RED/YEL DISC $4-5
❑ ❑ KOR GE9404 **STICKER SHEET,** 1994 $1-1.25
❑ ❑ KOR GE9405 **RULER/RONALD,** 1994 $3-4
❑ ❑ KOR GE9406 TRAYLINER/OPENING, 1995 $2-3

COMMENTS: REGIONAL DISTRIBUTION: NETHERLANDS; NEW
ZEALAND, KOREA: 1994. NED GE9401 FROM: NETHER-
LANDS HAPPY MEAL FANCLUB, POSTBUS 9310, 1006 AH IN
AMSTERDAM - 1995/1994. ZEA GE9402 WAS DISTRIBUTED:
NEW ZEALAND - 1994. McDONALD'S HAS CONSISTENTLY
ENCOURAGED YOUNG CUSTOMERS TO JOIN RONALD
McDONALD'S BIRTHDAY CLUBS.

OUT FOR FUN/SPLASH TIME FUN HAPPY MEAL, 1994

❑ ❑ GUA OU9410 HM BAG, 1992, SPANISH GRAPHICS $1-1.25
❑ ❑ GUA OU9401 **BALLOON BALL,** 1992, RONALD/BLU BEACH
BALL/BLOW UP BALL INSIDE $1-1.25
❑ ❑ GUA OU9402 **BUBBLE SHOE WAND,** 1992 2P RED/YEL
$1-1.50
❑ ❑ GUA OU9403 **SAND PAIL,** 1992, RON/FRIENDS ON BEACH/
YEL HANDLE $1-1.50
❑ ❑ GUA OU9404 **SUNGLASSES,** 1992, 1P BLU/GRN $1-1.25

COMMENTS: REGIONAL DISTRIBUTION: CHILE, ARGENTINA,
GUATEMALA, PANAMA, SINGAPORE: MAY/JUNE 1994.

ZEA GE9402

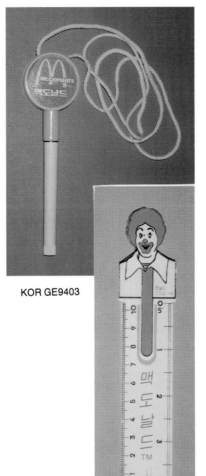

KOR GE9403

KOR GE9406

KOR GE9405

NED GE9401

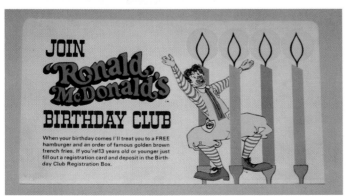

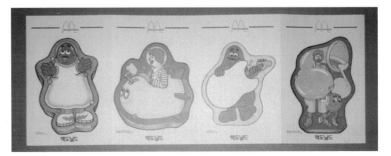

KOR GE9404

USA

USA OU9364

PLAY-DOH/SPIELKNETE JUNIOR TUTE/HAPPY MEAL, 1994

❏ ❏	UK PL9410 HM BOX, 1994, INFORMATION	$2-3
❏ ❏	UK PL9411 HM BOX, 1994, PETS CORNER	$2-3
❏ ❏	UK PL9412 HM BOX, 1994, SNACKS	$2-3
❏ ❏	UK PL9413 HM BOX, 1994, ZOO SHOP	$2-3
❏ ❏	GER PL9430 HM BAG, 1993, JUNIOR TUTE/#57 or 58 or 59 or 60 or 61	$2-3
❏ ❏	HOL PL9410 HM BOX, 1994, TYRANNO REX/RED	$2-3
❏ ❏	HOL PL9411 HM BOX, 1994, STEGOSAURUS/YEL	$2-3
❏ ❏	HOL PL9412 HM BOX, 1994, TRICERATOPS/GREEN	$2-3
❏ ❏	HOL PL9413 HM BOX, 1994, DIMETRIDON/BLUE	$2-3

***IDENTICAL CANS: GER/HOL PL9401/02/03/04**

❏ ❏	*** PL9401 **PLAY-DOH - BLUE,** 1994, W RON/BLU PLAS DIMETRIDON MOLD	$4-5
❏ ❏	*** PL9402 **PLAY-DOH - GREEN,** 1994, W RON/GRN PLAS TRICERATOPS MOLD	$4-5
❏ ❏	*** PL9403 **PLAY-DOH - RED,** 1994, W HAMB/RED PLAS TYRANO MOLD	$4-5
❏ ❏	*** PL9404 **PLAY-DOH - YELLOW,** 1994, W FRY KID/YEL PLAS STEGO MOLD	$4-5

❏ ❏	GER PL9450 BUTTON/EGGS, 1994, PAPER	$1-1.25
❏ ❏	HOL PL9450 BUTTON, 1994, BRACHIOSAURUS	$2.50-3
❏ ❏	HOL PL9451 BUTTON, 1994, TYRANNOSAURUS	$2.50-3
❏ ❏	NED PL9455 TRAYLINER, 1994, PLAY-DOH HAPPY MEAL	$3-4
❏ ❏	GER PL9365 TRANSLITE/LG, 1993	$25-40

COMMENTS: NATIONAL DISTRIBUTION: HOLLAND: JANUARY 19-FEBRUARY 22, 1994; UK: MAY 6-JUNE 1994; BELGIUM/HUNGARY/SWITZERLAND/SCANDANAVIA: JANUARY 1994; REGIONAL DISTRIBUTION: GERMANY - NOVEMBER 1994.

UK PL9413   UK PL9412   UK PL9411   UK PL9410

GERMANY

GER PL9430

HOL PL9410

GER PL9430

HOL PL9411

HOL PL9413

GERMANY

HOL PL9412

HOLLAND

GER PL9301   GER PL9302   GER PL9303   GER PL9304

GER PL9450

HOL PL9450   HOL PL9451

GER PL9465

POCKET PALS PROMOTION, 1994

❏ ❏ *** PO9401 **DOLL - BIRDIE,** 1994, 4"/STUFFED $4-6
❏ ❏ *** PO9402 **DOLL - GRIMACE,** 1994, 4"/STUFFED $4-6
❏ ❏ *** PO9403 **DOLL - HAMBURGLAR,** 1994, 4"/STUFFED $4-6
❏ ❏ *** PO9404 **DOLL - RONALD,** 1994, 5"/STUFFED $4-6
❏ ❏ JPN PO9444 CREW POSTER, 1994, POCKET PALS HAPPY MEAL $12-15

COMMENTS: REGIONAL DISTRIBUTION: AUSTRALIA/JAPAN: 1994.

PUZZLE PROMOTION, 1994

❏ ❏ AUS PU9401 **PUZZLE - BIRDIE,** 1994, FLYING $3-4
❏ ❏ AUS PU9402 **PUZZLE - GRIMACE,** 1994, EXERCISING $3-4
❏ ❏ AUS PU9403 **PUZZLE - HAMBURGLAR,** 1994, SMILING

$3-4
❏ ❏ AUS PU9404 **PUZZLE - RONALD,** 1994, SMILING $3-4

COMMENTS: REGIONAL DISTRIBUTION: AUSTRALIA: 1994.

PUZZELVERRASSINGEN HAPPY MEAL, 1994

*** IDENTICAL PUZZLES: GER/NET PU9401/02
❏ ❏ *** PU9401 **PUZZLE,** 1994, RON ON ISLAND $4-6
❏ ❏ *** PU9402 **PUZZLE,** 1994, RON PICNIC/CASTLE $4-6

COMMENTS: REGIONAL DISTRIBUTION: GERMANY/NETHER-LANDS - MAY 4-24, 1994

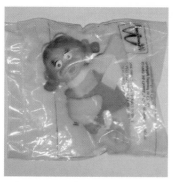

SIN PO9401　　　　　SIN PO9402

AUS PU9404

AUS PU9402

AUS PU9403　　　　AUS PU9401

SIN PL9403　　　　　SIN PL9404

JPN PO9444

GERMANY PU9401

238

NET PU9402

RONALD CELEBRATES HAPPY BIRTHDAY/LES GRANDS CLASSIQUES HAPPY MEAL, 1994

☐ ☐	CAN FI9420 HM BOX, 1994, CANDIES/FIND ALL THE	$2-3
☐ ☐	CAN FI9421 HM BOX, 1994, PARTY/RONALD INVITED	$2-3
☐ ☐	CAN FI9422 HM BOX, 1994, PORTRAIT/BERENSTAIN BEARS	$2-3
☐ ☐	CAN FI9423 HM BOX, 1994, PARADE/BIRTHDAY PARTY	$2-3
☐ ☐	CAN FI9416 **U-3 RONALD McDONALD,** 1994, IN RED HM BOX	$1.50-2
☐ ☐	CAN FI9401 **WK 1 RONALD McDONALD,** 1994, IN RED HM BOX WAVING/1P	$1.50
☐ ☐	CAN FI9402 **WK 1 BARBIE,** 1994, PNK BALLERINA/PURP STAND	$1-1.50
☐ ☐	CAN FI9403 **WK 1 HOT WHEELS,** 1994, BLU HW CAR IN ORG TRACK	$1-1.50
☐ ☐	CAN FI9404 **WK 2 E.T.,** 1994, W PURP HAT ON BLU STAGE	$1-1.50
☐ ☐	CAN FI9405 **WK 2 SONIC THE HEDGEHOG,** 1994, ON PNK TV	$1-1.50
☐ ☐	CAN FI9406 **WK 2 BERENSTAIN BEARS,** 1994, ON YEL SEESAW	$1-1.50
☐ ☐	CAN FI9407 **WK 3 CABBAGE PATCH KIDS,** 1994, ON BLU ROCKING HORSE	$1-1.50
☐ ☐	CAN FI9408 **WK 3 TONKA,** 1994, YEL TRUCK CARRYING RED PACKAGE	$1-1.50
☐ ☐	CAN FI9409 **WK 3 101 DALMATIANS,** 1994, DOGS ON BLK/WHT BOX	$1-1.50
☐ ☐	CAN FI9410 **WK 4 PEANUTS,** 1994, IN GRN CALLIOPE	$1-1.50
☐ ☐	CAN FI9411 **WK 4 MUPPET BABIES,** 1994, MISS PIGGY/**KERMIT W WHT TIE** ON BLU BASE	$2-2.50

CAN FI9409   CAN FI9412   CAN FI9411   CAN FI9410   CAN FI9413   CAN FI9414   CAN FI9415

CAN FI9401   CAN FI9402   CAN FI9403   CAN FI9406   CAN FI9405   CAN FI9404   CAN FI9408   CAN FI9407

CAN FI9417   CAN FI9411

❏ ❏ CAN FI9417 **WK 4 MUPPET BABIES,** 1994, MISS PIGGY/
KERMIT W BLU TIE ON BLU BASE $2-2.50
❏ ❏ CAN FI9412 **WK 4 LITTLE MERMAID,** 1994, W FLOUNDER
ON BLU BASE $1-1.50
❏ ❏ CAN FI9413 **WK 5 TINY TOONS,** 1994, W PNK CAKE/WHT
CANDLE $1-1.50
❏ ❏ CAN FI9414 **WK 5 LOONEY TUNES,** 1994, BUGS/
SYLVESTER W HORN/SYMBOLS $1-1.50
❏ ❏ CAN FI9415 **WK 5 HAPPY MEAL GUYS,** 1994, HAMB/FRIES/
SKAKE $1-1.50

❏ ❏ CAN FI9442 COUNTER CARD, 1994 $4-5

COMMENTS: NATIONAL DISTRIBUTION: CANADA: OCTOBER 28-
DECEMBER 1, 1994; PUERTO RICO: (REGIONALLY)
NOVEMBER 1994 AND AGAIN IN APRIL 1995. CALLED, "ALL
TIME FAVORITES" IN CANADA; SAME AS FIFTEENTH
ANNIVERSARY/BIRTHDAY OF USA HAPPY MEAL. DUE TO
MIXING OF USA AND CANADIAN TOYS IN DISTRIBUTION,
CAN FI9417 COULD HAVE BEEN DISTRIBUTED INSTEAD OF
CAN FI9411. BOTH MISS PIGGY/KERMIT WHT TIE AND BLUE
TIE VARIATION ARE APPEARING IN THE USA AND CANADA,
LOOSE.

RONALD McDONALD PUZZLE PACK PROMOTION, 1994
❏ ❏ *** RO9401 **PUZZLE CARD - WORD SEARCH,** 1994, PAPER
          $1-1.25
❏ ❏ *** RO9402 **PUZZLE CARD - CROSSWORD,** 1994, PAPER
          $1-1.25
❏ ❏ *** RO9403 **PUZZLE CARD - HIDDEN HAMBURGERS,** 1994,
PAPER $1-1.25
❏ ❏ *** RO9404 **PUZZLE CARD - SPOTTO,** 1994, PAPER $1-1.25
❏ ❏ *** RO9405 **PUZZLE CARD - MAZE,** 1994, PAPER $1-1.25

COMMENTS: REGIONAL DISTRIBUTION: EUROPE: 1994. PREMI-
UMS GIVEN TO CHILREN AT DRIVE-THRU WINDOWS AS
"KID'S BUMPER DRIVE THRU PUZZLE PACKS".

SIDEWALK CHALK/McDONALDLAND HAPPY MEAL, 1994
❏ ❏ AUS SI9401 **CHALK - BIRDIE,** 1994, MOLDED CHALK/FLAT
BACK $4-6
❏ ❏ AUS SI9402 **CHALK - GRIMACE,** 1994, MOLDED CHALK/
FLAT BACK $4-6
❏ ❏ AUS SI9403 **CHALK - HAMBURGLAR,** 1994, MOLDED
CHALK/FLAT BACK $4-6
❏ ❏ AUS SI9404 **CHALK - RONALD,** 1994, MOLDED CHALK/FLAT
BACK $4-6

COMMENTS: REGIONAL DISTRIBUTION: AUSTRALIA: SEPTEM-
BER 1994. EACH CHALK WAS 3 1/2"-4" TALL AND 1/2" THICK,
SHAPED LIKE THE CHARACTERS.

**SNOW WHITE AND THE SEVEN DWARFS HAPPY MEAL,
1994**
❏ ❏ AUS SN9410 HM BOX, 1994, SNEEZY/SLEEPY/DOPEY $3-4
❏ ❏ AUS SN9401 **PLACEMAT - SW,** 1994, DANCING W DWARFS
          $7-10
❏ ❏ AUS SN9402 **PLACEMAT - SW,** 1994, CROSSING BRIDGE/
OFF TO WORK $7-10
❏ ❏ AUS SN9403 **PLACEMAT - SW,** 1994, W FOREST FRIENDS/
ANIMALS $7-10

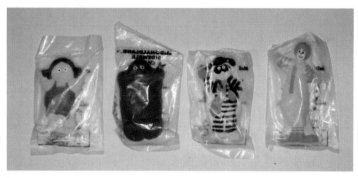

AUS SI9401   AUS SI9402   AUS SI9403   AUS SI9404

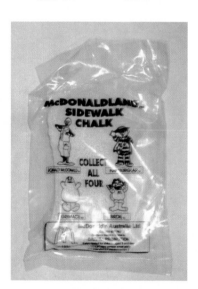

AUSTRALIA

AUS SN9410

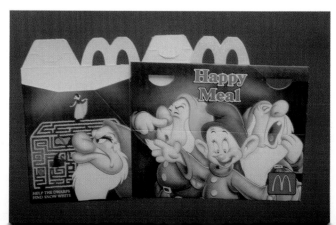

❏ ❏ AUS SN9404 **PLACEMAT - SW,** 1994, WAKING UP/MEETING
 DWARFS $7-10
❏ ❏ AUS SN9442 COUNTER CARD, 1994 $4-6

COMMENTS: REGIONAL DISTRIBUTION: AUSTRALIA: NOVEM-
 BER/DECEMBER 1994.

SOAP BUBBLE GAME/SEIGENBLASEN-SPIEL HAPPY MEAL, 1994
❏ ❏ GER BU9401 **BUBBLE BLOWER - BIRDIE,** 1994, W HAT/
 BUBBLE LIQ/WAND/3" $4-6
❏ ❏ GER BU9402 **BUBBLE BLOWER - HAMBURGLAR,** 1994, W
 BLK HAT/BUBBLE LIQ/WAND/3" $4-6
❏ ❏ GER BU9403 **BUBBLE BLOWER - RONALD,** 1994, W HAT/
 BUBBLE LIQ/WAND/3" $4-6

COMMENTS: REGIONAL DISTRIBUTION: GERMANY, FRANCE:
 JULY-AUGUST 1994.

SONIC THE HEDGEHOG JUNIOR TUTE/HAPPY MEAL, 1995/1994

 *** IDENTICAL BOXES: FRA/UK SO9410/11/12/13
❏ ❏ *** SO9410 HM BOX, 1994, POLAR ICE REGION $2-3
❏ ❏ *** SO9411 HM BOX, 1994, MODERN CITY $2-3
❏ ❏ *** SO9412 HM BOX, 1994, PALACE AT EDGE OF MTS $2-3
❏ ❏ *** SO9413 HM BOX, 1994, JUNGLE $2-3

❏ ❏ CAN SO9430 HM BAG, 1994, SONIC $1-1.25

AUS SN9401

AUS SN9402

FRA SO9401 FRA SO9402 FRA SO9403

AUS SN9403

GERMANY

CAN SO9430

AUS SN9404

AUS SN9442

241

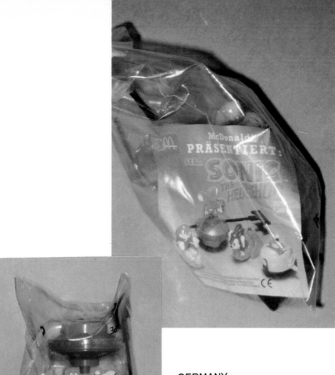

*** **IDENTICAL TOYS: BEL/CAN/GER/UK SO9501/02/03/04**

❏ ❏ *** SO9401 **DR. IVO ROBOTNIK,** 1993, GREY AUTO/HAND
CRANK $1-1.50

❏ ❏ *** SO9402 **KNUCKLES,** 1993, WHITE CLOUD W RED FIG,
1993 $1-1.50

❏ ❏ *** SO9403 **MILES/TAILS/PROW,** 1993, **BLU PROWER/ORG
TAILS/BLK PULL/3P** $1-1.50

❏ ❏ *** SO9404 **SONIC/HEDGEHOG,** 1993, BLU SONIC W ORG
BASE/2P $1-1.50

❏ ❏ BEL SO9444 CREW POSTER, 1994, $15-20
❏ ❏ BEL SO9426 DISPLAY W 4 PREMS, 1993 $25-40
❏ ❏ UK SO9426 DISPLAY W 4 PREMS, 1993 $25-40

COMMENTS: NATIONAL DISTRIBUTION: CANADA: DECEMBER
1994; GERMANY/UK: FEBRUARY 1995; PUERTO RICO: 1994.
*** SO9401/02/04 = USA SO9401/02/04. USA SO9403 WAS
RECALLED AND REDESIGNED FOR DISTRIBUTION IN
EUROPE. See USA SONIC 3 THE HEDGEHOG HAPPY MEAL,
1995.

GERMANY

UK SO9512

UK SO9510

UK SO9513

UK SO9511

242

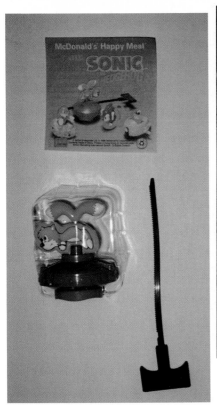

BEL SO9444

AUS SG9402

BEL SO9403

AUS ST9401   AUS ST9402   AUS ST9403   AUS ST9404

STRAW GRIPPERS HAPPY MEAL, 1994
- ❏ ❏ AUS SG9401 **BIRDIE,** 1994, W PLASTIC STRAW HOLER $2-3
- ❏ ❏ AUS SG9402 **GRIMACE,** 1994, W PLASTIC STRAW HOLER $2-3
- ❏ ❏ AUS SG9403 **HAMBURGLAR,** 1994, W PLASTIC STRAW HOLER $2-3
- ❏ ❏ AUS SG9404 **RONALD,** 1994, W PLASTIC STRAW HOLER $2-3

COMMENTS: REGIONAL DISTRIBUTION: AUSTRALIA - 1994. PREMIUMS ARE NOT THE SAME AS STRAW GRIPPERS PROMOTION, 1994.

STRAW GRIPPERS PROMOTION, 1994
- ❏ ❏ AUS ST9401 **BIRDIE,** 1994, ON CLEAR PLASTIC/2 STRAW HOLES $2-3
- ❏ ❏ AUS ST9402 **GRIMACE,** 1994, ON CLEAR PLASTIC/2 STRAW HOLES $2-3
- ❏ ❏ AUS ST9403 **HAMBURGLAR,** 1994, ON CLEAR PLASTIC/2 STRAW HOLES $2-3
- ❏ ❏ AUS ST9404 **RONALD,** 1994, ON CLEAR PLASTIC/2 STRAW HOLES $2-3

COMMENTS: REGIONAL DISTRIBUTION: AUSTRALIA: 1994. PREMIUMS ARE NOT THE SAME AS STRAW GRIPPERS HAPPY MEAL, 1994.

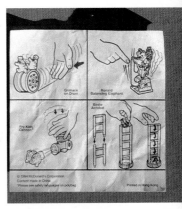

UNDER THE BIG TOP HAPPY MEAL, 1995/1994
- ❏ ❏ ZEA UN9401 **LADDER - BIRDIE,** 1994, BIRDIE ACROBAT/FLIPS/3P $4-5
- ❏ ❏ ZEA UN9402 **BARREL - GRIMACE,** 1994, DRUM/ROLLS $4-5
- ❏ ❏ ZEA UN9403 **CANNON - FRY KIDS,** 1994, PUMP/SHOOT/2P $7-10
- ❏ ❏ ZEA UN9404 **ELEPHANT -RON,** 1994, BALANCING/RIDING/2P $4-5

COMMENTS: REGIONAL DISTRIBUTION: HONG KONG/SINGAPORE: 1994; NATIONAL DISTRIBUTION: NEW ZEALAND: MARCH 1995. ZEA UN9503 FRY KIDS CANNON WAS RECALLED.

243   ZEA UN9401   ZEA UN9402   ZEA UN9403   ZEA UN9404

WALT DISNEY WORLD HAPPY MEAL, 1994

❏ ❏ JPN WA9401 **MICKEY,** 1994, IN BLU MONORAIL $5-7
❏ ❏ JPN WA9402 **GOOFY,** 1994, IN RED JEEP $5-7
❏ ❏ JPN WA9403 **CHIP/DALE,** 1994, IN AIRPLANE $5-7
❏ ❏ JPN WA9404 **MINNIE,** 1994, IN CANOE/WHEELS $5-7
❏ ❏ JPN WA9405 **DONALD,** 1994, ON FLYING DUMBO $5-7
❏ ❏ JPN WA9406 **PLUTO,** 1994, IN LOG RIDE/WHEELS $5-7
❏ ❏ JPN WA9455 TRAYLINER, 1994 $1-1.25

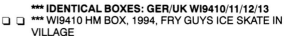
JPN WA9455

COMMENTS: REGIONAL DISTRIBUTION: JAPAN: JULY 1994.

WINTER SPORTS JUNIOR TUTE/HAPPY MEAL, 1995/1994

*** IDENTICAL BOXES: GER/UK WI9410/11/12/13
❏ ❏ *** WI9410 HM BOX, 1994, FRY GUYS ICE SKATE IN VILLAGE $2-3
❏ ❏ *** WI9411 HM BOX, 1994, RONALD/SKI LIFT HOUSE/DOWN HILL $2-3
❏ ❏ *** WI9412 HM BOX, 1994, GRIMACE/FRY GUYS SNOW SURF/GRI ICE SKATING $2-3
❏ ❏ *** WI9413 HM BOX, 1994, BIRDIE SKI SLALOM/START/FINISH/LODGE $2-3

*** IDENTICAL TOYS: GER/NET/JPN/UK WI9401/02/03/04
❏ ❏ *** WI9401 **BIRDIE ICE SKATING,** 1994, ON WHT CLOUD/2P W BLK PULL HANDLE $3-4
❏ ❏ *** WI9402 **GRIMACE IN SNOW PLOW,** 1994, ON GRN SNOW PLOW/1P $3-4
❏ ❏ *** WI9403 **HAMB IN SNOWMOBILE,** 1994, ON RED SNOW-MOBILE PULLING YEL SLED $3-4
❏ ❏ *** WI9404 **RONALD ON SKIS,** 1994, ON YEL SKIS $3-4

❏ ❏ UK WI9426 DISPLAY/PREMIUMS, 1994 $125-150
❏ ❏ BEL WI9444 CREW POSTER, 1994, $-------
❏ ❏ UK WI9464 TRANSLITE/SM, 1994 $4-7
❏ ❏ UK WI9465 TRANSLITE/LG, 1994 $8-12

COMMENTS: NATIONAL DISTRIBUTION: UK: FEBRUARY 25 - MARCH 1994; EUROPE: NOVEMBER 1994; JAPAN TEST IN DECEMBER 1994; GERMANY: JANUARY 1995. DIFFERENT SETS OF HM BOXES HAVE AND DO NOT HAVE WORDS, "WINTER SPORTS" ON FRONT BOX PANEL.

JPN WA9401   JAPAN

UK WI9413   UK WI9411   UK WI9412   UK WI9410

UK WI9401   UK WI9402   UK WI9403   UK WI9404

FRA WI9411

GERMANY

UK WI9426

244

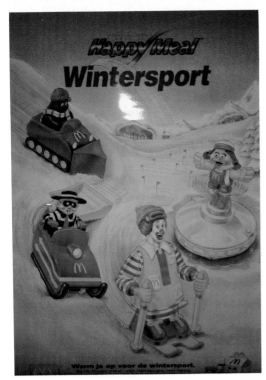

GER WI9465

BELGIUM

BEL WI9444

HOL OR9430

WORLD CUP/ORANJEPAKKET PROMOTION, 1994

☐ ☐ HOL OR9430 HM BAG, 1994, HUP HOLLAND $2-3
☐ ☐ HOL OR9406 **HAT,** 1994, AANVALLUUUUUHH/WORLD CUP
USA94 $3-4
☐ ☐ HOL OR9407 **FACE PAINT,** 1994, RED/WHT/BLU W ORG
DECAL $3-4
☐ ☐ HOL OR9408 **WHISTLE,** 1994, ORG W ORG SHOE LACE
STRING $3-4
☐ ☐ HOL OR9455 TRAYLINER, 1994, ORANJEPAKKET $1-2

COMMENTS: NATIONAL DISTRIBUTION: HOLLAND - MAY 25-JUNE
26, 1994.

HOL OR9406

HOL OR9408

UK CA9401

UK CA9402

HOL OR9455

WORLD CUP '94 SHOOT-OUT SCRATCH CARD PROMO-TION, 1994

❏ ❏ UK CA9401 **AMERICAN AIRLINES,** 1994, SCRATCH CARD
     $1-1.25
❏ ❏ UK CA9402 **HOLLYWOOD,** 1994, SCRATCH CARD $1-1.25
❏ ❏ UK CA9403 **STADIUM,** 1994, SCRATCH CARD $1-1.25
❏ ❏ UK CA9404 **WORLD CUP TROPHY,** 1994, SCRATCH CARD
     $1-1.25

COMMENTS: REGIONAL DISTRIBUTION: UK - 1994. CARDS WERE
FREE WITH EACH VISIT.

UK CA9404   UK CA9403

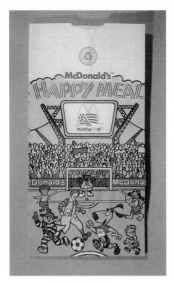

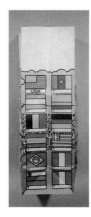

FRA WO9430

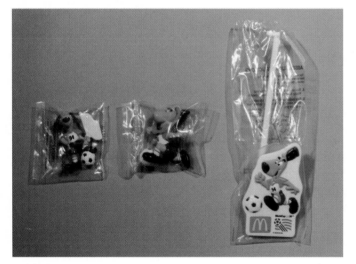

AUS WO9401   AUS WO9402   AUS WO9404

UK WO9402   UK WO9403   UK WO9405   UK WO9404

GERMANY

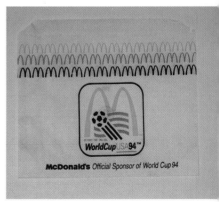

WORLD CUP USA 94/WORLD CUP FUN/WORLD CUP/ WERELDBEKER JUNIOR TUTE/HAPPY MEAL, 1994

- ❑ ❑ BEL WO9410 HM BOX, 1994, MCD HM/RON IN RESTAURANT FORMING ARCHES $2-3
- ❑ ❑ UK WO9410 HM BOX, 1994, MCD HM/RON IN RESTAURANT FORMING ARCHES $2-3
- ❑ ❑ FRA WO9430 HM BAG, 1994, WORLD CUP FLAGS/SAUDIA ARABIAN FLAG $5-7

- ❑ ❑ AUS WO9401 **DOG W BALL,** 1994, 1P DOG W BALL FIGU- RINE $3-4
- ❑ ❑ AUS WO9402 **KEY RING,** 1994, 1P DOG W BALL W RING $3-4
- ❑ ❑ AUS WO9404 **WACKY WAVER,** 1994, DOG W BALL/MCD LOGO/SUCTION CUP $3-4

- ****** IDENTICAL TOY: AUS/GER/GUA/NET/UK WO9402***
- ❑ ❑ *** WO9402 **WATER BOTTLE,** 1994, 3" SOCCER BALL W WORLD CUP LOGO/BLK LID/WHT/STRAW $3-4

- ****** IDENTICAL TOYS: GER/NET/UK WO9403/04***
- ❑ ❑ *** WO9403 **WRIST WALLET,** 1994, WHT W ZIPPER/VELCRO/ WORLD CUP LOGO $3-4
- ❑ ❑ *** WO9404 **CLAPPER,** 1994. 8" NOISE MAKER/CLAPPER W WORLD CUP LOGO $3-4

- ****** IDENTICAL TOY: NET/UK WO9405***
- ❑ ❑ *** WO9405 **SOCCER BALL,** 1994, 6" SOCCER BALL/BLK/ WHT PLASTIC W WORLD CUP LOGO $3-4

- ❑ ❑ CAN WO9406 **SOCCER BALL,** 1994, WHT/LEATHER LOOK W WORLDCUPUSA94 $3-5

- ❑ ❑ BEL WO9444 CREW POSTER/LG, 1994 $15-20
- ❑ ❑ FRA WO9445 REGISTER TOPPER, 1994, EACH PREMIUM $5-7
- ❑ ❑ CAN WO9455 TRAYLINER, 1994, GOLDENARCHIE/MINI FOOTBALLS $1-1.25
- ❑ ❑ GER WO9465 TRANSLITE/LG, 1994 $20-35

COMMENTS: NATIONAL DISTRIBUTION: AUSTRALIA (4 PREMI- UMS): MAY 27, 1994; GERMANY (3 PREMIUMS): JUNE 1994. FRANCE DISTRIBUTED: GER WO9402-04 WITH BAG FRA WO9401. UK/NETHERLANDS/FRANCE/BELGIUM (4 PREMI- UMS) NATIONAL DISTRIBUTION: MAY 25-JUNE 28, 1994; COSTA RICA, PANAMA, VENEZUELA, ARGENTINA: 1994; SAUDIA ARABIA REQUESTED HM BAG BE RECALLED. BEL WO9410 = UK WO9410 EXCEPT FOR YEAR PRINTED/ COUNTRY IN WHICH BOX WAS PRINTED. WORLD CUP FUN (GERMANY): JUNE 1994; WORLD CUP MASCOTS (AUSTRA- LIA): MAY 1994; WORLD CUP DRINK BOTTLE (SOCCER BALL): JUNE 1994.

Coupe du Monde

FRA WO9445

BEL WO9444

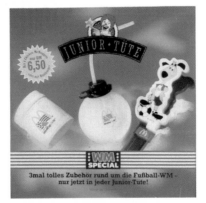

GER WO9465

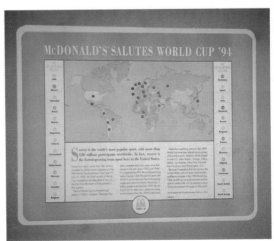

JAPAN

JPN YO9401

USA AS9264

YOMIURI NIPPON FOOTBALL CLUB PROMOTION, 1994
❑ ❑ JPN YO9401 **CARD SET,** 1994, 12 CARDS/SOCCER $50-75

COMMENTS: REGIONAL DISTRIBUTION: JAPAN - 1994.

YOUNG ASTRONAUTS/JUNGE ASTRONAUTEN JUNIOR TUTE/HAPPY MEAL, 1994
❑ ❑ GER AS9410 HM BAG, 1993, WHT JR TUTE BAG $1-1.25
❑ ❑ GER AS9401 **COMMAND MODULE/KOMMANDO ZENTRALEN,** 1991, 13P/CARDBOARD $1-1.50
❑ ❑ GER AS9202 **LUNAR ROVER,** 1991, 13P/CARDBOARD $1-1.50
❑ ❑ GER AS9403 **SATELLITE DISH/SATELLITENSTATION,** 1991, 8P/CARDBOARD $1-1.50
❑ ❑ GER AS9404 **SPACE SHUTTLE/RAUMFAHRE,** 1991, 10P/ CARDBOARD $1-1.50

COMMENTS: REGIONAL DISTRIBUTION: GERMANY: JULY/ AUGUST 1994 DURING CLEAN-UP WEEK. GER AS9401/03/ 04 = USA AS9201/03/0404, LOOSE OUT OF PACKAGE.

GER AS9403
GER AS9401
GER AS9404

GERMANY

1995

101 DALMATIONS HAPPY MEAL, 1995/1994

*** IDENTICAL BOXES: MEX/UK ON9110/11/12/13
❑ ❑ *** ON9110 HM BOX, 1994, THE DEN $1-1.50
❑ ❑ *** ON9111 HM BOX, 1994, THE PARK $1-1.50
❑ ❑ *** ON9112 HM BOX, 1994, OLD HOUSE $1-1.50
❑ ❑ *** ON9113 HM BOX, 1994, BARN $1-1.50

*** IDENTICAL TOYS: AUS/UK
❑ ❑ *** ON9100 **SET 1 PONGO THE DOG,** 1990, BLK/WHT DALMATION STANDING $1-2
❑ ❑ *** ON9102 **SET 3 COLONEL/SGT.TIBS,** 1990, SHEEP DOG W CAT $1-2
❑ ❑ *** ON9103 **SET 4 CRUELA DE VIL,** 1990, YEL/BLK VILLAIN-ESS $1-2

- ☐ ☐ UK ON9501 **SET 2 LUCKY THE PUP,** 1990, BLK/WHT DALMATION PUP SITTING W RED COLLAR $1-2
- ☐ ☐ AUS ON9504 **PATCH/BLANKET,** 1994, **DALMATION ON YEL BLANKET** $4-5

- ☐ ☐ AUS ON9542 COUNTER CARD, 1995 $4-5
- ☐ ☐ HOL ON9555 TRAYLINER, 1995 $1-1.25

COMMENTS: REGIONAL DISTRIBUTION: AUSTRALIA: APRIL 1995; NATIONAL DISTRIBUTION: HOL/UK: JANUARY 1995. SETS 1/ 2/3/4 = USA ON9100/01/02/03 (See USA 101 DALMATION HAPPY MEAL, 1991).

HOL ON9555

AUSTRALIA

UK

UK

AUS ON9542

MEX ON9110

USA ON9100 USA ON9101 USA ON9102 USA ON9103

249

FRANCE

AIRPORT/McDONALDLAND HAPPY MEAL, 1995

- ❏ ❏ UK AI9510 HM BOX, 1995, RON/GRI IN CONTROL TOWER $1-1.50
- ❏ ❏ UK AI9511 HM BOX, 1995, CHARS IN TERMINAL/WINDOW $1-1.50
- ❏ ❏ UK AI9512 HM BOX, 1995, CHARS ON OBSERVATION DECK/ PLANE LIFT OFF $1-1.50
- ❏ ❏ UK AI9513 HM BOX, 1995, RON/BIRDIE AT DEPARTURE AREA $1-1.50

   *** **IDENTICAL TOYS: HOL/UK TR9501/02/03/04**
- ❏ ❏ *** AI9501 **BIRDIE IN HELICOPTER,** 1995, RED/YEL HELI- COPTER $3-4
- ❏ ❏ *** AI9502 **GRIMACE PILOTING AIRPLANE,** 1995, YEL/RED AIRPLANE $3-4
- ❏ ❏ *** AI9503 **HAMBURGLAR IN UTILITY TRUCK,** 1995, RED TRUCK $3-4
- ❏ ❏ *** AI9504 **RONALD IN BAGGAGE LOADER,** 1995, RED/YEL BAGAGE TRAM LOADER W BLU LADDER $3-4

- ❏ ❏ UK AI9526 DISPLAY, 1995 $75-100
- ❏ ❏ UK AI9565 TRANSLITE, 1995 $8-12

COMMENTS: NATIONAL DISTRIBUTION: HOLLAND - MARCH/ APRIL 1995; UK - 1995; JAPAN - 1995.

UK AI9510

UK AI9513

UK AI9511

UK AI9512

UK AI9501

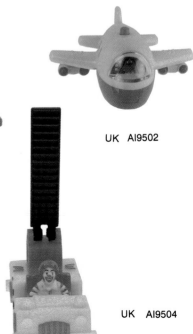

UK AI9502

UK AI9503

UK AI9504

AMAZING WILDLIFE HAPPY MEAL, 1995

❏ ❏ CAN AM9510 HM BOX, 1994, ELEPHANT/KOALA $1-1.50
❏ ❏ CAN AM9511 HM BOX, 1994, TURTLE/CAMEL $1-1.50
❏ ❏ CAN AM9512 HM BOX, 1994, LION/MONKEY $1-1.50
❏ ❏ CAN AM9513 HM BOX, 1994, POLAR BEAR/TIGER $1-1.50
❏ ❏ CAN AM9501 **ASIATIC LION**, 1994, BEIGE/TAN STUFFED
LION $1-1.25
❏ ❏ CAN AM9502 **CHIMPANZEE**, 1994, BRN/TAN STUFFED
CHIMPANZEE $1-1.25
❏ ❏ CAN AM9503 **AFRICAN ELEPHANT,** 1994, GRY STUFFED
ELEPHANT $1-1.25
❏ ❏ CAN AM9504 **KOALA,** 1994, TAN/WHT STUFFED BEAR
$1-1.25
❏ ❏ CAN AM9505 **DROMEDARY CAMEL,** 1994, BRN STUFFED
CAMEL $1-1.25
❏ ❏ CAN AM9506 **GALAPAGOS TORTOISE,** 1994, GRN STUFFED
TORTOISE $1-1.25
❏ ❏ CAN AM9507 **POLAR BEAR,** 1994, WHT STUFFED BEAR
$1-1.25
❏ ❏ CAN AM9508 **SIBERIAN TIGER,** 1994, GOLD/BLK/WHT
STUFFED TIGER $1-1.25
❏ ❏ CAN AM9526 DISPLAY, 1994, W 8 PREMIUMS $15-25
❏ ❏ CAN AM9544 CREW POSTER, 1995 $1.50-3
❏ ❏ CAN AM9546 PUZZLE, 1995, NEVER ENDING/PAPER $1-1.25
❏ ❏ CAN AM9547 CARDS/4, 1995, AMAZING STENCIL CARDS/4P
$1-1.25

COMMENTS: NATIONAL DISTRIBUTION: CANADA: APRIL 1-28,
1995. THE ADVERTISING TIE-IN PARTNER WAS THE
CANADIAN WILDLIFE FEDERATION. PROMOTION IN-
CLUDED PROMO AD FOR RANGER RICK MAGAZINE.

USA

CAN AM9501   CAN AM9502   CAN AM9504   CAN AM9503

CAN AM9505   CAN AM9506   CAN AM9508   CAN AM9507

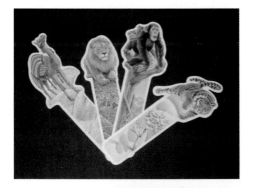

CANADA

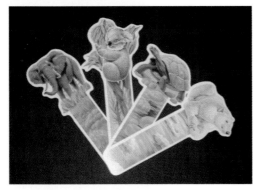

CANADA

CAN AM9511

CAN AM9510

251

CAN AM9512

CAN AM9513

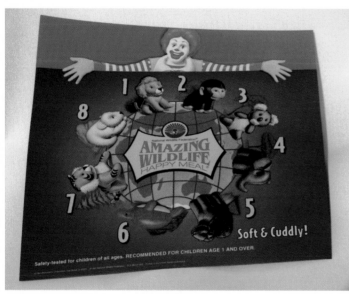

AM9564

CAN AM9546

COMMENTS: REGIONAL DISTRIBUTION: AUSTRALIA, NEW ZEALAND: 1995.

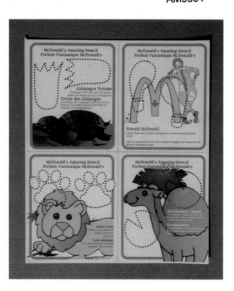

CAN AM9547

AUS GE9501

AUS GE9501

ZEA GE9501

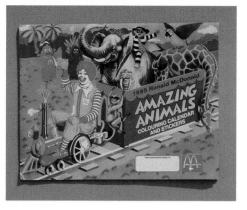

ZEA GE9505

JAPAN

BARBIE/HOT WHEELS HAPPY MEAL, 1995

- ❑ ❑ UK BA9510 HM BOX, 1995 $1-1.50
- ❑ ❑ UK BA9511 HM BOX, 1995 $1-1.50
- ❑ ❑ UK BA9512 HM BOX, 1995 $1-1.50
- ❑ ❑ UK BA9513 HM BOX, 1995 $1-1.50

- ❑ ❑ JPN BA9403 **CAMP BARBIE,** 1994, PNK JACKET/BLONDE HAIR/BLU SHORTS/GRN BASE $1.50-2.50
- ❑ ❑ JPN BA9306 **SECRET HEART,** 1993, WHT/ROSE LONG GOWN/HOLDING RED HEART/LONG BLOND HAIR $1.50-2.50
- ❑ ❑ JPN BA9307 **TWINKLE LIGHTS,** 1993, PINK/WHT GOWN/ WHT PURSE/LONG BLONDE SYN HAIR $1.50-2.50
- ❑ ❑ JPN BA9407 **JEWEL/GLITTER BRIDE,** 1994, WHT LONG DRESS/BLONDE HAIR/PNK FLOWERS $1.50-2.50

- ❑ ❑ JPN HW9413 **TURBINE 4-2,** 1994, BLU TURBINE/JET CAR $1-1.50
- ❑ ❑ JPN HW9309 **MCD FUNNY CAR,** 1993, RED/WHT/ "McDONALD'S" ON SIDE $1-1.50
- ❑ ❑ JPN HW9312 **HOT WHEELS FUNNY CAR,** 1993, WHT/RED/ YEL "HOT WHEELS" ON SIDE FUNNY CAR $1-1.50
- ❑ ❑ JPN HW9517 **#27 HOT WHEELS,** 1994, **BLU W YEL MCD LOGO/YEL #27 ON HOOD** $3-5

- ❑ ❑ UK BA9302 **HOLLYWOOD HAIR,** 1993, GOLD SHORT DRESS/**BLU STAR BASE** $1.50-2.50
- ❑ ❑ UK BA9307 **TWINKLE LIGHTS,** 1993, PINK/WHT GOWN/WHT PURSE/LONG BLONDE SYN HAIR $1.50-2.50
- ❑ ❑ UK HW9310 **QUAKER STATE RACER #62,** 1993, GRN QUAKER STATE #62 $1-1.50
- ❑ ❑ UK HW9312 **HOT WHEELS FUNNY CAR,** 1993, WHT/RED/ YEL "HOT WHEELS" ON SIDE FUNNY CAR $1-1.50

- ❑ ❑ UK BA9526 DISPLAY, 1995   35-50
- ❑ ❑ JPN BA9544 COUNTER CARD, 1995 $5-7
- ❑ ❑ JPN BA9555 TRAYLINER, 1995 $1-1.25

COMMENTS: NATIONAL DISTRIBUTION: UK: AUGUST 1995; JAPAN - 1995. UK BA9307/10 AND HW9310/12 = USA BA9307/ 10 AND HW9310/12 (See USA BARBIE/HOW WHEELS HAPPY MEAL, 1993). THE USA DISTRIBUTED 8 BARBIES AND 8 HOT WHEELS DURING THE 1993 HM PROMOTION.

JPN BA9407   JPN BA9307   JPN BA9306   JPN BA9403

JPN BA9555

253   JPN HW9517   JPN HW9312   JPN HW9309   JPN HW9413

ZEA BE9501

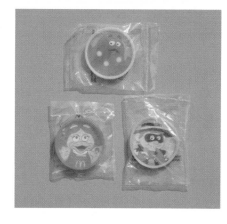

ZEA BE9503

BEAD GAME PROMOTION, 1995
❑ ❑ ZEA BE9501 **BEAD GAME - BIRDIE,** 1995, PNK/CIRCLE $3-4
❑ ❑ ZEA BE9502 **BEAD GAME - GRIMACE,** 1995, YEL/CIRCLE $3-4
❑ ❑ ZEA BE9503 **BEAD GAME - HAMBURGLAR,** 1995, GRN/CIRCLE $3-4
❑ ❑ ZEA BE9504 **BEAD GAME - RONALD,** 1995, RED/CIRCLE $3-4

COMMENTS: REGIONAL DISTRIBUTION: NEW ZEALAND: 1995

CANADA/GENERIC PROMOTION, 1995
❑ ❑ CAN GE9501 **CALENDAR '95,** 1995, UNDERWATER WORLD $2-3

COMMENTS: REGIONAL DISTRIBUTION: CANADA: 1995.

DISNEYLAND ADVENTURES 40 YEARS HAPPY MEAL, 1995
❑ ❑ CAN DI9510 HM BOX, 1995, ALADDIN OASIS/DANCERS $1-1.50
❑ ❑ CAN DI9511 HM BOX, 1995, FANTASMIC/PIRATES $1-1.50
❑ ❑ CAN DI9512 HM BOX, 1995, LION KING CELEBRATION $1-1.50
❑ ❑ CAN DI9513 HM BOX, 1995, SPACE MOUNTAIN/MICKEY MOUSE $1-1.50

CAN GE9501

CAN DI9511

CAN DI9510

CAN DI9512

CAN DI9513

254

□ □ CAN DI9509 **U-3 WINNIE THE POOH/THUNDER MOUNTAIN**, 1995, IN TRAIN W GRN CAB/**NO VIEWER** $2-2.50

□ □ CAN DI9501 **BRER BEAR ON SPLASH MOUNTAIN**, 1995, IN BRN LOG BOAT/VIEWER $1.25-1.50

□ □ CAN DI9502 **ALADDIN & JASMINE AT ALADDIN'S OASIS**, 1995, ON ELEPHANT/PURP VIEWER $1.25-1.50

□ □ CAN DI9503 **SIMBA IN THE LION KING CELEBRATION**, 1995, ON ROCK/MOUNTAIN/BRN VIEWER $1.25-1.50

□ □ CAN DI9504 **MICKEY MOUSE ON SPACE MOUNTAIN**, 1995, IN RED SPACE CAR/VIEWER $1.25-1.50

□ □ CAN DI9505 **ROGER RABBIT IN MICKEY'S TOONTOWN**, 1995, IN YEL/BLU CAR/VIEWER $1.25-1.50

□ □ CAN DI9506 **WINNIE/POOH ON BIG THUNDER MOUNTAIN**, 1995, RED TRAIN W BLK OR GRN CAB/**VIEWER** $1.25-1.50

□ □ CAN DI9507 **PETER PAN IN FANTASMIC!**, 1995, IN ORG BOAT/VIEWER $1.25-1.50

□ □ CAN DI9508 **KING LOUIE ON THE JUNGLE CRUISE**, 1995, IN GRN/YEL JUNGLE BOAT/VIEWER $1.25-1.50

□ □ CAN DI9526 DISPLAY, 1995, W 8 PREMIUMS $35-50

□ □ CAN DI9543 CREW REFERENCE SHEET, 1995, BLK/WHT PIC $1-1.50

□ □ CAN DI9544 CREW POSTER, 1995 $1.50-3

□ □ CAN DI9550 CREW BADGE, 1995, PAPER $1.50-2.50

□ □ CAN DI9564 TRANSLITE/SM, 1995 $5-7

COMMENTS: NATIONAL DISTRIBUTION: CANADA: JUNE 1 - 31, 1995. CAN DI9509 AND CAN DI9506 ARE NOT THE SAME; CAN DI9506 HAS VIEWER (CAB IN GRN OR BLK VERSIONS) AND U-3 DOES NOT HAVE VIEWER.

CAN DI9509

CAN DI9550

CANADA

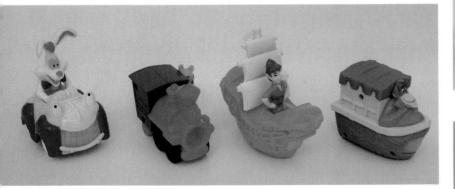

CAN DI9501   CAN DI9502   CAN DI9503   CAN DI9504

CAN DI9505   CAN DI9506   CAN DI9507   CAN DI9508

CAN DI9526

CAN DI9564

CAN DI9543

JPN DO9501   JPN DO9502   JPN DO9504

UK DR9412

DOLL PROMOTION, 1995

❑ ❑ JPN DO9501 **DOLL - BIRDIE,** 1995, 2 2/1" W KEY RING $3-4
❑ ❑ JPN DO9502 **DOLL - GRIMACE,** 1995, 2 1/2" W KEY RING
                                                          $3-4
❑ ❑ JPN DO9503 **DOLL - HAMBURGLAR,** 1995, 2" W KEY RING
                                                          $3-4
❑ ❑ JPN DO9504 **DOLL - RONALD,** 1995, 3" W KEY RING $3-4

COMMENTS: REGIONAL DISTRIBUTION: JAPAN: 1995 AS SELF
LIQUIDATOR.

DRIVE AND FLY/SPEEDIES/CLASSICS HAPPY MEAL, 1995

*** IDENTICAL TOYS: HOL/UK DR9501/02/03/04
❑ ❑ *** DR9501 **AIRPLANE - FRY KID,** 1994, IN BLU PLANE $4-5
❑ ❑ *** DR9502 **BUS - HAMBURGLAR,** 1994, IN GRN DOUBLE
DECKER BUS $4-5
❑ ❑ *** DR9503 **CAR - BIRDIE,** 1994, IN SILVER AUTO $4-5
❑ ❑ *** DR9504 **CAR - RONALD,** 1994, IN RED CAR W LOGO ON
HOOD $4-5

❑ ❑ UK DR9526 DISPLAY, 1995 $75-100
❑ ❑ HOL DR9555 TRAYLINER, 1995 $1-1.25
❑ ❑ UK DR9565 TRANSLITE, 1995 $8-12
❑ ❑ UK DR9570 MANAGER'S GUIDE, 1995, PAPER $3-4

COMMENTS: NATIONAL DISTRIBUTION: HOLLAND: JANUARY 4-
FEBRUARY 7, 1995; UK: DECEMBER 15-JANUARY 15, 1995;
EUROPE: MARCH 1995. CALLED, "SPEEDIES" IN HOLLAND
AND "DRIVE AND FLY HAPPY MEAL" IN THE UK; "CLASSICS"
IN OTHER PARTS OF EUROPE.

HOL SP9501-04

UK DR9410

UK DR9411

UK DR9413

UK

UK DR9403   UK DR9401   UK DR9402   UK DR9404

UK DR9526

HOL DR9555

EUROPE/NETHERLANDS GENERIC PROMOTION, 1995
- ❏ ❏ NET GE9501 **POSTCARD - RONALD,** 1995, JUMPING THRU HOOP $2-3
- ❏ ❏ NET GE9502 **GAME - FIND WAY TO MCD,** 1995, PAPER W PUNCHOUT CHARS $1-1.25
- ❏ ❏ LAT GE9555 TRAYLINER, 1995, LATVIA $1-1.25

COMMENTS: REGIONAL DISTRIBUTION: GERMANY/HOLLAND/ LATVIA: 1995.

UK DR9570

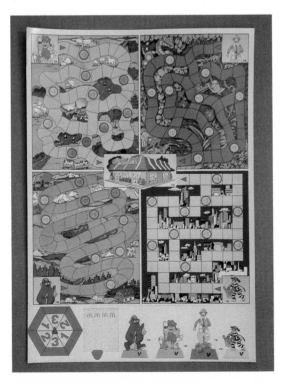

NET GE9502

LAT GE9555

JPN FU9501   JPN FU9502   JPN FU9503   JPN FU9504

FUZZIES PROMOTION, 1995

❑ ❑	JPN FU9501 **FRY GIRL**, 1995	$2-3
❑ ❑	JPN FU9502 **GRIMACE**, 1995	$2-3
❑ ❑	JPN FU9503 **HAMBURGLAR**, 1995	$2-3
❑ ❑	JPN FU9504 **BIRDIE**, 1995	$2-3

COMMENTS: REGIONAL DISTRIBUTION: JAPAN: 1995 AS SELF-
LIQUIDATOR AND/OR SOLD IN McDONALD'S RETAIL
SHOPS IN JAPAN.

INTERGALACTIC ADVENTURES, 1995

❑ ❑	UK IN9510 HM BOX, 1995, SPACESHIP	$1-1.50
❑ ❑	UK IN9511 HM BOX, 1995, SPACE CITY	$1-1.50
❑ ❑	UK IN9512 HM BOX, 1995, SPACE STATION	$1-1.50
❑ ❑	UK IN9513 HM BOX, 1995, ALIEN CITY	$1-1.50

❑ ❑ UK IN9501 **MCROBOT - MAN**, 1995, BLU W YEL VEHICLE
$3-4

❑ ❑ UK IN9502 **MOON BUGGY - GRIM**, 1995, PURP W GRN
VEHICLE $3-4

❑ ❑ UK IN9503 **SPACE SHUTTLE - RON/GRI**, 1995, WHT
SPACESHIP W BLU WEHICLE $3-4

❑ ❑ UK IN9504 **LUNAR ROVER - RON**, 1995, YEL RON W RED
VEHICLE $3-4

❑ ❑ UK IN9526 DISPLAY W 4 PREMS, 1995 $20-35

COMMENTS: NATIONAL DISTRIBUTION: UK: FEBRUARY-MARCH
1995; EUROPE - MAY 1995.

UK IN9501   UK IN9502   UK IN9503   UK IN9504

MCFARM HAPPY MEAL, 1995

❑ ❑	UK FA9510 HM BOX, 1995	$1-1.50
❑ ❑	UK FA9511 HM BOX, 1995	$1-1.50
❑ ❑	UK FA9512 HM BOX, 1995	$1-1.50
❑ ❑	UK FA9513 HM BOX, 1995	$1-1.50

❑ ❑ UK FA9501 **BIRDIE/WHEELBARROW**, 1995, PUSHING
BRN WHEELBARROW W DUCKS/2P $4-5

❑ ❑ UK FA9502 **GRIMACE/PICK-UP TRUCK**, 1995, IN RED PICK-
UP TRUCK $4-5

❑ ❑ UK FA9503 **HAMBURGLAR/HARVESTER**, 1995, IN RED
HARVESTER $4-5

❑ ❑ UK FA9504 **RONALD/TRACTOR**, 1995, IN GRN TRACTOR
$4-5

❑ ❑	UK FA9526 DISPLAY, 1995	$25-40
❑ ❑	UK FA9565 TRANSLITE, 1995	$8-12

COMMENTS: NATIONAL DISTRIBUTION: UK: 1995.

MCRODEO HAPPY MEAL, 1995

❑ ❑	UK RO9510 HM BOX, 1995	$1-1.50
❑ ❑	UK RO9511 HM BOX, 1995	$1-1.50
❑ ❑	UK RO9512 HM BOX, 1995	$1-1.50
❑ ❑	UK RO9513 HM BOX, 1995	$1-1.50

***IDENTICAL TOYS: GER/MEX/ZEA/UK RO9501/02/03/04

❑ ❑ *** RO9501 **BIRDIE/LASSO**, 1995, W BEIGE LASSO $4-5
❑ ❑ *** RO9502 **GRIMACE/HORSE**, 1995, ON BRN HORSE $4-5
❑ ❑ *** RO9503 **HAMBURGLAR/COWBOY**, 1995, WEARING RED
PANTS/BLK HAT $4-5
❑ ❑ *** RO9504 **RONALD/BARREL**, 1995, IN YEL BARREL $4-5

❑ ❑	*** RO9526 DISPLAY, 1995	$25-40
❑ ❑	UK RO9565 TRANSLITE, 1995	$8-12

ZEA RO9501   ZEA RO9502   ZEA RO9503   ZEA RO9504

COMMENTS: NATIONAL DISTRIBUTION: GERMANY, PANAMA, NEW ZEALAND, UK: MAY 5-JUNE 1995; JAPAN TESTED IN NOVEMBER 1994; GERMANY: MAY 1995; MEXICO: MARCH/APRIL 1995.

MUPPET WORKSHOP HAPPY MEAL, 1995

❑ ❑ CAN MU9510 HM BOX, 1995, BIRD PUPPET $1-1.50
❑ ❑ CAN MU9511 HM BOX, 1995, DOG PUPPET $1-1.50
❑ ❑ CAN MU9512 HM BOX, 1995, MONSTER PUPPET $1-1.50
❑ ❑ CAN MU9513 HM BOX, 1995, WHAT-NOT PUPPET $1-1.50
❑ ❑ CAN MU9505 **U-3 WHAT-NOT,** 1995, YEL MONSTER/PURP COWBOY HAT/RED GUITAR/4P $1.25-1.50

*** IDENTICAL TOYS: CAN/MEX MU9501/02/03/04

❑ ❑ *** **MU9501 WK 1 BIRD,** 1995, TURQ BIRD/RED HAT/PURP BOW/4P $1-1.25
❑ ❑ *** **MU9502 WK 2 DOG,** 1995, PNK DOG/ORG BIRD HAT/GRN CAMERA/4P $1-1.25
❑ ❑ *** **MU9503 WK 3 MONSTER,** 1995, GRN MONSTER/ORG HAT/BLU BEAR/4P $1-1.25
❑ ❑ *** **MU9504 WK 4 WHAT-NOT,** 1995, YEL MONSTER/PURP COWBOY HAT/RED GUITAR/4P $1-1.25

❑ ❑ CAN MU9526 DISPLAY, 1995, W 4 PREMIUMS $15-20
❑ ❑ CAN MU9543 CREW REF SHEET, 1995, BLK/WHT PIC $1-1.50
❑ ❑ CAN MU9544 CREW POSTER, 1995 $1.50-3
❑ ❑ CAN MU9564 TRANSLITE/SM, 1995 $3-5

COMMENTS: NATIONAL DISTRIBUTION: CANADA: MARCH 1995; ARGENTINA, COSTA RICA, MEXICO, PANAMA, URUGUAY, VENZUELA: MARCH 1995.

POCAHONTAS HAPPY MEAL, 1995

❑ ❑ UK PC9510 HM BOX, 1995 $1-1.50
❑ ❑ UK PC9511 HM BOX, 1995 $1-1.50
❑ ❑ UK PC9512 HM BOX, 1995 $1-1.50
❑ ❑ UK PC9513 HM BOX, 1995 $1-1.50
❑ ❑ UK PC9501 **POCAHONTAS,** 1995 $4-5
❑ ❑ UK PC9502 **CAPT JOHN SMITH,** 1995 $4-5
❑ ❑ UK PC9503 **JOHN RADCLIFF,** 1995 $4-5
❑ ❑ UK PC9504 **GRANDMA'S WILLOW TREE,** 1995 $4-5
❑ ❑ UK PC9526 DISPLAY, 1995 $50-65
❑ ❑ UK PC9565 TRANSLITE/LG, 1995 $20-25

COMMENTS: NATIONAL DISTRIBUTION: UK: 1995.

MEX MU9502

USA MU9520

MEX MU9503

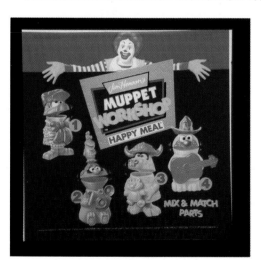

USA MU9564

CAN MU9501   CAN MU9502   CAN MU9503   CAN MU9504

POLLY POCKET / ATTACK PACK HAPPY MEAL, 1995

❑ ❑ CAN PO9530 HM BAG, 1995, POLLY POCKET/ATTACK PACK $1-1.25
❑ ❑ CAN PO9509 **U-3 WATCH,** 1995, YEL CASE/TURQ DIAL $1.25-1.50
❑ ❑ CAN HW9510 **U-3 TRUCK,** 1995, GRY/BLK/RED TRUCK $1.25-1.50
❑ ❑ CAN PO9501 **RING,** 1995, PNK/YEL/GRN POLLY POCKET ON FLOWER PEDAL $1-1.25

CAN PO9530

□ □ CAN PO9502 **LOCKET,** 1995, PNK HEART LOCKET W PNK
CORD $1-1.25
□ □ CAN PO9503 **WATCH,** 1995, YEL CASE/TURQ DIAL $1-1.25
□ □ CAN PO9504 **BRACELET,** 1995, PNK/TURQ BUTTERFLY
CASE/YEL STRAP $1-1.25
□ □ CAN HW9505 **TRUCK,** 1995, GRY/BLK/RED TRUCK $1-1.25
□ □ CAN HW9506 **BATTLE BIRD,** 1995, GRN/WHT AIRPLANE/
BIRD $1-1.25
□ □ CAN HW9507 **LUNAR INVADER,** 1995, YEL/GRY LUNAR
MODULE $1-1.25
□ □ CAN HW9508 **SEA CREATURE,** 1995, TURQ/WHT SEA
CREATURE $1-1.25

□ □ CAN PO9526 DISPLAY, 1995, W 4 PREMIUMS $15-20
□ □ CAN PO9543 CREW REFERENC, 1995, BLK/WHT PIC $1-
1.50
□ □ CAN PO9544 CREW POSTER, 1995 $1.50-3
□ □ CAN PO9545 BOOKLET-PP/AP, 1995, ANIMATION BOOKLET
     $1-1.25
□ □ CAN PO9564 TRANSLITE/SM, 1995 $3-5

COMMENTS: NATIONAL DISTRIBUTION: CANADA: FEBRUARY 3-
MARCH 2, 1995. CAN PO9501-10 = USA PO9501-10.

PUZZLE HAPPY MEAL, 1995
□ □ AUS PU9501 **PUZZLE - BIRDIE,** 1995, SKIPPING $4-5
□ □ AUS PU9502 **PUZZLE - GRIMACE,** 1995, EXERCISING $4-5
□ □ AUS PU9503 **PUZZLE - HAMBURGLAR,** 1995, SCOOTING
     $4-5
□ □ AUS PU9504 **PUZZLE - RONALD,** 1995, SKIING $4-5

COMMENTS: REGIONAL DISTRIBUTION: AUSTRALIA: 1995.

SPACE RESCUE HAPPY MEAL, 1995
□ □ CAN SP9530 HM BAG, 1995, SPACE RESCUE $1-1.25

□ □ CAN SP9505 **U-3 ASTRO VIEWER,** 1994, GRN/PURP W WHT
LABEL $1.25-1.50
□ □ CAN SP9501 **ASTRO VIEWER,** 1994, GRN/PURP W PNK
LABEL $1-1.25
□ □ CAN SP9502 **TELE COMMUNICATOR,** 1994, ORG/GRN
     $1-1.25

USA PO9543

AUS PU9501   AUS PU9504

CAN PO9564

AUS PU9502

□ □ CAN SP9503 **SPACE SLATE,** 1994, BLU/PURP/ORG W PURP
PEN/2P $1-1.25
□ □ CAN SP9504 **LUNAR GRABBER,** 1994, BLU/GRN/ORG
                                         $1-1.25

□ □ CAN SP9526 DISPLAY, 1995, W 4 PREMIUMS $15-20
□ □ CAN SP9542 COUNTER CARD, 1995 $3-4
□ □ CAN SP9543 CREW REFERE SHEET, 1995, BLK/WHT PIC
                                         $1-1.50
□ □ CAN SP9544 CREW POSTER, 1995 $1.50-3
□ □ CAN SP9564 TRANSLITE/SM, 1995 $3-5

COMMENTS: NATIONAL DISTRIBUTION: CANADA: MARCH 3-31,
1995. CAN SP9501 = CAN SP9505, LOOSE OUT OF
PACKAGE. CAN SP9501-05 = USA SP9501-05.

SPIDER-MAN HAPPY MEAL, 1995
□ □ CAN SM9530 HM BAG, 1995, SPIDERMAN $1-1.25

□ □ CAN SM9509 **U-3 AMAZING SPIDER-MAN,** 1995, RED/BLU
SPIDER-MAN $1.50-2
□ □ CAN SM9501 **AMAZING SPIDER-MAN,** 1995, RED/BLU
SPIDER-MAN $1.25-1.50
□ □ CAN SM9502 **SCORPION STINGSTRIKER,** 1995, GRN
SCORPION VEHICLE W PLIER CLAWS $1.25-1.50
□ □ CAN SM9503 **DR. OCTOPUS,** 1995, YEL/GRN MAN W GRY
TENTACLES $1.25-1.50
□ □ CAN SM9504 **SPIDER-MAN WEBRUNNER,** 1995, SPIDER-
MAN IN WHT/RED/BLU SPIDER VEHICLE $1.25-1.50
□ □ CAN SM9505 **MARY JANE WATSON,** 1995, PNK COAT/YEL
SHIRT/W RED or GRN CLIP-ON DRESS/3P $1.25-1.50
□ □ CAN SM9506 **VENOM TRANSPORT,** 1995, BLK/WHT/RED
SPIDER VEHICLE $1.25-1.50
□ □ CAN SM9507 **SPIDER-SENSE PETER PARKER,** 1995, BRN
SHIRT/BLU PANTS/HALF FACE $1.25-1.50
□ □ CAN SM9508 **HOBGOBLIN LANDGLIDER,** 1995, PURP/ORG/
GRY VEHICLE $1.25-1.50

□ □ CAN SM9526 DISPLAY, 1995, W 8 PREMIUMS $35-50
□ □ CAN SM9543 CREW REFER SHEET, 1995, BLK/WHT PIC
                                         $1-1.50
□ □ CAN SM9544 CREW POSTER, 1995 $1.50-3
□ □ CAN SM9564 TRANSLITE/SM, 1995 $5-7

COMMENTS: NATIONAL DISTRIBUTION: CANADA: MAY: 1995.
CAN SM9501 = CAN SM95O9, LOOSE OUT OF PACKAGE.
CAN SM9501-09 = USA SM9501-09. SPIDER-MAN CHARAC-
TER NAMES AND LIKENESSES ARE TRADEMARK AND
COPYRIGHT: MARVEL ENTERTAINMENT GROUP, INC.

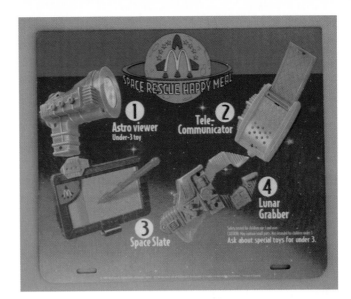

CAN SP9542

CAN SM9530

USA

CAN SM9501-04

USA

CAN SM9505-08

AUS SU9501   AUS SU9502   AUS SU9503   AUS SU9504

SPEEDSTERS HAPPY MEAL, 1995

❏	❏	UK SS9510 HM BOX, 1995	$1-1.50
❏	❏	UK SS9511 HM BOX, 1995	$1-1.50
❏	❏	UK SS9512 HM BOX, 1995	$1-1.50
❏	❏	UK SS9513 HM BOX, 1995	$1-1.50
❏	❏	UK SS9501 **BIRDIE/JEEP,** 1995, IN PNK JEEP/CONVERT-IBLE/GARAGE/2P	$4-5
❏	❏	UK SS9502 **GRIMACE/GO-KART,** 1995, IN LT BLU GO-KART/GARAGE/2P	$4-5
❏	❏	UK SS9503 **HAMBURGLAR/BIKE,** 1995, ON RED BIKE/GARAGE/2P	$4-5
❏	❏	UK SS9504 **RONALD/BOAT,** 1995, IN DK BLU BOAT/BOAT HOUSE/2P	$4-5
❏	❏	UK SS9526 DISPLAY, 1995	$25-40
❏	❏	UK SS9565 TRANSLITE, 1995	$8-12

COMMENTS: NATIONAL DISTRIBUTION: UK: 1995.

SUMMER FUN HAPPY MEAL, 1995

❏	❏	AUS SU9501 **PAIL,** 1994, RED W YEL HANDLE	$2-2.50
❏	❏	AUS SU9502 **RAKE,** 1994, PURP	$2-2.50
❏	❏	AUS SU9503 **SHOVEL,** 1994, YEL	$2-2.50
❏	❏	AUS SU9504 **MOLD-STAR FISH,** 1994, HOT PNK	$2-2.50

COMMENTS: REGIONAL DISTRIBUTION: AUSTRALIA: JANUARY (SUMMER) 1995.

TRICKY TRACKERS/NEW YEAR PARADE HAPPY MEAL, 1995

❏	❏	SIN TR9510 HM BOX, 1995, FRY KIDS/KITES	$1-1.50

     *** IDENTICAL TOYS: SIN/ZEA TR9501/02/03/04

❏	❏	*** TR9501 **TRACK/FRIES,** 1995, YEL W FF/2P	$5-7
❏	❏	*** TR9502 **TRACK/BIG MAC,** 1995, ORG W BIG MAC/2P	$5-7
❏	❏	*** TR9503 **TRACK/HAMB,** 1995, RED W HAMBURGER/2P	$5-7
❏	❏	*** TR9504 **TRACK/SHAKE,** 1995, BLU W SHAKE/2P	$5-7

SIN TR9503

SIN TR9501

JPN TR9502   JPN TR9501   JPN TR9503   JPN TR9504

SINGAPORE

COMMENTS: NATIONAL DISTRIBUTION: NEW ZEALAND: JANU-
ARY 1995; SINGAPORE: FEBRUARY 1995; JAPAN TESTED
IN JANUARY AND RAN IN OCTOBER 1994; ARGENTINA:
MAY 1994; COSTA RICA, PANAMA, VENEZUELA, CHILE:
SEPTEMBER 1994. SIN TR9510 HM BOX IS DATED 1995.
EACH VEHICLE CAME WITH A CHARACTER STICKER PLUS
SCENERY STICKERS FOR BOARD. TRACKS ARE
INTERCONNECTIBLE; CONNECT TOGETHER TO CREATE
ONE LARGER TRACK.

WATER FUN HAPPY MEAL, 1995

❏ ❏	UK WA9510 HM BOX, 1995		$1-1.50
❏ ❏	UK WA9511 HM BOX, 1995		$1-1.50
❏ ❏	UK WA9512 HM BOX, 1995		$1-1.50
❏ ❏	UK WA9513 HM BOX, 1995		$1-1.50

JPN TR9503

❏ ❏ UK WA9501 **SQUIRTER - FROG,** 1995, GRN/RUBBER/
ROUND $2.50-3
❏ ❏ UK WA9502 **SQUIRTER - PIG,** 1995, PNK/RUBBER/ROUND
                                                                $2.50-3
❏ ❏ UK WA9503 **SQUIRTER - SHARK,** 1995, BLU/GREY/RUBBER/
ROUND $2.50-3
❏ ❏ UK WA9504 **SQUIRTER - CAT,** 1995, ORG/RUBBER/ROUND
$2.50-3

❏ ❏ UK WA9526 DISPLAY, 1995 $15-20
❏ ❏ UK WA9565 TRANSLITE, 1995 $5-7

COMMENTS: NATIONAL DISTRIBUTION: UK: JULY 1995.

JAPAN

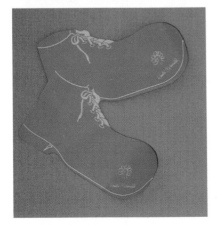

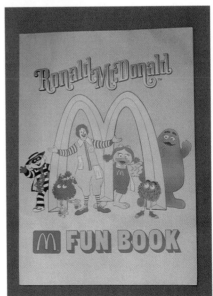

...Means Daring to Dream of the Future!

THANK YOU
FOR COMING TO McDonald's

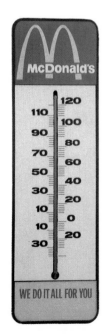

McDonald's

120
110
90
70
50
30
10
10
30

100
80
60
40
20
0
20

WE DO IT ALL FOR YOU

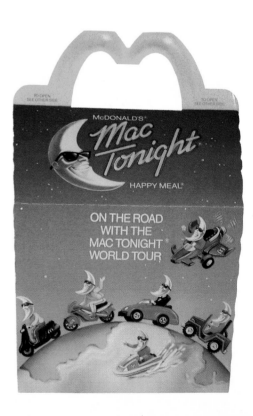

McDONALD'S
Mac Tonight
HAPPY MEAL

ON THE ROAD
WITH THE
MAC TONIGHT
WORLD TOUR

INDEX

N